PERSPECTIVES ON VIOLENCE AND VIOLENT DEATH

Edited by

Robert G. Stevenson
Mercy College—New York

Gerry R. Cox
University of Wisconsin–La Crosse

Death, Value and Meaning Series
Series Editor: Dale V. Lund

LONDON AND NEW YORK

First published 2008 by Baywood Publishing Company, Inc.

2 Park Square, Milton Park, Abingdon, Oxon OX14 4RN
711 Third Avenue, New York, NY 10017, USA

Routledge is an imprint of the Taylor & Francis Group, an informa business

First issued in paperback 2017

Copyright © 2008 Taylor & Francis

All rights reserved. No part of this book may be reprinted or reproduced or utilised in any form or by any electronic, mechanical, or other means, now known or hereafter invented, including photocopying and recording, or in any information storage or retrieval system, without permission in writing from the publishers.

Notice:
Product or corporate names may be trademarks or registered trademarks, and are used only for identification and explanation without intent to infringe.

Library of Congress Catalog Number: 2006051205
ISBN-13: 978-0-89503-313-0 (hbk)

Library of Congress Cataloging-in-Publication Data

Perspectives on violence and violent death / edited by Robert G. Stevenson, Gerry R. Cox.
     p. cm. -- (Death, value, and meaning series)
  ISBN-13: 978-0-89503-313-0
  ISBN-10: 0-89503-313-5
 1. Violence. 2. Violent deaths. I. Stevenson, Robert. II. Cox, Gerry R.

  HM1116.P48 2007
  303.6--dc22

                       2006051205

ISBN 978-0-89503-313-0 (hbk)
ISBN 978-0-415-78509-9 (pbk)

Dedication

We dedicate this book to the memory of John D. Morgan, friend,
colleague, and mentor, with thanks for his leadership, help, and example.
We dedicate it as well to Herman Feifel and Stan Henen.
All three of these men were instrumental in the initial IWG work group
that was the genesis of this book. May their untiring efforts
on behalf of others long be remembered.
To Eileen Patricia Stevenson and to our children Sean Casey Stevenson,
Robert Louis Stevenson, Eileen Conrad Stevenson,
and to our granddaughter Kiera Ryann Stevenson.
To Linda Cox and to our children Father Christopher Cox,
Andrea Sullivan, Kelly Huggins, Gregory Cox, and Theresa Motes,
and to our grandchildren Isaac Motes, John Sullivan, Elanor Sullivan,
Olivia Motes, Finley Huggins, Declan Huggins, and Eamon Sullivan.

Preface

In the twentieth century, the world experienced two major world wars and countless other wars. Many millions died violent deaths from murder, death squads, purges, riots, revolutions, ethnic cleansing, rape, robbery, domestic violence, suicide, gang violence, terrorist acts, genocide, and in many other ways. As we entered the twenty-first century, we experienced September 11th, Red Lake School deaths, suicide bombers, and still more mass death by governments, revolutionaries, terrorists, and still more wars. The need to better understand violence and violent death, to become aware of the many forms of violence, and to better know how to survive in the aftermath violent death is the focus of this work.

PART I:
THE NATURE OF VIOLENCE

These five chapters look at the nature of violence as it is seen in today's world. It begins with an overview by Robert G. Stevenson, a noted educator and leader in managing violence in schools. "Good Violence/Bad Violence: Its Impact on Children and Suggested Responses" offers an overview of the book by explaining opposing views of violence, surviving violence, how to cope with violence, and why societies of the world need to understand and control violence. Chapter 2, "Violence in the Family: Spirituality/Religion as Culprit and Comfort" by Reverend Richard Gilbert, helps readers to better understand that family violence is a part of our communities and affects all those around us. Gilbert, director of the World Pastoral Care Center and long-time practicing chaplain, offers an approach to ministering to those who are culprits and to comfort those who are victims. In Chapter 3, "Conflict and Violence in the Workplace: An Existentialist Analysis," Neil Thompson illustrates a masterful model of workplace conflict and violence from an existentialist position and the perspective of a social worker. Gregory Paul Wegner, a noted historian of the Holocaust, next presents "Violence and the Dehumanization of Victims in Auschwitz and Beyond: Remembering Through Literature," a powerful examination of Holocaust actions. In the next chapter, "Religious Violence and x / PERSPECTIVES ON VIOLENCE AND VIOLENT DEATH

Weapons of Mass Destruction," Timothy Kullman looks at religious actors in the arena of violence.

PART II:
ENCOUNTERS WITH VIOLENCE

This section includes four chapters that look at specific encounters with violence. It begins with "Resisting the Magnet: A Study of South African Children's Engagements with Neighborhood Violence" by Jenny Parkes, who examines the ability of children in South Africa to manage violence. She offers suggestions from them that give some insight into how to better manage violence. Carr Maher, in "Silent Night, Violent Night: An Encounter With Unexpected Violence," chronicles a tragic story of Christmas violence in a family and the impact of that unexpected violence on some of the police officers who responded. "Hispanic Families and Mass Casualties: The First 48 Hours" by Fernando Cabrera, examines the response of family members of those who perished when American Airlines flight 587 plunged into New York City shortly after takeoff. As a pastor and counselor, he offers solid suggestions for counselors and care-givers to use during the first 48 hours, with special attention to the needs of Hispanic families. The next chapter, "Grief and Guilt in the Military" by Carr Maher, offers an interesting perspective for managing the grief and "survivors guilt" of military personnel. It also speaks of the debt that those who have not served may owe to those who do.

PART III:
EMPIRICAL STUDIES

Each of these four chapters reports the results of specific studies related to violence and its effects. The first of these chapters, "Characteristics of Homicide: Victimization Across the Life Span" by Kimberly A. Vogt, examines the inci-dence of homicide across the life span. It provides insight into the extent of homicide today by examining violence and the factors of gender, race, age, culture, social structure, and the impact of violence on grief. The next chapter, "Grief and Attachment Within the Context of Family Violence" by Kimberly A. Rapoza and Kathleen Malley-Morrison, examines the connections between attachment, interpersonal violence, loss, and grief. In particular, the authors focus on the ways in which attachment theory can add to our understanding of the role of grief in violence. "Bereavement Following Violent Death: An Assault on Life and Meaning" by Joseph M. Currier, Jason M. Holland, Rachel A. Coleman, and Robert A. Neimeyer provides details and results of a study of grief and meaning making in the wake of violent death. The fourth chapter in this section, "Violence In Our Own Backyard: September 11th Revisited" by Barbara

Melamed, examines reactions to September 11th in a study of survivors. This is a follow-up survey and reexamination of data initially gathered immediately after the attacks of September 11, 2001.

PART IV:
ALTERNATIVES TO VIOLENCE/
COPING WITH VIOLENCE

These final four chapters examine violence with particular emphasis on alternatives to break the chain of violence. Sir Colin Murray Parkes, noted English psychiatrist and pioneer in the field of thanatology, offers "Making and Breaking the Cycles of Violence," wherein he develops strategies for ending the cycles of violence on personal, family, group/community, and national levels. Gerry Cox's chapter, "Coping with Violent Death: The Role of Spirituality," presents a model of spiritual coping as a means of surviving violent death. "From Violence to Peace: Posthomicide Memorials" by Inge Corless and Phyllis R. Silverman, discusses the ways in which families find solace and comfort after the violent death of a family member. It examines ways in which they memorialize those who died and how they act to prevent further violence by focusing on Boston's Garden of Peace. Finally, we end this volume as we started it, by looking again at our young people and their schools. In "Talk it Out! Walk it Out! Wait it Out! Take Ten: An Intercultural Approach to Creating Safer Schools," Kim Overdyck and Jay Caponigro offer a promising program that presents alternatives to violence in what may well be a first step in the globalization of nonviolence.

The book concludes with three more sections. The first is Appendix A, "Violence: A Statement of Assumptions and Principles." This statement was a three-year project prepared by members of The International Work Group On Death, Dying, and Bereavement. The second section, Appendix B, is a quick summary of guidelines offered by authors of several of the chapters. Each is linked to its author so that a reader may quickly go to the appropriate section of the book, if they wish, for a fuller explanation. The final section, Appendix C, is an extensive bibliography on violence and grief, compiled by Dick Gilbert.

Acknowledgments

All projects involve many more people than those whose names appear on the cover of the book. This project is no exception. While it is impossible to thank all who made this project successful, John D. Morgan, the series editor when we began, is at the top of the list. His friendship and support over many years have been of immeasurable value to us. His work at King's College, his excellent International Death, Grief, and Bereavement Conference, and his work as series editor kept us inspired and active in the death-awareness movement. We thank the members of the International Work Group on Death, Dying, and Bereavement for their intellectual stimulation, support, and friendship. We thank the members of IWG who contributed materials that are included in this book and those members who contributed to the book by their support, review, and scholarship. We would also like to thank Stuart Cohen and the Baywood staff for their patience and support. We thank our colleagues at Mercy College and the University of Wisconsin–La Crosse. We especially thank all of those who contributed to this volume for all of your efforts to help make this project successful.

xiii

Table of Contents

Preface. ix
Acknowledgments xiii

PART I
Introduction—The Nature of Violence

Chapter 1
Good Violence/Bad Violence: Its Impact on Children and
Suggested Responses. 3
Robert G. Stevenson

Chapter 2
Violence in the Family: Spirituality/Religion as Culprit and Comfort. . . . 23
Reverend Richard B. Gilbert

Chapter 3
Conflict and Violence in the Workplace: An Existentialist Analysis 45
Neil Thompson

Chapter 4
Violence and the Dehumanization of Victims in Auschwitz
and Beyond: Remembering Through Literature 59
Gregory Paul Wegner

Chapter 5
Religious Violence and Weapons of Mass Destruction. 79
Timothy Kullman

PART II
Encounters with Violence

Chapter 6
Resisting the Magnet: A Study of South African Children's
Engagements with Neighborhood Violence 97
Jenny Parkes

vi / PERSPECTIVES ON VIOLENCE AND VIOLENT DEATH

Chapter 7
Silent Night, Violent Night: An Encounter With Unexpected Violence . . . 107
Carr Maher

Chapter 8
Hispanic Families and Mass Casualties: The First 48 Hours. 119
Fernando Cabrera

Chapter 9
Grief and Guilt in the Military 127
Carr Maher

PART III
Empirical Studies

Chapter 10
Characteristics of Homicide: Victimization Across the Life Span 135
Kimberly A. Vogt

Chapter 11
Grief and Attachment Within the Context of Family Violence. 151
Kimberly A. Rapoza and Kathleen Malley-Morrison

Chapter 12
Bereavement Following Violent Death: An Assault on
Life and Meaning 177
*Joseph M. Currier, Jason M. Holland, Rachel A. Coleman,
and Robert A. Neimeyer*

Chapter 13
Violence in Our Own Backyard: September 11th Revisited 203
Barbara Melamed

PART IV
Alternatives to Violence/Coping with Violence

Chapter 14
Making and Breaking Cycles of Violence 223
Colin Murray Parkes

Chapter 15
Coping with Violent Death: The Role of Spirituality 239
Gerry R. Cox

TABLE OF CONTENTS / vii

Chapter 16
From Violence to Peace: Posthomicide Memorials 255
   Inge B. Corless and Phyllis R. Silverman

Chapter 17
Talk it Out! Walk it Out! Wait it Out! Take Ten:
An Intercultural Approach to Creating Safer Schools 265
   Kim Overdyck and Jay Caponigro

Appendix A
Violence: A Statement of Assumptions and Principles (IWG). 291

Appendix B
Summary of Guidelines, Protocols, and Procedures 305

Appendix C
Bibliography: Perspectives on Violence 309
   Reverend Richard B. Gilbert

Contributors. 321
Index 329

PART I

Introduction—
The Nature of Violence

CHAPTER 1
Good Violence/Bad Violence: Its Impact on Children and Suggested Responses

Robert G. Stevenson

Many people see the twenty-first century as a dangerous time. Even a cursory glance back at the twentieth century will reveal that violence and its aftermath occurred frequently through all of those years. That is why some say that there was a steady increase through the century. Others point to the violent deaths of the Second World War as a high point and say that there are fewer violent deaths today than the millions who perished in that war. However, this statement takes into account only violent *death*. There are many forms of violence, and not all of these lead to, or result from, a death.

In March of 2005, two noted conservative speakers were assaulted in separate incidents. While making appearances at college campuses, the two men, Pat Buchanan and William Kristol, were hit with salad dressing and a pie respectively (Associated Press, 2005). The likelihood of physical harm was minor, but the public humiliation was quite real. This may seem to have no connection with lethal violence, but in both cases the attackers believed that their cause was good enough to justify their actions. They believed that the end justified the means. The same philosophy can be seen in the violence that erupts when world leaders meet to conduct an economic summit or to discuss free trade. These attacks are a part (small to be sure) of an increasing tolerance for violence as a means of solving problems.

In light of developments in the first few years of this new millennium, violence and its aftermath are clearly problems. Violence is not a single problem; it can take many forms. People are urgently seeking answers to these problems of violence. Some individuals and groups work to limit violence in a particular area. Others want to address broader issues and wish to limit violence in all of its many forms. If

4 / PERSPECTIVES ON VIOLENCE AND VIOLENT DEATH

people do not want violence to continue at its present level, decisions have to be made. We know that no decision can be better than the information upon which it is based. That is the seminal idea that led to this volume.

The idea for this book started with a meeting of members of the International Work Group on Death, Dying, and Bereavement (IWG) at King's College in London, Ontario, Canada in 1993. The IWG began in 1974 at a conference in Columbia, Maryland. Today, it is an international group with over 200 members from 6 continents. These leaders in the study of death, dying, and bereavement examine important issues in those fields and produce work products designed to disseminate their findings to the widest possible audience. At the London conference, the topic of one of the work groups was violence. Over the next three years, thirty committee members produced a document that contained statements about violence, assumptions and principles concerning violence, and definitions of key terms. The committee members were unanimous in their approval of this document. Its publication was approved by the full IWG membership and Board of Directors, and it appeared in 1997 as "Document on Violence and Grief" produced by the IWG in *OMEGA—Journal of Death and Dying*, Volume 36(3), pp. 259-272. (The original document appears, with the publisher's permission, as an appendix to this volume.)

The contributors to *Perspectives on Violence and Violent Death* come from several countries. Each of their chapters speaks to violence in one or more of its many forms. The chapters range from reflective essays to empirical studies. It is our hope that the information contained in this work will be of benefit to those who seek to make decisions related to violence. Those decision makers may be private individuals, group spokespersons, or government officials. The ability to make decisions may be theirs, but if we all will be affected by their consequences, the decisions are ours as well.

This book is not definitive. It is not the last word on any issues related to violence and the grief that follows. It offers insights in the form of thoughts and feelings as well as the results of some formal studies. If it is true that no decision can be better than the information on which it is based, then each of these contributions can be of value. The title of this book states what this is. This work is a collection of "perspectives on violence and violent death." Hopefully, the images presented here will be clear to all who take the time to view them.

Violence has reached a point where it enters our lives on a daily basis. Every newscast carries stories of violent death, whether accidental or intentional. The news axiom, "If it bleeds, it leads" has never been truer than it is today (Reuters, 2005). Headlines report casualty counts among troops and civilians, dead and injured from terrorist acts and military action, cases of domestic violence and child abuse, and sudden violent outbursts of nature itself (Stevenson, 2003, 2004). In this work, unless a particular contributor states otherwise, *violence* is defined as "the exertion by an agent of any force or action that injures or abuses whether physically, psychologically, emotionally or spiritually" (IWG, 1997).

That definition includes both lethal and nonlethal acts. Words can also impart violence through the threat of its use. *Threat* is defined as "communication of what will be done to hurt or punish someone" (IWG, 1997).

Following violence, whether in word or in deed, there is loss. When we look at the impact of loss, it is important to differentiate between bereavement and grief. *Bereavement* refers to an event, a point in time. It is the forcible loss of someone or something precious. *Grief* is a highly personal response to loss. It is a process through which an individual acknowledges the loss and finds a place for the reality of it in his or her life.

The definition, nature, and meaning of violence could fill a text. However, based on the work of IWG (1997), there are statements than can be made about violence.

- Violence takes place in a particular context. No violent act or word exists in a vacuum; therefore, to understand the nature of violence and its effects, one must examine the event in context. Violence can also take place because of failure to act. Once again, it is important to look at the context of the inaction.
- Violence exists on many levels. There is violence that directly affects individuals. However, there is also familial, social, political, cultural, and institutional violence. The impact of these types of violence will eventually affect individuals, but it may be some time after the actual event.
- Violence can be cyclical and may be transmitted from person to person, from parent to child, and from generation to generation. The cyclical nature of violence is examined in greater detail in this book by Colin Murray Parkes. Perpetrators of violence may, themselves, have been victims of violence. A violent response to violence may cause further violence. However, there are responses to violence that can reduce further violence. If this were not true, there would be no reason for a book such as this or, when violence has occurred, for any attempt at intervention aimed at reducing violence. If we are to remain hopeful, it is important to remember that the cycle of violence can be broken.
- Violence has many variables. It may be overt or covert. It may occur as a single acute case or a chronic pattern. It may be premeditated or sudden and unexpected, even by the perpetrator. Violence can be intentional or accidental. However, violence that is accidental or unpremeditated is not necessarily any less profound in its effect.
- Violence may be delivered with malicious intent, but it can also result from the best of intentions.
- Violence affects an individual in many ways. One act can have physical, psychological, social, emotional, and spiritual consequences with which an individual may have to cope. The type of death can have an impact on the grief process.

6 / PERSPECTIVES ON VIOLENCE AND VIOLENT DEATH

- Identifying the reasons for violent behavior can help understand the causation behind the act. However, it is important to remember that most societies still believe that an individual needs to be held accountable for the consequences of his or her actions. Explaining the cause of an action, or of the choice to act, does not necessarily excuse the action or exonerate the perpetrator.
- Violence involves us all, whether or not we choose to respond to it. This is truly a case wherein those who are not part of the solution may well be part of the problem. Too many people, and institutions, seem willing to look away and allow the cycle of violence to continue. The choice to take action to break the cycle of violence is an important one. Ideally, that choice will be based on knowledge and experience and not merely the result of passionate emotions.

DEFINING VIOLENCE

According to the definition cited above, violence can result from the exertion of *any* force that injures or abuses. Why then have so many people focused exclusively on *guns* as the cause of violence? Why have many of these same people failed to distinguish between the *causes* of violence and the *means* used to inflict violence? After the events at Columbine High School in Littleton, Colorado, a national conference of the NRA was pressured to move to another date and another state, away from Colorado. The popular news media acted as though anyone who advocated responsible gun ownership was, at the very least, bizarre and perhaps even criminal or psychotic. This can be seen in the reaction of people from other countries to the easy access to firearms in the United States. This strong reaction has not diminished with the passage of time. In one popular television show (Boston Public, December 4, 2000), students who sought to form a gun club with NRA sponsorship were discriminated against by the administration and then held up to public ridicule by a teacher they admired for what the show presented as the students' bizarre preoccupation with firearms.

If guns were the cause of the violence, all of this inflammatory rhetoric might be warranted. However, even though guns seem to grab headlines, what of knives or razors? These are more common in schools than guns and have been for some time. It was a knife that caused the violence that brought me to the district I was helping on the day that the Columbine incident occurred. In another district, one angry student poured gasoline over the engine of a teacher's car. If the teacher had started that engine, he would have been engulfed in a fireball. It was a warning by another student that saved his life.

What about the bombs constructed from propane tanks by the troubled young men at Columbine? Those improvised explosive devices (IEDs) did not work. If guns had not been available and those bombs had received more attention in their construction, the death toll might have been far higher. What do we understand of the plan they discussed to commandeer an airplane and crash it into a major city? Others took that threat more seriously, and the result was seen in New York, Washington, D.C., and in a farmer's field in Pennsylvania. Where is the outrage over these terrible threats? Why have we not heard calls to restrict knives and razors, to restrict gasoline, propane grills, aluminum baseball bats, or airplanes rising to the same level as the call to ban firearms? The answer is that we, as a society, always seek quick and achievable solutions to our problems. We want "guns" to be the problem so that, in banning them, the problem can be "solved." Research is cited to "prove" that guns are the cause of violence in schools, but this research may be seriously flawed. In fact, much of what is accepted as research supported "fact" may be called into question if the research itself is examined closely. Readers who wish to examine this premise are directed to *Issues in School Violence Research* (Furlong, Morrison, Skiba, & Cornell, 2004).

Guns, and their availability, seem to be something we can change. There are certainly problems connected to guns. Most people do not believe that hunters and sportsmen need automatic or assault weapons, at least not until Bambi begins to return fire. Most such weapons are far less accurate than hunting rifles and seem decidedly inappropriate for the uses claimed for them. However, restrictions placed on automatic weapons and assault rifles would not have kept several students from using hunting rifles against innocent victims in schools.

Registration of firearms and licensing of gun owners also seem to be reasonable steps to take. However, in cases wherein guns were stolen, or were used by individuals with licenses and no criminal background, this also seems inadequate in preventing their illegal use. Finally, why is there so little gun-related violence in some societies, such as Switzerland, where firearms are found in many households? The answer may be that the cause of violence is not the gun or the availability of guns. We have become distracted, in part, because we have confused the means of inflicting violence with the cause of the violence. Violence has been carried out with guns, but the cause of the problem runs deeper.

It has been assumed that the grief process after violent loss is different from the grief that follows other, anticipated losses. In this volume, there are chapters that examine the reaction of individuals to violent losses (Cabrera, Cox, Melamed, Vogt, Wegner) and examining the difference between types of grief after violent vs. nonviolent losses (Currier, Holland, Coleman, Neimeyer). However, there may be an earlier issue that still remains unexamined; namely, the belief that there is such a thing as "good" violence.

GOOD VIOLENCE vs. BAD VIOLENCE

In the course of supervising graduate-school interns in the Mercy College counseling program, I visit schools in New York City and throughout its metropolitan

8 / PERSPECTIVES ON VIOLENCE AND VIOLENT DEATH

area. In one of these schools, a counselor stated that her greatest concern in the school was violence among the students. She reported that fighting was epidemic. Episodes of violence began as soon as school started each day. She feared that one or more of her students might be killed in this regular violence. This was not a troubled high school. It was a grammar school with grades kindergarten through fifth grade. The fighting started with children in kindergarten. These children believe that wrongs can be made right through violence. Where did they get such beliefs? Domestic violence can have this sort of effect on the behavior of children. However, the problem of violence among the young may have other sources as well.

In Hollywood films, there is a formula that allows violence to be used to redress violence. The violence of motion pictures, whether American, European, or Asian, is often extreme. Some dismiss this as "cartoon" violence. The cartoons of today's world can be violent indeed. The violence heaped on Wile E. Coyote, Daffy Duck, or Elmer Fudd has been changed to pictures of bullets ripping through flesh with blood splashing on everything and everyone nearby. Cartoon violence, if anything, has become more realistic, not less. However, it is in motion pictures that we see violence systematically presented as a "solution" to problems. This type of violence can be described as "good" violence. The worse the nature of the original act, the greater will be the allowable response. The judicious application of good violence is used to reestablish balance in the cinematic world.

It is an easy task to compile a list of films wherein the hero uses violence and a huge body-count to redress evil deeds. The films of Charles Bronson (especially the *Death Wish* series) seem a logical place to start. The films of Sylvester Stallone (*Nighthawks, Cliffhanger, Demolition Man, The Specialist, Judge Dredd*, the *Rambo* series), Arnold Schwarzenegger (*Eraser, True Lies, Total Recall, Raw Deal, Commando, The Terminator* series, the *Conan* series, etc.), Bruce Willis (*Last Man Standing, The Fifth Element*, and the *Die Hard* series), and Mel Gibson (*The Patriot, Braveheart, We Were Soldiers,* the *Lethal Weapon* series, and the *Mad Max/Road Warrior* series) are the first ones that are used to make this point. These films are sometimes dismissed as escapist fantasy. It is said that they are seen as too exaggerated to be considered "real" by any audience. It is pointed out that in many of the tales collected centuries ago by the Brothers Grimm, there was violence and death. Two of the three little pigs are killed (as is the wolf). The Giant falls to his death as he pursues Jack down the beanstalk. Gretel pushes the witch into a burning oven, where she dies. However, the violence in those folk tales was not accompanied by *graphic pictures* of blood, gore, and death; and not every film or image needs blood and gore to be violent.

It is a Harrison Ford film (and not one of the Indiana Jones epics) that shows how far the belief in good violence can go. *Witness* (1985) was a film about a young Amish boy who witnesses a murder when traveling with his mother. Ford plays police detective Captain John Book, who is assigned to protect the young man. In the course of his assignment, he takes on the persona of an Amish man. These people believe in nonviolence. In accordance with their beliefs, there is no such thing as good violence. One scene shows some of the Amish families on a shopping trip into a nearby town. Some of the town bullies are taunting the men, certain they will not fight to defend themselves or their families. The bullies then begin to pick on Detective Book. He warns them to stop, saying they will regret what they are doing. They only go farther in tormenting him. Finally, when they put their hands on him, he proceeds to give each of them a sound beating.

When the town bullies, young men in their twenties who should have known better, got what some might call their "just desserts," the movie audience cheered loudly and applauded. Lost on them was the look on the faces of the men that Book was defending. They were strong enough to have used force in their own defense had they chosen to do so. They displayed far greater strength by choosing not to use force. What Book did violated their deeply held beliefs. The fact that he did it while representing their community (by his dress and in the role he was playing) made the violation even worse. None of this mattered to the audience. This was good violence, the kind they expected and anticipated. In their minds, it set things right. Yes, the evil men (police detectives) were defeated in the end with good violence as they tried to kill the young witness; however, that confrontation scene, and the cheering that accompanied it, provided evidence of just what the audience felt about the violence they were watching.

There are parallels to this in the real world. Mahatma Gandhi, leader of India's struggle for independence, came to oppose violent force of any type, and had the strength of character to lead others to do the same. However, in the real world there are few Gandhis, and it should be remembered that this apostle of nonviolence was, himself, shot to death by a disgruntled follower. In the United States, Reverend Dr. Martin Luther King tried continually to control those that would have led the civil rights struggle down a violent path. He too was martyred for his cause. Both men refused to take life, but gave up their own for their cause. They died, but their cause lived on. These men stand out because they refused to accept violence, to say that the end justified the means used to achieve it. In many places, such rejection of violence flies in the face of growing national policies.

The Second World War is offered as an example of a "just" war, and therefore, good violence. Today, some point to the invasion of Iraq as good violence, since it removed a tyrant from power, who had inflicted violence, suffering, and countless deaths on his own people. However, as the fighting continued for months and years after the invasion, with most of the victims being the same Iraqis that the invading forces sought to protect, there are also those who question what was gained. Also, the first rationale for the invasion was the presence of weapons of mass destruction, but such weapons were never found and seem to have not been there in the first place. However, that is not the argument that pertains most strongly to this discussion.

10 / PERSPECTIVES ON VIOLENCE AND VIOLENT DEATH

The point to be made here is that like good/bad violence, there are apparently good/bad weapons of mass destruction. The argument is made that the presence of nuclear weapons kept the Cold War cold. The United States still possesses enough weapons of mass destruction to erase all life on this planet. That threat is a "good" one if it maintains peace because, after all, the United States is one of the "good guys." Many other states possess nuclear weapons, but that is "allowed" because once you have them, it is too dangerous to try to take them away. Saddam Hussein was a "bad" guy, and so the threat that he might someday possess the same weapons was enough to prompt an invasion of Iraq by the United States and England (both nuclear powers) with a number of allies. With certainty of the justice of a cause comes a certainty that any means used to achieve that noble cause will be "good."

There is a moral argument, one that is used to justify war, that force (violence) can be used to resist force (violence). Thus, violence used in self-defense is good. Every "true believer" in a cause can thus use violence to defend their cause or people from presumed attack. Germany used violence as a "final solution" to protect the "purity" of their race and culture. The results are discussed in Greg Wegner's chapter in this book. Religious extremists use violence (and mass deaths of noncombatants) to defend beliefs or people from attack by alien philosophies, religious beliefs, or simply cultural differences. This is shown in Timothy Kullman's chapter, *Religious Violence and Weapons of Mass Destruction*.

These beliefs can even be reduced at a more personal level to factors present in domestic violence. The abuser can make a case, and they sometimes do, that the violence was "necessary" to defend the family and its members. The political issues inherent in such beliefs are not a major focus of this work. What this book seeks to show are views of violence in many forms, the beliefs that may lead to violence, and the ways people seek to cope with the aftermath of violence. Perhaps it is logical to start our examination of violence by looking at its impact on children. They represent our future, and the lessons they are learning about violence today will resonate for many decades yet to come.

CHILDREN, SCHOOLS, AND THE
IMPACT OF VIOLENCE

In the United States there is steadily growing concern about violence. My own background is that of a teacher for almost 40 years and, for a few of those years, a member of the New York Guard. My time with the New York Guard, 88th Brigade, especially in the days and weeks after September 11, 2001, gave me insight into issues of security and violence prevention (Stevenson, 2003). However, it is the three decades that I spent as a teacher and counselor that gave me far more experience with the grief that follows violence. Students saw violence in their homes and their communities. They experienced it from peers and from strangers. In most cases, they brought their concerns to school with them. There were many times when violence in school was a direct result of earlier violence outside the school. My experience leads me to start this work about violence with a look at the violence that affects children and schools.

Events in recent years have caused much of that concern to be focused on schools. In March of 2005, a student at Red Lake High School in Minnesota shot family members and then went to his school, where he killed nine students and staff (Forliti, 2005). This represented the worst school shooting since the 1999 shootings at Columbine High School in Colorado. That day saw the deaths of 12 students, 2 faculty members and the 2 teen gunmen. Unlike the violence against schools and students in some other countries, such as Israel where armed men have killed students and taken hostages in schools on more than one occasion, this violence comes from students themselves.

The problem of violence in American schools is not a new one. What is different is that in the most recent cases, the weapons used (rifles, shotguns, handguns, and improvised explosive devices) have caused death tolls from violence to escalate sharply. Some of these cases are related to themes from violent computer simulations or role-play games. There are many individuals and groups seeking an appropriate response to this increase in violence. Some have taken the easy route by blaming it all on a single cause. Press releases from these people all seem to contain a variation of the following quote:

> It is all the result of _____ (fill in the blank with any of the following: guns, computer games, drugs, rock music, television, movies, or even the schools themselves).

Whatever the commentators personal agenda, it is simply transposed onto the violent episode and becomes the "cause." Experience has shown that violence is almost always due to multiple factors. There is not a single cause—and people should be very wary of those who say that there is. Also, not all violent actions have roots in the greater society.

There are troubled individuals whose moral judgments are influenced by pathological narcissism, or who feel they can no longer cope with depression, or a perceived lack of control over their lives. Their actions come from within the individual. Violence can lead to suicide attempts. We know there is a fine line between suicide and homicide. We know that one can become the other in the blink of an eye. However, for many years we focused almost exclusively on one issue (suicide) while, in many areas, paying little attention to the other (homicide). Whatever the cause, for many students and families, schools are no longer seen as a safe place. When that happens, fear grows; and this fear can prompt attempts at self-protection.

12 / PERSPECTIVES ON VIOLENCE AND VIOLENT DEATH

"VIOLENCE IS THE LAST RESORT OF FOOLS"

In Bergen County, New Jersey, a student brought a stun gun to school in March 2005. When stopped and questioned as to why he had a weapon, he said it was for self-protection. Young women in New York City have been found hiding razor blades in their mouths to bring them into school. Why? Again the reason given was self-protection. The fact is, these "defensive" actions frighten others and cause more people to be fearful, prompting more students to want to carry weapons for their own defense. It becomes only a matter of time until something will occur—not "if it happens" but "when it happens."

In order to understand an action or event, there is a need to correctly identify its causes and its effects. The media provides "special investigations" that claim to do just this. They feature stories of how this school or that has sought to reduce violence. There are two policies that seem to get the most play in the papers and on television: declaring "safe zones," and having "lockdowns" to find and confiscate contraband items.

- Declaring safe zones (drug/weapon free): From a violent perpetrator's point of view, this has created "target rich" areas where he (or, far less often, she) need not fear immediate reprisal. If a person has decided to use a weapon illegally, should we be surprised that another "rule" or "declaration" will do little to stop that action?
- Lockdowns: This technique of search and remove has never worked at keeping drugs and weapons out of prisons. It has not even been very effective at curtailing violence in those same prisons. In those institutions, control is at a maximum level, and still such policies do not work in the way officials would like. Why should we believe that such policies work in schools? Or, is the real purpose of such policies simply to create the illusion of safety?

It is merely an illusion when we blame the weapon for the violence more than the decisions and actions of the person carrying it. Michael Crichton, in his book *Rising Sun*, has a Japanese character say, "In our country we try to fix the problem. In America you try to fix the blame." If guns themselves were the cause of violence, why is it that there is not a similar problem in countries where there are guns in almost every home, such as in Switzerland?

There is also the belief that intelligent people do not need to resort to violence. If this is true, then violence can be seen as the result of the "dumbing down" of our society. Radio personalities, such as Sean Hannity or Rush Limbaugh, would lay violence at the doorstep of ineffective schools and permissive liberal parents. These are "bumper-sticker" solutions to violence—"Ban Guns from School, Not Prayers." The fact is, most students would never bring a gun to school or feel that they would be safer if they did. Such quick-fix slogans make no attempt to look at the deeper issues that cause some students to see violence as good—but they do get good ratings.

There is also the idea that violence comes from the "animal" side of human nature, not its higher, spiritual component. If this is true, does it mean that a country's leaders are acting on animalistic emotions when they choose violent solutions? What does it mean when looking at the men and women of a country's military? These young people show a love of country and its ideals. They serve at their country's will in its defense. Is their desire to serve and protect based on animalistic emotion? Once again, an attempt at a simple answer seems to miss the mark.

GUIDELINES FOR COPING WITH VIOLENCE IN SCHOOLS

Are there interventions that have worked to reduce violence in schools? Yes, there are guidelines that have worked in North American schools. Examining these may prove useful in dealing with violence outside of the schools as well. The following guidelines have been used in coping with violence in schools:

- CREATE A SENSE OF CONNECTION BETWEEN STUDENTS AND STAFF

  It is known that when students feel they belong as members of a school community, there is far less likelihood of violent behavior on their part. Creating that identification with the school is a first step. When students believe they are cared about as individuals, the entire school community can change. Here are four exercises that can help a school community to move in that direction.

  - Safety Net Awareness: In small groups or individual classes, students are presented with a scenario (violence, suicidal feelings, abuse, sexual harassment). This can be hypothetical or, as has been done with success, right after an incident has occurred. In that case, the recent incident becomes the case study. Students are then asked, "If this happened to you, to whom in this school would you turn?" As students suggest people, they are asked to share why they might choose that person. Each name is written on the board and the students see the list of possible support grow longer and longer. Students are discouraged from giving a position instead of a person's name as well as from merely repeating a previous answer. A repeated answer is acceptable, but each student who responds is encouraged to provide a new name. Participation should be voluntary, but the group leader may want to make a mental note of students who do not answer for possible individual follow-up.
  - Peer Leaders: Adolescents are more likely to share information about abuse, episodes of violence, sexual concerns, or fears of personal safety

14 / PERSPECTIVES ON VIOLENCE AND VIOLENT DEATH

with peers than with adults. Peer leaders (who are given any of a number of titles) are students who are trained as listeners and know how to make referrals. It is not a peer leaders job to assess the degree of risk in any particular student—they do not have enough training or experience for that. They are there to allow students to have a catharsis and "get out" things they are holding inside. They can also help students to make connections with professionals to whom they might not otherwise have turned. Peers may be better able to identify young people for referrals, because adults may have trouble distinguishing between troubled youth and those who are simply nonconformists or "making a statement."

– Memorials: When a current or former member of a school community dies, there is a memorial for that person. Some schools have one day a year when flags are lowered to half-mast in memory of those who have died in the previous year. This sends the message that every student (past or present) is connected. Every one of them does matter. To ban such memorials (as some schools have done) says to a students that they could be here one day and gone the next and the school would move on unchanged. The message to each member of a school community of a "no memorial" policy is that "you do not matter."

– Symbols of Safety: In classes there should be a way for students to show that they are stressed and may not be able to function normally. One way students typically do this is by simply cutting class. However, there may be an alternative here. One high school teacher brought to class a teddy bear that had belonged to his son. Any student who felt stressed, or had suffered a loss, could put "Teddy" on his or her desk. The student remained present and could still hear what was going on, but would not be called on. The student could participate, but it would be voluntary. It led to a reduction in cutting and a higher percentage of class attendance in that class. It gave students a feeling of greater personal control. Often, the fact that they could take a time out if they felt it was needed was enough. Most days Teddy stayed on the teacher's desk. It allowed one other, unexpected benefit. Students began to take the bear and put it on a friend's desk to show they knew of some issue in the student's life, and they were there for support.

• IDENTIFY ALL MEMBERS OF THE SCHOOL COMMUNITY WITH BADGES, PINS, OR SOME OTHER VISIBLE SCHOOL SYMBOL
This serves two purposes: (1) it helps staff and students to identify outsiders and (2) it can strengthen pride in members of the school community. If this is adopted, it is important that all staff, teachers, and administrators follow the same regulations as the students. To do this only with students can create feelings of powerlessness and be seen as a negative policy designed simply to give the staff (or administration) greater control.

- ZERO TOLERANCE FOR VIOLENCE
This does not mean automatic suspension or expulsion for any violent episode. Each episode must be seen within its context. Circumstances must be taken into account. However, the important point to remember is that there must be *appropriate consequences* in every case. When necessary, a violent student may have to be removed from the school to alternative placement, but this must be a last resort. For students who derive greater benefit from being a member of the school community, this consequence of such removal is more severe. For those students with little or no connection, there may be no personal feeling of loss, but it may still be necessary for the safety of others.
- SECURITY PERSONNEL
These men and women should know the students by face and name. Their role, providing security to all members of the school community, should be reinforced by stressing that they play a positive role. They must not be there simply to control or punish. Also, existing space should be assessed (with the help of trained professionals) to insure that blind spots or other features of school architecture do not create places where safety may be compromised.
- REEXAMINE THE CURRICULUM
This involves finding alternatives to films, books, and other media that promote violence as an effective problem-solving technique.
- EDUCATE PEOPLE ABOUT VIOLENCE
Methods should be pursued in order to raise awareness in the entire community of the many forms that violence can take, stressing that violence comes as a choice of the perpetrator, not through the fault of the victim.
- TEACH THE LIFE CYCLE OF CRISIS RESPONSE
If violence occurs in a cycle, it is helpful to know what steps should be followed to cope with it most effectively. In the United States, the Federal Emergency Management Agency (FEMA) produces materials based on a four-part cycle. The four steps are: preparation, response, recovery, and mitigation. There are materials available online to any interested party. Perhaps the most important step is mitigation. After a violent episode, key people gather to ask, "What have we learned from this?" and "How can we do better in the future?" Sometimes, after an episode of violence, the decision makers seek only to put it behind them and to move on. When this is done, there may be other episodes, perhaps more severe, in the future. Even when there is an effective response, it is important to study it so that the good points can be amplified.
  - Get everyone involved (students, parents, teachers, staff, administrators, and members from the community).
  - Establish principles of effective response and recovery in advance of a crisis (preparation). Assess responsibility. This is part of the recovery

16 / PERSPECTIVES ON VIOLENCE AND VIOLENT DEATH

phase. Remember that there may be victims at many levels (and some victims may be the perpetrators themselves).

- Avoid spreading blame for any episode of violence to so many ("we are all responsible") that no one is accountable for what happened. Assigning responsibility helps with effective mitigation. Start by having each member of a school community examine his or her own actions and the role he or she may have played in what took place.
- Use the principles of Critical Incident Stress Debriefing with students and staff. Know in advance who may be called on to carry out such a program.
- Set time limits on each phase of recovery. Open-ended programs can have a negative effect and can drain energy from caregivers. It is better to establish a new date at the end of the allotted time, than to allow people to think that the process may go on "forever."

Most of these points relate to a school community that is trying to anticipate and be prepared for the event of violence. When an episode of violence has already occurred, there are other points that must be considered. If the consequences for those involved are to be appropriate, then accurate information is essential. The following guidelines for response are intended to gain information to determine what actions should be taken next. It is offered in the form of questions.

What Was the *Level* of the Violence in this Particular Incident?

Violence may occur on many levels. Was the violence in this case individual, familial, social, cultural, or institutional? Did it occur on many levels at the same time? If we focus our response too narrowly, we run the risk of trying to remedy the violent behavior of one or more individuals, while failing to address a violent family, cultural, or institutional setting that may have been, and continues to be, a contributing factor in that student's behavior.

What Exactly Happened?

To answer this, one must know if

- the violence was overt, covert, acute, chronic, or a combination of two or more of these. Each of these factors can play a role in the reactions of victims and the responses of perpetrators to later attempts at assistance.
- the violence was intentional or unintentional, spontaneous or premeditated? Whether a deliberate act, or an accident, violence has occurred. The presence or absence of intent may influence responses, including determining the degree of culpability and possible punishment. The role played by an impulsive act versus planned violence is also important in determining the

best response. Zero tolerance of violence, followed by automatic expulsion, is a policy that sounds good, but handicaps decision makers, limits their ability to recognize individual differences, and has tended to foster a view of mandated responses as unfair. If the response is seen as unfair, it may be considered to merely be violence in another form. If a school response is defended as appropriate because the school has the authority to enforce its will, the emotional, and psychological impact of such actions can also meet the general definition of violence. This may reinforce, not break, the cycle of violence.

- this violence occurred because of some action or because of a failure to act? In the wake of violence, there is a widespread need to affix blame. If there was someone (or something) that was a causative agent, that person or thing will receive much of the blame and become a target of the anger that follows an episode of violence. If the violence resulted from a failure to act, blame and anger may remain unfocused. They may then be directed toward anyone who attempts to assist in recovery from the violence or to reestablish routine. If the violence was the result of action by one or more people, it is important to look at the perpetrators as well as at the action.

What Do We Know About the Perpetrator(s) of the Violence?

Sometimes the cause of violence may be due to circumstances that are not readily apparent: prior violence is a notable factor; as is an expression of grief; or as a reaction to victimization, especially when punishment is involved that may seem arbitrary or excessive.

Identifying the reasons for violent behavior does not necessarily excuse the action or exonerate the perpetrator. The perpetrator may have *believed* that his or her life was threatened, regardless of whether a threat really existed. Does this justify a violent act? What if the perpetrator of the violence suffered from an impaired ability to make an appropriate judgment? Alcohol, drugs, addiction, and affective disorders can be factors in causing violent behavior. Their continued use in attempting to cope with past violence may serve only to continue the cycle of violence.

What Was the Immediate Trigger of this Violence?

The student who tried to incinerate a teacher by pouring gasoline on the teacher's car engine did so because he was grieving the sudden, violent death of a coach to whom the student had felt close ties. The thwarted violence came after a statement about the deceased by the teacher. The student felt this statement showed a lack of respect for his former coach.

It is known that individuals exposed to violence, especially violent deaths, either directly or indirectly, may be impaired in their capacity to make judgments,

18 / PERSPECTIVES ON VIOLENCE AND VIOLENT DEATH

to plan appropriate action, or to act wisely. Violent death may result in grief that differs from grief that follows nonviolent death. A judge, who was aware of these two factors, had the student returned to school and to mandatory grief counseling, rather than placing him in a state correctional facility. The students and staff members angered by this "mild" response to a potentially deadly action, also needed counseling to be able to understand how this decision represented justice. No violent act exists in a vacuum, and a serious attempt must be made to understand all of the factors involved. Understanding the causes of violent behavior may provide a basis for preventing violence.

What Responses Followed the Violent Episode?

Responses to violence are extremely important: they can either contribute to further violence or, conversely, reduce the likelihood of further violence, thus paving the way to break the cycle of violence. Individuals grieving violent death may be confronted with multiple, complex tasks with relation to both the deceased and the perpetrator of the violence, which may make appropriate positive responses difficult to determine.

How Have the Survivors of the Violence Reacted?

This question must be answered to properly meet the diverse needs of those individuals coping with the aftermath of violence. The reactions of those affected by violent death may be influenced by a number of factors, including

- the nature and circumstances of the event,
- any physical or mental trauma sustained by the survivor(s),
- the degree of displacement from homes, networks, and communities,
- the developmental level of the survivor(s),
- trauma and violence in the social and political milieu,
- identification with the dead person(s) and the perpetrator(s),
- the nature and quality of the relationship between the survivor(s) and the victim(s) of violence,
- the nature and quality of the relationship between the perpetrator(s) and the victim(s),
- the interaction among survivors,
- the interaction between the survivor(s) and society,
- previous and concurrent losses and their resolution,
- the number of losses incurred,
- previous and concurrent victimization and its resolution,
- internal strengths (e.g., spiritual beliefs, psychological health),
- external supports (e.g., family, community, society, economic resources),
- direct experience of the loss (e.g., did the person see the actual event or learn of it from others),

- perceived impact of the loss,
- perceived responsibility for the death,
- availability of the body or other reminders of the deceased,
- physical condition of the dead body,
- the nature of the funeral and other rituals,
- the persistence of threat,
- the recurrence of loss (Parkes, 1981).

Have the Survivors of the Violence Had an Opportunity to Process and Give Meaning To What They Have Experienced?

The reactions of those involved in violence (whether as perpetrators, victims, or observers) reflect the meaning(s) they attribute to the experience. What are these meanings? The individuals involved need an opportunity to process and give meaning to what has taken place.

Once we are able to answer these questions, the next step is to establish an environment in which the individuals and the school can recover from the violence that has occurred and begin to build safeguards against its recurrence. In short, they need to take steps to break the cycle of violence.

GRIEVING A VIOLENT DEATH

For some time, counselors have acted on the belief that violent death has different characteristics that have an impact on the grief process of survivors. These include the following:

- A VIOLENT DEATH IS TYPICALLY SUDDEN AND NOT ANTICI- PATED: Grief is more likely to be complicated after a sudden death. The violence of the death itself is magnified by the way it tears apart the lives of survivors.
- A VIOLENT DEATH CAN MAGNIFY THE EFFECTS OF OTHER STRESSORS: The presence of stress when violence occurs complicates the grief process. Existing and new problems, taken together, may be more difficult for a person to handle and may provoke a more extreme response.
- FEELINGS OF REGRET AND GUILT MAY COMPLICATE GRIEF: This can persist even when survivors know such feelings are not based on real events.
- SURVIVORS EXPERIENCE A LOSS OF CONTROL: This can result in a coping style of "submission." In such a coping style, the person gives control over his or her life to others to avoid feeling responsible for being so emotionally out of control.

20 / PERSPECTIVES ON VIOLENCE AND VIOLENT DEATH

- THE MEDIA AND THE REACTIONS OF SOCIETY CAN COMPLI-CATE GRIEF: When we do not know what to do or say, we typically do or say nothing. This silence can complicate grief.

Moving On

The following are suggestions that can help grieving individuals to move on after a violent death:

- Accept the grief. Be tolerant of perceived shortcomings (short temper, attention span, avoidance, lack of energy, lack of feelings that others seem to have).
- Talk about the death if you can. Be patient with misstatements by yourself and others.
- Keep busy, but not too busy. Sometimes people try to avoid unpleasant feelings through the distraction of work. This may cause the individual to become physically run down and possibly sick.
- Take care of yourself: eat well and exercise. Stress takes a physical toll and can impair the immune system. Taking care of personal needs will help one to cope with grief and possibly to be available to help others.
- Be aware of your surroundings and remain alert to any possible threat. Doing this as a conscious choice may help to overcome feelings of helplessness and vulnerability.
- Externalize you grief (symbols, journals, sharing with others). Choosing some symbol as a expression, or representation of the loss can be helpful to the grief process. This practice is as old as history itself. After a temporary absence, symbols showing that a person is grieving are again being seen on a regular basis.
- Deal with the guilt (real or imagined). It is a part of the human condition that we can feel guilty over almost anything. It does not matter that the things we feel guilty about never happened. We can even feel guilty about feeling guilty in the first place. If ignored or denied, these feelings of guilt (often tied to a belief that the individual provoked, or could have prevented the violence) can complicate the grief process.
- Accept your understanding of the death.
- Draw on your spiritual background. Some secular counselors are reluctant to touch issues related to personal spiritual or religious beliefs. However, most religions have beliefs, rituals, and traditions that can provide support in the aftermath of violence.
- Understand (but do not ignore) negative coping by yourself and others. Such negative coping can include anger, inappropriate humor, self-injury, denial, or apathy (simply withdrawing from life).

CONCLUSION

As was stated at the beginning of this chapter, the topic of violence is so large, and we are learning so much about what causes it and its subsequent effects, that it cannot be covered fully in any one volume. In addition, the differences in perceptions of violence among various nations, cultures, and beliefs play a role in defining violence, identifying its effects, and choosing appropriate responses when violence has occurred. The authors of the chapters in this one volume come from different backgrounds, but in reading their contributions, it is important to remember that they hold many things in common. They seek to understand the nature of violence and its causes. They wish to identify ways in which people (whether in a universal sense or within a particular group or culture) seek to cope with violence. And they understand that the success of a coping strategy or intervention in one area does not mean there will be an equal degree of success in others. They agree that violence doesn't affect only those who had connections to the victims of violence. They know that individuals grieving losses from violence are confronted with multiple, complex tasks relating to both the victims of the violence and the perpetrator of the violence. Finally, they know that the process of "meaning making" is an important one for those who have been involved in violence. The reactions of those involved in violence (whether as perpetrators, victims, or observers) will reflect the meaning(s) they attribute to the experience.

Readers of this volume who wish to apply its information in their own areas need to adapt what they read to fit their personal context. Together, caring people seek wisdom to be able to make effective choices related to the problems of violence. To achieve this wisdom, we need to have a fuller understanding of all aspects of violence and the grief that follows it. A starting point in understanding the many aspects of this topic is a solid foundation of fact-based knowledge. Hopefully this chapter and those that follow will add to that knowledge.

REFERENCES

Associated Press. (2005). "Pat Buchanan doused with salad dressing." Posted Friday, April 1, 2005 9:48 AM EST (1448 GMT).

Forliti, A. (2005). "First Funerals Held for Minn. Victims." Posted March 26, 2005 Associated Press.

Furlong, M, Morrison, G., Skiba, R., & Cornell, D. (Eds.). (2004). *Issues in School Violence Research,* Binghamton, NY: Haworth Press.

IWG. (1997). Document on violence and grief. *Omega: Journal of Death and Dying, 36*(3), 259-272.

Parkes, C. M. (1981). Evaluation of a Bereavement Service. *Journal of Preventive Psychiatry, 1,* 179-188.

Reuters. (2005). "Man kills one, injures others in Germany church." Posted 04/03/05 Reuters, Ltd.

Stevenson, R. (2003). Soldiers and students: Lessons in coping with loss and grief. *Illness, Crisis and Loss, 11*(3), 242-257.

Stevenson, R. (2004). Where have we come from? Where do we go from here? Thirty years of death education in schools. *Illness, Crisis and Loss, 12*(3), 231-238.

CHAPTER 2

Violence in the Family: Spirituality/Religion as Culprit and Comfort

Reverend Richard B. Gilbert, PhD, CT

"Where two or three people are gathered . . . there shall a perpetrator and a victim be." While it isn't quite the wording offered in the Christian scriptures, it is a compelling reminder to the Christian community, and to all religious communities, that violence, and for this chapter, domestic violence (violence in the family), is rampant in society, in our congregations and in our homes.

THE CHALLENGES AND STORIES

Congregations of all religions connote some expression of sanctuary. This may be an ornate space filled with stained glass and religious symbols or a simple room in the corner of a multipurpose room serving nursing-home residents. It tells the visitor that the space is sacred, a place where God dwells, and where we are free and safe to explore our questions, doubts, longings, and joys. Note the word "safe." Sanctuary means safe. To be in a sanctuary is to be in a safe place where no harm can come to us.

From theory to reality, it is time to issue a wake-up call to all religions, religious leaders and religious communities (none are immune or excused) that domestic violence is real and it is in our congregations. We must acknowledge this reality with a decisive, thoughtful, and collaborative plan of action to be both proactive and reactive in responding to victims *and* perpetrators within our primary responsibility of safety. We will discuss this further.

The second reality is that not only is domestic violence present in the lives of our congregants or the worshippers sitting next to us or in ourselves, but we must begin to address the teachings, practices, social and cultural attitudes and

24 / PERSPECTIVES ON VIOLENCE AND VIOLENT DEATH

customs, even the very scriptures that we teach and preach, as culprits that contribute to the problems of domestic violence. It is no longer acceptable to tell victimized spouses, generally women, that St. Paul (Ephesians 5:21-25) reminds us that the husband is the head of the household and, "If you were just a better wife, your husband wouldn't hit you." This happens. We also need to understand that many of our clergy are so weary, unhealthy in their ability to stay focused in demanding jobs with often very dysfunctional congregations, it results in a level of fear that, if we move out of our "boxes" of scripting, the official things that we must say, we will lose our jobs.

Some denominations are inherently threatened and threatening around issues of family violence. Some oppress women. The same scriptures that, to the Christian community, suggest that we are all one, equal, through the one baptism, also prompt us to suggest, however, that women are not equal, at least in terms of presiding at the altar or preaching from the pulpit. They can teach, clean, baby sit, and work in the kitchen, but some things can be done only by men. That doesn't mean that these teachings condone domestic violence, but the undercurrent of such teachings erodes an already complex "family system" that facilitates the dominance of men, the perpetuation of secrets, and the lack of safety that produces one "face" at worship or other religious gatherings and an entirely different one at home.

"Male headship sets the stage for domestic violence. I don't subscribe to that in any way, shape, or form. When we talk about a man and a woman in the sacrament of matrimony, we're talking about a partnership, people working together. One partner is just as much the expression of God's creation as the other" (Fr. Michael McDermott, quoted in Miles, 2000, p. 28).

Denominational Structures

Ritter and O'Neill (1996) wrote a breakthrough work on denominational struggles with power and control and their inherent susceptibility to abuse practices and behaviors. Even when these behaviors are not sanctioned by the religion, but opposed vigorously, their argument is that the risks are so woven into the fabric of their rituals, teachings, and life patterns, that the risk is always there. In fairness, it must be stated that many of these dynamics are in *all* religions and denominations in one way or another, but the radical nature of the styles they studied warranted our further attention.

> Many members of righteous religion require their churches to be philosophically reasonable, morally helpful, spiritually illuminating, and communally supportive. In this regard, they look to their religion to validate the unconditional goodness of the human being and God's unconditional love for each. Christians earnestly wish for moral guidelines that are sufficiently flexible so as to be relevant to their life circumstances without distorting the underlying Christian principles. In other words, they want the church to help

them become one with Christ within the context of their lives. Believers long for models of sacred lives with which they can identify, and for shaping stories broad enough to encompass their own human experiences. Finally, Christians want to be included in the community of faith and counted among God's children.

What a growing number of Catholics and Fundamentalists are experiencing, however, are church structures that fail to meet their expectations and spiritual needs and may, in fact, even thwart them. For example, they are continually threatened with exclusion and eternal punishment at the hands of an angry parental God unless they abide by the dictates of righteous law and authority. Members encounter a belief system that assumes that they are flawed and evil children, and that only out of fear will they stay in line. In this regard, believers are terrified into obedience by frequent references to Satan, hell, and a final judgment presided over by a jealous and wrathful God.

Like a negative or conditional parent, authoritarian churches interpret law and scripture in a manner so absolute and rigid that mere mortals seldom can achieve the perfection demanded. This creates a situation wherein the children of faith often feel guilty for not measuring up and pleasing a perfect parent. Many Fundamentalists and Catholics are thus made to feel shameful and unworthy by constant reminders of their fallen and evil natures. This sense of being defective at their very core leaves them at the mercy of the dictates and leadership of righteous religion (Ritter & O'Neill, 1996, pp. 13-14).

It would seem logical that the primary task of religion is to lay the groundwork for and nurture the spiritual voice of its members (Ritter & O'Neill, 1996, p. 15).

To be a good member of an authoritarian church is often to live with a divided self. One side is outwardly conforming and compliant, dutiful and faithful; whereas an inner, perhaps secret, side strives to express itself (Ritter & O'Neill, 1996, pp. 15-16).

Many of these religious approaches are appealing. We want absolutes in a world torn apart by a war many of us do not understand, economic challenges, skyrocketing health care costs, job problems, family dynamics. Absolutes that appear neat and tidy are seductive. If we follow the absolutes, we contend, as do many religious leaders and practices, we can make every social or personal issue equally black and white and thus manageable. Absolutes seldom work.

Righteous religion impresses upon its members that it speaks with the voice of God and thus can be relied upon as a bastion of absolute truth. . . . Thus, to obey the church was to obey God (Ritter & O'Neill, 1996, p. 19).

Denial of a Universal

Before you rip the chapter out of the book because you do not agree with the above, and we did preface it with the reminder that these dynamics, in varying

26 / PERSPECTIVES ON VIOLENCE AND VIOLENT DEATH

degrees, are inherent in any religious system and not true across the board in every congregation in a denomination, we must acknowledge that the pressures and injustices surrounding domestic violence require us to examine who we are, our beliefs and practices, and be prepared to question things that might need to be changed.

Al Miles (2000) has developed a significant ministry in awakening congregations to their responsibilities with regard to domestic violence. He has also suffered a good bit of verbal and social abuse for taking such stands. He persists because perpetrators persist. If domestic violence is a universal, then it is also a local issue. We have no excuse for our denial or blindness, and certainly not for any contributions we make to the problem, but must continue to address it in thoughtful and meaningful ways. Here are two of his anecdotes:

> After meeting with her pastor, Rita immediately called my office. Her description of the session shocked me. "I told Pastor Carl all about Walt's violence," she began, her words nearly suffocated by tears. "He stared at me for a long time then finally replied, 'I just can't believe it. I've known Walt since he was a little kid. He wouldn't harm a flea. Why have you waited all these years to tell this story? Are you sure you're not exaggerating things? You could ruin your marriage and Walt's fine practice [Walt was a prominent surgeon in the community.] He's such a great guy." Rita said she felt raped by her minister's words (Miles, 2000, p. 24).

> The pastor of another local parish heard about this sermon from one of his female parishioners who had visited Steve's church the Sunday I spoke. "You opened up a huge can of worms," said the minister when he phoned me five days after the service. "I've pastored this church for more than six years," he continued in a very loud tone, "but until this week no woman had ever brought up to me the issue of being abused by her husband. The woman from my church who attended your service is a wonderful Christian wife and mother. She has never made waves. But your sermon agitated her. She now claims her husband, who is one of the finest Christian men I have ever known, has been abusing her for years." According to this pastor, my sermon also caused other women worshiping in his congregation to "fall away from the truth." The spiritual leader tried to explain to me what this phrase meant. "The parishioner who attended your sermon has now riled several other so-called victims worshiping in my congregation," the pastor lamented. "They tried to tell me about their own Christian husbands abusing them. The women want to begin a support group for abuse victims and they asked to hold the meetings in the church on Saturdays. They even requested that I begin speaking about domestic violence from the pulpit. Why couldn't you have just left well enough alone?" (Miles, 2000, p. 54).

There is a case for clergy who must function as generalists. They are human, they are bound in by myriad expressed and unexpressed expectations of their job. If they have 500 members, they have 500 job descriptions. Some relationships are, at best, unhelpful, and many are dysfunctional. Codependence is rife in many congregations, sometimes fed into by needy clergy. All of us have our comfort levels around various tasks in the ministry, and as generalists, we are bound to be more competent in some areas than in others. It is important that we have basic competencies in all of these areas, effectively network, and know how to "walk with" parishioners to the specialists and programs best equipped to serve our parishioners. We understand that with Alcoholics Anonymous. Why can't we get it right with domestic violence? We are human. We have too many expectations. We have our levels of competency. That is reality. What should never be real is our slipping into the role of a new perpetrator, especially considering what is projected on us as men and women of God.

There have been reports at various times concerning some of the more closed denominations and sects (Amish, Mormons, Hasidic Jews), but they have been hard to document. The power of shunning, of being ostracized by your faith community has furthered their victimization and silenced their tears. Occasionally there are reports of those who rise above these fears because they have chosen to be survivors.

Faith and religious tradition are woven through most cases of IPV (intimate partner violence). In the Christian tradition particularly, there have been numerous incidents wherein their behaviors have been "justified," at least by the perpetrator and, as we have seen, often validated by others.

Most of the studies examining the rates of abuse within religiously identified couples have focused upon Christian denominations. Church attendance has been examined as a factor in intimate partner violence. Researchers found the lowest rates of spousal abuse among those couples attending church weekly or more . . . (Ware, Levitt, & Bayer, 2003). It was the men who reported "moderate attendance" that were identified as the typical Christian offenders, not the rare attendees. Ellison, Bartoski, and Anderson (1999) found male-perpetrated abuse was more likely when men held more conservative beliefs about the inerrancy and authority of the Bible than their partners and when men attended services more frequently than partners. There have been a few interview studies exploring batterers' religious beliefs. Shupe, Stacey, and Hazelwood (1987) found that most of the violent men rationalized that their violence was biblically acceptable and helped the family run more smoothly. Further, their wives struggled to reconcile similar beliefs with the pain of battering. These findings raise questions about the teachings that these men are internalizing from their religion and its doctrines on family. As it is not the intention of religious leaders to promote IPV, Ellison, Bartoski, and Anderson (1999) suggest that the messages taught in faith communities may not be accurately communicated to or comprehended by these moderately committed members (pp. 56-57).

With the growth of multicultural dynamics in many communities, including religious diversity, our neighborhood scenes have changed. We are becoming more aware of domestic violence in other cultures, cultures that we often do not understand and, for cultural if not for religious reasons, fail to recognize as

28 / PERSPECTIVES ON VIOLENCE AND VIOLENT DEATH

inappropriate behavior. Two specialists from Illinois are preparing to travel to Russia to help them deal with the previously denied domestic violence. Many cultures that keep women as subservient tend to experience domestic violence, often encased in a normative status as defined by the culture so that the culture itself becomes a perpetrator and heightens the level of victimization (Ware, Levitt, & Bayer, 2003).

Most studies on abuse and religion have been conducted within the context of the Christian tradition. One study with Islamic-Palestinian men (Haj-Yahia, 1998) indicated men who justified wife beating held more patriarchal and nonegalitarian marital role expectations, as evaluated by the Familial Patriarchal Belief Scale (Smith, 1990) and the Marriage Role Expectation Inventory (Dunn & DeBonis, 1979), and identified themselves as more religious (Haj-Yahia, 1998). Also, the more strongly the Palestinian men endorsed negative and traditional attitudes toward women on the Attitudes Towards Women Scale (Spence & Helmreich, 1978), the greater was their tendency to justify wife beating (Haj-Yahia, 1998, p. 57).

Victimization of Groups

For people who observe the religious world view, many would think (especially among Christians), that the only issue of the day is sexuality (i.e., homosexuality). It is another example of victimization, the denomination of scripture with spot passages, and an urgent issue that condemns and isolates people in ways that leave them victims.

Many have moved beyond their victimization to either steer clear of religion altogether or to form their own religions and denominations. The "reconstructionist" movement is active in Christian and Jewish circles. New movements to free up people and their beliefs around a variety of issues, including sexuality and gender, are becoming more common. In my Anglican communion, it is safe to say that there are no less than 30 independent expressions of Anglicanism in the United States, most divided around a particular theological or social point.

Just as family violence can increase around and against a gay family member, so does it go throughout congregations and denominations. This leads to isolation, lack of trust, a sense of distancing from God, and a forced secretiveness that compromises a person's self worth and sense of value before God and lessens the strength and community sense of a congregation.

> Torment, secrecy, conflict, misery and shame. Wherever you look—a movie like *Priest*, or faggots and fundamentalists shouting each other down on *Oprah* and *Ricki* and the rest, or tabloid tales of pervert priests in sex scandals, or broadsheet pontification about outed bishops and the Church being torn apart, or patronizing documentaries—the message seems clear: homosexuality plus religion can only equal bad news. And yet, for a large number of lesbian, gay and bisexual people, both spirituality and sexuality are sources of joy and strength (Sweasey, 1997, p. ix).

If spirituality is that which enables us to feel connected and find value, meaning and hope, and religion, for many, provide interpretations and rituals to accompany those spiritual riches, then anything that corrupts or compromises those dynamics would be considered abusive.

When people are oppressed and victimized, they learn, if they are to survive, to either become distanced from the source of those burdens or become indifferent to them. Some seek new expressions religiously and spiritually, even if they have to invent them. Some simply denounce God, church, and religion as irrelevant because it is essential for their sense of safety. For many it is not just frustration on a practical level, but a spiritual crisis of abandonment as people find themselves cut off from God, at least the God as presented to them, and thus without any spiritual clarity.

> My question is not, why should religions accept lesbian, gay, and bisexual people? We know the answers to that by now, even if religious authorities refuse to hear them. My question is why should queers want anything to do with religion? Religion has not, traditionally, been very welcoming towards queer people, and continues to advertise its hostility. The Catholic Church calls homosexuality an "intrinsic moral evil" and "an objective moral disorder." Texts from the Qur'an are used to justify executing gay men in fundamentalist Islamic nations, and stir up hatred elsewhere. A former Chief Rabbi in Great Britain looked forward to the day when genetic engineering might rid the world of homosexuals. The religious right in America claims homophobia is fundamental to its faith. Even the relatively liberal Church of England won't (officially) ordain practicing homosexuals and declares that we "fall short of the ideal." Heterosexuality is the eleventh commandment: followers of these and other faiths have experienced miserable inner torment, as well as prejudice and harassment, when they break it. People who do not hold religious beliefs—the majority, at least in Europe—are none the less hampered in their struggles against homophobia by the political power, and alleged moral authority, of religious institutions (Sweasey, 1997, p. 3).

It seems a human need for many to find their self worth and strength in power and control. It could be suggested that people generally need someone they can perceive as subservient to them, less than they are, so that they can rise above them and increase their "marketability." It is something like an upstairs/downstairs social structure, even within religious communities. The patterns of judgment, social isolation, and abuse are prevalent, and not only contrary to most religious teachings, but an abuse rooted in the very faith we seek to proclaim and live by.

The Spiritual Dilemma and the Loss of Faith

Several decades ago there were substantive studies shared suggesting that, at least in the United States, 60–70% of people in need of spiritual, emotional, and other support would go to a minister first. There were many factors involved in this. Of course there were trust and safety issues, although it often was a naïve

30 / PERSPECTIVES ON VIOLENCE AND VIOLENT DEATH

assumption that clergy were sufficiently equipped or emotionally available on every issue. There were the spiritual overtones related to life issues. There also was the general ease of availability vs. the cost, inaccessibility, and stigma factors associated with mental-health programs. In addition, many of the specialty groups and programs now available were not as readily available at that time.

In the latter years of the last century, there were shifts. Insurance funding made it easier to go to a therapist. Support groups abounded, including in bereavement. There was an emerging commitment to social factors on the local, state, and national levels. New attitudes around religion, even with a rapid growth of interest in spiritual matters, left some suspicious of the church, organized religion, and religious leaders. Sadly, many congregations and religious leaders, by their choices, attitudes, lack of interest, funding priorities, and in some cases, their preaching and teaching, put out many "not welcome here" signs that forced people to seek their spiritual (and other) support elsewhere.

Many religious communities and leaders worked valiantly around many of these issues, including domestic violence, supporting existing agencies, assisting with fundraising, crisis intervention, and leadership, through their preaching, teaching, and counseling, and, most of all, their willingness to stay informed and equipped. Oftentimes good people and religious communities were thwarted by professionals unwilling to deal with their own religious and spiritual baggage, a growing societal indifference to the religious establishment, and even the church/state issue.

The number of people seeking out a religious leader or congregation first for support is increasing. Some denominations are doing a better job on skills and issues awareness, as are the reconstructionist movements in many religions, which offer the traditions and rituals without the bigotry. Managed Care, already a tragedy in medical care, has spilled over into mental health with radical cuts in funding. Even those with health-insurance plans that provide coverage for counseling and therapy have witnessed a significant drop in their eligible benefits and sessions coverage. Many providers, especially those related to domestic violence, do not benefit from third party reimbursement and must rely on government and foundation grants as well as fundraising. This has proven harder for many agencies with the continued cuts in government funding (further marginalizing the victims) as well as the economic issues of the times that must stretch fewer dollars to more programs and agencies.

Clergy and congregations are thus being sought out early in the journey of victimization and violence by need, sometimes by default, but always with the hope and expectation that there will be safety, informed support, and access to the courage and resources needed to choose to be a survivor. This still is, at best, an assumption with selected providers, but it gives us the arena within which to educate these resources and keep after them with regard to their ill-informed approaches, problems with doctrines and denominational expectations, and their need to take risks professionally in a prophetic way which often pushes them out on a very frail limb when viewed by congregants.

There is a second, and perhaps more challenging, reason why many victims seek out their religious leaders and communities. Congregations, however defined, are supposed to understand sanctuary and be safe places. We are supposed to be expressions of hospitality and support. Even more important, we need to understand that to be victimized is to leave us so shaken in our *ability* to trust (in fact, victims must be very cautious about any future trust if they are to remain safe) that our ability and reason to trust in God is often damaged beyond repair.

"Faith communities can be an important resource to those women who face intimate partner violence (IPV). Studies have indicated that women often tend to disclose marital violence to faith leader; therefore leaders' understanding of IPV is critical for swift intervention and prevention" (Ware, Levitt, & Bayer, 2003, p. 56).

There are many definitions of spirituality.

> Rabbi Sarah's understanding of spirituality contains elements that many others would agree with: having a deeper sense of oneself, addressing the whole of life, and a connection with something bigger. It is also far more than just a set of ideas: spirituality is rooted in life-as-lived, as well as affecting how life is lived. . . . Religion's trying to make you what you're not. Spirituality is trying to make you who you are (Sweasey, 1997, p. 12).

Nancy Nason-Clark (1997) speaks about the battered woman around pastoral care concerns and responses. While this quote is under the heading of "Evangelical Clergy and Wife Abuse: Knowledge and Response," and speaks in specific ways to this general audience, it is an important observation for all of us to consider.

> Celebrating family life, along with its traditional values and patterns, has become a cornerstone of the contemporary Christian message. As a result, pastors—evangelical and liberal alike—have found themselves defining marriage and family patterns, offering advice to enhance marital satisfaction, and counseling those family members whose experience does not match the ideal preached from church pulpits. Parishioner demand for pastoral one-to-one counseling has grown exponentially in recent years, though there is little evidence that clergy themselves are more predisposed—or trained—to offer it. Clearly, the more family life is placed on a sacred pedestal, the wider the gap between the rhetoric and the reality (p. 57).

Consider a few stories on the severity of the matter from the *faith* perspective as well as the sense of being "turned away at the door." The following excerpt is from a larger narrative about a visit between a chaplain and a victim of domestic violence in a shelter:

> At the appointed time I (the chaplain) was ushered into a quiet room for conversation. While I sensed that the eyes of the woman in the living room

32 / PERSPECTIVES ON VIOLENCE AND VIOLENT DEATH

were following me (it is a safety issue for the clients, so the stare was understood and appropriate), something told me that this person was checking me out with a very specific agenda in mind. She was my client.

Jane [fictitious name] was dressed well, giving the appearance of a professional woman ready to go to work. It was a noticeable contrast from some of the other clients who were watching me. While watching me carefully she also seemed to be contently reading a magazine.

I invited her to select a place to sit down that was comfortable for her as I introduced myself. Before I could even sit down the calm composure became the eye of a hurricane. She had gone on the offensive. Standing, waving her fist at me, a face red from the intensity yet with tears streaming down her face. She shouted, *Don't you dare tell me that God loves me. I won't have it. . . . Do you hear me? God let his son get beat up and now he let me get beat up, over and over again. My husband, some pillar of the church!, he sat in the front pew every Sunday. Everyone loves him. He greets everyone, sings the hymns louder than everyone, stays after to listen to everyone's stories . . . then comes home and beats me up. I sang a hymn wrong. I didn't quite get the gist of the sermon. I don't look holy enough when I pray. God let his son get beat up and he did nothing to keep me safe . . . even when I prayed. Some shepherd he is.*

There was then a pause in the dialog and the shouting continued, at times targeting the chaplain as "God's representative." The chaplain was working very hard to stay patiently focused, not react to the specific points and, because he knew the husband referred to, to tend to how he personally felt in this given scenario. The story resumes . . .

I don't know why I would expect you to be any different. All ministers are alike, aren't they?! How could I tell our pastor that his little pet, the layman he trusted and counted on, was an abuser? How could I tell him about the swings that follow a sermon about love. The yelling when things don't go right at work? The threats when the kids aren't as he wants them to be? My pastor wouldn't believe it. I tried to tell him. I tried to tell him that things weren't right, that I was scared, that some nights I just wanted to run away. He could only say something stupid, like, "Well, there are times when we all want to run away." He couldn't hear a thing that I had to say. He just promised "to pray for me."

Pray? Ha! That's a laugh. A lot of good that does. I pray for peace, and get conflict. I pray for safety and I am afraid to close my eyes and sleep. I asked God to show me what I was doing wrong and the only message I got was from my husband, telling me that everything is my fault.

Either I am the worst of sinners, the lousiest of Christians, or "The Lord is my Shepherd" means absolutely nothing to me or to anyone. God just doesn't care, or seems to play favorites. Maybe if I served on more church committees, sang the hymns better, saved more from my "food allotment" to make the offering bigger, my husband would respect me more (Gilbert & Gilbert, 2002, p. 283).

To be a victim is to feel violated, ripped apart, exposed, raw; and unless we belong to a religious context that pounds similar dynamics or expressions before

VIOLENCE IN THE FAMILY / 33

us, these are unfamiliar dynamics that emerge from and through our feeling a loss of safety that thrusts us into new feelings, new responsibilities, and new doubts. It can redefine who we are, how we function, our life meaning, our beliefs, *and* our ability to believe. What relevance does a God of love have when everything in our life setting contradicts not only love, but all that we believe God represents? We come to our religious leaders with not only the rawness of the horror of abuse, including the meaning (especially the *theological* meaning) of family, but also the very practical alarms racing through us as we consider the needs of family and children, and the secondary issues of finance, future safety, housing, health insurance, and the myriad other issues that often choke feelings with the harshness of reality.

Those of us who work in bereavement are now learning, thanks in no small part to the recent research of Therese Rando, that there is a difference between being traumatized and being bereaved. The losses that accompany any family violence are numerous and require much work on the part of very fragile, often spirit-broken people. When you add to that burden the pain and complexity of mourning, now complicated by various factors including fear and the real or projected lack of safety, then you have women, men, and children in need of sanctuary, purpose, meaning, and hope. In our praxis section we will discuss this in further detail, but here it is essential that all caregivers, especially clergy, be informed; safe themselves, as well as providing safety for those in their care; emotionally healthy and focused; and able to distinguish between any personal, biblical or denominational baggage that may be present so that it does not become a new scandal for the person who has been victimized. Victims need time, space, and safety to explore all of what they are experiencing, thinking and feeling; including their disappointments with God (or their beliefs), their religious communities, even the minister with whom they are speaking.

A *Christianity Today* (2005) editorial piece on tsunamis reflected on the issues of tragedy and violence and their impact on faith systems. It offers something to this discussion:

> When people take any traditional Christian line of comment by itself, they can paint a devilish picture of God. But each traditional line of thought has some basis in revelation and gives us an important piece of the picture.
>
> Here's a list. God allows evil events in order to bring greater good; God allows evil in order to challenge us to spiritual growth and maturity; God may allow tragedy, but he rewards us with greater blessings in heaven; God is in control of whatever happens, and his ways are inscrutable; God punishes the wicked with disasters. Each of these has an important element of truth, but when isolated from the Bible's big picture, the statements distort our understanding of God. . . .
>
> Formulated outside its biblical context, the conundrum of evil casts God in the role of a mechanical engineer who is responsible for designing a system and keeping it functional. But the God of the Bible does not merely keep

34 / PERSPECTIVES ON VIOLENCE AND VIOLENT DEATH

> things in working order. If that were his primary role, the infidels and
> unbelievers would have a point. The dynamic God of the Bible is a savior, not
> a mechanic. And through the Incarnation, he is a participant in our suffering,
> not the distant observer posited by deists (p. 28).

Not all of you buy into those specific images, or even those scriptures, but it is imperative that we understand that to be a victim is not only contradictory to the mainline religions in our land, but a significant spiritual crisis for those thrust into the deep recesses of victimization. How does it sit when some minister says, "God loves you?" The stinging words (Gilbert & Gilbert, 2002) shared above highlight the folly and tragedy of pious platitudes that not only offer little comfort or relief, but easily become a further victimization.

Clergy (and others) talk about trust and faith with people who trusted and suffered because of it. Discussions lead to prayer, and victims say, "I prayed and prayed and God did nothing to stop my husband." It is pointed out (and this error is not limited to clergy!) that the victim is better off without the perpetrator, but the victim wrestles with powerful fear (and justly so) because of the continued threat of guns; the lack of a place to live; the further disruption of the lives of children by relocating and removing them from their schools; uncertain employment and financial circumstances; and the issues of housing, health insurance, and retirement. Victims, if their sense of inquiry hasn't been totally beaten out of them, demand answers when there aren't any, seek a God who often has let them down, feel further compromised by religious leaders and communities (whether that is a fair accusation or not), but grasp for the thinnest straw in their barren wilderness to even *want* to dare to live anew.

Clergy have much to offer symbolically. They, by virtue of their office, represent sanctuary or safety. People may not know how to approach clergy; may not know ones to call; may approach one blindly; or may be unable to discern their level of compassion, competence or even if they are safe. Again, clergy are not the only ones to face this necessary scrutinization. They also get unfair treatment from experts in the field. Many of them are one-time victims, who may not have addressed their own spiritual and religious issues, and can project their religious indifference or bias onto the victims in their care. While the clergy who are working very hard with and for victims are wonderful, competent, and caring, they need to be committed to collaborative approaches to problem solving, and they need to be embraced by others who seek that same collaboration.

People go to a religious leader because they expect something. It may be trust, safety, answers, direction, reconciliation, or several of these at the same time. Each bears a different meaning depending on the faith tradition and the needs of the victim, but the religious leader chosen, whether by last-ditch effort or choice, is sought out with the hope (a rare commodity for victims) that there can be some relief and release.

VIOLENCE IN THE FAMILY / 35

Wesley Carr, retired Dean of Westminster Abbey, is internationally recognized for his writing and speaking on pastoral care and his frequently strong words to clergy. "Pastoral work expressed in care for others has been central to the Church's life from its earliest days" (1997, p. 7). A study of the current literature on pastoral care, especially works by respected authors like Dean Hoge, Donald Cozzens, and Eugene Peterson, highlight, as documented in Gilbert's *Healing the Holy Helpers: Healthy Clergy for the Third Millennium* (2003), that the clergy, as individuals and as a professional group, are often in severe professional, vocational, and health crises, and face an unheralded pace of change, unrealistic expectations, and overwhelming challenges (many of which find them very ill-equipped). In some ways, we find clergy experiencing their own victimization. That may be the one bridge or point of connection to victims of violence.

Clergy will find restoration of vocation and health, even against insurmountable odds and expectations, as they go back to being who they are and what they are *called* to be. Carr continues, ". . . Ministry, whether by ordained or lay people, which is concerned with the well-being of communities or of individuals" (1997, p. 9). Clergy are entrusted with a symbolic role and presence, as prophets and, in some sense, "keepers of truth," suggesting to others that, when approaching clergy (and we will discuss their responsibilities further in the closing chapter) they are safe, they will receive empathetic listening and wise counsel and, in some way, feel drawn closer to the God they seek, the God they feel may well have abandoned them.

Set adrift in very turbulent congregations (as well as other settings), clergy are easily distracted by chores and unreasonable expectations. Some are openly chastised for "straying too much from Jesus by getting involved in social matters," but many valiantly strive to be what they are called to be, even engaging those same critics in a collaborative ministry of service.

Clergy often bear the brunt of our anger toward God. We project onto clergy our pictures of God (as well as the feelings behind those pictures) and project onto God the pictures (and disappointments) we often feel with clergy. It can become an unfair conversation, sometimes even hostile. The clergy are the professionals in the scenario and need to expect these tensions, respect them, even facilitate them, confident in their role and competence so that the victim, if the victim chooses, can dare to move beyond the present issues to a clearer picture of self-worth and hope-filled, safe living. Carr (1997) clarifies this point, "Ministers are servants who are confident enough in their own authority to risk it being examined and used by others as a means to recover or discover their own" (p. 190). In that arena of mutual respect and vulnerability, there can be healing.

Clergy, like the victims who seek them out, must be aware of the boxes they are in, that threaten them or that may be projected onto them by others. A simple example. "What does a single, celibate clergyperson know about intimacy and marriage?" is as faulty as saying that, "Because I do not drink, how could I possibly understand the powers of addiction?" It isn't our story; it is about being

36 / PERSPECTIVES ON VIOLENCE AND VIOLENT DEATH

a guest in the story of another person. At the same time, many clergy face very serious boxes that bind them and can limit their effectiveness. The earlier quote from Nason-Clark states it well. If we are bound by very specific teachings on scripture, marriage, and family, especially in today's climate, and additionally, if our "jobs" depend on upholding the "company line," how free will we be to really commit to safety first, not saving the marriage? Clergy have failed to listen to threats, including weapons, in an effort to bring husband and wife together, because they take on the mission of saving the marriage. It not only shuts the victim down in the presence of the perpetrator, it leaves the minister's safety perilously threatened.

Nonclergy must acknowledge their role as spiritual caregivers. Matters of the spirit are not limited to clergy and are not limited to people of similar tradition and belief. They are about acknowledging that the "tough-God questions" are there, are appropriate, are unanswerable, and remain potential open doors for victims, that bring all of us into the work of spiritual caregiving. It is important that those who are not as comfortable in these areas, especially those not tuned into personal biases or unresolved issues, be very clear on boundaries. Protecting the client is equally a boundary issue: setting limits around what we can and cannot offer and also knowing religious leaders we can safely call on to assist the client. Collaboration is essential, and is built on doing appropriate networking while setting aside our own agendas and biases. We may not believe in God. We may have no use for religion or clergy. But that doesn't have to be thrust upon the victim.

Nason-Clark (1997) shared several quotes from women in various focus groups. One shared,

> I hid from the church because I didn't feel safe, that wasn't a safe place for me to come and talk without feeling like I was being judged and condemned and put down. . . . I don't know if a lot of our pastors would even recognize abuse because they're not trained to . . . they should be much, much, much more aware. . . . They've never lived or experienced it, so they don't know what to say (p. 121).

A second woman commented,

> I guess I see the church perhaps as a, a safe haven. A place where if they're at the end of their rope and have nowhere to go I would hope that the church would be one place . . . where they could be given some love and immediate attention (p. 121).

It isn't just about competent, safe clergy who nonjudgmentally stay empathetically present with those who seek them out. It isn't just about being very cautious about offering "the company line." It is not just a crisis of socialization, safety, family, health, and self-esteem. It is a crisis of *faith*. Everything that the victim has treasured about God, faith, religion, ethical values, or the standards for living that became their code for life is threatened. As they have fallen deeper into their valley of despair the distance between them and God has widened to a gap considered insurmountable. It also means that clergy must address, as the victim is willing, the failures in the congregation or the work of the minister: times when the rituals or practices have hurt rather than blessed, and also when the language and practices of *that* religious expression or structure may no longer suit the victim. A healthy clergyperson will not be threatened by this.

For some, God is a second perpetrator. As the husband or significant other let them down, so did God! It may offend some conservative readers, but the reality is that the victim has to decide to give God a second chance (God can handle it!), and God may be redefined, be "on probation," and the minister may have to identify other words (faith and trust may be out) so that the victim can find a new spiritual pathway that is safe and comforting.

Also helpful for providers are the new bereavement approaches offered in recent years under the careful watch of Dr. Therese Rando (1993) and The Reverend Dr. Kenneth Doka (1989, 2002). Rando has pushed the perspectives surrounding complicated mourning and the implications of these complications on the griever and on caregivers. Victims face the complications of mourning, along with the myriad losses that accompany victimization. Her extensive studies, writing, and speaking have helped us identify individuals who are at risk for more complex and complicated grief experiences, thus generally requiring a more therapeutic, often different, approach for intervention and care.

Rando has expanded her recent studies with important insights about the weight born by trauma and bereavement (loss). We often frustrate grievers because we approach circumstances primarily as care for the bereaved, failing to understand (and thus compromising the effectiveness of the care and the griever's journey, as well), that many such people need considerable time, space, and clarity to deal with the fact of having been traumatized, before they can even grasp the pain of loss. Think of these implications for victims and also for those of us who provide care.

Doka has introduced "disenfranchised grief" to grief work. Disenfranchised grief is defined as a loss that "Cannot be openly acknowledged, socially validated, or publicly mourned" (2002, p. xiii). Victims of domestic violence have experienced long periods of traumatization, words, psychological games, social isolation, physical abuse, on top of the death of many feelings, dreams, marriages and families as we idealistically believe they should be. Many victims are so traumatized by guilt and shame—the fear of being "found out"—along with the ongoing control and power exerted by the perpetrator, that they fear any expression of their victimization. It is an enormous issue around therapy and feelings, but above all, safety. It is a population of the disenfranchised.

When you build on these brief discussions of traumatic loss and disenfranchised grief while caring for victims, you gain further insight into the spiritual and religious dimensions of victimization. Victims may need to restructure their faith perspectives and redefine theological truths in their healing process. It is

38 / PERSPECTIVES ON VIOLENCE AND VIOLENT DEATH

enormously traumatic to feel betrayed by God, to feel that you have failed in the eyes of God, and to bear a level of shame from that failure that can weigh more heavily than the bruises and broken bones It is hard enough, because of the ongoing control of the perpetrator, to come to terms with one's victimization and to seek help. How much harder is it to acknowledge such deep anger and resentment toward God or the growing sense of shame that one can experience when told over and over again that one has failed God and "deserves victimization?"

Violence shatters the spiritual self and destroys centeredness. It is a byproduct of abuse. "Soul appears, then, to be a concept of the self that speaks of the whole person integrated in his or her unique way. Trauma disrupts or destroys this integration of the total person" (McBride, 1998, p. 13).

How does one repair or replace a "lost soul?" How does one restore that sense of harmony or balance suggested by McBride? Trauma shoves us away from points of peace, safety, and harmony; and the trauma of victimization, itself a spiritual crisis, must be mourned and "repaired" along with other "fragments" of person, life, and story.

> Trauma occurs when one loses a sense of having a safe place to retreat within or outside oneself to deal with frightening emotions and experiences. . . . Trauma made them feel cut off from God, from others and even from themselves. . . . How can a viable spiritual life exist in the midst of all this? How can a connection with God be established (or re-established) in the midst of radical separation? (McBride, 1998, pp. 12-13).

This, then, becomes the crucial issue for pastoral care and why many victims approach a clergy person. They may need a safe person (sanctuary) on whom to lash out at God and to perhaps even hope that the restoration of soul, that integrated and harmonious inner self, that has been pounded out of them, might happen. Clergy must be informed about domestic violence, and be aware of the limits of their abilities in pastoral care (along with their rightful place as pastoral caregivers); also acknowledging that, at times, they may be the one voice in the collaboration of voices to raise these serious complicated aspects of spiritual crisis. The traumatized face an enormous crunching of their psyche, even their desire to live. When such despair and disbelief are expressed against God, society (and sometimes specific clergy or religious teachings and practices), either refuses to believe the depths of this anguish or condemns it altogether. This paints the clergyperson or religion as the perpetrator and forces the victim into the deeper silence and depression that generally accompany the disenfranchised.

Clergy will need to address their own issues and pursue stronger competencies in this area. They will need to tend to their own feelings, including fear. This fear is real. It generally is not fear of the victim, but it can be fear of the issues and also the fear of what these issues can do as the knowledge of them ripples through the congregation. This fear can also be heightened by our own vocational and professional challenges and lack of health.

VIOLENCE IN THE FAMILY / 39

Yes, if pastors begin to admit that victims worship among us; if in our sermons, classrooms, and prayers we identify domestic violence as a morally reprehensible act, then victims will come out in droves to seek our support. Is this the so-called "can of worms" many ministers are afraid of opening? Why? (Miles, 2000, p. 55).

PRAXIS

This section is offered as a "to do" list for clergy, other ministers of care, and other professionals to aid them in finding helpful and easily personalized ways to engage people in the issues and to respond effectively and safely.

1. *Accept the reality that domestic violence exists; it exists in larger numbers and in your congregation or place of ministry.*
   - One in three women is sexually assaulted in her lifetime
   - Every 7.4 seconds in the United States a woman is physically assaulted in her home
   - 95% of batterers are men
   - 75% of abused women reported that their children had been abused physically or sexually by their abusers
   - 65%-95% of incarcerated women are victims of prior abuse
   - 1/3 of women seeking emergency room treatment are victims of domestic violence
   - 25% of pregnant women are abused during pregnancy
   - Each of us is affected by the prevalence of abuse in our culture
   - 66%-80% of victims of sexual assault know their offenders
   - 64% of rapes and 84% of attempted rapes are never reported
   - More than 50% of women will experience violence from intimate partners
   - Spouse/partner beating results in more injuries requiring medical treatment than rape, auto accidents, and muggings combined.

2. *Know your boundaries, but don't be afraid to stretch them*

As with many professions, there are generalists and specialists. In the language of pastoral care, this is often identified as pastoral care, pastoral counseling, and pastoral psychotherapy. While there are some contemporary trends that suggest that there is no difference, this author contends that there is a difference, often measured in terms of competence, but always in terms of relationship. The generalist in ministry is the shepherd, one who seeks and embraces the "lost" and, recognizing the need for care, guides them to the specialist. When the pastor gets in over his or her head, it can lead to not only the victimization that emerges from incompetence but also on some occasions, the clergyperson (who is also a victim, bearing too much of the burden or story) can damage the pastor/person relationship if he or she doesn't carefully self monitor. There is a place for the pastoral counselor and the pastoral psychotherapist, as specialists, to help fight victimization. Generally they are involved for the short haul. The pastor/generalist

40 / PERSPECTIVES ON VIOLENCE AND VIOLENT DEATH

is then free to stand aside during the psychotherapy, protecting the privacy of those discussions, in order to be the shepherd over the long haul of the restorative process.

Clergy have much to offer. While speaking to what clergy bring to the bereavement team, these insights are equally relevant here. It is a dualism in pastoral care because these resources are valid and necessary both for the victim and also the members of the collaborative team (Gilbert, 2002).

- Help explore the deeper spiritual issues in a safe and informed way
- Symbolic presence of another "word" or perspective
- Linkage to religious communities, traditions, and values
- Administers sacraments and rituals as requested by the victim
- Represents sanctuary or safety
- Integrates spirituality into the individual's journey as an option and gift as well as in his or her approach to the team
- Advocacy, including advocacy before and to God (p. 186)

Clergy assist with "assessment" and "treatment." To assess is to give meaning. Chaplains in health care, crunched for time and staff, find it harder to assess spiritually and easier to shove it into the medical model. Assessment around spiritual matters is always done by that individual, not the provider. To feel loved, nurtured, valued, hopeful, respected, nourished, and safe are the hallmarks of a healthy spirituality. The absence of any one of these, however prompted (and certainly that is common in domestic violence), sparks the spiritual crisis. The medical model might suggest, "This person *feels guilty* because she has doubts about God's relevance in her life." The medical model would then prescribe a course of action to address the identified issue or need. The pastoral model understands what it means to be a guest in a person's story and *invites* the person to "invite the pastoral person 'in,'" exploring, for example, the *possibility* of guilt, what this person determines that to mean, and how they might address it together.

Pastoral caregivers are in a better position to examine religious expressions that may have been flawed, or at least unhelpful, before the victimization. A cartoon shows a child listening to a radio, the singer proclaiming, "God is watching over you," to which she replies, "Oh no, not God AND Santa Claus." Part of this spiritual discernment is to help explore what the person's understanding of God (beliefs) was before this victimization and whether or not it was helpful or healthy. Through careful pastoral support, as well as aid from others in the caregiving team, the victim may not only reach survivorship, but a life worth living.

3. *Don't be surprised if you meet resistance*

Resistance is no stranger to pastoral care and pastoral caregiving. Even healthy spirituality leaves room for denial and doubt (despite what some preachers may tell you). The resistance here may come as a surprise, be very hurtful (as well as clouding the minister's sense of vocation and job security), and therefore run the risk of confusing or further victimizing the already distraught parishioner or client.

If clergy are generalists, their task is to join with others rather than being the lone rangers in domestic violence cases. We have too many of those already. Some congregations get caught up in the issues of domestic violence and want to do their own programs. For some, it is well meaning; for others it is a typical expression of their need to be in control. Oftentimes these sparks of interest run their course and are fueled by well-intended energy that doesn't always bring the expertise, and long-term stamina, needed for effective and safe programming.

Clergy need to understand that they might experience resistance when they approach established domestic-violence programs to offer even competent and compassionate care of the highest professional order. Many shelter and agency workers are themselves victims and may also have experienced bad outcomes with clergy, congregations, God, or religion. Some simply have not addressed their own spiritual issues. Others bear the cumulative result of frequent complaints from victims expressing their spiritual outrage or religious disappointment.

Some caregivers do overprotect, thus failing to maintain healthy boundaries and do some things that might be better for the clients. Others have tried repeatedly to engage clergy and congregations, only to give up in total frustration and disgust.

Some clergy are going through their own victimization as they address the demands and challenges of ministry in this new millennium. Many are still trying to discern their role and place. While settings and expectations often change, or at least evolve, their *vocation* does not change. Clergy must be persistent in reaching out to victims and to those providing for their care. They must do it as compassionate shepherds who understand the issues, are healthy within themselves, understand collaborative teamwork, and are patient enough to "earn their way onto the team."

As tough and scrutinizing as professionals in the field of domestic violence may be, especially the client advocates, it doesn't necessarily match the turmoil that clergy may feel from parishioners or denominational leaders and structures. For clergy to be and stay healthy themselves, and around these issues, they may well be challenging traditional views of scripture, doctrine, polity, and practice. When this happens, congregational leaders, members, and judicatory leaders may start questioning the minister. You can see why it is sometimes safer, yet tragic, simply to stay neutral on these and many other issues. To do the right thing comes at a cost. In addition, many parishioners do not expect their pastors to be engaged in things "outside the Bible." As one person commented while shaking my hand (with great reluctance that made her hand feel like a cold fish) after my presentation on the Christian response to violence, "I came here to hear about Jesus, not domestic violence." How can anyone "hear Jesus" and not hear the cries of the victims?

42 / PERSPECTIVES ON VIOLENCE AND VIOLENT DEATH

Consensus seldom exists in ministry, even within the same congregation. Whether it be within a congregation, throughout a denomination or religion, or collectively among religious leaders of a parish, denomination, or neighborhood, we would get little done if we waited for everyone to agree. We must take risks, bearing the consequences; and clergy are encouraged to find the few in leadership or in the pews ready to get involved: those who are willing to take the risk, to seek out a few other clergy (you will never get all of them), or neighbors and friends willing to step forward because it is the right thing to do. It isn't about numbers; it *is* about doing what we can to right a terrible wrong.

CONCLUSION

Domestic violence is real. It is ugly. It is wrong. It is sinful. It destroys lives (often literally), individual aspirations and dreams, relationships, families, friendships, neighborhoods, workplaces, congregations, nations—the world. It is no longer valid to be in denial about a very real and pervasive problem, *especially a problem that, intentionally or otherwise, we may have furthered in the name of God or our religious values and practices.* Are we to be comforters or culprits? You cannot own the latter until you willingly acknowledge it.

Miles (2000) says it best in his concluding remarks:

> Most ministers—females and males, conservatives, moderates, and liberals alike, from all ethnic and racial backgrounds—have done a very poor job of caring for victims of domestic violence and in dealing with those individuals who perpetuate this sin. We continue to deny the prevalence of the problem, especially within our own faith groups and among couples worshipping in our churches. We fail to recognize the connection between some of the doctrines we espouse, and the abuse and subjugation of females. And, while readily acknowledging the fear and helplessness this issue engenders, we refuse to seek the necessary training to help us care effectively for victims and confront perpetrators. We even fail to talk about or acknowledge the fact that some of our own male colleagues are themselves abusers (p. 185).

As we reflect on violence in and throughout the world, there is compelling evidence that it is time for all of us to choose actively and proactively for peace.

> Almighty God, whose will it is to hold both heaven and earth in the peace of your love: Give peace to your (Church), peace among nations, peace in our homes, and peace in our hearts. Amen. (adapted from *Prayers, Thanksgivings, and Litanies*, The Church Hymnal Corporation, 1973, p. 30).

REFERENCES

Carr, W. (1997). *Handbook of pastoral studies.* London: NLPC Resources.
Christianity Today. (2005). Tsunamis and birth pangs. *Christianity Today,* February 2005, p. 28.

Doka, K. (Ed.). (1989). *Disenfranchised grief: Recognizing hidden sorrow.* Lexington, MA: Lexington.

Doka, K. (Ed.). (2002). *Disenfranchised grief: New directions, challenges, and strategies for practice.* Champaign, IL: Research Press.

Dunn, M., & DeBonis, N. (1979). *Teachers' and counselors' guide to accompany a marriage role expectations inventory.* Saluda, NC: Family Life Publications.

Ellison, C., Bartoski, J., & Anderson, K. (1999). Are there religious variations in intimate partner violence? *Journal of Family Issues, 20*(1): 87-113.

Gilbert, R. (200a). *Healing the holy helpers. Healthy clergy for the third millennium.* Unpublished dissertation. South Bend, IN: The Graduate Theological Foundation.

Gilbert, R. (2002b). Spirituality and religion: Risks for complicated mourning. In G. Cox, R. Bendiksen, & R. Stevenson (Eds.), *Complicated grieving and bereavement: Understanding and treating people experiencing loss* (Ch. 12). Amityville, NY: Baywood.

Gilbert, R., & Gilbert, S. (2002). The victim of domestic violence and sexual assault. In R. Gilbert (Ed.), *Healthcare & spirituality: Listening, assessing, caring* (Ch. 22). Amityville, NY: Baywood.

Haj-Yahia, M. (1998). A patriarchal perspective of beliefs about wife beating among Palestinian men from the West Bank and the Gaza Strip. *Journal of Family Issues, 19*(5): 595-621.

McBride, J. L. (1998). *Spiritual crisis: Surviving trauma to the soul.* Binghamton: Haworth.

Miles, A. (2000). *Domestic violence: What every pastor needs to know.* Minneapolis: Fortress.

Nason-Clark, N. (1997). *The battered wife: How Christians confront family violence.* Louisville: Westminster John Knox Press.

Rando, T. (1993). *Treatment of complicated mourning.* Champaign, IL: Research Press.

Ritter, K., & O'Neill, C. (1996). *Righteous religion: Unmasking the illusions of fundamentalism and authoritarian Catholicism.* Binghamton: Haworth.

Shupe, A., Stacey, W., & Hazelwood, L. (1987). *Violent men, violent couples: The dynamics of intimate partner violence.* Lexington, MA: Lexington Books.

Sweasey, P. (1997). *From queer to eternity: Spirituality in the lives of lesbian, gay & bisexual people.* London: Cassell.

Ware, K., Levitt, H., & Bayer, G. (2003). May God help you: Faith leaders' perspectives of Intimate Partner Violence within their communities. *Journal of Religion & Abuse, 5*(2), 55-81.

CHAPTER 3

Conflict and Violence in the Workplace: An Existentialist Analysis

Neil Thompson

Existentialism as a philosophical school has waxed and waned in its influence on social thought. The emergence of poststructuralist and postmodernist thinking has, to a certain extent, occupied some of the territory previously associated with existentialist thought. However, this is not to say that existentialism no longer has anything to offer. Indeed, this chapter will argue that existentialist concepts can be very useful in clarifying conflict and violence in the workplace, and thereby acting as a guide to addressing the problems involved. The fact that the philosophy is no longer fashionable in no way detracts from its explanatory power or its usefulness as a basis for action.

I shall begin by providing a brief outline of some of the main tenets of existentialist thought. Space does not permit a detailed exposition, but guidelines on further reading are provided below. After introducing existentialism in broad outline, I shall show how it can be helpful in explaining conflict in the workplace. From this I shall proceed to examine violence in the workplace in reference to existentialist thought. Finally, I shall briefly outline how existentialism can help to guide our actions in responding to the problems of workplace conflict and violence.

EXISTENTIALISM

Being and Nothingness (Sartre, 1958), a classic work in the existentialist canon, carries the subtitle *An Essay on Phenomenological Ontology*. This refers to the two key component parts of existentialism: phenomenology and ontology. I shall briefly outline each in turn.

Phenomenology

Moran (2000) makes apt comment when he argues that

> Phenomenology was announced by Edmund Husserl in 1900-1901 as a bold, radically new way of doing philosophy, an attempt to bring philosophy back from abstract metaphysical speculation wrapped up in pseudo-problems, in order to come into contact with the matters themselves, with concrete living experience (p. xiii).

Different thinkers have developed phenomenology in different directions, but what they all have in common is an emphasis on perception and meaning making. Phenomenon, a word of Greek derivation, can be defined as that which is perceived, so phenomenology can be seen as a school of thought based on the importance of perception and, by extension, the role of interpretation in making sense of what we perceive. That is, phenomenology is concerned with meaning making. As Merleau-Ponty (1962) clarifies, meaning is not something that lies within the individual or in the objective world around him or her. Rather, it lies in the relationship between the individual (subjectivity) and the wider circumstances (objectivity).

Phenomenology is based not on looking for absolute meaning or uncovering eternal truths, but on exploring how meanings are created through our engagement with the social world. This approach can therefore help cast light on conflict and violence by linking such phenomena to the process of meaning making.

A key part of phenomenology is the recognition of the importance of the subjective dimension—the role of the individual in interpreting and thus making sense of experience. However, it is not purely a matter of subjective interpretation; there is also the objective dimension to consider, the world "out there" that presents itself to our senses. Sartre (1982) understood the two dimensions of experience: the subjective (or inner) and objective (or outer) to be engaged in a dialectical relationship; that is, the subjective and objective dimensions interact and influence each other. The objective circumstances that we find ourselves in will influence our perception of the world and, in turn, our perception of the world will influence those objective circumstances (for example, in terms of how we react to them and, in doing so, act upon them). The "dialectic of subjectivity and objectivity" can therefore be seen as a central part of Sartrean existentialism.

Ontology

Ontology is the study of being and is concerned with how reality is defined and experienced.

> Ontology is the study of being, an analysis of the deeper questions which underlie our various conceptualisations of the world. It is concerned with issues which relate to fundamental aspects of existence. What is being? What does it mean to exist? What is the relationship between being and non-being?

CONFLICT AND VIOLENCE IN THE WORKPLACE / 47

These are examples of ontological questions. They are difficult questions and so it is not surprising that the answers offered are not simple either (Thompson, 1992, pp. 28-29).

One important element of existentialist ontology is the recognition that human existence is simultaneously personal and social. This means that existentialism is critical of attempts to explain human experience that either (a) rely solely on individualistic, psychological approaches that fail to do justice to the social context; or (b) address the social context, but somehow lose sight of the human actor within that context. In attempting to understand conflict and violence, it is therefore necessary to take into account both psychological and sociological dimensions.

This ties in well with the notion of the dialectic of subjectivity and objectivity outlined above. Phenomenologically, it is important to recognize the inner and the outer, and the dialectical relationship between them. Similarly, from an ontological point of view, it is important to recognize individual experience as part of a wider sociological reality. From this we can deduce that, while it is a necessary condition to understand individual experience, it is not a sufficient condition, we also need to consider the wider context within which such experience arises.

Key Concepts

By applying phenomenology to ontological concerns, existentialism offers a rich philosophy that embraces a number of important concepts. Space does not permit a comprehensive analysis, so I shall limit myself to what I see as some of the central concepts that have a bearing on conflict and violence in the workplace.

- *Hell:* Sartre (1955) defined hell as other people. By this he meant that other people get in our way in our attempts to achieve our goals (a traffic jam is a good example of this, insofar as it illustrates how the wishes of other people to reach a particular destination can frustrate our own wishes to reach our chosen destination). This underlines that it is necessary, in trying to understand the actions of an individual, to locate the individual's behavior within the context of his or her relationships with others as well as the frustrations and conflicts that can be involved in those relationships.
- *Contingency:* Human existence is characterized by flux and uncertainty. Insecurity, then, is not a breakdown from a putative norm of security, rather, it is a basic feature of what it means to be a human being. What we usually refer to as security is, from an existentialist point of view, our ability to deal with insecurity.
- *Responsibility:* Making choices involves taking responsibility for our actions. Existentialism rejects deterministic approaches that deny responsibility for one's own decisions and ensuing actions. Individuals make choices

48 / PERSPECTIVES ON VIOLENCE AND VIOLENT DEATH

within the context of a wide range of social influences, but it is the person who makes the choice, not the social circumstances. Responsibility can be seen as the price we pay for freedom—if we reject the idea that our actions are governed by others or by circumstances beyond our control, then the conclusion we must draw is that we are responsible for our own choices and the actions (and inactions) to which they lead.

• *Identity:* Selfhood in existentialist terms is not a relatively fixed "personality," but rather a journey of self-creation through the decisions we make, the responses to those decisions, and the social circumstances in which they are made. In making choices on a daily basis, we subtly shape the patterns and structures that form our identity, our sense of who we are, who we have been (our roots) and where we are going (our future plans).

These are important concepts in their own right as part of a broader attempt to explain human behavior; but they are particularly relevant to casting light on the more specific sphere of conflict and violence in the workplace.

CONFLICT

Conflict can be said to arise when there is tension between two or more forces. In the workplace, this is likely to be a daily occurrence, if only because of inherent tensions between the employing organization and its employees (as a reflection of the broader social conflict between capital and labor). Indeed, it can be argued that workplaces are inherently conflictual. Every time there is a disagreement, a situation wherein one person reluctantly accedes to another's wishes or when there is the use of power to deal with a particular issue, there is, in effect, conflict.

An existentialist analysis of conflict would go a step beyond this and argue that conflict is intrinsic to human existence. In engaging with the social world, each of us will encounter other people whose wishes and plans run counter to our own—the "hell" of other people. It would be naïve to assume that we can achieve our aims without coming into conflict with others (for example, competition from other candidates for the promotion we seek or competition to acquire scarce resources). Organizations are, of course, based on power dynamics and power dynamics, by their very nature, involve conflicts—if there were no conflicts of interest, for example, there would be no need to exercise power.

However, this does not mean that such conflict has to manifest itself in unpleasant ways. Given that conflict is, in existentialist terms, such an integral part of everyday life, it is necessary to recognize that we have many ways of managing conflict without it becoming problematic or resulting in unpleasantness. This can be deceptive: because we tend to become very skilled in managing day-to-day occurrences of conflict, it is a very easy mistake to make to assume that conflict is largely absent. I would refer to this mistake as the "fallacy of

CONFLICT AND VIOLENCE IN THE WORKPLACE / 49

harmony"—the false assumption that everyday life is characterized primarily by harmony or consensus and that conflict is a breakdown from this putative norm. What is regarded as conflict is generally an *escalation* of conflict; that is, when everyday levels of conflict reach a new, higher level. This fallacy of harmony can be problematic in a number of ways:

- It can lead to conflict being seen as a failure and thus conceived in unduly negative terms (conflict can have positive as well as negative outcomes— many positive developments arise from conflict situations; for example, people who initially enter into conflict with one another may, in due course, develop great respect for one another for having stood by their principles and thus form the basis for working in partnership effectively in the future).
- It can desensitize us to conflict, with the result that we become blasé about the conflicts we encounter (because we do not recognize them as conflicts). This can leave us ill-prepared for dealing with more serious conflict issues.
- It can reduce confidence in managing conflicts by distracting attention from how much experience and skill we have in managing the tensions that arise on a daily basis. This again can leave us ill-prepared.

It is therefore important to recognize conflict as part of everyday reality, rather than an aberration from it. This means that conflict-management skills can be seen as a development of everyday people skills (Thompson, 2002), rather than a set of separate, specialist skills reserved for expert "troubleshoooters" (although some conflict situations can require highly specialized mediation skills if the conflict has escalated or become entrenched).

A central part of conflict is communication. This applies in two senses. First, conflict is in itself a form of communication; that is, communication often occurs by means of conflict. For example, if I fall out with a particular individual, the conflict is likely to manifest itself through my communications with that individual (content, style, frequency, and so on), and so the conflict itself becomes a vehicle of communication. Second, conflict commonly arises as a result of breakdowns in communication; for example, when someone's nonhostile intention is interpreted as an attack as a result of a communications mismatch (the two individuals being from different cultures perhaps) (Guirdham, 1999).

Communication is, of course, linked to understanding and, as the well-known figure within existentialist thought, Søren Kierkegaard (1996) so aptly put it: "The most sublime tragedy consists without doubt in being *misunderstood*" (p. 15). Much conflict arises, then, from misunderstanding which, in turn, can be traced back to communication difficulties.

One problem with how communication issues are handled within organizations is that there can be a tendency for them to be dealt with in a technical or mechanistic way that fails to do justice to the subtleties of the rich and complex

50 / PERSPECTIVES ON VIOLENCE AND VIOLENT DEATH

field of human communication (Thompson, 2003). In particular, the narrow approach to organizational communication often fails to address issues of identity and meaning making.

Traditional models of communication are based on a simplistic, tripartite model: broadcast or transmission of the message, reception of the message, and the "noise" or interference that can stand in the way of the former reaching the latter. This mechanistic model fails to take into account such vitally important issues as the role of culture (including organizational cultures) in shaping communicative encounters; that is, it is not sufficiently phenomenological, as cultures are a major influence of processes of meaning making.

Similarly, narrow, mechanistic conceptions of communication neglect the important role of identity. We are not simply passive receivers of information from others or from our environment more broadly. Information processing can be seen as an active process, in part filtered through the medium of identity; that is, how I interpret sensory information will depend in part on how I perceive (and conceive) myself. For example, if I feel confident in my professional role, I may interpret a friend's aspersions about my capabilities as a joke and respond accordingly, with no conflict involved. However, if I lack confidence in my professional capabilities, I may interpret the comment made by my friend as a subtle attack on me, rather than as an example of humor, and thus experience the situation as a conflictual one.

However, it would be a mistake to attribute too much importance to communication in seeking to explain conflict. As was noted earlier, existentialist ontology is based on the premise that human existence is simultaneously personal and social. In order to understand human experience, it is therefore important to consider wider sociological factors as well as psychological ones.

One sociological aspect of conflict is, of course, power. It would be naïve not to recognize the role of power in shaping the experience of conflict. Power, like communication, is also a concept that is prone to oversimplification. It is not simply a matter of two types of people, those with power and those without. The reality is far more complex than this. Who has power, over what and over whom, will vary according to context and circumstances. Someone who is powerful within one context may have very little power in another (for example, a police officer may be quite powerful while in uniform, but far less so at other times when the symbolic power associated with a police uniform is absent).

There are also different types of power: relational power (manager/employee, for example), the power of knowledge, power deriving from skills, charismatic power, and so on. However, it is fair to say that whenever we encounter the exercise of power, we encounter potential or actual conflict. An understanding of conflict therefore needs to be based in part at least on an understanding of power.

Space does not permit a detailed analysis of power from an existentialist perspective, but one point that is worth emphasizing for present purposes is that power can be linked with the existentialist notion of "hell"—seeking to achieve

CONFLICT AND VIOLENCE IN THE WORKPLACE / 51

our objectives within a context of other people's plans and projects standing in our way—as well as that of identity. How an individual defines him- or herself will both depend on and produce power relations. It will depend on power relations insofar as others will play a part in shaping our sense of self. For example, a person who engages in workplace bullying or harassment may succeed in destroying the confidence of his or her victim and thereby affect the victim's sense of self through this process of the abuse of power (Thompson, 2000a). It will produce power relations based upon how one person relates to another, thus contributing to the power balance between them (for example, by showing excessive deference to somebody I respect, I may be contributing to an unequal power relationship, inviting that person to exercise power over me).

Contingency is another existentialist concept that is very applicable to our attempts to understand conflict. Accepting the contingency of human existence means accepting the possibility of conflict escalating at any time. We therefore need to develop skills in managing it, rather than adopt the "ostrich" approach of avoidance behavior (this is a point to which I shall return below). Indeed, this is a common problem with conflict management: the tendency to ignore conflict and hope that it will go away. Of course, sometimes conflicts will go away if we ignore them—they will peter out or be resolved without our intervention. However, such an approach involves playing a dangerous game. It involves taking the risk that such conflicts will escalate and get out of hand.

Rather than adopt the avoidance approach, a much wiser way of tackling conflict is to undertake a risk assessment: to evaluate what is involved in terms of

- How likely is it that this conflict will escalate (or even combust)?
- If it does, what is at stake? How much harm is it likely to do?
- What is the worst case scenario?
- How likely is this to come about?
- Can you afford to risk this happening?
- What steps can be taken to deal with this conflict?
- In terms of investing resources in such activities, how does this compare with the costs of the harm that can arise from the conflict being allowed to develop further?

This is not an exhaustive list of issues to address, but it does give a picture of the sorts of questions that are relevant to weighing the risks involved (the risks and potential costs of not dealing with the conflict versus the risks and costs of trying to address it). This illustrates well the concept of contingency—the recognition that there are no guarantees and that managing conflict is in effect a microcosm of the wider sphere of risk taking within the context of a world based more on contingency, risk, uncertainty, and insecurity than on fixity, stability, and certainty.

52 / PERSPECTIVES ON VIOLENCE AND VIOLENT DEATH

VIOLENCE

While some violence can arise without direct conflict; for example, when someone is acting under the influence of alcohol or drugs—in a high proportion of instances we can recognize a continuum: conflict → aggression → violence. That is, a considerable degree of violence can be seen to involve an escalation of conflict through aggression, although it has to be recognized that:

(I)   conflict does not necessarily lead to aggression; indeed, most conflict is managed very effectively without recourse to aggression at all; and

(ii) aggression does not necessarily lead to violence. Aggression can often be used as a form of bluff, with the person who is displaying an aggressive attitude having no intention of resorting to violence. For example, a customer or client of an organization may use aggression as a means of seeking to gain advantage in some way, perhaps to obtain additional resources.

It is also important to recognize that aggression is often understood in essentialist terms; that is, as something fixed and beyond the control of the individual. It is commonly presented as if the result of an uncontrollable biological urge: "I couldn't help it; I just lost control and hit him." However, this is not consistent with the existentialist notion of responsibility. We are the authors of our own actions, and this includes aggressive or violent actions. This is an example of the existentialist notion of "bad faith," which involves a lie to oneself in taking refuge in excuses for our behavior: "It's my nature . . . ," "I had no choice . . . ," and so on. Bad faith stands in the way of taking responsibility for our actions and is therefore an obstacle to empowerment and self-development.

How, then, can we account for what appears to be an uncontrollable urge by using existentialist concepts? Here the work of Jean-Paul Sartre can be particularly helpful. He sought to explain masochism and sadism in terms of how we deal with some of the existentialist challenges of human existence. He was interested in how an individual's self-perception owes a great deal to the perception of others (the "look of the Other," as Sartre called it). He conceptualized masochism as a (misguided) attempt to feel "real" and thus deal with the challenge of contingency and the insecurity it can bring. By allowing another person to inflict pain, the masochist can feel more "objective" or concrete and thus less prone to the insecurity of a fluid identity based on contingency and responsibility. It is an attempt to find an easy (yet doomed to failure) way out of the anguish associated with being an existentially free individual who not only has to take responsibility for his or her actions, but also for the sense of self we derive from our actions.

Sadism in particular (and to a large extent violence in general) can be seen to be a parallel strategy also based on bad faith. The person inflicting the violence seeks to feel more real by treating another person as an object (objectification).

CONFLICT AND VIOLENCE IN THE WORKPLACE / 53

This is done within a context of contingency, insecurity, and responsibility for our own identity, and it thereby seeks a form of solace in harming others. Sartre points out that this, too, is a strategy doomed to failure, with the result that the perpetrator of violence feels the need to inflict further violence because they remain dissatisfied in their attempt to gain a sense of security.

The existentialist notion of "hell is other people" is also relevant when it comes to explaining violence, as it shows that there are constant opportunities for conflict to lead to frustration and thus potentially through to aggression and then violence. When this is combined with the existentialist concept of contingency and the insecurity associated with it, we can see the potential for violence to arise, particularly for someone who has not developed the interpersonal skills needed to manage low level, everyday conflict.

Identity issues can also be relevant to violence. This can apply in (at least) two ways. First, being violent may, for some people, be part of their sense of self; that is, they may pride themselves (and thus define themselves) in terms of their reputation for violence. In effect, this is an example of the use of violence as a form of exercise of power or, to be more precise, abuse of power. Second, violence may be an individual's response to when an aspect of their identity is threatened or disrespected. For example, someone who feels insulted may respond with violence because they feel that there has been a significant violation of their sense of self; that is, when the self-respect that forms part of identity is undermined, the response is likely to be an angry one that may well result in violence.

The issue of identity can be particularly relevant to the workplace. This can apply in relation to staff: an employee's identity is likely to be influenced in part at least by their work role. Similarly, it can relate to clients of the organization: in many cases, a person's identity may in part be influenced by their status as a client of a particular organization (for example, a member of a sporting club or a student at a university). The role of identity can therefore be very significant in the workplace.

Threats to identity through the undermining of self-respect can thus at times be a source of anger and, in turn, violence. Anger is an emotional response that does not necessarily lead to violence or even aggression. However, anger can clearly be linked with violence in some circumstances. Newhill (2003) makes an important contribution to our understanding of these issues when she draws on the work of Charles (1999) to establish the following list of factors that can contribute to an "anger epidemic":

- *Compressed time*: the constant experience of having too many things to do and too little time to do them in.
- *Communication overload*: the constant bombardment of information simultaneously from multiple sources 24 hours a day.
- *Disconnectedness*: being physically or electronically connected to others but without meaningful emotional intimacy that is nurturing and supportive . . .

54 / PERSPECTIVES ON VIOLENCE AND VIOLENT DEATH

- *Cost*: not having enough money and resources to live comfortably while living in a society of unbridled consumerism, entitlement, and enormous wealth for a relatively small proportion of the population.
- *Competition*: increasing demands to achieve status, power, and profit with fewer resources available to achieve them.
- *Customer contact*: too many people to deal with, especially in the service area (including social work services), and contacts that are cold, unpleasant, uncaring, and frustrating, leading to an "assembly-line" feeling (managed care may be an example).
- *Computers*: coping with the kinds of technology, increasing dependence on computers to function at home and work, as well as being constantly on call due to e-mail, faxes, cell phones, pagers, and so forth.
- *Change*: social and technological change that moves faster than the ability of many people to adapt comfortably.
- *Coming of age*: significant changes in the nature, experiences, and expectations of the various life cycle stages due to both sociological influences and changes brought about by medical and health care advances.
- *Complexity*: coping with all these aspects (pp. 24-25).

This quotation paints an important picture of the strains of modern life that can be a source of anger and thus potential violence. It should be noted that most if not all of these are directly or indirectly related to the workplace.

When we add to this our existentialist understanding of the prevalence of low level conflict in everyday life, we can begin to move away from an individualistic, essentialist conception of "the violent character" toward a much more sophisticated understanding. In particular, we can recognize the need to incorporate a sociological perspective, to draw upon an understanding of not only what factors can lead to violence, but also (given the prevalence of conflict and potential sources of anger) what factors can inhibit violence (the role of socialization into society's norms and values, for example).

TACKLING CONFLICT AND VIOLENCE IN THE WORKPLACE

The discussions in this chapter of conflict and violence have shown that we are dealing with a very complex set of issues, and we have only scratched the surface in some respects. It should therefore be clear that it would be very unwise to attempt to come up with simple solutions to the problems that conflict and violence can generate. However, it is possible to draw out a small number of practice guidelines that can help to rise to the challenge of conflict and violence in the workplace.

Of course, what has been stated so far in this chapter can be seen to apply to conflict and violence in general, but here my focus is specifically on workplace conflict and violence; partly because the workplace provides a microcosm of wider society in some ways, and partly because, when focusing on practical

CONFLICT AND VIOLENCE IN THE WORKPLACE / 55

solutions, it is important to look at the specific circumstances in question (reflecting the point made earlier that there are dangers involved in focusing too narrowly on the individual).

The workplace presents many challenges in terms of conflict and violence. While some workplace settings are particularly prone to violence (police work, for example), all workplaces involve some degree of risk, whether from clients (dissatisfied customers in a retail setting; drunken users of emergency room services, and so on) or from colleagues (for example, as a result of one colleague having an affair with the partner of another colleague).

The following guidelines are offered as a platform for tackling problems: a foundation on which to build a more substantive strategy for handling conflict and violence in the workplace.

1. *It is important to invest in developing interpersonal skills.* Given that conflict is an everyday matter, it is important to be aware of the central role of interpersonal skills in managing the minutiae of day-to-day interactions to prevent conflicts from escalating and to draw out the positives where possible. There is much to be gained from ensuring that staff are well-versed in interpersonal skills (for example, through the provision of appropriate training).

2. *We need to base our understanding on the dialectic of subjectivity and objectivity.* There is a long-standing tendency to reduce complex psychosocial matters to individual concerns by adopting a narrow perspective that prioritizes the personal dimension at the expense of a balanced consideration of the wider issues. In order to address conflict and violence issues satisfactorily, we need to avoid individualizing the situation and make sure we adopt a more balanced perspective that also takes into consideration the wider contextual factors.

3. *We need to develop the skills involved in managing contingency.* Managing contingency means, in effect, managing insecurity. As mentioned earlier, in existentialist terms, achieving a sense of security amounts to being able to manage the insecurity of human existence. It is not a matter of seeking a chimerical security based on a false sense of fixity. This is a complex undertaking and can be a real challenge of leadership: to develop and sustain a workplace culture where staff feel sufficiently well-supported to be able to deal with the insecurities of wrestling with the flux of working life in a complex and constantly changing workplace arena.

4. *It is important to respect identity.* Workplaces can boost or undermine self-esteem and self-respect. In order to minimize conflict and violence, it is important to make sure that factors that undermine selfhood (bullying and harassment, for example) are not allowed to feature. This is another challenge of leadership.

56 / PERSPECTIVES ON VIOLENCE AND VIOLENT DEATH

CONCLUSION

The subject of conflict and violence in the workplace is a very complex one that raises a wide range of significant issues. One chapter cannot do justice to these complexities, and so my aim has been the more modest one of introducing a number of existentialist concepts and beginning to map out how they can help us develop our understanding of conflict and violence in the workplace.

While the ideas presented take us forward to a certain extent, the discussion also shows just how far we have to go to develop a more comprehensive existentialist theory of conflict and violence. In this respect, this chapter should be seen as a contribution to a process rather than any attempt at producing a definitive understanding in its own right. As such, I trust it can make a positive contribution to the appreciation of the subtleties and complexities of this important aspect of social life.

GUIDE TO FURTHER READING

Sartre produced an extensive literature on existentialism. A simple guide to his early work is Sartre (1948), while his later work is presented in Sartre (1963). For more detailed and in-depth expositions, see Sartre (1958) and Sartre (1982). There are numerous commentaries on Sartre's work. My own favorite is Barnes (1974).

Existentialism as a foundation for social-work practice is discussed in detail in Thompson (1992) and in more summary form in Thompson (2000b).

A very good overall introduction to existentialism is to be found in MacQuarrie (1973).

REFERENCES

Barnes, H. E. (1974). *Sartre.* London: Quartet.

Charles, C. L. (1999). *Why is everyone so cranky?* New York: Hyperion Press.

Guirdham, M. (1999). *Communicating Across Cultures*, London, Macmillan.

Kierkegaard, S. (1996). *Papers and journals: A selection.* Harmondsworth and New York: Penguin.

MacQuarrie, J. (1973). *Existentialism.* Harmondsworth: Penguin.

Merleau-Ponty, M. (1962). *Phenomenology of perception.* London: Routledge.

Moran, D. (2000). *Introduction to phenomenology.* London: Routledge.

Newhill, C. E. (2003). *Client violence in social work practice: Prevention, intervention and research.* London and New York: Guilford Press.

Sartre, J-P. (1948). *Existentialism and humanism.* London: Methuen.

Sartre, J-P. (1955). *No exit and three other plays.* New York: Vintage.

Sartre, J-P. (1958). *Being and nothingness: An essay on phenomenological ontology.* London: Methuen.

Sartre, J-P. (1963). *Search for a method.* New York: Vintage Books.

Sartre, J-P. (1982). *Critique of dialectical reason.* London: Verso.

Thompson, N. (1992). *Existentialism and social work.* Aldershot and Vermont: Ashgate.

Thompson, N. (2000a). *Tackling bullying and harassment in the workplace.* Birmingham: Pepar Publications.

Thompson, N. (2000b). Existentialist practice. In P. Stepney & D. Ford (Eds.), *Social work models, methods and theories.* Lyme Regis: Russell House Publishing.

Thompson, N. (2002). *People skills* (2nd ed.), Basingstoke and New York: Palgrave Macmillan.

Thompson, N. (2003). *Communication and language: A handbook of theory and practice.* Basingstoke and New York: Palgrave Macmillan.

CHAPTER 4
Violence and the Dehumanization of Victims in Auschwitz and Beyond: Remembering Through Literature

Gregory Paul Wegner

> All questions pertaining to Auschwitz lead to anguish. Whether or not the death of one million children has meaning, either way man is negated and condemned.
>
> Elie Wiesel, *One Generation After* (1972), p. 56

> Life in a concentration camp tore open the human soul and exposed its depths. Is it surprising that in those depths we found only human qualities which in their very nature were a mixture of good and evil?
>
> Viktor Frankl, *Man's Search for Meaning* (1984), p. 94

Some sixty years have passed since the end of the death camps that so powerfully symbolized the racist and anti-Semitic agenda of Nazi Germany. Never before had a modern state marked itself so indelibly through the industrialization of mass murder and the brutally efficient annihilation of human beings. Nazi crimes against humanity, to borrow a legal phrase from the Nuremberg Trials, continue to raise questions of a deeply moral nature. Who is ultimately responsible for the perpetration of such horrendous crimes? What made the working of such violence possible, and what does this imply about the relationship among perpetrator, victim, and bystander? What legacy is left for those who survived mass shootings, hangings, and executions across Europe under the Nazi boot?

These are only three of a legion of complex and difficult questions about the Holocaust that continue to challenge the thinking of historians, poets, artists, theologians, and social scientists to this very day. The ashes of the dead at Auschwitz cooled six decades ago, but their passing casts a long and deep shadow over not only the relationship between the individual and the state, but also what it means to be human.

60 / PERSPECTIVES ON VIOLENCE AND VIOLENT DEATH

THE ROLE OF LITERATURE

Literature represents a means of trying to explain the unexplainable in human experience, even something as horrific and disturbing as genocide and mass murder. In this chapter, voices of mourning emerge from several Holocaust survivors, primarily through the medium of prose with support from poetry in two parts of the essay. Their experience of loss, oftentimes articulated in the literature decades after 1945, could in some way be related to the struggle with what Elie Wiesel called the almost impossible task of communicating the unfathomable to those who never experienced the horror of the death camps. It is therefore with great humility that readers are brought within this select circle of writing.

The literature is vast. Thus, the idea of exploring selected works from Holocaust survivors regarding violence and dehumanization may appear to be a tall order for a chapter of any collected work. The literary voices of Elie Wiesel, Primo Levi, and Tadeusz Barowski, considered in this essay, remain selective in light of the myriad books and essays published by not only them, but by many other Holocaust survivors as well. Collectively, they inform readers about the human struggle to come to terms with a variety of losses in the face of a regime dedicated to their dehumanization and demise.

DEHUMANIZATION AS LEGAL PRINCIPLE

Legalizing and bureaucratizing the process of dehumanization in the Third Reich had profound implications for both perpetrator and victim. As Raul Hilberg (1985) noted in his groundbreaking work, *The Destruction of the European Jews,* the Nazi oppression of the Jews passed through several phases, each designed to strip victims of their humanity. He identified these stages as definition by decree, concentration, mobile killing squads, deportations, and killing-center operations (Hilberg, 1985). Such a process did not exist in a historical vacuum. The Nazis exploited an already well-established history of religious and economic anti-Semitic hatred with roots going back to the Middle Ages (Katz, 1994, pp. 225-400, 529-577).

That Catholic and Protestant churches reflected certain anti-Semitic traditions was certainly not lost on Nazi propagandists. Repeatedly exploited by the Nazis for its strident anti-Jewish tone was Martin Luther's incendiary pamphlet, "On The Jews and Their Lies" from 1543. Though not an advocate of murdering the Jews, Luther tapped an already old prejudice by identifying Jews with the Devil. In his towering rage, Luther demonized Jews and called for violent measures against those in the Jewish community who refused to be converted to Christianity. Luther called Christians to, among other things, burn down Jewish synagogues and schools, raze Jewish homes, remove Talmudic writings, prohibit usury, and forbid rabbis to teach (Luther in Sherman & Lehmann, 1971, pp. 121-306; Smith, 2002, p. 309). Although it would be grossly ahistorical to make Luther's anti-Jewish attacks responsible for the gas chambers of Auschwitz, his work is mentioned here because it provided an important part of a larger justification of brutality against Jews by Nazi propaganda.

What set Hitler apart from all other rulers of modern states was his emphasis on racial and "quasi-scientific" justifications for anti-Semitic hatred above and beyond the more traditional religious and economic forms of anti-Semitism. Under the Third Reich, a broad legal framework for legitimizing the separation of Jews from the rest of the population came through the initiation of the Nuremberg Laws in September of 1935. As legally designated non-Aryans, Jews not only lost citizenship and political rights, they also were not allowed to marry Aryan Germans. Under this legislation, a Jew was defined as anyone who claimed at least one Jewish grandparent. The emphasis on preserving the myth of "purity of bloodlines," legitimized under this legislation, defined Nazi Germany as first and foremost a biological state. Documentation of bloodlines became a matter of life and death.

Six years later, in September of 1941, Jews were required by law to wear the Yellow Star of David on their clothing to set them apart from the general population. From 1933 to 1944, a multitude of specific laws prohibited Jews from engaging in everything from entering swimming pools and beaches, owning pets, attending schools, and visiting barber shops to having meat, eggs, or milk. The Nazis remained so obsessed in legally restricting the Jews that, even as late as November of 1944, a special regulation was handed down forbidding Jews the use of warming rooms. By this time, there were only 15,000 Jews left in Germany out of a previous total of 500,000 in 1933. Most German Jews had already suffered deportation, execution or fled the country (Anti-Defamation League, 1978, p. 265; Ginzel, 1984, pp. 8-12; Richter, 2000, pp. 168-172).

"Definition by decree" set down a moral and legal judgment on who was essentially human or subhuman (*Untermenschen*), thus providing support for further isolation and persecution (Hilberg, 1985, pp. 12-26). The victims suffered economically from Nazi-enforced boycotts and decrees removing them from their professions. The "Night of the Broken Glass" or "Crystal Night" in November of 1938 resulted in the Nazi destruction of numerous Jewish synagogues and businesses across Germany, along with the arrest of 26,000 who ended up in concentration camps. In one of the most cynical of all Nazi legal actions, the government fined the entire Jewish community 1 million marks in what became know as a "debt of atonement" for the resulting damage (Noakes & Pridham, 1975, p. 467). Between Crystal Night and the outbreak of war with Poland in September of 1939, the Nazi state promulgated no less than 200 anti-Semitic laws (Walk, 1996).

The reality of war provided a critical context for a serious escalation of persecutions that eventually culminated in the creation of the death camps. The war with Poland eventually opened Nazi plans for the establishment of ghettos in Lodz, Warsaw, and other locations in occupied areas under Nazi rule. Apparently

62 / PERSPECTIVES ON VIOLENCE AND VIOLENT DEATH

confident of ultimate victory over the Russians in the east, Nazi leaders set into motion during October of 1941 a process that became known as the *Endlösung* or "final solution" to the Jewish question. Mass executions of Jews in the Soviet Union had already begun in June of 1941, augmented by the activities of mobile killing squads or *Einsatzgruppen* organized and manned by SS units. By the end of 1941, these squads had murdered 500,000 people. In December of that same year, Jews were killed in gas vans at Chelmo, a death camp in Poland. Eventually, Poland became the site for five other death camps, originally designed for the sole purpose of murdering Jews. These included Auschwitz, the largest camp of them all, along with Treblinka, Sobibor, Maidanek, and Belzec.

An important distinction must be made between concentration and death camps since both of these institutions obviously figured rather prominently in the literature left by survivors. Concentration camps, first opened in 1933 with Dachau, imprisoned hundreds of thousands of political prisoners including Communists, Social Democrats, homosexuals, Free Masons, Jehovah's Witnesses, Jews, Soviet POWs, and Sinti and Roma. Many fell victim to direct execution through gassings, shootings, and hangings, while others perished under extreme and inhumane conditions leading to starvation and disease. The brutal exploitation of inmates as forced laborers also figures prominently in the writings of camp survivors.

By contrast, the death camps claimed a singular purpose: the industrialized mass murder of its victims. The numbers of those who perished under all forms of Nazi mass murder both inside and outside the concentration and death camps remains almost incomprehensible. An estimated 250,000 Sinti and Roma (Gypsies) died during the Holocaust, along with about 5,750,000 Jews and as many as 3.3 million Soviet prisoners of war. Tens of thousands of homosexuals lost their lives. In what was called the T-4 killings, over 70,000 mentally ill and disabled people were among the first to die in gas chambers, used at selected mental hospitals across the Reich. The victims of the T-4 killings were among the very first of the Nazi victims (Berenbaum, 1993, p. 127; Burleigh, 1997, p. 126; Fleming, 1984, p. 217; Gilbert, 1985, p. 824; Gilbert, 1993, p. 244).

The vast system of railroads connecting the camps run by pencil-pushing bureaucrats with their long lists of victims and timetables, constituted a critically important factor in the efficient and well-ordered Nazi system of mass execution (Browning, 1992). Enzo Traverso, capturing the spirit of this thinking in the following passage, suggests that Nazi violence targeted against Jews was not always motivated by anti-Semitic hatred.

> In the vast majority of these cases, the zeal of these bureaucrats of the Final Solution did not stem from anti-Semitism—not that they were unaffected by it, far from it. Hatred of the Jews was not the motive for their behavior. Their zeal in applying measures of persecution and in setting up the logistical apparatus of extermination was prompted as much by professional habit as by a generalized indifference. It was the bureaucracy that organized the application of the Nuremberg Laws, the census of the Jews and the partial

Jews, the expropriation of Jewish property within the framework of measures for the "Aryanization" of the economy, the herding of Jews into ghettos and their subsequent deportation, the management of the concentration camps and of the killing centers (Traverso, 2003, p. 43).

The tremendous Nazi investment in rolling stock and SS security personnel to support the smooth and timely administration of these killing centers offers a humbling reminder that this was first and foremost a "war against the Jews" (Hitler's speech, January 30, 1939, cited in Domarus, 1962). The enemies list articulated by the Nazis was long. In the midst of all of these persecuted groups, it was the Jews who remained marked by Hitler and his minions for total annihilation down to the last man, woman, and child.

This does not suggest in any way that non-Jewish victims who lost their lives under the Nazis remain any less important to remember in history or literature. To engage in arguments over a comparative catalogue of suffering would be most counterproductive and an insult to the dead. Most of the survivors who eventually wrote about their experiences in the Holocaust, regardless of their social or religious backgrounds as victims, appeared to have entered an extended period of mourning after 1945. Decades would pass before some would take up the pen to record their recollections about this moment in history that changed their lives forever. Very soon, the survivors of the Holocaust and witnesses to the Nazi policy of mass murder will be gone. For years to come, the literature that they created will remain an omnipresent call to remembrance.

Much of this literature comes to us from those who were relatively young at the time of the Holocaust. The elderly, infirm, and very small children often were among the first to fall to disease, starvation, or immediate selection for the gas chambers. A good share of the literary selections came from survivors who were teenagers or in their twenties when the death camps were operating, primarily from 1942 until their liberation in 1945. Some participated in the forced marches to places like Bergen-Belsen as the Russians neared Auschwitz and the other camps in Poland. The voices heard in these pieces come from Jews and non-Jews, as well as those whose religious faith deepened or dissipated in the face of brutality from the hands of not only the Nazis but also other camp personnel—including inmates. Camp conditions and the struggle for survival held the potential for turning human beings into beasts. What follows in this foray into literature is not meant to outline a chamber of horrors, but to probe a deeper understanding about how surviving victims tried to deal with the forms of violence that surrounded them.

THE QUESTION OF SURVIVAL

Violence, as Holocaust survivor testimony affirms, could be a gross affront not only to the body, but also to the spirit. Those who arrived at the "kingdom of death" (Dawidowicz, 1986, p. 129) in Auschwitz and other camps came on cattle

64 / PERSPECTIVES ON VIOLENCE AND VIOLENT DEATH

cars, often at the end of a long and harrowing journey. The process of dehumanization and Nazi psychology united in what became rolling coffins for some of the victims. The cattle trains symbolized the Nazi strategy of treating the victims like animals while further degrading them in a host of ways. Crammed in tightly, often upwards of eighty people to one cattle car, passengers struggled with little space to move and a severe shortage of water and food. Maintaining privacy was not possible. A single pail in the corner often served as a makeshift latrine.

A fifteen-year-old Jewish boy from Sighet in Hungary made the journey with his family on one of the cattle cars to Auschwitz in 1944. The young Elie Wiesel had grown up in his village with a strong desire to study the mystical cabbala and the Talmud. The searing experience of the Holocaust, preserved in the harrowing book *Night,* changed his faith forever. The book reads like a novel as well as a memoir. "The race toward death," he wrote, began with the German arrest of the Jewish leaders in the community. The heavy hand of Nazi legality manifested itself once again with the decree that all Jews must remain in their homes for three days "upon pain of death." The Nazis did not have to work this dragnet themselves. The Hungarian police, as willing accomplices, readily assisted in making sure that Jews turned over all gold and jewels to the authorities that same day. Three days later, the Jewish community moved into a ghetto surrounded by barbed wire (Wiesel, 1982, pp. 8-26).

Deportation soon followed. Suffering physical indignities was only a part of the story Elie shared with readers about the train trip. Some lost their minds. Madame Schächter, a woman who had already suffering from a painful separation from her husband and two oldest sons from an earlier deportation, had hysterical visions of Jews dying "in a terrible fire." Frightened passengers thought her insane and tried to silence her.

The death trains ran unceasingly from all over occupied Europe 24 hours a day. Another form of terror, the terror of not knowing, came to many victims shortly after their arrival. The railroad platform at Birkenau acted as a kind of receiving center for Auschwitz (see Figure 1). Arriving late at night, Elie Wiesel remembered what became one of the most painful separations of his life. Yet, because the Nazis wanted to avoid riots and a disruption of the killing process, the dreadful implications of separating from his mother and sister did not become clear until later. Moving to the left line or right, as it turned out, was a profoundly real entry to either continued life in the form of forced labor or a more immediate death by gassing. The elderly, sick and infirm, pregnant women, babies, and small children, marked for annihilation under the direction of indifferent SS batons, came to their end by coming to this fateful crossroads. In the following passage, Elie Wiesel's recollections offer readers a sense of impending loss in the face of a selection system singularly dedicated to their destruction:

> An SS non-commissioned officer came to meet us, a truncheon in his hand. He gave the order: "Men to the left. Women to the right." Eight words spoken

Figure 1. Railroad tracks into the main gate at Birkenau. (Photo by Gregory Paul Wegner)

66 / PERSPECTIVES ON VIOLENCE AND VIOLENT DEATH

> quietly, indifferently, without emotion. Eight short, simple words. Yet that was the moment when I parted from my mother. I had not had time to think, but already I felt the pressure of my father's hand: we were alone. For a part of a second I glimpsed my mother and sisters moving away to the right. Tzipora held mother's hand. I saw them disappear into the distance; my mother was stroking my sister's fair hair, as though to protect her, while I walked with my father and the other men. And I did not know that in that place, at that moment, I was parting from my mother and Tzipora forever. I went on walking. My father held onto my hand (Wiesel, 1982, p. 27).

In a synthesis of recollections on camp life from a host of Holocaust survivors and writers, Terrence de Pres observed that, "prisoners were *systematically* subjected to filth. They were the deliberate target of excremental assault" (des Pres, 1976, p. 63). This was true on the trip to the camps as well as after arrival. There was a brutal logic to the Nazi architectural plans created for Auschwitz. The latrines were deliberately placed a certain distance away from the washrooms so that diseases could be spread more rapidly among the victims (Van Pelt, 1993, pp. 104-110). Diarrhea and dysentery were common maladies. Even going to the latrine could be life threatening. Staying on the toilet too long earned inmates severe beatings or worse. Even getting to the latrine on time was an ordeal for many.

> Imagine what it would be like to be forbidden to go to the toilet; imagine that you are suffering from increasingly severe dysentery, caused and aggravated by a diet of cabbage soup as well as by constant cold. Naturally, you would try to go anyway. Sometimes you might succeed. But your absences would be noticed and you would be beaten, knocked down and trampled on. By now, you would know what the risks were, but urgency would oblige you to repeat the attempt, cost what it might. . . . I soon learn to deal with the dysentery by tying strings around the lower end of my drawers (Maurel, 1958, pp. 38-39).

The struggle for survival often revolved around taking care of bodily functions and securing enough food and water. An underground economy emerged from these necessities where trading for a higher ration in the form of an extra piece of bread could spell the difference between life and death—a death that brought a reprieve before the grim reaper. With degradation and defilement a calculated part of daily camp culture, one may well ask how any of the inmates survived this onslaught against body and soul. Part of the answer is found in the writings of Primo Levi, an Italian Jew, who came to Auschwitz as *Häftling* (prisoner) #174517 from his native Turin in 1944. His new name, he remembered, was the number tattooed on his arm "in bluish characters under the skin" (Levi, 1986, pp. 16-17).

Michael Jacobs, a teenager when he arrived in Auschwitz, recalled the ritual of tattooing: "As you stretched out your arm, they gave you a number . . . and as they gave me my tattoo number, B-4990, the SS man came to me, and he said to me, 'Do you know what this number's all about?' I said, 'No, sir.' 'Okay, let me tell you now. You are being dehumanized'" (Berenbaum, 1993, p. 147).

Levi soon learned that the first rule in Auschwitz was not to ask questions about why something was so. One day, tortured by thirst, he reached outside the window of his barracks to break off an icicle. Immediately, a big prowling guard confronted him and brutally snatched the icicle away. *"Warum?"* Primo asked in German. *"Hier ist kein warum"* (there is no why here), the guard answered, and pushed him aside. The explanation for this dictatorial response was "repugnant but simple" for the inmates. In the death camps, "everything is forbidden, not for hidden reasons, but because the camp has been created for that purpose." One of the keys to staying alive at Auschwitz was to learn this lesson well, and to learn it as soon as possible (Levi, 1986, pp. 16-17).

Levi was an acute observer of the human condition, one of the most insightful in the realm of Holocaust literature. His narrative is tightly woven around the language of the *Lager* or camp itself, so much so that the various linguistic expressions used in the everyday culture of the place almost require the reader to be multilingual. New prisoners sometimes became lost in this "perpetual Babel, in which everyone shouts orders and threats in languages never heard before, and woe betide whoever fails to grasp the meaning" (Levi, 1986, p. 53). Greek, German, French, Yiddish, Russian, Italian, Hebrew, and Polish expressions spread across his recollections. Levi recognized the limits of language to encompass the horror of Auschwitz for those who never lived through its hell.

As Lawrence Langer observed, we often take for granted the place accorded to common language in articulating human needs, creating bonds with others, and defining the moral boundaries of the world in which we live (Langer, 1998, p. 28). Auschwitz and its confusion of tongues made such assumptions superfluous. We enter into a very different linguistic universe that made survival all the more challenging and difficult. Forty years after the liberation of Auschwitz, writing in *The Drowned and the Saved,* Levi wrote in sympathetic tones about the many human beings in the camp who became victims by "drowning one by one in the stormy sea of not-understanding." The "Lager jargon" did not connect to their mother tongues. They remained linguistic aliens in a camp that imprisoned and murdered people from over 30 countries (Levi, 1998, p. 96).

The prisoners often communicated with words that marked a state of being, a medical condition, or a specific role, some with sinister implications. A *Muselmann* was a member of the walking dead in the advanced stages of starvation or disease. The empty and dead stares of these victims and their aimless behavior usually signaled to other inmates that they were on their way to the gas chambers. They were living skeletons. The *Muselmann* was often among those singled out during the daily selection process when the sick and weak were separated from the rest of the camp population for execution. The *Muselmann* remains prominent in Holocaust literature because, at least in part, he symbolized the loss of hope and a reminder that calculated oppression can destroy the human spirit.

68 / PERSPECTIVES ON VIOLENCE AND VIOLENT DEATH

Most victims who came to Auschwitz and the five other death camps did not leave these places alive (see Figure 2). Many did not live beyond three months. A crust of bread and thin, watery soup for the daily diet was another part of the persecutor's calculation in hastening the end of those deemed subhuman. Shoes became objects of survival. Getting a pair that did not cause blisters was considered a major victory. Woe to those whose shoes became "instruments of torture" causing painful sores leading to fatal infections. Levi tells us that these afflicted souls usually arrived last at a forced labor site and thus became targets for severe beatings. As a last resort, coming to the *Ka-Be* or *Krankenbau* (infirmary) and taking the diagnosis of *dicke Füsse* or swollen feet was perilous since, to the SS, there existed no cure for the condition. Another doorway opened for the gas chambers (Levi, 1986, pp. 21-22).

Somehow, after all that his eyes witnessed, Primo Levi sensed the necessity of appealing to yet unborn generations to tell them about the cultural necessity to remember what happened in places like Auschwitz. Implicit in his poetic expression is a warning about the immorality of forgetting about the individual human beings who perished in the camps.

> You who live safe
> In your warm houses,
> You who find, returning in the evening,
> Hot food and friendly faces:
> Consider if this is a man
> Who dies because of a yes or no.
> Consider if this is a woman,
> Without hair and without name
> With no more strength to remember,
> Her eyes empty and her womb cold
> Like a frog in winter.
> Mediate that this came about:
> I commend these words to you.
> Carve them into your hearts
> At home, in the street,
> Going to bed, rising;
> Repeat them to your children,
> Or may your house fall apart,
> May illness impede you,
> May your children turn their faces from you.
>
> (Levi, 1986, frontal page).

The literary insights and recollections of Primo Levi and Elie Wiesel obviously deserve much more attention than can be offered in these pages. They provide literary critics, historians, social scientists, and artists with intellectual grist for years to come (Dresden, 1991; Rosenfeld, 1980; Schlant, 1999; Schwarz, 1999).

There is another survivor voice among many, one non-Jewish and Polish in origin, which beckons the reader. He is Tasdeusz Borowski, a writer of essays,

Figure 2. The electrified fence at Auschwitz.
(Photo by Gregory Paul Wegner)

70 / PERSPECTIVES ON VIOLENCE AND VIOLENT DEATH

poems, short stories, and history. After imprisonment in the Warsaw Ghetto for two months, Borowski was sent to Auschwitz in 1943 where he worked as a hospital orderly. His most famous work, *This Way to the Gas, Ladies and Gentlemen* (1976), is a collection of short stories, several of which are written from the perspective of a deputy Kapo named Vorarbeiter Tadeusz, who acts as narrator. A Kapo was a prisoner who was chosen by camp authorities to supervise works crews or to help the block elder to supervise the barracks. For this, Kapos usually received extra privileges and rations. In this division of labor, the Nazis exercised a degree of control through delegating authority at the lower levels. This extended to the crematoriums where prisoners themselves disposed of the bodies.

In employing this literary device, Borowski identifies with the Kapo. In doing so, the author made a moral decision to accept "mutual responsibility, mutual participation, and mutual guilt for the concentration camp" (Borowski, 1976, pp. 21-22). Borowski recognized that, even as a prisoner, he was one of the cogs in a larger machine that ran the camp. There is a certain matter-of-fact tone in much of Borowski's writing. As John Roth and Michael Berenbaum noted, he challenges readers to dispense with the easy categorization of good and evil as well as criminals and victims in the camps (Roth & Berenbaum, 1989, p. 154). Under this author's script, conventional morality receded into the background and disappeared. In its place, there emerged in Auschwitz a brutal "survival of the fittest" and "the rule of the jungle" (Schwarz, 1999, p. 133). Human existence is reduced to securing another blanket to get through the cold, securing a decent pair of shoes, an extra bowl of soup or piece of bread.

As central as this reality is to Borowski's vision of Auschwitz, he also invites us to contemplate an equally important truth at the heart of industrialized mass murder. Like factory production, annihilating human beings can become so efficient and machine-like that the question of morality becomes temptingly irrelevant. The rationalized system of mass killing can itself become so smooth in its operation that many of the victims are barely noticed except for the numbers that identify them. Like Wiesel and Levi, Borowski makes sure that we do not forget.

In what is most assuredly a classic passage in Holocaust literature, the Polish scholar takes us to the haunting "People Who Walked On." Seen through the eyes of hospital orderly Kapo Tadeusz, who plays both narrator and protagonist, we are invited to witness a Sunday soccer game at Auschwitz:

> I was the goalkeeper. As always on Sundays, a sizeable crowd of hospital orderlies and convalescent patients had gathered to watch the game. Keeping goal, I had my back to the ramp. The ball went out and rolled all the way to the fence. I ran after it, and as I reached to pick it up, I happened to glance at the ramp. A train had arrived. People were emerging from the cattle cars and walking in the direction of the little wood. All I could see from where I stood were bright splashes of color. The women, it seemed, were wearing summer dresses; it was the first time that season. The men had taken off their coats, and

their white shirts stood out sharply against the green of the trees. The procession moved along slowly growing in size as more and more people poured from the freight cars. And then it stopped. The people sat down on the grass and gazed in our direction. I returned with the ball and kicked it back inside the field. It traveled from one foot to another and, in a wide arc, returned to the goal. I kicked it towards a corner. Again it rolled out into the grass. Once more I ran to retrieve it. But as I reached down, I stopped in amazement—the ramp was empty. Out of the whole colorful summer procession, not one person remained. The train too was gone. . . . Between two throw-ins in a soccer game, right behind my back, three thousand people had been put to death (Borowski, 1976, pp. 83-84).

We among the living in the twenty-first century are still challenged by the inherent limitations posed by language in grasping the meaning of the Holocaust or any of the other genocides that transpired since that time. Survivor literature remains humble in nature because it never claims the fulfillment of an impossible and presumptuous task. Language, expressed through the power of the word and art, was all the survivors had in connecting us to their experiences. Borowski's passage, for example, remains powerful because both of an economy of words and the manner by which the reader is drawn into a timeframe. There is a profound passing of human beings marked by an indifferent assembly-line-like process. Among the lost were a multitude of children. Some survived to tell a story, while others who perished left a precious legacy of art and literature for the living.

THE VOICES OF CHILDREN

The sheer scope and depth of loss regarding children who perished remains one of the most brutal aspects of the Holocaust legacy. While historians generally agree that some 1.5 million Jewish children died from the Holocaust, the number of non-Jewish children who perished is less clear. But numbers, as we have seen, do not by themselves convey the full weight of loss suffered by humanity with the passing of millions of innocent young people. Indeed, this chapter symbolizes an attempt to transcend the exquisite order of numbers to preserve human voices. Because Nazi ideologues wanted to make sure that future Jewish progeny would not populate the world, Jewish children were almost nonexistent at Auschwitz and the other death and concentration camps. Moreover, before Auschwitz was in full operation, an untold number of children died with their parents during the mass executions carried out by the mobile killing squads or *Einsatzgruppen* during 1941 and 1942, primarily in the occupied Baltic States and the Soviet Union. Auschwitz, the largest cemetery in the world, became the biggest place of execution for pregnant woman and babies in modern history.

The memory of murdered children would forever haunt Elie Wiesel, who wrote: "Never shall I forget that smoke. Never shall I forget the faces of the little children, whose bodies I saw turned into wreaths of smoke beneath a silent blue

72 / PERSPECTIVES ON VIOLENCE AND VIOLENT DEATH

sky" (Wiesel, 1982, p. 32). The one group of children that stood any chance of survival were those tall enough to pass as adults. Elie Wiesel was among the children in this group. It is therefore not surprising that only one Jewish child was to be found in the Women's Camp in the Auschwitz/Birkenau complex until the close of 1943. Many children died in transit to the camps or beforehand in the ghetto. Some Jewish and non-Jewish children survived to bear witness to the greatest moral travesties in their existence. The memoirs of a Jewish boy described infanticide by SS guards in the ghetto of Lodz with newborns speared by SS bayonets after being pushed out of windows. In Radom, a Polish Catholic teenager and later resistance fighter watched with horror from a nearby window as an SS officer committed the unspeakable act as Jews were rounded up in the ghetto for deportation.

> As I pressed against the glass, I saw an officer make a flinging movement with his arm, and something rose up into the sky like a fat bird. With his other hand he aimed his pistol, and the bird plummeted to the ground besides its screaming mother, and the officer shot the mother, too. But it was not a bird. It was not a bird. It was not a bird (Opdyke, 1999, p. 117).

Older children, who were swallowed up in the madness of the camps and never lived long enough to see liberation in 1945, remain special witnesses of violence and dehumanization. The world already embraced Anne Frank through her diaries, one of the most published pieces of adolescent literature (Frank, 1952). As precious as they are in capturing the thoughts of a young Jewish girl in occupied Amsterdam, these diaries represent only a partial picture of her Holocaust experience. There is another critically important aspect of Anne's life, her last days in Bergen-Belsen, that demands closer attention. The utter degradation of the place, along with starvation and the onslaught of typhoid fever, assaulted Anne's faith in the essential goodness of humanity (Landwer, 1991, p. 74; Müller, 1998, pp. 243-258).

Without considering this part of Anne's struggle, we essentially strip her of part of her humanity. As S. Lillian Kremer pointed out, readers of Anne Frank's diary "can be charmed by her brightness, humor, and curiosity and beguiled by her unquenchable hopefulness, because it is the writing of a person removed from the atrocities and hoping to survive." The reader "is spared life outside the attic and life awaiting her after capture" (Kremer, 1999, p. 71). Anne's body lies buried in an anonymous mass grave at Bergen-Belsen. Certainly, succeeding generations of school children who read her diary should come to know about the larger context of Anne Frank's story. Without this context, there is a danger that the violence, dehumanization, and brutality that she and other victims suffered will be overlooked, forgotten, or distorted.

Lawrence Langer warns about a "tradition of avoidance" since "much of our language about the Holocaust is designed to console instead of confront" (Langer, 1995, p. 5). Confronting the reality of the Holocaust through literature requires the consideration of multiple perspectives, including those that do not avoid the dark realities of horror and terror. Anne Frank remains part of a literary tradition in Holocaust literature: teenage diarists who perished in the storm of Nazi violence. They somehow managed to leave behind their thoughts on paper, probably not knowing that people would read them for years to come.

A recent collection of these dairies, gathered into one volume by Jacob Boas, integrates the perspectives of five Jewish teenagers from different parts of Europe. David Rubinowicz, Yitzhak Rudashevski, Moshe Flinker, Eva Heyman, and Anne Frank are not survivors. They all perished in the camps. Each brings his or her personal interpretation and meaning to what happened around them. Eva recounted her fears and the pall of silence that fell over her family as they prepared for a move to the ghetto and the loss of their way of life. Yitzhak and Moshe, in sharp contrast to Anne, convey a sense of impending doom. Yitzhak described the painful humiliation of his community and a gnawing sense of helplessness in the face of Nazi oppression. "It hurt me," he wrote, "that I saw absolutely no way out." Moshe's final entry was a prayer borne of loss and mourning. He looked out of his window and saw "a sky covered with bloody clouds." His afternoon prayer of lamentation was also a prayer for deliverance:

> We are the bleeding clouds, and from the sea of blood have we come. We have come to you from the place where your brothers are, to bring you greetings from your people. We are witnesses; we are sent by our people to show you their trouble; we were brought into being by an inferno of suffering; and we are a sign of peace to you. . . . Two thousand years have we brought into this world children who are doomed to suffer. Lord our God, is this still not enough? . . . Wilt thou forget us forever, Lord of Israel? . . . Pity us, have mercy Lord, on thy people, do not tarry, do not wait, for soon, it will be too late (Boas, 1995, pp. 46-47, 112-113).

The prayer is even more poignant because it really was too late for all five of these young diarists. Moshe was not the only one to appeal to God in the midst of darkness. "Where was God at Auschwitz?" is a question that Elie Wiesel continues to ask today and for which he claims to have no answer. Living with a question that has no answer grates against the tradition of certainty and reductionism that marks the culture of the West. What emerges for the living in reading the Holocaust literature penned by children may be more questions than answers. Not the least of these questions asks about why a nation steeped in Christian traditions could legitimize the mass murder of children.

There are other voices that we dare not ignore. The poetry and art from children in Terezin concentration camp, also known as the Theresienstadt ghetto (1942-1944), represents an important literary legacy. Of the 15,000 Jewish children deported from Theresienstadt to Auschwitz, only 100 survived. An enterprising teacher named Friedl Dicker-Brandeis conducted art classes in the camp to serve as a kind of refuge from the surrounding horror. The children created about

74 / PERSPECTIVES ON VIOLENCE AND VIOLENT DEATH

5,000 drawings and a number of poems. What makes this collection so valuable is that it preserves the human face and artistic expression of the young victims in the midst of genocide. The drawings and poems reflected their dreams and anxieties as well as an incredible longing for flowers, happiness, home, spring, and butterflies. Interspersed throughout the collection are expressions of fear about the dark and repressive forces around them. Eva Pickova, a 12-year-old from Nymburk, left behind a mournful poem expressing a desire to live, even though death and sorrow prevailed around her.

Fear
Today the ghetto knows a different fear,
Close in its grip, Death wields an icy scythe.
An evil sickness spreads a terror in its wake,
The victims of its shadow weep and writhe.

Today a father's heartbeat tells his fright
and mothers bend their heads into their hands.
Now children choke and die with typhus here,
A bitter tax is taken from their bands.

My heart still beats inside my breast
While friends depart for other worlds.
Perhaps it's better—who can say?—
Than watching this, to die today?

No, no my God, we want to live!
Not watch our numbers melt away.
We want to have a better world,
We want to work—we must not die!
(*I Never Saw Another Butterfly,* 1993, pp. 55, 99).

CONCLUSION

Visitors to the United States Holocaust Memorial Museum in Washington are invited to take a small gray card before beginning their tour of the museum on the fourth floor. Each "identification card" includes a picture and story about a victim of the Holocaust along with words about the fate of that person as survivor or murdered victim. In a sense, this essay resembles one of these gray cards, writ large with literature as the medium. Holocaust writers both famous and obscure leave us with stories about "Auschwitz and beyond" that should give us pause about the legacy of one of the most monstrous crimes in modern times.

Many of the victims of the Holocaust remain nameless and unknown. What these authors have done through their literature is to provide a human face to the incomprehensible suffering and loss suffered by the oppressed. They also were not afraid to keep before us the omnipresent and disturbing question of what it means to be human. The dehumanization of victims was not exclusive to the Holocaust. These writers have provided a sense of place and immediacy to this dimension of Nazi policy.

The industrialization of death and mass murder remains a hallmark of the Third Reich. Still, the violence on which the Holocaust was predicated claimed precursors that made it possible in the first place. As Wiesel, Levi, and Borowski would remind us, even death itself was dehumanized by the Nazis.

Enzo Traverso's thinking on the origins of Nazi violence connects us once again us to a vital historical context within which the literature was created. The Holocaust is not simply explained away as a powerful and inexplicable anomaly. Auschwitz symbolized a coalescence of thinking with strong links to the ideologies of racial supremacy widely popular in Europe during the nineteenth and twentieth centuries. Dehumanization and mass murder may have been brought to a new level of technological sophistication by the Nazis, but the technical and cultural antecedents for their application were already present well before 1933. As Traverso noted, Europe had "become accustomed to massacre" through, for example, the genocide of 1.5 million Armenians at the hands of the Ottoman Empire during World War I. The event did not elicit any significant protest. Persecuted European Jews some two decades later suffered from a similar global indifference.

To profoundly disturb the thinking of human beings about moral responsibility and the relationship between the individual and the state is one of the great legacies of Holocaust literature. Whether this has had any real impact on creating a stronger commitment to social justice remains highly debatable. Genocide, the ultimate form of dehumanization, still remains a part of the international political landscape as attested by events in Cambodia, Rwanda, and Bosnia. In returning to the circle of literary writings espoused in this journey, we hope to reaffirm the wisdom inherent in the words of Primo Levi. He admonishes us that, "The story of the death camps should be understood by everyone as a sinister alarm signal" (Levi, 1986, p. 3). Recent developments suggest that the world has not been listening.

REFERENCES

Anti-Defamation League. (1978). *The Holocaust: A chronology of social education.* New York: ADL.

Boas, J. (1995). *We are witnesses: Five diaries of teenagers who died in the Holocaust.* New York: Scholastic.

Borowski, T. (1976). *This way to the gas, ladies and gentlemen,* B. Vedder (Trans.). New York: Penguin.

Berenbaum, M. (1993). *The world must know.* New York: Little Brown.

Browning, C. (1992). *The path to genocide: Essays on launching the final solution.* New York: Cambridge University Press.

Burleigh, M. (1997). *Ethics and extermination: Reflections on Nazi genocide.* New York: Cambridge University Press.

76 / PERSPECTIVES ON VIOLENCE AND VIOLENT DEATH

Dawidowicz, L. (1986). *The war against the Jews, 1933-1945.* New York: Free Press.

des Pres, T. (1976). *The survivor: An anatomy of life in the death camps.* New York: Pocket Books.

Domarus, M. (Ed.). (1962). *Hitler: Reden und Proklamationen, 1932-1945* (2 vols.). Würzburg: Schmidt, Neustadt a.d. Aisch.

Dresden, S. (1991). *Persecution, extermination, literature,* H. Schogt (Trans.). Toronto: University of Toronto Press.

Fleming, G. (1984). *Hitler and the final solution.* Berkeley: University of California Press.

Frank, A. (1952). *Diary of a young girl.* New York: Doubleday.

Frankl, V. (1984). *Man's search for meaning.* New York: Simon and Schuster.

Gilbert, M. (1985). *The Holocaust.* New York: Holt, Rinehart and Winston.

Gilbert, M. (1993). *Atlas of the Holocaust.* New York: Morrow.

Ginzel, G. (1984). *Jüdischer Alltag in Deutschland, 1933-1945.* Düsseldorf: Droste.

Hilberg, R. (1985). *The destruction of the European Jews.* New York: Holmes and Meier.

I never saw another butterfly: Children's drawings and poems from Terezin concentration camp 1942-1944. (1993). New York: Schocken Books.

Katz, S. (1994). *The Holocaust in historical context* (Vol. 1). New York: Oxford University Press.

Kremer, S. L. (1999). *Women's Holocaust writing: Memory and imagination.* Lincoln: University of Nebraska Press.

Landwer, W. (1991). *The last seven months of Anne Frank.* New York: Random House.

Langer, L. (1995). *Admitting the Holocaust: Collected essays.* New York: Oxford University Press.

Langer, L. (1998). *Pre-empting the Holocaust.* New Haven: Yale University Press.

Levi, P. (1986). Survival in Auschwitz. In *If this is a man* (pp. 5-132). New York: Summit Books.

Levi, P. (1998). *The drowned and the saved,* R. Rosenthal (Trans.). New York: Simon and Schuster.

Luther M. (1543). On the Jews and their lies. In *Luther's works* (54 vols.), M. Bertram (Trans), vol. 47, *The Christian in society, II* (pp. 121-306), F. Sherman & H. Lehmann (Eds.). Philadelphia (1971).

Maurel, M. (1958). *An ordinary camp,* M. Summers (Trans.). New York: Simon and Schuster.

Müller, M. (1998). *Anne Frank: The biography.* New York: Holt.

Noakes, J., & Pridham, G. (Eds.). (1975). *Documents on Nazism, 1919-1945.* New York: Viking Press.

Opdyke, I. (1999). *In my hands.* New York: Dell.

Richter, H. (2000). *Damals war es Friedrich.* München: Deutsche Taschenbuch.

Rosenfeld, A. (1980). *A double dying: Reflections on Holocaust literature.* Bloomington, IN: Indian University Press.

Roth, J., & Berenbaum, M. (Eds.). (1989). *Holocaust: Religious and philosophical implications.* St. Paul, MN: Paragon House.

Schlant, E. (1999). *The language of silence: West German literature and the Holocaust.* London: Routledge.

Schwarz, D. (1999). *Imagining the Holocaust.* New York: St. Martin's Press.

Smith, H. (Ed.). (2002). *The Holocaust and other genocides.* Nashville, TN: Vanderbilt University Press.

Traverso, E. (2003). *The origins of Nazi violence*, J. Lloyd (Trans.). New York: New Press.

Van Pelt, R. (1993). Auschwitz: From architect's promise to inmate's perdition. *Modernism, 1,* 104-110.

Walk, J. (1996). *Das Sonderrecht für die Juden in NS-Staat. 2. Auflage.* Heidelberg: Müller.

Wiesel, E. (1972). *One generation after.* Translated from the French by L. Edelman & E. Wiesel. New York: Schocken Books.

Wiesel, E. (1982). *Night.* New York: Bantam.

CHAPTER 5
Religious Violence and Weapons of Mass Destruction*

Timothy Kullman

This chapter reviews the growing threat of religious violence, the potential use of weapons of mass destruction (WMD) as a tool to achieve a "religious goal," the expanse of global transfer systems as the mechanism for ideological extremist groups to obtain WMD, and the ideological evolution of two very different groups, the Aum Shinrikoy Movement in Japan and the Al Qaeda terrorist organization, in their development of an apocalyptic mindset. The groups were chosen because they are global in reach and their difference compels us to recognize that they represent both a dangerous trend that defies region, and they represent a diversity of apocalyptic ideological belief.

THE THREAT OF RELIGIOUS VIOLENCE

Religious-based violence has a dark and troubling presence from the earliest moments of human history. Wholesale slaughter in the name of numerous gods and deities is perhaps one of the most profound examples of collective irrationality evidenced in the human condition. Belief in "ultimate truths" has the power to suspend the everyday secular order of normal human behavior. The nearly universal compulsion to believe in a great truth that exists beyond the everyday

---

*In any discussion of violence and grief, the topic of religious extremism, as an element of terrorism and as a cause of violence, is bound to arise. Since the grief following losses connected to violence may vary depending on the type of the violence, it is important to have a factual understanding of the nature of the violent act. There are some who see this as a topic linked only to modern Islamists. This is not the case. This chapter looks at the topic of terrorism as a tool of apocalyptic ideologies and gives historical perspective. It is included here for that reason.

80 / PERSPECTIVES ON VIOLENCE AND VIOLENT DEATH

human condition has, at numerous times throughout history, triggered some of the most savage and barbaric actions of people toward various nonbelievers and enemies of "the truth."

History is replete with examples of mass slaughter in the name of religion. A couple of examples out of thousands will suffice. Haught relates one of many examples of religious carnage during a battle for Jerusalem during a Crusade in 1098. Chronicler Raymond of Aguilers recorded: "Wonderful things were to be seen. Numbers of the Saracens were beheaded. . . . Others were shot with arrows or forced to jump from towers: others were tortured for several days, then burned in flames. In the streets were seen piles of heads and hands and feet. . . . In the Temple of Solomon, the horses waded in blood up to their knees, nay, up to their bridle. It was a just and marvelous judgment of God, that this place should be filled with the blood of the unbelievers" (Haught, 1990, pp. 25-26). The late leader of Iran, the Ayatollah Khomeini, motivated hundreds of thousands of young men to be used in human wave assaults against the better-equipped Iraqi army in their border dispute during the 1980s. Khomeini raised death in combat to the glories of religious martyrdom. The enemy wasn't the Satanic West, but a secular Muslim society that opposed his Islamic Revolution. In a 1984 speech, Khomeini proclaimed, "War is a blessing for the world and all nations. It is God who incites men to fight and kill. The Koran says, 'Fight until all corruptions and all rebellion have ceased.' The wars the Prophet led against the infidels were a blessing for all humanity. . . . Thanks to God our young people are now, to the limits of their means, putting God's commandments into action. They know that to kill the unbelievers is one of man's greatest missions" (Iadicola & Shupe, 2003, p. 179). The prolonged war that lasted from 1980-1988 virtually wiped out an entire generation of Iranian men, all in the name of pleasing God.

The growing danger for mass genocide of apocalyptic proportions is exacerbated by the numerous claims to the truth and the ever-increasing efficiency of Weapons of Mass Destruction (WMD). Hannah Arendt states, "The technical development of the implements of violence has now reached the point where no political goal could conceivably correspond to their destructive potential or justify their actual use in armed conflict" (Arendt, 1970, p. 3). She further states that violence applied to human affairs runs the risk of being overwhelmed by the means for which it (violence) was justified. The nature of human aggression hasn't changed, but the retaliatory response has been magnified to a critical level as chemical, biological, radiological, and nuclear weapons research has evolved to a state that threatens human survival. Arendts' contribution is a reference to the nuclear escalation at the height of the Cold War. Her insight was pertinent in a time of superpower struggles with the measured goal of deterrence. The goals of Al Qaeda and Aum Shinrikyo are anything but deterrence. The ideological perspective of Al Qaeda and Aum Shinrikyo sees the world as decadent and immoral. Using very different philosophies, they both seek to purge the world of the evil secular Western influences using any means necessary. To accomplish these apocalyptic goals, the acquisition of WMD has been a priority. With the Aum Shinrikyo attacks on the Tokyo subways in 1995, we saw that the desire to create an apocalyptic scenario was not just rhetoric, but represented a significant threat to civilization. Had the quality of the sarin nerve agent been more lethal, thousands would have perished. Aum Shinrikyo signaled a new threat to global stability, and such threats should be taken with the utmost seriousness (Olson, 1999).

THE THREAT OF WEAPONS ACQUISITION
TO GLOBAL STABILITY

Several factors contributed to Aum Shinrikyo's ability to acquire WMD, and many of the same factors may very well contribute to the likelihood of Al Qaeda obtaining the same WMD. The factors include motivation driven by a powerful ideology, the increasing fluidity of international borders and global trade factors, and the accumulation of vast financial networks to obtain needed materials and skilled scientists.

Ideological Influences on Aum Shinrikyo

Shoko Asahara (birth name, Chizuo Matsumoto) founded Aum Shinsen no Kai in 1984 and changed the name to Aum Shinrikyo, which means "teaching of the supreme truth," in 1987. Aum Shinrikyo is an apocalyptic cult that blends philosophical precepts from a wide array of sources including Buddhism, Taoism, Hinduism, Yoga, Shamanism, New Age philosophy, and Christianity (Lifton, 1999). The eclectic blend of fresh ideas was appealing to a wide range of Japanese society, especially the youth. Membership ranged into the tens of thousands, with a sizable number of adherents in Russia and the United States.

Asahara's preoccupation with mass death is represented in his adoption of Shiva as a prominent figure in his apocalyptic ideology. Shiva is the Hindu god associated with salvation through world destruction (Lifton, 1999). His interest in Christianity is primarily the "end times" belief found in the Book of Revelations (Juergensmeyer, 2000). Asahara stated on many occasions that he was the reincarnation of Jesus Christ and the first "enlightened one" since the Buddha (Olson, 1999). Asahara's interest in Nostradamus stemmed from his intrigue with precise calculations for major world events, including the end of the world, and he admired Hitler's concept of a thousand year Reich (Benjamin & Simon, 2002).

Asahara adopted the Buddhist term *Po'a* for his own apocalyptic use. Po'a refers to rites performed for the dead to ease their passage into the next realm. By 1994, Asahara was speaking about doing Po'a for the whole world. The only survivors would be the adherents of Aum Shinrikyo because of their purity (Benjamin & Simon, 2002). The decadence and debauchery of the world had

82 / PERSPECTIVES ON VIOLENCE AND VIOLENT DEATH

created collective bad karma, and the only solution was to kill all nonbelievers to save the world. This perverted rationale leads to the logical conclusion that to heal you, I will have to kill you (Lifton, 1999). It is important to note that the vast majority of his followers (estimates range wildly from 20,000 to 40,000, the widely varying estimates can perhaps be accounted for by separating truly dedicated followers from casual members), except for those in his inner circle, were not aware of his apocalyptic intentions. Nuclear anxiety resulting from a post-Hiroshima life experience has had a significant influence upon Asahara's apocalyptic end-time vision. Horrifying visions of world destruction had become prominent images in postwar Japanese culture (Lifton, 1999).

The combination of charisma, an eclectic blending of traditional and modern beliefs, and Asahara's alleged superhuman powers of insight and physical prowess allowed him to demand complete allegiance from the most dedicated followers. The chosen were brought into closed totalistic communities where all activities and behaviors could be completely controlled (Lifton, 1999). Techniques used to control disciples in this totalistic community included severe forms of ascetic performance such as fasting, long periods of meditation, celibacy, a prohibition against ejaculation, intense breathing exercises, irregular sleep patterns, and long work periods. Techniques to get individuals to admit past misbehaviors included drug induced "narco initiation" to compel the disciple to purge past impurities (Lifton, 1999).

Aum Shinrikyo recruited a large number of scientists in an attempt to legitimate Asahara's spiritual claims and to develop WMD. His "scientific spirituality" ranged from Tantric sexual initiations or "transfers of energy" to the belief that brainwave research could reveal a scientific basis for stages of spiritual attainment. Asahara once declared, "A religion which cannot be scientifically proven is fake" (Lifton, 1999, p. 23). With his chief scientist, Hideo Murai, Asahara developed a headset that allegedly contained the guru's brain waves, which could be transmitted to disciples to achieve "perfect salvation initiation." In an Aum publication, Asahara states, "With the help of instruments like the Astral Teleporter, which faithfully reproduces the vibration of my mantra through electric signals; a device that awakens Kundalini through magnetic fields; an FET (Field Effect Transistor), which correctly reads waves sent out by each chakra; an electroencephalograph connected to a computer; and so on. I have finally succeeded in scientifically verifying the teachings of the saints of the past, especially those of Buddha Sakyamuni" (Lifton, 1999, p. 116). Asahara's scientific endeavors to blend belief with science deteriorated into a surreal blend of pseudoscience and science fiction.

Ideological Influences on Al Qaeda

Al Qaeda's belief in the religiously sanctioned mass slaughter of untold numbers of nonbelievers is rooted in the ideology of the Muslim Brotherhood. The

RELIGIOUS VIOLENCE AND WEAPONS OF MASS DESTRUCTION / 83

twentieth century roots of Muslim extremism can be traced to the Muslim Brotherhood, formally established in Egypt in 1928 by Hasan Al-Banna (Benjamin & Simon, 2002). Other contributors to its ideological formation included Sayyid Qutb and Sayyid Abul-Ala Mawdudi (Benjamin & Simon, 2002). The earliest ideological roots of Muslim extremism can be traced to Taqi al-Din Ibn Taymiyya in the thirteenth century and the religious and economic alliance of Ibn Abd al-Wahhab and Muhammad Al Sa'ud in the seventeenth century (Schwartz, 2002). The Wahhab/Sa'ud alliance eventually led to the establishment of the Saudi Arabian kingdom early in the twentieth century. The Wahhab influence is instrumental in the development of Abdullah Azzam and Osama bin Laden's construction of Al Qaeda. The ideological sentiments existed prior to the creation of the Muslim Brotherhood, but the formal solidifying of its precepts gave it tremendous momentum as it began to spread out of Egypt into Syria and eventually into dozens of countries. The core ideology of the Muslim Brotherhood rests on five major points:

1. Resist foreign domination: Any review of the history of the modern Middle East will be full of examples of Western Colonial dominance. In the nineteenth century, Great Britain and France exercised economic, political, and military influence over large sections of the Middle East as well as Africa and Asia. With the beginning of the twentieth century and the collapse of the Ottoman Empire at the end of the First World War, coupled with the realization of the growing importance of Persian Gulf oil, Western colonial presence and access to cheap oil became vital to sustained economic growth. When the League of Nations partitioned off large tracts of the former Ottoman Empire under French and British Mandates, it further solidified Western control over much of the Middle East. Al-Banna experienced firsthand the power and influence of Great Britain in his native Egypt (Benjamin & Simon, 2002). Al-Banna saw the occupation of Egypt by British troops as a detriment to Egyptian identity and sovereignty.

2. Stop the spread of Western culture, particularly the spread of loose moral values and Christian missionary activity: The Brotherhood rejected both the influence of Christianity, which they saw as a threat to the practice of Islam and quite possibly its extinction, and the secular attitudes of sexuality, feminism, and mores, which promoted a separation of religious practice and everyday life.

3. Restore the Islamic Caliphate: The Caliphate refers to the restoration of the messengers of the Prophet (Muhammad) as the institution to restore the Law of God by reestablishing the Sharia, a community governed by God's revealed law. The two Muslim sects, the Sunnis and the Shi'as, disagree as to who is the rightful descendent. But as a response to perceived moral decay caused by Western political and social influences, the extremist components in both sects believe that a return to Islam and the Quran as the Word of God is the only way to revive Islamic civilization and combat the threat of foreign influences (Esposito, 1992). The Islamic revolution of the Ayatollah Khomeini in Iran in 1979 was Shi'a in origin, and the rise of the Mujahedeen to fight the Soviet Union in Afghanistan

84 / PERSPECTIVES ON VIOLENCE AND VIOLENT DEATH

during the 1980s was primarily Sunni, even though it attracted fighters from all over the world.

4. Restore Muslim pride, power, and rule by acknowledging past Islamic empires and civilizations: By returning to former models of Islamic success, Muslim societies could overcome the influences of Western modernization, nationalism, and Marxism (Esposito, 1992).

5. Harness science and technology, and use them within an Islamic-oriented and guided context in order to avoid the Westernization and secularization of Muslim society (Esposito, 1992, p. 123).

Hasan Al-Banna was instrumental in redefining the concept of jihad. In its most basic meaning, jihad signifies the battle of self-discipline in leading a virtuous life and resisting evil in one's own life. Jihad represents the lifelong struggle against the devil and all negative influences. The broader definition means the struggle to spread and defend Islam (Esposito, 1992, p. 33). Islam believes the world is a continuous struggle between believers and non-believers and that, "it is a Muslim's duty to wage war against polytheists, apostates (abandonment of faith), and People of the Book (Jews and Christians) who refuse Muslim rule" (Esposito, 1992, p. 33). To contribute to the global spread of Islam is every Muslim's duty, and to die in that endeavor is to achieve martyrdom and, as in Christianity, to be rewarded with paradise (Esposito, 1992).

Al-Banna succeeded in combining the two traditional definitions and reasserting the goal of Muslim's to expel the foreign dominators and restore traditional Islamic order. Originally created as a youth and social organization, the Brotherhood developed as a powerful political entity dedicated to reinstating the Caliphate. The Caliphate, which had been reduced to a ceremonial office, was formally abolished in 1924 by Kemal Ataturk, the republican leader of Turkey, in a move toward secular modernity. This reform movement and the threat of this tendency to spread to other Islamic societies, along with general Western influences, would be essential cornerstones in the creation and development of the Brotherhood (Berman, 2003).

With the military overthrow of Egyptian King Farouk by Gamal Abdel Nasser in 1952 and the establishment of a Pan-Arabist nationalist government, there were preliminary indications that the Brotherhood would be in support of the new regime. But rifts occurred over the unwillingness of the new government to ban alcohol and Egypt's political associations with Great Britain and the Soviet Union. The Brotherhood sought a political direction that would reinvigorate an Islamic state, not one that would move Egypt towards a Western secular state (Benjamin & Simon, 2002).

The growing threat that the Brotherhood posed for the Egyptian government resulted in the eventual banning of the Brotherhood, which succeeded in spreading the movement into many other countries, and with the assassination of Al-Banna in 1949, the Brotherhood's leading intellectual, Sayyid Qutb, became active in the movement. Qutb represents the most radical and influential philosophical strategists of the Brotherhood (Berman, 2003).

Qutb memorized the Qur'an by age ten, received a formal education in Cairo, and worked for a time in the Egyptian Ministry of Education. He traveled to the United States and received a Master's Degree in Education from the University of Northern Colorado at Greeley. His extended exposure to American culture disgusted Qutb. Materialism, loose sexual practices, racism, and general American policies convinced Qutb of the inherent decadence of American culture. In his *Islam: The Religion of the Future,* Qutb states, "The human quality of modern life was sliding downward. Man's inspiration, intelligence and morality were degenerating. Sexual relations were deteriorating to a level lower than the beasts. Man was miserable, anxious and skeptical, his basic functions inoperative, debilitated and atrophied, suffering from affliction, distress, nervous and psychological diseases, perversion, idiocy, insanity and crime. Man was roving without destination . . ." (Berman, 2003, pp. 68-69).

Upon returning home, Qutb joined the Brotherhood and with the death of Al-Banna, he became the intellectual spokesman for the Brotherhood. Over the years, there were several bans imposed on the Brotherhood, resulting in driving many of its intellectual leaders to Saudi Arabia, where they were welcome and given positions in Saudi universities. One such example was Qutb's brother Muhammad, who became a professor of Islamic Studies, where one of his students was Osama bin Laden (Berman, 2003).

Sayyid Qutb refused to flee Egypt, where he was incarcerated for years with thousands of other members of the Brotherhood. With the attempted assassination of Nasser in 1965, the suppression and executions continued with Qutb finally being hanged in 1966 (Esposito, 1992). During his long periods of incarceration (Qutb was briefly released only to be rearrested), Qutb became more radicalized and incredibly prolific. In addition to his *Milestones, Social Justice in Islam* and *Islam: The Religion of the Future*, Qutb produced a 30 volume commentary on various chapters in the Quran called *In the Shade of the Qur'an* (Berman, 2003). In death, Qutb achieved not only the status of martyr, but he became the leading intellectual icon for the Brotherhood; and in virtually all fundamentalist Islamic movements from the 1950s to the present, he is still revered, along with Hasan Al-Banna and Sayyid Abul-Ala Mawdudi.

Mawdudi represents the expansion of the anti-Colonial Wahhab-Saudi fundamentalist ideology into India and Pakistan. He was born in India, but with the creation of Pakistan in 1947, Mawdudi, along with millions of Indian Muslims, migrated to the newly created state (Benjamin & Simon, 2002). Influenced by the writings of Ibn Taymiyya and Sayyid Qutb, Mawdudi became the founder of Pakistan's Jamaat-i-Islami religious party (Juergensmeyer, 2000). Mawdudi sought religious purification and opposed colonialism and Western influences including nationalism, feminism, and secularism. In defense of his radicalism, Mawdudi states, "Islam is a revolutionary doctrine and system that overthrows

86 / PERSPECTIVES ON VIOLENCE AND VIOLENT DEATH

governments. It seeks to overturn the whole universal social order . . . and establish its structure anew. . . . Islam seeks the world. It is not satisfied by a piece of land but demands the whole universe. . . . Jihad is at the same time offensive and defensive. . . . The Islamic party does not hesitate to utilize the means of war to implement its goal" (Schwartz, 2002, p. 143). Mawdudi provided a rationalization for Islamic fundamentalist ideology and its establishing a Sharia-(Islamic law) based state.

In 1979, two major events revitalized the fundamentalist Islamic movement and gave it its current global momentum. The overthrow of the U.S.-supported Shah of Iran (Muhammad Reza Pahlavi) by followers of the Ayatollah Khomeini shocked the West and many Gulf-state monarchies (Hiro, 2002). With the invasion of Afghanistan by the Soviet Union, Islamic fighters came from around the world in support of the Mujahedeen (freedom fighters) in their struggle against the Soviet Union. The United States, along with Great Britain, sent substantial resources to assist the Mujahedeen with the hopes of creating political unrest in Soviet Central Asia (Rashid, 2002). The end result was a defeated Soviet Union and a resurgent global Islamic fundamentalist movement that provided Muslim fundamentalists worldwide with the confidence to be able to combat and defeat superpowers anywhere in the world.

With the defeat of the Soviet Union, the Islamic fundamentalist turned toward their next enemy, the United States. The decade-long struggle against the Soviets gave the Jihadi fighters years to perfect their tactics, strategies, and organizational efficiency on and off the battlefield. Al Qaeda (The Base) traces its origins to the Afghan struggle. Abdullah Azzam, Osama bin Laden, and Ayman Al-Zawahiri met in Afghanistan, and toward the end of that conflict, became the architects of Al Qaeda, the first truly global terrorist organizational network.

FLUIDITY OF INTERNATIONAL BORDERS AND GLOBAL TRADE

Adding to the rapid development of underground weapons networks is the geometric expansion of globalization policies and practices. There are many definitions of globalization. For Bagley, "globalization refers to the shrinkage of distance on a global scale through the emergence and thickening of 'nets of connection'—economic, technological, social, political and environmental" (Bagley, 2001, p. 2). Burbules and Torres define globalization using a number of criteria including: the emergence of supranational institutions whose decisions shape and constrain the policy options for any particular nation-state; the overwhelming impact of global economic processes, including processes of production, consumption, trade, capital flow and monetary interdependence; the rise of neo-liberalism as a hegemonic policy discourse and globalization as the emergence of new global cultural forms (Burbules & Torres, 2000).

RELIGIOUS VIOLENCE AND WEAPONS OF MASS DESTRUCTION / 87

Further complicating the threat of the spread of WMD is the continued expansion of underground banking networks where funds transfers occur outside the traditional systems of banking and can't be tracked using electronic means. Informal Value Transfer Systems (IVTS) are used extensively worldwide by legitimate groups as well as criminal organizations (Passas, 1999).

With the escalating threat of WMD, it may be helpful to gain a historical perspective on the impending menace. In 1947 the Bulletin of Atomic Scientists established in 1947 the "Doomsday Clock" as a way to symbolize the threat of nuclear danger. The closer the minute hand was to midnight reflected the heightened or reduced level of nuclear danger, depending on world events. With the accelerated arms race in 1984, the Clock was moved to three minutes to midnight. With the end of the Cold War in 1990, the Clock is rolled back to 10 minutes to midnight. In 1991, with the signing of the Strategic Arms Reduction Treaty (START) by the United States and the Soviet Union and the announcement of further unilateral cuts in tactical and strategic nuclear weapons, the Clock read 17 minutes to midnight. Unfortunately, with the continued reports of extensive military spending and the risk of nuclear materials not being adequately secured in the former Soviet Union, the Clock was moved forward to 14 minutes to midnight in 1995. The Clock was moved forward again in 1998 to nine minutes to midnight with India and Pakistan resuming nuclear tests. In 2002, the Clock was set at its current position of seven minutes to midnight because of the United States withdrawing from the Anti-Ballistic Missile Treaty and because of the threat posed by terrorists in their attempt at acquiring nuclear and biological weapons (Bulletin of the Atomic Scientists, 2005).

With the resurgence of religious fanaticism and the fluid dynamics of global trade and commerce assisting transnational criminal organizations, global stability is a tenuous proposition. Perhaps we don't face complete planetary annihilation as during the Cold War, but any major biological, chemical, radiological, or nuclear attack that could decimate a major city or region would have catastrophic effects for decades. Massive loss of life, ecological disaster, and economic disruption in one region would have a cascading effect on other regions due to the ever-shrinking "nets of connection" and the total interdependency of economic, technological, social, and political systems.

Aum Shinrikyo's Quest for WMD

With a powerful and alluring ideology in place, Asahara began to accumulate the wealth that would be necessary to put his apocalyptic vision into motion. Aum Shinrikyo accumulated a significant fortune by utilizing a variety of money-making ventures. Money was collected through donations, tithing (giving a tenth of one's annual income), selling religious paraphernalia, videotapes, and book sales. Training courses and seminars conducted by members, and a computer

88 / PERSPECTIVES ON VIOLENCE AND VIOLENT DEATH

manufacturing enterprise contributed to the wealth generated by Aum Shinrikyo. Its net worth in March, 1995 was around $1.5 billion (Olson, 1999).

Asahara's compulsion to recruit large numbers of scientists as mentioned earlier was twofold: to establish a scientific basis for his spiritual truths and the much darker intention, to develop WMD to assist in the fulfilling of his apocalyptic end-time vision of global destruction where only those trained and purified through his spiritual science would survive.

With his charisma and idealistic visions, Asahara had no problem recruiting potential scientific disciples. He would give public speeches arguing that the scientific research (on which Aum spent millions annually) was more advantageous and exciting than traditional research done in the government or universities. He was successful in his recruitment efforts, but as his vision of creating Armageddon unfolded, it became apparent that many of the scientists and engineers were young, and their knowledge of how to make weapons-grade WMD was seriously lacking (Benjamin & Simon, 2002). Despite the scientific flaws, they were to achieve a frightful level of weapons production.

Aum's failure to recruit Russian chemical-weapons engineers in 1994 occurred after an accident in the summer of 1993 closed Satyan 7, Aum's crude facility for producing sarin gas (Olson, 1999). The first laboratory to experiment with biological weapons was in place in 1990, but was replaced with new labs in Kamakuishki and Tokyo.

Aum began its experimentation with chemical agents including sarin, VX, phosgene, and sodium cyanide (Allison, 2004). They cultured and tested a variety of biological agents including Q fever, cholera, anthrax, and botulinum toxin. Asahara led a team of Aum doctors and nurses to Zaire in central Africa to obtain the Ebola virus with the hope of being able to weaponize it. Fortunately, all attempts to weaponize Ebola have been unsuccessful (Schwan, 2004). Documents seized during the arrest of many of its membership provided evidence that Aum purchased property in Australia that contained uranium deposits and attempted to purchase mining licenses (Allison, 2004). Aum hoped to mine uranium and ship it back to Japan to develop nuclear weapons. Other documents showed the groups attempt to purchase a Mark IVxp Interforometer, which could have been used to measure the spherical surface of a fissile core used in nuclear weapons (Allison, 2004).

Aum Shinrikyo carried out nine biological weapons attacks from 1990 to 1995. In the first attack they attempted to release botulinum toxin with spray equipment from the back of a truck. The attack failed because the toxin was improperly prepared. Aum then switched to Bacillus anthracis (anthrax) and attempted to release it from its Tokyo laboratory. This failure was the result of the scientists developing a vaccine strain instead of a weapons grade-strain (Schwan, 2004).

The first of Aum's successful biological attacks occurred on June 27, 1994. In response to a real estate dispute, Asahara ordered a sarin gas attack on the dormitory residence of three of the judges involved in the dispute. Seven died and five hundred were hospitalized (Olson, 1999).

The attack on March 20, 1995 shocked and stunned the world and catapulted the possibility of a large-scale biological terrorist attack into a fact. Five bags of sarin were placed on five trains in the Tokyo subway system and punctured. With the liquid spreading, it began evaporating, and commuters began choking, and panic spread rapidly. Because of the poor quality of the sarin, the death toll was only 12, but nearly 1,000 were hospitalized. Had the sarin potency been greater, hundreds or thousands could have perished (Olson, 1999).

Within 2 weeks, several hundred Aum followers were arrested, and 189 have been convicted. Asahara and 12 of his inner circle were sentenced to death (Herman, 2005). Asahara was sentenced February 27, 2004 with the appeals process still ongoing (Hornyak, 2005). The 10th anniversary has dredged up feelings of panic and sadness for the thousands of victims. Many of the victims still suffer a decade later (Herman, 2005).

Despite the collective trauma experienced by thousands of Japanese citizens, Aum Shinrikyo has changed its name to Aleph, has denounced violence and, despite close police surveillance, continues to recruit new members (Hornyak, 2005).

Al Qaeda's Quest for WMD

The financial network of Al Qaeda resembles that found in a multinational corporation. Their income stream comes from private donations, the diversion of funds from legitimate charitable organizations, as well as their own "front" charities. Legitimate businesses include ventures in construction, transportation, fruit and vegetable production, road construction, leather, sweetmeats, corn and cattle hybrids, food processing, furniture, trucks, cars, tractors, sugar, fertilizer, iron, insecticide, fishing, hospital equipment, dairy products, wood, diamonds, olives, and camels (Gunaratna, 2002).

The world's response to 9/11 set in motion a major international effort to curtail the spread and influence of global terrorism. A major effort centered on revealing and disrupting the financial networks that proved so successful—and elusive to international investigations. Many of Al Qaeda's financial networks were disrupted, but Al Qaeda's ability to morph and adapt is one of their trademarks. Complicating the process is its extensive use of Informal Value Transfer Systems (IVTS). The system used primarily in the Middle East is called the *hawala* system. Hawala means "transfer" in Arabic. Payments using the hawala method are inexpensive as well as quick and are used when traditional banking services are unavailable, unreliable, or too expensive (Passas, 2005). The system is efficient and is based on long-term trust and alliances between families or gangs (Passas, 2005).

90 / PERSPECTIVES ON VIOLENCE AND VIOLENT DEATH

With the collapse of the Soviet Union in 1991, the growing Soviet organized crime syndicates reached maturity. The process had begun with the Soviet reform efforts of the mid-1980s with Mikhail Gorbachev's economic restructuring (perestroika) program and his parallel openness (glasnost) policy (Bagley, 2001). With a weakening Soviet central economy, Soviet organized crime began to flourish, with quickly expanding operations in worldwide money-laundering alliances, narcotics and weapons trafficking, financial scams, and assassinations.

Globalization has assisted in the expansion of strategic alliances among global criminal enterprises and with the weakening of state controls over border security and trade regulations, the 14 independent states that arose out of the former Soviet Union are prime exporters of organized crime, including the potential for WMD transfers (Bagley, 2001). Jessica Stern reported on Al Qaeda developing relationships with organized criminal groups in Central Asia, the former Soviet Union, and the Caucasus, and on numerous occasions of Al Qaeda attempting to acquire everything from botulinum and salmonella toxin to cyanide and enriched uranium (Stern, 2003).

When Al Qaeda moved its headquarters to the Sudan in 1991, the first order was given to its lieutenants to attempt to acquire chemical, biological, radiological, and nuclear weapons (CBRN). Al Qaeda's international structure allowed it to set up business fronts specifically for the acquisition of weapons of all kinds (Stern, 2003). Bin Laden believed that Muslim nations could successfully defend themselves against the United States, especially if they could acquire CBRN weapons. Bin Laden states, "Muslim nations should not be lax in possessing nuclear, chemical, and biological weapons . . . it is the duty of every Muslim to struggle for its (United States) annihilation" (Scheuer, 2003, p. 186). Bin Laden further states, "I am carrying out a duty. It would be a sin for Muslims not to try and possess the weapons that would prevent the infidels from inflicting harm on Muslims (Stern, 2003, p. 255). Al Qaeda has consistently reiterated this message of hoping to develop weapons that would cause such catastrophic loss, that the United States would rethink its actions in the world. Ayman Zawahiri, bin Laden's deputy, has stated in his memoirs, "the targets and the type of weapons must be selected carefully to cause damage to the enemy's structure and deter it enough to make it stop its brutality" (Stern, 2003, p. 255).

When Al Qaeda became established in the Sudan, Central Intelligence Agency (CIA) information suggested that the Sudanese government had agreed to the production of chemical weapons to be used specifically against U.S. troops stationed in Saudi Arabia. There are also intelligence reports that show the director of Iraq's nuclear weapons program, Khidhir Hamza, had been in touch with Al Qaeda members with the purpose of purchasing components for making nuclear weapons (Stern, 2003). Instruction manuals that contained recipes for making biological and chemical weapons were discovered when Al Qaeda agents were arrested in Milan, Italy, and Frankfurt, Germany in December, 2000

(Stern, 2003). Captured documents during the Afghanistan campaign revealed that Al Qaeda had the necessary materials for producing botulinum, and salmonella toxin, as well as cyanide, and were close to developing a potent strain of anthrax.

For Al Qaeda, or any extremist organization, to strike a devastating blow to the United States or other Western countries, they wouldn't even need to acquire a fully operational nuclear bomb. Even though the biggest fear acknowledged by former Homeland Security Secretary Tom Ridge is nuclear, terrorists could accomplish significant devastation with a radiological or dirty bomb. A radiological bomb consists of a conventional explosive surrounded by any type of radiological material, resulting in the extensive dispersal of radiological matter. The amount of material available for a radiological attack is staggering. A Harvard study in 2003 states that there are 130 civilian nuclear research labs scattered around the world, with many of them having minimal security (Brzezinski, 2004). Other material can be found in nuclear power stations, reactors, discarded radiological medical equipment, cesium, or strontium (Brzezinski, 2004).

With the ideological foundation firmly established, the development of an international organization, and with the legitimization of the slaughter of non-believers, we begin to see the extraordinary threat Al Qaeda poses. They have the desire and the financial and organizational means to obtain WMD.

Al Qaeda's continued communication and associations with global criminal organizations significantly increases the likelihood that if Al Qaeda is not yet in possession of WMD, then they certainly will be in the future.

CONCLUSIONS

The Doomsday Clock may be a symbolic reference, but the threats to global stability are very real. A powerful ideology can be harnessed with modern communication systems producing a global tool to motivate adherents to action. Increasing interdependency and fluidity in global systems has contributed to the ability of terrorist organizations to finance, obtain, and transport WMD. Technology has contributed to terrorist success with sophisticated communication, financial transfer systems, and by significantly increasing the potential casualty totals.

The solutions must also be global in scope. The best way to combat the growing threat is a coordinated international effort in sharing intelligence data concerning the movement of individuals, finances, and weaponry. The first order of concern should be the securing of nuclear material in the Soviet Union and a security reevaluation of all biological and chemical weapons facilities. There should be a global concerted effort to determine what can be done to create economic, educational, and cultural alternatives in regions where extremist groups prosper. Perhaps we can never completely defeat terrorist organizations, but strategies to improve political relationships and the general quality of life for potential future

92 / PERSPECTIVES ON VIOLENCE AND VIOLENT DEATH

terrorists may reduce the likelihood of individuals choosing the terrorist path. The problem is daunting in its complexity. The difficulty in coordination of all the agencies within Homeland Security gives us some indication of the difficulty of the task at hand.

In addition to the massive problems concerning a global integration of security systems, such as software, funding, language, and varying national commitments, there are the evolving challenges to future governance. Changing political systems, demographic challenges, and power struggles are just a few of the challenges facing leaders and policymakers in the twenty-first century. The National Intelligence Council has identified many of the concerns for the future. Questions raised include, will the emerging economies in Russia and Central Asia move toward democracy, or will they slip back toward authoritarianism? Can democratic progress be made in key Middle Eastern countries? Will the demographic youth bulges expected in the Middle East and West African countries contribute to the growing radical Islamic movement? Will Muslim immigration into Western European countries be inclusive, or will there be obstacles to full integration? Will terrorism substantially increase the cost of doing business and adversely affect trade patterns and financial markets? Will rising numbers of unemployed youth create a sense of alienation and increase their likelihood of terrorist recruitment? Will organized crime syndicates expand their influence and destabilize regions? Will the spread of anti-Americanism increase our insecurity (National Intelligence Council, 2005)?

All of these questions point to the factors and conditions that will exacerbate or reduce the potential for future terrorist attacks. How we decide to confront these questions could determine the possibility or probability of the use of WMD.

REFERENCES

Allison, G. (2004). *Nuclear terrorism: The ultimate preventable catastrophe.* New York: Times Books. Henry Holt and Company.

Arendt, H. (1970). *On violence.* New York: Harcourt, Brace & World Inc.

Bagley, B. (2001). *Globalization and transnational organized crime: The Russian mafia in Latin America and the Caribbean.* Retrieved March 1, 2005 from the World Wide Web:
http://www.mamacoca.org/feb2002/art_bagley_globalization_organized_crime_en.html.

Benjamin, D., & Simon, S. (2002). *The age of sacred terror.* New York: Random House Inc.

Berman, P. (2003). *Terror and liberalism.* New York: W. W. Norton & Company.

Brzezinski, M. (2004). *Fortress America: On the front lines of homeland security—An inside look at the coming surveillance state.* New York: Bantam Books.

Bulletin of the Atomic Scientists. (2005). Retrieved February 28, 2005 from the World Wide Web: http://www.thebulletin.org/doomsday_clock/timeline.htm.

Burbules, N., & Torres, C. (2000). *Globalization and education: Critical perspectives.* New York: Routledge.

Esposito, J. (1992). *The Islamic threat: Myth or reality?* New York: Oxford University Press.

Gunaratna, R. (2002). *Inside Al-Qaeda: Global network of terror.* New York: Columbia University Press.

Haught, J. (1990). *Holy horrors: An illustrated history of religious murder and madness. Buffalo.* New York: Prometheus Books.

Herman, S. (2005). *Japan remembers sarin gas attack 10 years later.* Retrieved March, 19, 2005 from the World Wide Web:
http://www.voanews.com/english/2005-03-19-voal1.cfm?renderforprint=1.

Hiro, D. (2002). *War without end: The rise of Islamist terrorism and global response.* New York: Routledge.

Hornyak, T. (2005). *10 years after Aum sarin gas attack, pseudo-religions thriving in Japan.* Retrieved March 19, 2005 from the World Wide Web:
http://www.japantoday.com/e/?content=feature&id=871.

Iadicola, P., & Shupe, A. (2003). *Violence, inequality and human freedom.* Lanham, MD: Rowman & Littlefield Publishers Inc.

Juergensmeyer, M. (2000). *Terror in the mind of God: The global rise of religious violence.* Berkeley, CA: University of California Press.

Lifton, R. (1999). *Destroying the world to save it: Aum Shinrikyo, apocalyptic violence, and the new global terrorism.* New York: Metropolitan Books/Henry Holt and Co.

National Intelligence Council. (2005). *The contradictions of globalization.* Report of the National Intelligence Council's 2020 Project. Retrieved January 19, 2005 from the World Wide Web: http://www.cia/gov/NIC_globaltrend2020_sl.html.

Olson, K. (1999). *Aum Shinrikyo: Once and future threat?* Center for Disease Control (CDC). Emerging Infectious Diseases. Retrieved January 31, 2005 from the World Wide Web: http://www.cdc.gov/ncidod/EID/vol5no4/olson.htm.

Passas, N. (2005). *Informal value transfer systems, terrorism and money laundering.* Department of Justice funded report. Document No.: 208301. Award Number: 2002-IJ-CX-0001.

Passas, N. (1999). *Informal value transfer systems and criminal organizations: A study into so-called underground banking networks.* Retrieved February 15, 2005 from the World Wide Web: http://www.minjust.nl:8080/b_organ/wodc/publications/ivts.pdf.

Rashid, A. (2002). *Jihad: The rise of militant Islam in Central Asia.* New York: Penguin Books.

Scheuer, M. (2003). *Through our enemies' eyes: Osama bin Laden, radical Islam, and the future of America.* Washington, DC: Brassey's Inc.

Schwan, W. (2004). Bioterrorism: Should I be worried? In A. Nyatepe-Coo & D. Zeisler-Vralsted (Eds.), *Understanding terrorism: Threats in an uncertain world* (pp. 223-238). Upper Saddle River, NJ: Pearson Prentice Hall.

Schwartz, S. (2002). *The two faces of Islam: Saudi fundamentalism and its role in terrorism.* New York: Anchor Books.

Stern, J. (2003). *Terror in the name of God: Why religious militants kill.* New York: HarperCollins Publishers.

PART II

Encounters with Violence

CHAPTER 6

Resisting the Magnet: A Study of South African Children's Engagements with Neighborhood Violence

Jenny Parkes

South Africa is a country in the process of immense change. Its first democratic elections in 1994 heralded the advent of democracy and ended the brutal and repressive apartheid regime. With democracy, a vast program of reforms has begun, aiming to promote human rights, equality, and social justice. But apartheid, and colonialism, have left a legacy of continuing disparities in economic and social circumstances, high levels of unemployment, and rates of violent crime among the highest in the world, particularly in poorer communities, where people are 80 times more likely than the rich to be victims of violent crime (Hamber, 2000). Violence enters into children's lives in multiple realms—in the neighborhood, in schools, and in families: "violence is part of a dynamic and systemic cycle that appears to have its origin in the apartheid years when institutionalized violence became a way of life in our homes, schools, and communities" (Matthews, Griggs, & Caine, 1999).

This chapter considers what it means to children in South Africa to live with violence. Research in this area has frequently conceptualized children as passive victims, caught up in a "cycle of violence," which turns innocent children into violent adults. Studies have highlighted the problem and the negative consequences of violence on children's education (Human Rights Watch, 2001), emotions (Henderson, 1999; Seedat, Nyamai, Njenga, Vythilingum, & Stein, 2004), and behavior (van der Merwe & Dawes, 2000). But very little research has looked at how children cope, how most children do *not* take up violent lifestyles; and children have rarely been asked for their perspectives. In this chapter, using

98 / PERSPECTIVES ON VIOLENCE AND VIOLENT DEATH

material from my PhD research, I will explore how children actively construct beliefs and practices in relation to the violence in their neighborhoods (Parkes, 2005). Through understanding these processes of meaning construction, I believe that we can begin to change violent social relationships.

BACKGROUND TO THE STUDY

The study focused on a group of primary-school children living at the start of the twenty-first century in a working-class neighborhood of Cape Town, where there were high levels of unemployment and substance abuse, overcrowded living conditions, and high levels of violence, with widespread gangsterism. The children, who were between 8 and 15-years-old, spent many hours talking with me about their lives, discussing with me and with each other their relationships, their conflicts, and the violence they encountered at school, at home, or in the neighborhood; violence they witnessed or heard about, participated in, or ran away from. Interweaving ethnographic and participatory research methods, I worked over several months with children individually and in friendship groups, using discussion, drama, art, and games to generate rich data about the sensitive and taboo subjects of violence and conflict.

In considering children's perspectives about violence, a theoretical challenge was to analyze how children's perspectives are socially *constructed* (Gergen, 1999) and at the same time, how they are *constructive*. In making sense of violence, children draw on the locally available "knowledges," the taken-for-granted beliefs and practices of their neighborhoods, learned at home, at school, and through the media. Children's perspectives are then constructed through past and present relationships. So, when I ask a child about violence in the neighborhood, her response will be influenced by her relationship with me, an adult (foreign, female), and may be quite different from what she would say to her friend or her father. She may be thinking of violence witnessed on the way home from school yesterday, what she heard last week at church or mosque, or what she saw on television last night. Or she may be remembering a conversation she overheard between her mother and aunt, or her mother's words to her about where to play or not to play. And her mother's views will be influenced by her own life experiences, and for both, their perspectives will be connected with their social identities as female, black, and working class. In interacting with me, she actively engages with these social relationships.

> When we enter human life, it is as if we walk on stage into a play whose enactment is already in progress—a play whose somewhat open plot determines what part we may play and towards what denouements we may be heading. Others on stage already have a sense of what the play is about, enough of a sense to make negotiations with a newcomer possible (Bruner, 1990, p. 34).

RESISTING THE MAGNET / 99

And if these previous interactions have influenced the perspectives and practices we have now, then what about this present interaction? What impact might it have on the future? Talk is constructive, a form of social action: "discourse builds objects, worlds, minds and social relations. It doesn't just reflect them" (Wetherell, 2001). This gives the analysis of talk immense potential. As children talk about violent social relations, they co-create ways of engaging with violence. Analysis of their talk can tell us not just their opinions, but where those opinions come from, how they are constructed through social relations, how they are repeated, patterned, and how they change.

The analysis of children's talk about violence in the neighborhood generated the metaphor of violence as a magnet, which both repels and attracts children.

VIOLENCE THAT REPELS

Violence entered into the social relations of children in this study in multiple forms—in their relations with each other and with adults at school and at home—but the violence that most concerned children was the violence in the neighborhood. Patterns emerged in the ways in which children talked about this violence with two contrasting forms of violence dominating children's talk: the *drink-drugs-violence* repertoire and the *predatory violence* repertoire.

The drink-drugs-violence repertoire was characterized by the gradual loss of control, leading to violence, whether because of alcohol, drugs, or a minor conflict escalating into violent conflict, as in these responses in individual interviews to my question about the causes of neighborhood problems.

> **Fatima:** This drinking, they drinking and this alcohol is just making them so dizzy, and then they catch on all the nonsense.
>
> **Clinton:** I think it's of drinking, drinking problems and smoking weed, that is my suggestion because mostly um, here at, again at the back, just by the park, before you get the park, uh, the gangsters call it "a yard." That's where they go drink and smoke weed, and when they come out of there, then they're "high wire" then they start this problems.

With adults within this context expected to protect, regulate, and control many aspects of children's lives, Fatima and Clinton are highly critical of the lack of self-control of those adults, who "catch on all the nonsense." The violence in these narratives spills in an uncontrolled way to others, so that children become endangered almost by accident. In contrast to this is predatory violence, where the violence is viewed as intentional, and children view themselves (and others) as prey.

> **Ayesha:** There's people laying on the fields sometimes that can catch you, and then they can kill you.

100 / PERSPECTIVES ON VIOLENCE AND VIOLENT DEATH

> **Alex:** If you, if there's somebody outside and they call you, and they give you, and they want to give you sweets you mustn't go [. . .] because then they're just going to grab you into the car, and they going to ride away.
> **Robin:** And they rape you.

While children's narratives of violent incidents they have experienced more often involved the first repertoire, their talk suggested that it is this repertoire of predatory violence that engendered more fear, perhaps because it more clearly rendered children as prey, as potential victims rather than bystanders and so inevitably disempowered them. Often, though, there was a confluence of both these forms of violence.

Some of the most haunting narratives included two contrasting features— they emphasized both the *horror* and the *everyday nature of the violence*. Ryan told me about a time when he was walking home and heard gunshots.

> **Ryan:** A girl was in a fight—in a gangster fight—so they shot her here in the back and here in the stomach.
> **Jenny:** Okay. And what happened afterwards, do you know?
> **Ryan:** They took her to hospital. When they came there she was already dead.
> **Jenny:** And was she in one of the gangs, or was she a young girl?
> **Ryan:** She was a young girl. She was on her way to school.

As in many of the children's narratives, Ryan's repulsion is stressed by the graphic imagery—the location of wounds on the body of the girl who has been shot in the crossfire of a gang fight. But at the same time, there is a sense that this could happen to anyone; that it is an everyday event—she was just "on her way to school." And it is this that makes the violence even more haunting. Several children talked about a brutal murder that happened "just around the corner."

> **Odette:** This lady what was hanging up her washing, and then all the gangsters came over the wall, and then they put the black bag over her neck, and then she was dead next time, and then her son came home, and then her son called the police.

Again, the imagery Odette uses is graphic, presenting the violence as extreme and exceptional, and at the same time it is mundane—the victim was just going about her daily life, she was "hanging up her washing." Often children talked about violence as if it was an everyday event; they shared their practice of hiding under the bed when they heard shooting; they talked of gang fights "every Friday." There was then a juxtaposition of the ubiquitous, everyday nature of the violence in this talk and the graphic descriptions that emphasized the exceptional nature of the violence. Children were clearly repelled by these forms of violence, and there was no evidence of a desensitizing or numbing effect. The overriding emotion expressed was a sense of powerlessness—they empathized with the victims, who, like them, were just going about their day-to-day lives when they were caught up in violence, either accidentally through being in the wrong place at the wrong time, or intentionally, through the predatory actions of the perpetrators. Children were repelled by violence that positioned them as helpless, which cast them as the victims, which rendered them powerless.

THE ATTRACTION OF VIOLENCE

While usually children were repelled by neighborhood violence, permeating their narratives were examples where the relationship with violence was much more ambivalent. Sometimes in our group discussions there seemed to be competition to recount incidents of crime and violence. Some of these narratives had all the hallmarks of a "good story"—setting the scene, creating an atmosphere, a clear sequence, and lively humor and action—as if these narratives had been told and retold, perhaps becoming family stories. Often they were stories of bravery, resourcefulness, and resilience, and often it was the men and boys in the family who successfully resisted violence, as when Rushaanah's father and uncles tried to prevent a break-in, "my uncle with a gun . . . the other one went with a . . . a iron. . . . And my daddy went with a broomstick" or when eight-year-old Alex tells how he and his father went with pellet guns to challenge an intruder.

Children then seemed to be attracted to telling stories about violence; violence could be exciting, but in these stories, it is not the violence that attracts, but the successful resistance to violence and threat. It was only in retrospect that these became "good" stories, and there will be many stories they will choose not to tell. These "good" stories contrasted markedly with others that lacked these narrative features. So Melissa told me at length about a violent conflict between rival gangs, in which her parents, her brother and her uncles were injured. In telling this story, her sentences were fragmented, the narrative difficult to follow. She told me, "they still want to kill my uncle and my auntie . . . they're coming, and they're going to hit our house also." The events involve the people closest to Melissa, and there has not been the passing of enough time to help create distance from these events, to select memories, to turn them into family stories, and so to regain some sense of control.

The successful resistance described in the "good" stories often entailed the potential to use force by the children or their families, usually by the men and boys. Boys talked with pride about their resistance and, in contrast, with shame and frustration when they were not able to defend their families, as when David was unable to prevent his brother from being robbed. Bravery, fighting skill, and toughness carried high status for boys. In South Africa, with its long history of conflict and violence, masculinity and violence have been closely connected (Morrell, 2001). These tough masculinities were epitomized in local gang practices, and children spoke at length about the drug dealing, crime, and violence of the street gangs. While they were repelled by the ways in which gang violence

102 / PERSPECTIVES ON VIOLENCE AND VIOLENT DEATH

endangered and disempowered them, they could also be attracted to the tough masculinities embodied in gang practices.

Children were highly critical of gangs, but at the same time they talked of the status within the peer group of joining a gang.

> **Shandre:** I think that they want to be like the coolest in the area—they want to think that they are the coolest, and then they like rob people and that, and then they go to jail, and then they're out again, and they think they rough—cool—that they went to jail, and then they're out again and that. And sometimes if you have friends, and then the one join the gang just to show his friends that he is in a gang, and he can be with the cool guys, as they say.

Gangs were associated with a potent combination of coolness, fearlessness, and violence. Shandre's words show how gang membership can offer strength, power, and a sense of inclusion or belonging: "he can be with the cool guys."

The older boys, at 13-years-old, were the most fascinated by the gangs—both determined not to become gangsters themselves, and proud of their knowledge about the gangs.

> **Luke:** I can name, Jenny, almost all the gangs here, I know all this gangs here [. . . .] But I know them so they won't try anything with me.

This proximity to gangs enabled some boys to gain status without actually participating in or supporting gang violence. Luke presents himself as tough and protected by his acquaintance with gang members. But his ambiguous positioning of himself as both close to and distanced from gangs may be difficult to maintain. For boys, there were tensions in the relationship with violence. Boys in this study engaged in multiple forms of masculinity, many of them quite contrary to gangs and violence, but tough masculinities carried high social capital, generating uneasy relationships with violence.

For the girls, too, there was sometimes ambivalence, though compliance was a more socially acceptable performance of femininity than toughness. While the girls in this study positioned themselves as caring, obedient, and compliant, they were often reluctant to take up associated positions of passivity and helplessness. Some of the girls, while hostile to the gangs, yearned for the freedom from constraint they were seen to offer. Both boys and girls were repelled by the violence in their neighborhoods, which endangered and disempowered them. But where violence appeared to empower, like a magnet, violence could attract. This simultaneous attraction and repulsion created ambiguous and uneasy relationships with violence.

RESISTING THE MAGNET

Children's perceptions of violence in their neighborhoods were connected with power and control. When violence is associated with control, when it is seen as

RESISTING THE MAGNET / 103

empowering, it entices. When children have so little control over their lives, then these glimmers of power must be tempting. But the children in this study much more often talked of their repulsion and, in their talk, they constructed ways to resist the magnet of violence. A key task for children in resisting the magnet was to shift the magnetism, reducing the attraction to violence.

This process can be illustrated by returning to extracts of children's talk discussed above. When Ryan, for example, recounted the shooting of a girl caught in the crossfire of a gang fight, he said "she was a young girl." When Fatima talked of a robbery in the street, the victim was "a pensioner." In their choice of narratives in which women, children, or the elderly were victims, the children disempowered the perpetrator by the suggestion that he was able to injure only the weakest members of society. Rather than the violent act displaying the perpetrator's ability to exert control over others, the imbalance of power displayed his impotence and the futility of acts of extreme violence. But being positioned as weak disempowers the victims as well as the perpetrators, and children were reluctant to position themselves as victims. So in their selection of narratives, children often talked about victims who were deemed to be weaker than the narrator; so boys talked about the victims being girls, while the victims girls talked of were old people or babies. In this way, they wrested control from the perpetrator and avoided, when they could, casting themselves as helpless.

In illustrating the attraction of gangs, I used this extract from a discussion with Shandre:

> **Shandre:** I think that they want to be like the coolest in the area—they want to *think* that they are the coolest, and then they like rob people and that, and then they go to jail, and then they're out again, and *they think* they rough—cool—that they went to jail, and then they're out again and that. And sometimes if you have friends, and then the one join the gang just to show his friends that he is in a gang, and he can be with the cool guys, *as they say*.

But re-reading the extract reveals ways in which she deconstructs the power of gangs. In particular, like many of the children when they talked about gangs, she uses the words "they think," challenging the association of gang membership with being cool or rough. The power then is an illusion.

Frequently, children talked about gangs as a trap that ensnares young people, and reduces rather than increases power or control: "like they say, 'you live a *skollie*, you die a *skollie*.' You can say you'll lose your life quick if you're a *skollie*, or you'll go to prison." So rather than gain power and riches, the consequence of becoming a gangster, or in Afrikaans, *skollie*, is death or prison. Children often talked about the violent punishments gangs administer to members who try to leave; so rather than sources of freedom, control, and social support, gangs were reconstructed as coercive and disempowering.

104 / PERSPECTIVES ON VIOLENCE AND VIOLENT DEATH

CONTROL, CONNECTION, COHERENCE

At the heart of the magnet of violence lies power. For children in this study, much of the violence in their lives disempowered them, casting them as victims, and they were repelled by such violence. Within this context, children had little power; they were some of the least powerful members of a neighborhood already weakened and fractured by social and economic stresses. Where violence could award power, as in gang membership, such violence could attract. But children resisted this attraction through challenging the power of violence, and so they were able to resist the magnet. Through resourceful positioning of themselves and others, the children in this study were able to deconstruct the power of violence as illusory. For some children, this had costs, forcing choices in which distancing the self from violence might entail giving up forms of power, like the power and status of violent and tough masculinities. At the same time though, children wrested *control*, seeking agency in their retelling of stories about violence.

Within this context, wherein children identified a need for support and protection in violent interactions, *connection* and inclusion in friendship and family groups had particular resonance. Friends provided social support through sharing company, offering advice, keeping secrets, and listening when children talked about their problems. Families, too, were sites of support, with mothers in particular offering advice, managing daily routines, setting rules to keep children safe. Through connection within families and friendship groups, children resisted violence. But social support could take violent forms; for example, in the use of physical punishment, fighting to protect each other, and sometimes in negotiating their inclusion in friendship groups, children excluded others, thus increasing potential conflict and violence.

Through constructing rules and narratives, we try to organize, order, and bring coherence to our experience (Bruner, 1990; Haste, 1987). These rules and narratives are passed on through our cultural communities, and children actively interpret them in ways that may be reproductive, but may also generate change. In trying to make sense of the violence in their lives, children sometimes created rules and narratives that reinforced violent practices, as in their talk about retaliation: "you hit me, I hit you" and retribution: "they must feel before they listen." But in their construction of narratives that resisted the magnet, they were clearly striving for *coherence* in ways that contested violence. Within the changing context of South Africa, children were also able to engage in a new language of rights, freedom, and equality, in which alternative nonviolent masculinities are becoming more widespread (Morrell, 2001). Children were beginning to use the language of rights and to question inequities, as in Jacqueline's challenge, "children also have rights, but then who wants to listen to our rights?"

Striving for control, connection, and coherence were key processes through which children made sense of violence. They generated rules and narratives to bring coherence. They strove for connection, to belong to networks of people who supported and protected them. They strove for control, to have some kind of agency in managing social relationships. But these strivings generated tensions, and in managing these tensions, children sometimes reproduced and perpetuated violence. Yet, these strivings also enabled children to contest violent social relations. Unexpectedly, the research process itself seemed to illustrate how this could work. At the start of their participation in the research, children saw punishment by adults—teachers, parents, or police—as the solution to problems of violence. But after participating in the research, many more children proposed talk and verbal persuasion as solutions. Clinton, for example, reflected on how to solve the problems of gangs: "if the police or headmaster or the government can just get all the gangsters into one group, and maybe they can talk them out of it. Talk some sense into them." Louise proposed, "telling the people that it's dangerous to shoot around," and when I asked her who should tell them, she replied, "the children or the parents or the people." Jacqueline suggested, "maybe if they should tell someone older who can handle the problem, and then maybe they can help, and they don't need to go out and get . . . do mischief." Verbal reasoning, problem solving, and social support were increasingly seen as solutions to problems of violence. These changes had not been intended and they appeared to stem from the experience of actively participating in friendship-group discussions, reflecting together on social problems and co-constructing new narratives. Building on these experiences, children strove for control, connection, and coherence to contest violence.

CONCLUSION

Violence reverberates in children's lives in complex ways, and we need to avoid the temptation to imagine easy solutions (Scheper-Hughes & Bourgois, 2004). Yet, in this chapter, I have shown how children, while caught up in these webs of social relations, can also strive for change. Interventions can have a crucial role in supporting these strivings. Encouragement of children's active participation could foster a sense of control and agency. Working with collaborative groups could develop problem-solving and negotiation skills and a sense of connection. Building on children's existing knowledge and co-creating nonviolent rules and narratives could generate coherence.

While it may be possible, in the safety of the research relationship, for children to co-construct less violent ways of engaging with others, the deeply rooted, historically constituted beliefs and practices that continue to feed into children's social relationships persist, and solutions remain elusive. Whether or not children can contribute to changing violent relations, this chapter shows that, given the opportunity, they will actively and creatively strive to do so.

REFERENCES

Bruner, J. (1990). *Acts of meaning*. Cambridge MA: Harvard University Press.

Gergen, K. J. (1999). *An invitation to social constructionism*. London: Sage.

Hamber, B. (2000). "Have no doubt it is fear in the land": An exploration of the continuing cycles of violence in South Africa. *Southern African Journal of Child and Adolescent Mental Health, 12*(1), 5-18.

Haste, H. (1987). Growing into rules. In J. Bruner & H. Haste (Eds.), *Making sense: The child's construction of the world* (pp. 163-195). London: Methuen.

Henderson, P. (1999). *Living with fragility: Children in new crossroads*. Unpublished Ph.D. thesis, University of Cape Town, Cape Town.

Human Rights Watch. (2001). *Scared at school: Sexual violence against girls in South African schools*. New York: Human Rights Watch.

Matthews, I., Griggs, M., & Caine, G. (1999). *The experience review of interventions and programmes dealing with youth violence in urban schools in South Africa*. Durban: Independent Projects Trust.

Morrell, R. (Ed.). (2001). *Changing men in Southern Africa*. Pietermaritzburg and London: University of Natal Press and Zed Books Ltd.

Parkes, J. (2005). *Children's engagements with violence: A study in a South African school*. Unpublished Ph.D. thesis, University of London Institute of Education, London.

Scheper-Hughes, N., & Bourgois, P. (Eds.). (2004). *Violence in war and peace: An anthology*. Oxford: Blackwell.

Seedat, S., Nyamai, C., Njenga, F., Vythilingum, B., & Stein, D. J. (2004). Trauma exposure and post-traumatic stress symptoms in urban African schools: Survey in Cape Town and Nairobi. *British Journal of Psychiatry, 184,* 169-175.

van der Merwe, A., & Dawes, A. (2000). Prosocial and antisocial tendencies in children exposed to community violence. *Southern African Journal of Child and Adolescent Mental Health, 12,* 19-37.

Wetherell, M. (2001). Themes in discourse research: The case of Diana. In M. Wetherell, S. Taylor, & S. J. Yates (Eds.), *Discourse theory and practice: A reader* (pp. 14-28). London: Sage.

CHAPTER 7

Silent Night, Violent Night: An Encounter with Unexpected Violence*

Carr Maher

It was always the same, red lights reflecting off storefronts, windshields, or wet pavement: the metric beat of flash-blank-flash-blank. Someone had told him once that if you looked at the lights long enough, you could actually hypnotize yourself. He never did. He never had the time. As a patrolman, it was always the same routine: set up the barriers, check the perimeter, or go see the boss, who is running the job. When he moved on to the trucks, it was find a place, get gear set up, and be ready. Now he was a "talker." Other departments had other names for them, but NYPD called them talkers. His job was simple: he talked to people, people who were in trouble, people who had managed to put themselves into situations where they or others were in great danger. His job was to talk them out of the problem. Sometimes it was by phone, sometimes it was by bullhorn. Usually, it was in person, face to face.[†]

He had a knack for this job. He had a certain charm, a way with words and a quick wit that helped take the edge off most situations. He had howled at the moon with drunks on top of bridges and cried with terrified teens whose girl-friends were pregnant. He had conned weapons away from hardened criminals and convinced a secretary not to shoot her boss because it was Tuesday. He had

---

*There is research on many aspects of domestic violence. However, research on the impact of this violence on the responding police officer is much less. This chapter is an account by a former officer of the incident that effectively ended his career. It provides an example of an encounter with violence felt to be both "unexpected" and "unnecessary." It is offered in the hope that it can add a new dimension to the examination of the impact of domestic violence.

[†]"Talkers" are members of the Hostage Negotiation Unit. Some departments call them "Crisis Management Specialists" or "Negotiators."

108 / PERSPECTIVES ON VIOLENCE AND VIOLENT DEATH

field-divorced a couple of rummies who were holding his and her shotguns on one another because their married life was hell. He had talked more jumpers off ledges and bridges than he cared to remember.

It was simple, really, just follow the steps.

A - Assess the situation yourself.
B - Breathe—take three good deep breaths before you did anything else. This relaxes you, so you don't start off on an immediate high.
C - Communicate with the bosses to explain what you need, and learn what they need.
D - Deploy whatever gear you need.
E - Evacuate. You can't call time out to take a leak when you're facing some guy waving a weapon around.
F - Feel the environment—don't "talk street" to Park Ave and never talk Park Ave to the street.
G - Get it done.

By the time he arrived, the guys from the trucks[1] have done their part, the simple Cs.

Control the scene,
Contain the individual,
Communicate exact information.

There was one other golden rule to always be remembered at the end of the tour— you are the one who is going to go home.

Yes, the scene was always the same on the exterior, always bustle and light. It was after you looked inside that the scenes all became different, and that's when a talented talker was really valuable. A good talker related to people and got them away from the mood they were in and made them compliant, the mood that had brought them here.

This he could do. This he had always done. He stepped from his car, walked up to the boss running the job, and got the first of his many surprises that night. The precinct operations lieutenant was running the job. There was no Emergency Service boss present. In fact, there were no Emergency Service Units on the scene at all. To his question, he received the answer, "We don't need them. It's just a drunk 'Dago' who fired a few shots at his wife and mother-in-law and locked

---

[1] "From the trucks"— Because emergency service work is so varied, the members of this unit patrol in a pickup truck equipped with every type of rescue gear imaginable. These units also have massive lighting displays used to search in dark places for weapons or illuminate a rescue site. The motto of the ESU, Emergency Service Unit, is "When a citizen needs help, he calls a cop. . . . When a cop needs help, he calls ESU." The unofficial motto of the trucks is "If you're so f___n smart, why are you running in when everyone else is running out?"

himself in the bathroom. He's got no place to go. You just talk him out, and we'll all get home in time to have a nice Christmas Eve with the family."

The officer had forgotten it was Christmas Eve. He walked back to the car and spoke with his driver, who told him dispatch had them logged on the call; then he went toward the house. Actually, it was an upstairs apartment above a store that sold carpeting. It was a long 13 steps up to where a Patrol Sergeant was standing in the hall.

Together they pieced together the story. "Jimmy" worked for the NYC Sanitation Department at one of the landfills full-time and worked part-time for one of the private bus companies at night. He was married to a real princess— a shrew with a voice that could scar glass and a heart as big as a very small grain of sand. Jimmy coped by not being there; he was seldom home because he was always working. Unfortunately, tonight was an overtime night, so no part-timers were needed, and Jimmy came home. He arrived to find not just his wife but also his mother-in-law present. Now, the wife was bad, but his mother-in-law was bad cubed. In mythology, she would have been, at least, a harpy and probably a gorgon. During his interview with her, she used such phrases as "that bastard son-in-law," "he's never been worth anything," and that wonderful catch phrase, "I told my daughter not to marry him."

A little further investigation revealed that the three had sat down to a small supper, which Jimmy couldn't or didn't finish because the two women, who had started drinking at about 4 PM had started in on him as soon as he arrived home. When he wasn't around, they went after each other. Grandkids were mentioned in an accusing way as well as the wonderful life of the sister who had moved out of range of the senior-most harpy and made only infrequent pilgrimages in from Huntington, accompanied by her dutiful spouse and three children. Jimmy, who didn't usually drink, retreated to the bedroom with a bottle of pretty good blended scotch whiskey and tried to drown out their torment by consuming the better part of it. Unfortunately, his anger wouldn't let him pass out, and the more he drank, the more enraged he became. He finally went to the dresser drawer and came out with a Colt revolver. It was one he had picked up to protect himself from rats when he was working the night shift at the landfill. He was seeing lots of rats at the moment, and he was going to shut them up once and for all. He walked into the living room and fired just once. Considering how drunk he was, he didn't do too badly. The shot missed both the wife and the mother-in-law, but did kill a very garish-looking lamp on the end table at the far end of the couch. He then retreated to the bathroom to get very, very sick and try to stop the ringing in his ears from the blast of the pistol.

The wife immediately reacted to the shot by screaming about the cost of the lamp. The mother-in-law suspected that, to her daughter, she would have been a more palatable victim and actually claimed that she was shocked into silence, for a whole 10 to 20 seconds, before she picked up the phone and called the police.

110 / PERSPECTIVES ON VIOLENCE AND VIOLENT DEATH

When the talker suggested that the women be escorted from the house, not only did they violently refuse, he found out they were not welcome in any of the neighbors' houses and the ops lou (Operations Lieutenant) had forbidden them from entering the precinct. One of the Patrolmen then approached and informed him that he knew Jimmy and the wife. He said that he felt sorry for Jimmy, and vouched that he was really a very good, hard-working, quiet guy. His biggest mistake was marrying a spendthrift who most of the time was too lazy to get her big butt off the couch to even cook. Also, the mother-in-law was something of a local legend. She had moved to the neighborhood about 30 years ago and still didn't have a single friend.

So, this is what he had to deal with—a man pushed by circumstances into a corner who, under the influence of a considerable amount of alcohol, had finally snapped and lashed out using an illegal weapon. In his anger, he had killed a lamp. With this established, the talker started toward the back of the apartment, where Jimmy was fortified in the bathroom. He called out, "Jimmy, Jimmy Delafortuna. My name is Detective Fox, and I have to talk to you."

"Go away," was the moaned reply. From the sound of the timbre of his voice, Jimmy still had his head in the bowl.

"Jimmy, I can't do that. Open the door, and let's talk about this."

"Just leave me alone," was the soft reply. At least the head was no longer in the bowl.

"Hey, Jimmy. Come on out. I've got to arrest you for the homicide of one lamp. You gonna come peaceable?"

This time the reply was louder and firmer, "You're arresting me for what?!"

"Jimmy, you shot the lamp in cold blood. You gotta be arrested."

"What?"

"Jimmy just shut up and listen. I got to read you your rights. You have the right to remain silent. If you give up that right, anything you say may be used in evidence against you in a court of law. You have the right to have an electrician present during questioning, and if you don't have one, the court will appoint one for you. Do you understand these rights as I have given them to you?"

With that, the bathroom door opened and there stood Jimmy still in his work clothes, leaning against the bathroom sink holding the pistol at his side. His expression was one of complete disbelief. "Homicide of a lamp, the right to an electrician, what sort of bull is that?"

"The kind that got you to open the door," the talker said smiling.

"Yeah, you got me with that, but there's no way I'm going out there and no way your arresting me."

"Ok, I'm not going anywhere and neither are you, so how about we talk some." And talk they did for almost five hours. They talked sports and jobs, wives and homes, hopes and expectations, and always about problems. They talked of everything and about nothing, and for four hours and forty-seven minutes, Jimmy stayed alive.

He did not hurt anyone else, and he did not hurt himself. The weapon never left his hand, but it wasn't pointed at anyone, and his finger had been coaxed out of the trigger guard. You see, the weapon was the key. It didn't matter if you were talking nursery rhymes or football stats, as long as he had the weapon, the situation wasn't safe. A sudden flair up of temper, and the situation could turn deadly. And, if that happened, it happened fast.

Movies always show this in slow motion. The subject always gets big eyes or screams or does something really dramatic, then the good guy wrestles the gun from his hand. As the subject is removed, safely cuffed, the good guy pats him on the back and says something like, "It'll be OK now." The truth is never like that.

Sociopaths usually smiled as they brought their weapon up to try to blow your head off. You didn't try to take the weapon from them. You ducked like hell and shot him as quick as possible, or hoped someone else would be able to. Psychopaths had a bad habit of having no emotional outlook on the situation; without an external sign, they just brought the weapon up and tried to kill you, themselves, or both. At no time do you ever take your eyes off the subject. You concentrate. You watch. You evaluate every minute movement, every slight nuance. If you lose concentration for a split second, someone is going to get hurt. So you develop the skill of talking while observing everything. Without seeming to observe, you talk to establish calm, to establish a rapport. You never let the subject get out of control. You talk him down from rage or up from depression. Once you stop talking, you have no chance; so you talk. And you get the subject to talk. You get him to plan for the future. You show him options, and you never close the door on hope. If they are to ever get past this moment, even the "baddest of the bad" need hope.

He may have slaughtered the entire convent of the Little Sisters of the Poor, but you had to show him the best way out was to give up, and let the process work. Of course, he was disturbed. You understood that he wasn't responsible for his actions. You may actually have wanted to kill him where he stood for what he did, but that wasn't your job. Your job was to get him to give in to the inevitable and surrender peacefully so nobody else would get hurt, even him.

Drug addicts and drunks were always the hardest. Their brains just do not function well, because when someone is on drugs or alcohol, the whole thought process becomes muddled, and it is a real challenge to keep them on track. The talker had once talked a drunken father who was wielding a knife into giving up a hostage, his young daughter. Then he talked the knife away from the father. At that point, the father climbed onto a window ledge and threatened to jump. He had walked to the father and pushed him out the window. The drunken father forgot he was on the first floor. Except for being somewhat muddy from falling in the rose garden, the man was fine. If only the current situation could move that way.

Jimmy wasn't a bad guy. He was just in over his head. Things got to be too much for him and, fueled by the drinking, he had snapped. He had still not hurt anyone, and in the general scheme of things, he was a threat to no one but

112 / PERSPECTIVES ON VIOLENCE AND VIOLENT DEATH

himself. He was in a pickle. That was a fact. But he did have value as a person, and he was entitled to walk away from this incident.

Unfortunately, that was not to be the case. Things were starting to unravel behind the scenes, and the slim thread that kept the situation under control had already started to unwind. The second most important individual in a lock-in situation is the talker's driver. While the talker was doing his job, the driver also had a job to do. First, he set up the tape recorder, because every word the talker or the subject said was important, if not for this case, then for the next. It was all a learning process. Slowly, a body of material was being built that would enable talkers to go through much less of a trial and error process in order to push the "right" buttons.

The driver's second job was to relay information from the talker to command and from command to the talker. The ear bud was the talker's lifeline. If he was in danger and extreme action was to be taken, he could request it through a code word into his mike and be advised when and how to move, all through his ear bud. A priest could be requested and his arrival announced through this set up. The driver was as much a key to the successful resolution of the problem as the talker.

Usually drivers and talkers were pairings that had worked together for a long period of time. Not on this night. Not on this Christmas Eve. The driver was a floater who worked the boats during the good weather and floated through the rest of SOD[2] during the winter. He had enough knowledge to set up the tape recorder, but not the skill or experience to accomplish his third task. That third task was to keep *everyone* off the talkers back.

Bosses tend to get impatient. Bosses wanted the streets clear. Bosses never understood the fact that it could take hours, or even days, to work through the subject's problem and to bring everyone out safely. The Bosses only wanted instant results, immediate gratification. A stand-off was not only a talker's problem, it was also a Boss's problem. From the point of view of the Boss, men are not on patrol. They are tied up doing perimeter duty. The longer this situation goes on, the more spectators will flock to the scene. One cynic suggested that there was a mathematical equation that could predict the exact size of a crowd that any given event would draw. Take the number of sector cars and multiply by the temperature, and that would give you the base number. Then factor in the precinct status—a status-one precinct would add 100 people; a status-two precinct 80 people; and on down to a status 5, which added only 20 people. With this formula, you could

---

[2] SOD—Special Operations Division—the citywide command that is in charge of the departments special units, such as Aviation, Emergency Service, Bomb Squad, Harbor, Mounted, and Highway units. During the winter months, there is less call for Harbor units, so some of their members are used to fill in other areas. Some cops look at it as a learning experience, others try to make it a "vacation on duty," and they do as little as possible. As a result, these folks tend to be floated more than the others. They may work three days at an ESU truck and then wind up polishing the windshield of a police helicopter for their next couple of tours. Floaters are necessary, but they are usually not liked.

SILENT NIGHT, VIOLENT NIGHT / 113

estimate the size of the crowd with which you would be dealing. What was very interesting was that it actually worked.

Yes, the "Oh! Squad" was always present; no matter the time of day or night they were there.[3] The Oh! squad was always dangerous. They could be mild mannered or hostile, but they were always present. With their presence, the potential for problems was multiplied with each passing minute. They moaned and groaned in unison.

At times they chanted things like, "Jump!" "Jump," they shouted to suicide attempts sitting on ledges. The crowd was known to be fickle, cheering the police one minute and booing the next. They were the audience many criminals played to, attempting to assure their release. Many hadn't a clue what was going on and were too far away to really see anything, but they wouldn't leave. They were a part of what was happening, and they took up valuable manpower that cost the city money every minute and hour that a situation continued.

Bosses were always responsible to bigger bosses, until finally you got to the PC (Police Commissioner) who was responsible to the Mayor. Of course, in this case, the Mayor wasn't to be bothered. After all, it was Christmas Eve. So, it fell to some Deputy Mayor to start asking the PC questions about how long this was going to take. The PC had no love for this Deputy Mayor. "Pissant politician," was his most frequent phrase for him, so the PC passed on his mantel of responsibility to the Chief of Patrol. The Chief really didn't want to be bothered, so he referred it to the Borough Chief. It was the Borough Chief who got the Inspector for the Division out of his Christmas Party to call the Precinct Commander at *his* Christmas Party to find out just what the delay was and why the buses on such and such an avenue were being detoured. Back up the chain came the reply that some fool had shot his mother-in-law and was locked in his bathroom.

Now, the Deputy Mayor, who had hopes one day of being a Mayor or alderman or dog catcher, wasn't satisfied with this explanation. It was necessary to get those buses back on schedule. The fact that at that time of night only one bus ran the entire route, and that it never had more than three passengers on board, never appears to have entered into his thought process. No, for the efficiency of the city's transportation network, the thing must end now. It must end immediately, if not sooner.

Nowhere in the flow of information was the SOD chief notified. No mention was made to the SOD Captain or to the Hostage Negotiation Team Supervisor. They were not disturbed. After all it was Christmas Eve. It was a "perp" who had shot someone, and he had to be arrested. So the order flowed back down the chain of command all the way down to the lowly Patrol Lieutenant. The Lieutenant wasn't too happy with it, but wasn't on the best speaking terms with his Captain

---

[3] "Oh! Squad"—The crowd that is drawn by any incident. They are also referred to as ghouls. These people have a sound they make as things develop in front of them. The most common sound is, "Ohhhhh!" Thus, the name.

114 / PERSPECTIVES ON VIOLENCE AND VIOLENT DEATH

and had been at the precinct holiday party before all this had started. The Lieutenant grabbed a Sergeant and told him to take six officers and to affect the arrest.

If the driver had been more experienced, or more aware of what was going on around him, he would have done what the talker's regular driver would have done. Calmly or not, he would have explained to the LT that he was no longer in charge and he should go back to supporting his men on the perimeter. If the LT still insisted, then an SOD supervisor could be summoned to the scene to explain it to him in boss-to-boss fashion. If necessary, the driver could have stopped the LT. The talker's regular driver had already done this once by holding an LT off the ground by the throat until the SOD boss arrived. It can be tough giving orders when your windpipe is slowly being closed off. But, failing all else, he could have and should have warned the talker that this was going on. He didn't!

The patrol LT grabbed the Sergeant and laid out his plan to him. He told the Sergeant exactly how they were going to grab this guy. The Sergeant, a veteran with more than twice the time on the job than the LT, was neither impressed nor inspired. He didn't like running down blind alleys, and the LT couldn't or wouldn't acknowledge where the talker was. SOD had an entire unit for this type of thing, and the talker hadn't requested them, so the Sergeant did something he wasn't supposed to do: he asked questions. Asking questions is almost always dangerous, even more so when the LT you were questioning had spent far more time in the classroom than on the street and had been hooked up to his rank by a brother who was a Borough Chief in Brooklyn.

Now, no one would ever say the LT wasn't bright. It was just that he wasn't smart and lacked the experience for his job. He knew that all of his men knew this. He was unpopular, just as the cripple in a herd can appear unpopular, because his lack of street smarts and lack of experience were going to get someone killed someday and none of the herd wanted to volunteer for that job. The sound of their discussion on the first floor radiated to the second, and this made Jimmy nervous. He was become more jittery, more worried.

The talker watched as several hours of work was being washed away by the noise. Jimmy's hand tensed on his gun, and the talker knew he was going to have to start all over. The sound died down. The argument ended and the LT, with his little assault party, climbed the stairs, entered the hallway and, with the LT leading, made the turn to confront . . . the back of the talker. Perhaps it was at that moment that the LT realized he had made a mistake. Perhaps that's the point where total sobriety hit him. But he was in a very bad place. He couldn't go forward, and he couldn't go back. He had to do *something*, so he did: he brought his weapon up and fired at Jimmy.

Exactly what he was thinking is unknown, but the chain of events he started went like this: the bullet from the LT's 38 cal. Smith and Wesson passed by the left ear of the talker. The muzzle blast in the hallway was loud enough to temporarily deafen everyone. Jimmy could not see the LT, but knew someone had just shot at him. He brought up his pistol and fired at the only target he had, the talker. He fired once. The bullet passed between the talker's left ear and left shoulder blade hitting nothing. The talker, while moving to his right, drew his weapon and fired three times. The first bullet from his .45 cal. automatic hit Jimmy dead in the sternum blowing pieces of bone and metal through his heart into his backbone, lifting him off his feet and slamming him into the back wall of the shower stall. The impact was great enough to fracture the back of his skull. He was already dead when the second bullet hit just below the first one, shattering the xyphoid process and rupturing his spleen and the descending aorta. The third bullet hit Jimmy in his right hip and shattered the bone in the pelvic hip junction.

Bouncing up off the floor, the talker continued to train his weapon on Jimmy while he moved forward. Standing on Jimmy's weapon he screamed, "Get an ambulance!"

For no good reason, the talker had just become an executioner, forced there by circumstance and ineptitude. He took quick stock of the situation. He was not shot, and that was a good thing. He was, for the time being, deaf. That was a bad thing. He was somewhat stunned, and that too was a bad thing. He was covered in blood, a bad thing. The blood was not his, good thing. He felt sick, normal thing. He was pissed off. This was a very bad thing.

Everything now would have a procedure, everything would follow a pattern. Looking back, the talker actually marveled at how the training took over. He turned to the Sergeant and handed him his weapon. "Read me my rights," he had said, and the Sergeant did so. He went to the LT. "You OK?" he asked. The LT was as deaf as he was and just nodded. "Not for long," he said.

He didn't know if the LT heard him or not. He really didn't care. He used all of his 6 foot 5 inch height and 220 pounds of trained muscle to punch the LT right between the eyes. The LT fell on the spot, and the talker then picked him up and threw him down the stairs. He was in the process of following down the stairs to further kick the sh## out of the LT, when the Sergeant intervened.

A shooting team came to investigate, as did Internal Affairs, Homicide, and the DA's office. The case was prepared for the grand jury, and the DA was pretty well convinced that he was going to be able to get a quick indictment— another case of police brutality. A poor man who was just defending his home had been shot three times at close range by this raging cop who assaulted his boss on the scene and then, against orders, shot this poor husband in his own bathroom. The after-scene investigation was slightly slanted, so the LT was now looking like a real hero who tried to save Jimmy's life.

Under the advice of his attorney, the talker said nothing. He only admitted that he had fired his weapon at Jimmy. At the Grand Jury procedure, the DA called only the LT and the driver. The one testified to what he remembered in his own peculiar way, and the other could testify only to what he saw, which had

116 / PERSPECTIVES ON VIOLENCE AND VIOLENT DEATH

not been very much. The Grand Jury voted a bill of indictment on homicide charges, and the wheels of justice ground away.

The talker was suspended from the force, without pay, pending the outcome of the trial. The LT was moved to another precinct and then to the bowels of One Police Plaza. The Sergeant always thought it was strange that he was never asked to testify before the Grand Jury. None of the other patrolmen were called either.

The talker, who swore to any who would listen that he did nothing wrong, was set up to guarantee that the DA would be reelected, and the LT would be covered. The case was in pretrial hearings when suddenly the DA's office vacated the indictment. The departmental trial was a mere formality, and the talker was returned to duty with all the back pay that was coming to him. It was only later that the talker found out that the Sergeant's brother, a State Senator, had impounded the tape and produced a copy that the DA's office couldn't shake.

The talker retired from the job. The incident cost him his marriage, the respect of his children and the respect of his co-workers. For seven years he suffered from sleepless nights and any loud noise brought back memories of that night and the surprised look on Jimmy's face when he had killed him. He still has not celebrated Christmas, not since that night more than 20 years ago. He still has problems with anger management, but this gets better and gets milder with age.

Three years after the incident, the driver committed suicide. The note he left tried to explain his part in what happened that night and how he had failed to protect his partner. The autopsy showed he would not have lived much longer because he was suffering from a nasty form of lung cancer. It is unknown if he knew about his condition.

The LT continued his career in the bowels of Police Plaza until his brother was forced to resign in the wake of a drug scandal. He was then also encouraged to retire, and he did. He managed to live in seclusion for five years after the incident before taking his off duty piece and putting a bullet in his own head. He left no note.

Jimmy's wife remarried. He was a bartender in a place in northern Queens. Her new husband had a fight with his boss, came home early one night and found her in bed with a carpenter. She and her lover died that night, each killed at close range by the single shotgun blast at close range. Her new husband got in his car, drove off and was the focus of a seven state manhunt until arrested in Pennsylvania. During the attempted arrest, he chose to shoot it out with police and died on the hood of his car. Supposedly his last words were he regretted only one thing in his life and that was not "shooting the b___h's mother too."

The mother-in-law continued to live in the neighborhood for 15 years after that Christmas Night. She attempted to sue the city and the Department, but was blocked in court. She remained as nasty as ever and was shunned by the neighborhood until her death. She died alone in her house. She apparently had been dead for some time when her body was found. Much of her face had been consumed by her cats.

The Sergeant went to SOD shortly after this incident. He became a much decorated member of the Emergency Services Unit and ultimately became a talker himself. After completing his time on the job, he retired. He is still very uncomfortable around Christmastime. He has been known to drink a little too heavily and doesn't sleep all that well. But, looking at the effects of the incident on the others, he got away lucky. Jimmy? Well, Jimmy never had a chance.

CHAPTER 8

Hispanic Families and Mass Casualties: The First 48 Hours

Fernando Cabrera

A Dominican mother faints. Her son begins to yell frantically in despair. At a nearby table, a Dominican man grabs a chair and throws it to the floor. This is not the horrific scene of a family feud. It is but one example of families who were just notified on November 12, 2001 that their family member had perished on American Airlines flight 587 just three minutes after take off, at 9:17 in the morning. The plane and all on board were bound for the Dominican Republic, but plunged to the ground in Queens, New York just after lifting off from Kennedy Airport, only a few miles away. The crash came at a time when many were still trying to cope with the aftermath of the September 11, 2001.

Since the tragic incidents of 9/11, many critical incident interventions have been developed, and numerous personnel have been trained in their use. However, none of these interventions, developed for cases of mass casualties in the United States, have specifically addressed possible application to the Hispanic community. This chapter addresses the intervention strategies applicable to Hispanic families and mass casualties during the first 48 hours after a critical incident. I base these recommendations on my direct experiences with the families who lost their loved ones on AA flight 587.

My positions as a pastor and as the program director of a graduate counseling program have enabled me to integrate and apply an eclectic approach to the issue of mass casualties and Hispanic families. I worked for 15 years in the Bronx community as a senior pastor of a contemporary and growing church, one that has a significantly large population of Hispanics. Also, having worked in the counseling field and directing the graduate counseling program at Mercy College has given me the opportunity to integrate a psychospiritual approach to issues related to critical incidents. The marriage of these two fields has prompted me to work as a chaplain for the Latin American Chaplain Association, the Red

120 / PERSPECTIVES ON VIOLENCE AND VIOLENT DEATH

Cross, and the Kings County Child Protective Service. My direct experiences with those who were in the World Trade Center towers, and with the families of those who perished on 9/11, were a prelude to the critical incident encountered with the families of American Airlines Flight 587. It is from that perspective I arrived at the following recommendations.

RECOMMENDATION 1: MEET PRIVATELY

During the hours following the crash of AA Flight 587, families were gathered at the main conference room of the Ramada Inn at John F. Kennedy Airport. Mayor Giuliani's staff were prepared to approach family members and confirmed whether their family member was confirmed as a passenger aboard the flight and deceased. Mayor Giuliani was asked by the Hispanic chaplains to meet with each family on an individual basis, due to the nature of the grieving process often exhibited among Dominicans. Based on his previous experience with survivors of mass casualties, the mayor made a decision to meet with families on a large scale. After an earlier air crash in 1996, TWA Flight 800, the mental-health community and city-hall staff worked with the families of those who had perished. Most of these families were Caucasian. All of the family members related to someone on TWA Flight 800 were gathered in the main hall at the Ramada Inn, and confirmation was provided as to whether their family member(s) was aboard that particular flight. The plan had worked smoothly and effectively.

Mayor Giuliani and some mental-health workers decided to approach the families of AA Flight 587 in the same manner. Since there was no precedent in working with Hispanic families after mass casualties in New York City, it seems the obvious approach was to follow the same plan that worked with the families of TWA Flight 800. Hispanic chaplains, who were familiar with the cultural expression of grief and loss demonstrated by Dominican families, advised otherwise. They were fearful that this "public" approach would produce an emotional chain reaction in the families that could result in chaos and pandemonium.

Soon after the first two families were informed of the presence of their loved ones on the flight, an atmosphere of desperation and panic took root in the hearts of the people in the conference room. Quickly, the Mayor heeded the call by the Hispanic clergy to allow families to be informed separately and privately. Thereafter, each family was escorted to a private room and, the family members were informed as to whether their loved one was present on AA Flight 587.

This private setting was ideal, since it allowed family members to express their grief privately and with the proper support. It allowed the containment of a possible unhealthy chain reaction among families present in the main conference room, and it focused the efforts of service providers, allowing them to concentrate emotional support on one family at a time. It brought the event to life for these bereaved family members in a safe setting.

RECOMMENDATION 2: SET THE RULES

Proper rules are needed to assure safety, confidentiality, and trust. Participation of each family member is voluntary. No breaks should be taken, since the meeting time for any one family will ideally be no longer than 20 minutes. Those in charge need to identify anyone who should not be at the meeting (for example, reporters or lawyers). There will be people who may have clearance to be in the building, but who should not be in the private meeting. Family members should not feel that they are on display or are providing others with a spectacle. Notes should not be taken at this first meeting. Taking notes may create a wall of fear and an atmosphere of distrust. Also, many Hispanic communities value greatly their privacy. Writing notes, even with good intentions, may create a disconnection. This is accentuated in cases where a criminal act may have been committed. It may send signals that you are working for the government or may be conducting an investigation.

RECOMMENDATION 3: MEET WITH A TEAM

A comprehensive team is crucial in providing proper intervention to families in the case of mass casualties, and this is especially true with Hispanic families. This team should include the following team members:

Mental Health Worker

This member of the team should be trained in and familiar with the use of at least one formal model of Critical Incident Stress Management. This will allow the person to help facilitate debriefing and may limit the initial shock. It is important to be aware that in Hispanic communities, people often view psychologists and social workers as professionals who work mainly with those who are "loco," the severely mentally ill. It may be appropriate to use the operative word "counselor" instead, which carries with it a less negative stereotype among Hispanic populations.

The goals of the Mental Health worker are to

- Focus on the rapid reduction of intense reactions,
- Keep affected family members functioning,
- Help family members share information, responses, and feelings about the incident,
- Supply information and skills to help with the coping process,
- Reaffirm that the families are valued and important,

122 / PERSPECTIVES ON VIOLENCE AND VIOLENT DEATH

- Instill confidence in the ability of the family member(s) to handle their reactions to this event, and
- Access additional support resources.

Chaplain or Clergy

Members of the clergy play a crucial role in establishing immediate and sustaining trust. In many Hispanic communities, it is the pastor, priest or *capellan* (chaplain) who are looked to in times of need or during and after crises. These team members are seen as icons of hope and relief in times of pain and despair. They bring an aura of stability to an atmosphere of chaos. It is the chaplain or clergy member who becomes a conduit of spiritual support. Even when an official chaplain is present as part of the team, the family Pastor or Minister should be allowed to be present as an important part of the support system for the family. The chaplain or clergyperson needs to be quickly advised of the protocol or procedure he or she is to follow. Not all chaplains or clergy are comfortable with this part of their duties, and it should never be assumed they know the most appropriate response or the best way to express it.

Law Enforcement Official

The sudden and traumatic death of a loved one can cause anyone to unexpectedly react in a dramatic manner. In the most acute case with which we worked, two sons and a daughter were notified of their mother's death on AA Flight 587. One son immediately proceeded to the bathroom and tried to inflict injury upon himself by striking his head into the glass mirror. The other son ran out quickly to the hallway, where he broke a plastic light fixture and attempted to cut his wrist. Law enforcement officials were strategically located in the hallway because of the possibility, even if unlikely, of such a response. These two brothers were stopped by the officers present and were taken quickly to a local hospital for treatment and observation.

The emotional and mental health condition of family members is seldom known upon their arrival at the meeting site. Some individuals may be intoxicated, medicated, or simply infuriated following the initial news of the disaster. The Hispanic community is a peaceful, law abiding, and respectful group of people. But in cases of mass casualties, where hundreds, even thousands of families and friends may show up at a debriefing, it is always best to be prepared for the possibility of such occurrences.

Government Representative

It is often a government official's responsibility to inform family members whether or not their loved one was present and is now deceased or injured due to a critical incident. It is the norm for someone from the Mayor's office to assume this role. Family members are asked the name of their loved one, and the government representative confirms whenever possible whether that person is listed as injured or deceased.

Ethnic Member(s) on the Team

It is advantageous, and sometimes crucial, for part of the team to be composed of Hispanics when dealing with Hispanics. Hearing the news in one's principal language has advantages. Language can unite people. It can bring a feeling of commonality in a time of crisis. Research indicates that people tend to express their personal and group identity and pride through language and accent (Altarriba & Santiago-Rivera, 1994; DeKlerk & Bosch, 1995; Mirsky, 1991; Padilla et al., 1991). It follows that any given group would be most comfortable when they are free to express themselves in their native language in a way that is consistent with their ethnic groups' accent and in the vernacular of their communities. It is more than a language issue. It is an identification issue. A Hispanic present among those in "authority" fosters trust, because they see someone with whom they can identify. When dealing with Hispanic families, the first 48 hours require immediate connection and receptivity. If a counselor is seen as an in-group member, he or she is seen as similar, sharing the same general background, values, and beliefs, and thus as able to empathize and understand the clients' world or perspectives or problems; a bridge can be made to establish rapport.

If an interpreter is needed, the following should be kept in mind:

- Interpreters should be seen as cultural consultants who can help define the cultural context of the client's experience and the specific cultural meanings of particular behaviors and metaphors. They become a conduit of crisis intervention.
- If there are two or three days of ongoing intervention, it is best to have the same individual interpret each session.
- It's not surprising if the Hispanic families initially form a stronger attachment to the interpreter than the chaplain/counselor. After all, it is the interpreter whom they see speaking to them.
- Eye contact should always be maintained with the family not the interpreter. This can facilitate a connection and avoid any unintended slight by lack of eye contact.

RECOMMENDATION 4:
INVITATION TO A FOOD COURT

Food, in Hispanic cultures, symbolizes community, togetherness, and family unity. Gathering around food enables families the opportunity to talk. It also allows family members to be physically replenished on a day when they will likely

124 / PERSPECTIVES ON VIOLENCE AND VIOLENT DEATH

be quickly physically and emotionally drained. Since meeting with family, even when multiple intervention teams are at work, can be a long, extensive process, it is advisable to be able to attend to their physical needs. In the events following the crash of AA Flight 587, the Red Cross immediately dispatched food and drinks to be made available at the Ramada Inn. Most families appreciated and participated in partaking of the food.

RECOMMENDATION 5: HEAR THEIR STORY

The gateway to engaging a conversation or discussion related to a critical incident with a Hispanic is by first eliciting and hearing his or her story. What was your relationship? How did you find out about the incident? Where were you at the time of the incident? What happened where you were? How did it happen?

The facts—the what, where, when, who—should be elicited from the Hispanic family members. Allowing each of them to tell his or her story can eventually help each to express an individual reaction. Once they engage in telling their story, they will engage in telling how they feel. Attempting to discuss feelings immediately, before hearing them tell their stories, may cause a Hispanic family member to raise a defensive emotional wall. The helper may even be regarded as disrespectful. Time should be taken to know the *familia* before exploring the feelings surrounding the loss and trauma.

Close attention should be paid to the family's concerns. In incidents that involve numerous families, misinformation can and will travel fast. It is important to short circuit misinformation quickly before it creates an atmosphere of mistrust.

One Hispanic woman told me that American Airlines had contacted her the night before, informing her that her sister's body had been identified and was ready to be claimed. It had been about nine hours after she had heard about the plane crash. I had been previously informed in a briefing that none of the bodies had been identified due to the severe burns caused in the crash. I quickly set up a meeting with the Medical Examiner for this Hispanic woman to assure her that the body of her sister had not yet been identified. It seems that when she received the call from American Airlines, it was to inform her that her sister was in the plane that had crashed. It had been a misunderstanding. She said to me after the meeting, "I feel better now. I just wanted to know the truth. It is speculation and uncertainty that drives me crazy."

RECOMMENDATION 6: FOLLOW UP

After the first meeting, it is beneficial to arrange for a second meeting within the first 48 hours. By building on the rapport established in the first 24 hours, communication of thoughts and feelings from family members are likely to increase. It is sometimes the case that those who were trying to be strong in the first 24 hours were having difficulty coping in the second 24 hours. This is especially true with the Hispanic male. In keeping with an often "macho" culture, he may try to be strong for the rest of the family. This can involve avoiding any expression of deep feelings of grief or loss. By the second day, profound sadness often sets in. If the Hispanic male was hesitant to speak in the first day, by the second day the opportunity will likely arise. He will probably be most comfortable if given the opportunity to share his feelings with another Hispanic male service provider. It is often seen as a sign of weakness for a Hispanic male to weep or cry in the presence of a female.

RECOMMENDATION 7:
DEBRIEFING THE DEBRIEFER

Any debriefer needs to be debriefed. I recall that after the first 12 hours of meeting with families, I was truly spent. We were short of Hispanic chaplains who spoke Spanish, especially any of Dominican descent. Most of the team members, from all of the teams, had already gone home for the night. Debriefing did not take place for any of the counselors or chaplains, including myself. I remember that when my wife picked me up, as soon as I entered the car, she asked me, "How did it go?" I began to weep profusely. I quickly recognized that debriefing had been skipped, and I was reacting to an overload of bad news. The next day, after completing my rounds with the families, I had the opportunity to debrief with other chaplains and mental-health workers. It was truly a moment of release, one that must be made available to each debriefer as soon as possible.

CONCLUSION

The events that followed the crash of AA Flight 587 taught us the value of understanding the target population we seek to help. A multicultural response is crucial in dealing with Hispanic families if we expect a healing response from them. The first 48 hours can accelerate the recovery and reduction of adverse reactions among Hispanic families when dealing with mass casualties. More research is needed in the area of mass casualties and Hispanics, as Hispanics have become the largest minority group in the United States. Whether it be an earthquake in the *barrios* of Los Angeles, a hurricane in the Hispanic community of Miami, or another incident like AA Flight 587, we must be prepared with the tools we need to make a significant difference. Those tools include the recommendations made here:

- Meet privately with the families and loved ones
- Set the rules before the meetings begin
- Establish the team and meet with them
- Have food available for the families

126 / PERSPECTIVES ON VIOLENCE AND VIOLENT DEATH

- Hear their stories—each person will have one
- Follow up on statements or promises made
- Debrief the debriefers

When dealing with Hispanic families, these recommendations may make a difficult situation a bit less threatening for all concerned.

REFERENCES

Altarriba, J., & Santiago-Rivera, A. L. (1994). Current perspectives on linguistic and cultural factors in counseling the Hispanic client. *Professional Psychology: Research and Practice, 25,* 388-397.

DeKlerk, V., & Bosch, B. (1995). Linguistic stereotypes: Nice accent—Nice person? *International Journal of the Sociology of Language, 116,* 17-37.

Mirsky, J. (1991). Language in migration: Separation individuation conflicts in relation to the mother tongue and the new language. *Psychotherapy, 28,* 618-624.

Padilla, A. M., Lindholm, K. J., Chen, A., Duran, R., Hakuta, K., Lambert, W., & Tucker, G. R. (1991). The English-only movement: Myths, reality, and implications for psychology. *American Psychologist, 46,* 120-130.

CHAPTER 9
Grief and Guilt in the Military

Carr Maher

> Outside of a battle lost, there is nothing so sad as a battle won.
>
> *Duke of Wellington spoken the night*
> *after his Victory at Waterloo*

> The Duke sat by the table and watched each time the door opened to scan the faces for any of his young gentlemen who survived the battle.
>
> *Earl of Somerset spoken on the night*
> *after the Battle of Waterloo*

A scene from a very bad movie, *Full Metal Jacket*, shows a group of U.S. Marines looking down at the corpse of one of their squad mates. They all mutter things of condolence to the corpse, except for one man who states flat out, "better you than me." It may sound trite, but to fully understand that line, and the grief that may follow it, you had to be there.

I suspect that most if not all of the individuals who read this will not have served in the military and have not faced combat conditions. Nothing that I put on the paper will convey to you the feelings that the average soldier feels when he is involved in combat. There is nothing in the civilian world that comes close to that experience. As human beings, we are really very ill-equipped for the battlefield. Whether we are talking about the fields of Agincourt, Waterloo, Gettysburg, the Somme, Bastogne, Chosin, Khe San, or the Highway of Death, none of our senses are insulated from the conditions of the battlefield. Let's examine what the senses are asked to endure in combat.

SIGHT

How frustrating is it to try to track that fly that buzzes your head at a picnic? How tough is it to try to pick up that elusive street sign on a darkened road? Much has been written about the combat stare, the thousand-yard stare that veteran

128 / PERSPECTIVES ON VIOLENCE AND VIOLENT DEATH

soldiers develop. In World War II, it was one of the ways that combat fatigue was diagnosed. A dead-eyed stare into space. What caused it?

Out there in that field is the enemy. You have seen his ability to kill, to maim, to hurt you and your friends firsthand. You must advance into that field, so you look, you stare at your patch of ground to try to find him before he finds you. You don't do this lightly because lives, your life is on the line. You must see him before he sees you, and so you strain your vision out to its maximum. If you are fortunate enough to see him before he sees you, you bring your weapon up to your shoulder, and you shoot at your target. You carefully put your sights on his form, and you pull the trigger, and hopefully you kill him before he kills you. You advance, and you stare out some more, looking for more targets.

You do this in its various forms every day you are in combat. Many times you'll also be involved at night, when the eyestrain becomes worse, more intense. Five days straight, ten days, twenty days. The eyes become the first thing to tell the strain. They develop the stare, the soldier develops the stare to stay alive. And what else do the eyes capture on the battlefield? Horrific death, terrible wounds, Dante's Inferno. Life and death on the battlefield is as much a matter of chance as skill, but if the soldier admits this, he couldn't function in the manner necessary to do his job, and so he files away what he sees and uses what skills he has learned to survive. The average infantry soldier in the American Civil War spent three years in the Army and only twenty days in combat. During World War I, the average infantry soldier spent four years in the Army and six days in combat. During World War II, the average infantry soldier spent four years in the Army and one hundred days in combat. In Korea, the average infantry soldier spent three years in the Army and thirty days in combat. In Viet Nam, the average infantry soldier spent three years in the Army and twenty days in combat. In the Gulf War, the average infantry soldier spent five years in the Army and three days in combat. How difficult is combat on the eyes? Look at the numbers, and then look at the eyes in the photos.

SOUND

Today, when rock bands perform onstage, most wear ear protection. When soldiers go to the range, they wear ear protection. It makes perfect sense, after all, the noise level is high in both instances. Hearing is critical to a combat soldier. Many a man survived the battlefield because he was able to identify the sound of a mortar round hitting the bottom of the tube, that hollow "thunk" that told you were about to receive an explosive package that could wipe out an entire squad. Also, the working of the bolt of a machine gun to ratchet in the first round is a sound you learn very quickly if you are to survive on the field of battle.

GRIEF AND GUILT IN THE MILITARY / 129

Unfortunately, hearing is the first sense that disappears on the battlefield. Whether you are firing at someone or someone is firing at you, it gets really noisy, really quick. It gets concussively noisy, and your hearing either shuts down or it gets overwhelmed. The only way a civilian can experience the initial sound of combat is to climb into a metal dumpster, pull the lid closed, and then have someone beat on it with a sledge hammer. Or, better yet, have several people with several sledge hammers of different sizes beat on it.

Unfortunately, hearing is also one of the first senses to stabilize after combat. The firing stops. You are still looking for the enemy, so you are still stressing your eyes. But your hearing comes back, and you hear the sounds.

Artists throughout history have made glorious paintings of battlefields showing the manly vigor and martial magic of the battlefield. They look good. Unfortunately, they cannot convey the sound. Men cannot scream in that pitch, moan that deep, or pray that loud. As your hearing returns, you pray that it would go back away. Your side, their side, animals that have wandered through the kill zones, all are crying, begging, screaming, praying for relief from their agony. You help where and when you can. You can't ignore the noise, but to do your job, you must file it away. You compartmentalize. How difficult is combat on the ears? Read the accounts; the first person accounts of soldiers will use terms like hell, bedlam, and worse than could be imagined.

SMELL

This one is going to be gross, so if you have a weak stomach, you may want to skip it. Gunpowder smells, heated metal smells, blood smells, burning flesh smells, unwashed flesh smells, urine smells, human defecation smells, burning wood smells, burning rubber smells. Combine them all, and that's what a battlefield smells like. The longer you are in a location, the more it smells.

How is the sense of smell affected by combat? If you have smelled one battlefield, you'll never forget it. There is nothing a civilian would be willing to do that can replicate it.

TASTE

Another of the gross ones for those of you with weak stomachs. We know much of taste is linked to our sense of smell, and we just covered that one. The only thing that will cover it for the civilian is to take a can of ravioli to your local manure pile, sit in the pile, and eat the ravioli without cooking it. It will develop a flavor all its own . . . still not quite there, but close. One other effect on taste is really quite remarkable. You never realize how good water tastes until you survive combat and drink from a warm canteen.

130 / PERSPECTIVES ON VIOLENCE AND VIOLENT DEATH

TOUCH

One of the mechanisms used to train U.S. Army Special Forces is to place them in the pit. The pit is ten yards long and filled with blood, mud, and sheep guts, and you have to crawl through it. Combat makes you dirty, filthy beyond your wildest imaginings. The ground is your friend. If you stay one with the ground you may survive. Mud is cradling, the earth shelters you, and you become one with it. On the other hand, when you take your dirty, filthy hands and try to stop the bleeding of your friend's wounds, blood is warm and slippery. The feel of a rubber poncho being carried to a helicopter containing the remains of a friend is one tactile memory that stays with you for life.

We covered how the battlefield can and does assault the soldier's senses. None of it is very nice. None of it can be remotely conceived as enjoyable. And I wrote this as an introduction to this article so those of you who have never experienced combat could have some idea of what I'm talking about. To understand soldiers and grief, you must understand the conditions faced and why the soldier fights in those conditions.

I have given you the conditions in which soldiers fight, now as to the why. Why do soldiers do what they do? Why did Dan Daly, Alvin York, Audie Murphy, and all the other heroes do what they did? Why do units continue to fight when by all reasonable measures they should be paralyzed by fear or fatigue? Soldiers enlist for many and various reasons, but they fight for *their friends*.

The bond of men working in a dangerous profession, counting on one another for survival, is the greatest motivator of why soldiers do what they do. The small unit trained together and learned each other's strengths and weaknesses, and gradually the sum of the whole became greater than the sum of its parts. Good soldiers look at what they have to do as a job. Sometimes the job is easy. Sometimes it is difficult. But it is still a job. The smallest unit, the fire team, eats together, sleeps together trains together. They in fact become *de facto* brothers. If each does his job properly, they understand their survival chances are tremendously enhanced. They encourage one another. They challenge one another. They push one another to a level not seen in the civilian world. They know exactly what they can and cannot do; as each talent is magnified, each deficiency is minimized by operating as a team. Soldiers fight not for lofty ideals, rather they fight for their brothers, and that is their strength. It is also their weakness. They will fight not letting down the side, till hell freezes over—but the sense of loss is greater when you lose a brother.

A SOLDIER'S GUILT

How do soldiers cope? How can they be helped to cope? Soldiers utilize two tools in handling their grief. The first is guilt.

GRIEF AND GUILT IN THE MILITARY / 131

Within the culture that man has developed over the years, killing has been consistently condemned. "Thou shall not kill" is one of the cornerstones of modern civilization. We take it very seriously. When an individual is convicted of homicide, it is so serious that he or she may be sentenced to death.

We put all sorts of safeguards in place to keep society free from people who kill, at times even taking the killer's life. Yet we take an average young person and give him a dispensation once he puts on the military uniform. We tell him, or today her, that he now has permission to kill other human beings because they are wearing a different uniform.

We proclaim as much as we can that war is not murder. Society is right. War is not murder. War is much, much worse. It is murder on so grand a scale that the majority of society simply cannot, or will not, comprehend it. It is social violence taken to the extreme power and then multiplied threefold. How does a soldier cope with this dichotomy?

He cries, when no one is looking at night, when no one can see. He sees those he has killed and cries for them. Veteran soldiers all have a "look" to them. They know one another by sight. They see into one another's souls and understand. The first part of a soldier's grief is for those they have had to kill. These were often young men, usually of a similar age, who have had their lives shortened and ended directly by the soldier's action. In the middle of a terrible firefight, soldiers have been known to scream at their enemy to go back because the slaughter was too great. The passage of time helps heal the veteran, helps him to deal with this grief. It does gradually subside, but not easily; and it leaves an emotional scar that can remain open if not treated with care.

The second and probably more powerful grief for the soldier is the loss of his friends. You have slept next to your friend, eaten with your friend, worked with your friend, and played with your friend. Now your friend is gone. Earlier, I described the members of a team as brothers. You never get over the loss of your brother, no matter how many years pass.

SURVIVOR'S GUILT

This leads to the ultimate guilt of the soldier. Why did I survive when better men were killed? During World War I the use of massed artillery brought the element of luck to the forefront of every battlefield. That element is still there today. Every combat veteran has been shot at. Every combat veteran has been shelled. Skill can militate against being shot, luck enters into whether or not an artillery shell kills you.

A shell hit one position, and six soldiers were knocked down by the blast. Two got up, dusted themselves off, and headed for cover. Two others were slightly wounded and limped away to get their wounds dressed. One was seriously hurt and had to be removed by the medics. One soldier just simply disappeared, and

132 / PERSPECTIVES ON VIOLENCE AND VIOLENT DEATH

only his dog tags and one boot remained. It could have been anyone of the six, but it was him. Why him? Why not one of the others? Luck, fate, chance, karma; you think back on it, and you wonder. In some small part of your mind, you say thank you. You're glad you're alive. . . . "No hard feelings, and I am sorry you're dead, but I'd be a lot sorrier if I was dead." And with that, you get the ultimate soldier guilt . . . you survived.

How do you help? Listen! As complicated as the causes and experience of survivor guilt may be, just listen. And don't be afraid. They won't tell you the horrible stories, only the silly ones, or the funny ones. But by telling that part of their story, they are remembering those who didn't come home. It can and does provide a catharsis for the veteran. When they have finished, just say thank you. A simple nod on Veterans Day or Memorial Day will usually do it.

If a soldier asks for help, get him to a veterans group. It is more than an act of kindness, it is, in some cases, very necessary. These veterans offer understanding, not judgment, and they know where more help is available.

For those reading this in a democracy, you owe your soldiers one other thing. These men and women have given much, both those who returned and those who did not, to allow us to have the lives we do. They paid the price to keep us safe. Show them by your action that their sacrifice mattered. Participate in your government. You may not go to parades that honor veterans or to memorial ceremonies and wreath laying, but on election day, vote. You owe them that much.

The last line of Tom Hanks in the movie *Saving Private Ryan* said, "Earn this." The movie and the line are fiction, but, in reality, there is nothing more to say.

PART III

Empirical Studies

CHAPTER 10

Characteristics of Homicide: Victimization Across the Life Span

Kimberly A. Vogt

Lethal violence exacts a devastating toll on humanity across all age groups. Although all are at risk of becoming the victim of a homicide, that risk is not equally distributed. According to the World Health Organization (WHO), lethal violence is one of the leading causes of death for 15–44 year-olds worldwide (Krug, Dahlberg, Mercy, Zwi, & Lozano, 2002). Of the many forms of lethal violence, homicide is among the most devastating. In the United States, homicide rates rose sharply from the mid 1960s to the 1980s and remained high into the early 1990s. In the 1990s, we saw a sharp decline to our current rate of 5.6 per 100,000 population in 2002 (Fox & Zawitz, 2004). This rate is comparable to U.S. homicide rates in the 1950s and early 1960s. In the United States, risk of homicide victimization is greatest among infants and in the late teens and young adulthood (Finkelhor & Ormrod, 2001). Figure 1 shows the trends in the risk of homicide by age group over the 26-year period between 1976 and 2002 (Fox & Zawitz, 2004). As can be seen, there was a small increase in homicides in the early 1980s and a large increase among people 14 to 24 during the early 1990s. Since the late 1990s, homicide rates have declined sharply among 14- to 34-year-olds and remained steady among other age groups. Differences in risk of death by homicide vary by gender, race and ethnicity, and age. This chapter examines the social characteristics of homicide victimization in the United States across the life span for children, teens and young adults, middle-aged adults, and the elderly. Additionally, a discussion of the impact on people left behind in the wake of a homicide is presented along with an overview of sociological explanations.

136 / PERSPECTIVES ON VIOLENCE AND VIOLENT DEATH

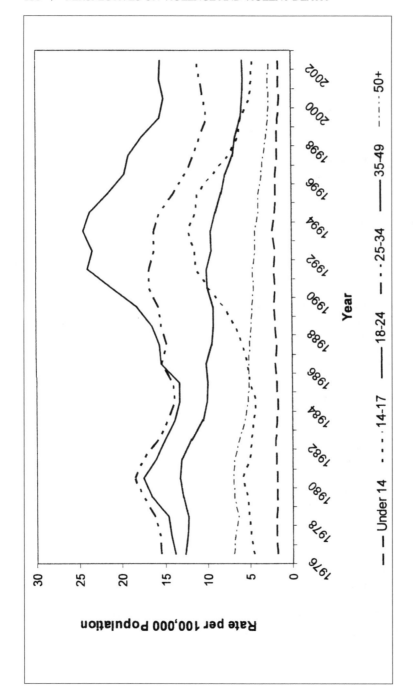

Figure 1. Trends in U.S. homicide by age group.
Source: James A. Fox and Marianne W. Zawitz, *Homicide Trends in the United States* (Washington, DC: Bureau of Justice Statistics, U.S. Department of Justice, 2004).

GENDER AND HOMICIDE

Males are disproportionately the victims of homicide. The WHO estimates that worldwide, "males accounted for 77% of all homicides and had rates that were more than three times those of females . . ." (Krug et al., 2002, p. 10). The U.S. ratio mirrors the worldwide ratio; males are killed at a ratio of 3:1 over females, making up approximately 75% of victims (Fox & Zawitz, 2004). The gender divide in homicide becomes noticeable during late adolescence, when rates of male victimization start to outstrip female victimization. The circumstances surrounding homicide for males and females often differ. Males are disproportionately killed by friends and acquaintances as a result of arguments, gang altercations, and sexual rivalry. Although women are killed at much lower rates than men, women are overrepresented in certain homicide circumstances such as intimate-partner violence. Gender-disaggregated homicide data present a picture of homicide that is richer in detail than aggregate-(total) homicide data and will be discussed in relationship to age-specific homicides presented later on in the chapter.

RACE AND HOMICIDE

In the United States, the risk of death by homicide varies by racial and ethnic group membership. African Americans have the highest rate of homicide across all age groups (Fox & Zawitz, 2004). Research on life expectancy and death in the United States in 1998 by the Centers for Disease Control (CDC) determined that the overall life expectancy for African Americans was six years less than that of whites, and that homicide accounted for almost 10% of that six-year difference (Potter, 2001). Fox and Zawitz's (2004) analysis of FBI supplemental homicide reports from 1976 to 2002 found that African Americans were six times more likely to be the victim of a homicide than their white counterparts across all age groups. This translates into a rate of 30.9 per 100,000 African Americans as compared with 4.9 per 100,000 whites. Although the rate of homicide among African Americans has been historically higher than that of whites, African American deaths by homicide skyrocketed during the late 1980s to mid 1990s (Blumstein, Rivara, & Rosenfeld, 2000). Blumstein and his colleagues argue that handgun and drug-related homicides, particularly for young African American victims, played a vital role in the increasing rate of homicide during the 1980s and 1990s (2000). It was the collapse of the crack-cocaine epidemic and economic prosperity that brought about the drop in this trend (Blumstein et al., 2000).

INFANTS AND CHILDREN

Homicides of children are not evenly distributed across the span of childhood. This section examines the victimization of children under the age of fourteen. The

138 / PERSPECTIVES ON VIOLENCE AND VIOLENT DEATH

high rate of child homicide in the United States is not a new phenomenon, having increased threefold from 1950 to 1994 (National Center for Health Statistics, 1995). Children who are very young (aged five and younger) are at greatest risk among children thirteen and younger. Finkelhor and Ormrod (2001) report that the homicide rate for children 5 and younger in the United States was 2.6 per 100,000 in 1997. Minority children suffer from higher levels of victimization than do nonminority children, with African American children, like their adult counterparts, suffering the most (Finkelhor & Ormrod, 2001; Lord, Boudreaux, Jarvis, Waldvogel, & Weeks, 2002).

The circumstances, weapon type, and gender ratios for homicides of children differ with the child's life-course stage, such as infant, toddler or preschool, primary-school age, and middle-school age (Alder & Polk, 2001; Christoffel, Anzinger, & Amari, 1983; Crittenden & Craig, 1990; Finkelhor & Ormrod, 2001). Because of physical dependency on adults, infant and preschool children tend to be killed by parents or caretakers in fatal situations of child abuse, physical punishment, or neglect (Alder & Polk, 2001; Crittenden & Craig, 1990; Finkelhor, 1997; Smithey, 1998), whereas middle-school-age children are more susceptible to violence outside the home (e.g., Finkelhor & Ormrod, 2001). Researchers tie this phenomenon to differences in socialization for girls and boys, maintaining that differing gender-role expectations and the resulting differences in routine activities of childhood explain differences in victimization risk for boys and girls as they grow older (Alder & Polk, 2001; Boudreaux, Lord, & Jarvis, 2001). As children move from the infant, toddler, and preschool developmental stages to the primary school and middle-school stages, they are less closely supervised by adults and more likely to explore risky activities such as gang membership. The difference in activity patterns for girls and boys produce an increased risk of homicide for boys as they grow older. Research by Vogt and Block (2003) using data from homicides of children from birth to age 14 in Chicago during the period 1965–1995 found that the risk of children being murdered tended to be as great or greater for infants and preschoolers than for middle-school-age children. The risk of victimization was higher for the youngest children when compared with middle-school-age children in 26 of the 31 years of the entire study period. In contrast, the victimization risk for children in the primary-school-age years tended to be lower than the risk for either older or younger children and showed no pattern of increase over time.

INFANTS AND TODDLERS

In the homicides of young children, parents and other family members are most often the offender. Finkelhor and Ormrod (2001) found that in the United States from 1984 to 1993, the number of homicides of young children increased by 38%, and that 71% of those were committed by family members. Vogt and Block's

(2003) study of child homicides in Chicago found that the younger the child victim, the more likely that the offender was one or both natural parents—77% of infants, 42% of toddlers and preschoolers, 21% of primary-school-age children, and 3% of middle-school-age children. Child abuse is a key factor in many homicides involving young children. Copeland (1985) found that over 91% of fatal child-abuse victims were age 3 or younger. In child abuse cases, almost 72% of the perpetrators were parents, stepparents, or boyfriends of the mother. In non-child abuse homicide cases, Copeland found that only 38% of victims were age 3 or younger. The offender in many cases is a male caretaker, who has become frustrated or impatient with the child and fatally abuses the child (Alder & Polk, 2001; Vogt & Block, 2003). Male acquaintances/boyfriends make up almost one-quarter of all killers of children under the age of 5 among U.S. homicides from 1976–2002 (Fox & Zawitz, 2004).

Alder and Polk's research (2001) found that women committed about half of the homicides of children. Women are disproportionately involved in neonaticides—the killing of children in the first 24 hours of life. Many of the women who commit neonaticide are isolated and under financial and emotional stress. Women who commit neonaticide are often unmarried and are younger than other female homicide offenders are. Women who commit fatal assaults on children are more likely to be sole caretakers of their children and under a lot of situational stress (Alder & Polk, 2001).

PRIMARY AND MIDDLE-SCHOOL-AGE CHILDREN

Homicides of children in middle childhood—primary and middle-school children—have been stable for over 20 years (Finkelhor & Ormrod, 2001). As children become older, gender of the victim becomes an important factor in risk of victimization. Boudreaux, Lord, and Jarvis (2001) argue that the routine activities of children now become a factor in their risk of homicide. Children in the primary-school age group are at the lowest risk of homicide because they are closely supervised. As children become older, they venture out on their own more often and put themselves at risk of other forms of victimization, including homicide by a stranger. Risk becomes gender dependent, based on social roles and expectations for boys and girls.

Children in middle childhood have unique risks related to their newfound independence. Boys are more likely to be involved in homicides related to guns. Girls are now at risk of sexual-assault homicides by acquaintances and strangers. Even so, this is the safest time for children when it comes to homicide. Children in this age group are better able to survive and escape physical assaults within the context of family life. They are away from home, at school in a protected environment, for much of their day. Since younger children are not often left unsupervised, they are at lower risk of homicides by strangers than older children

140 / PERSPECTIVES ON VIOLENCE AND VIOLENT DEATH

are. Children in this age group are not yet regularly exposed to gang violence, and few have access to firearms (Finkelhor & Ormrod, 2001).

However, low risk is not zero risk. Some children are still killed by parents and other caretakers as the end result of fatal child abuse (Boudreaux et al., 2001). And it is in middle childhood that firearms start to become a primary weapon of death, particularly for boys. Boys in middle childhood often die because of homicides related to gunplay; for example, showing off a firearm and shooting a friend. Girls in middle childhood are at risk of being victimized by strangers in sexual-assault and abduction homicides as they are allowed the freedom by families to engage in unsupervised play away from home (Boudreaux et al., 2001).

TEENAGERS AND YOUNG ADULTS

Teens and young adults in the 11-year age span from 14 to 24 years of age account for 28% of all homicide victims in the United States over the years 1976–2002 (Fox, 2005). Between 1985 and 1993 in the United States, the homicide victimization rate for 14–17-year-olds increased approximately 170% (Finkelhor & Ormrod, 2001).

Youth in their early teen years begin to show a pattern of victimization that resembles adult victimization. Gang altercations and arguments between friends and acquaintances turn deadly. For example, boys are disproportionately murdered by their friends and acquaintances, with firearms as the weapon of choice (Finkelhor & Ormrod, 2001). Teen males are often killed by other teen or young adult males in what Alder and Polk (2001) view as "masculinity contests," where in a confrontation, the commission of a crime, or a sexual rivalry, a homicide occurs. This pattern of victimization continues into young adulthood, affecting African American males disproportionately. African American males aged 18–24 have the highest victimization rate of any age group, with a rate of 102.3 per 100,000 population in 2002, compared with a rate of 12.7 for white males in this age group (Fox & Zawitz, 2004).

Researchers attempting to explain the extreme rate of homicide victimization among young people in the late 1980s and early 1990s have noted that homicide *offending* rates among teens and young adults increased in a pattern almost identical to that of homicide victims in this age group (Fox & Piquero, 2003). Because of some of the unique characteristics thought to bring about the increase, such as gang- and drug-related homicide and homicides with firearms, this is not surprising. Offenders and victims in circumstances related to gang and drug-related homicides are often close in age, creating the mirrored pattern of teen and young adult homicide victims. This was particularly true of teenage and young adult African American males. Blumstein and his colleagues (2000) found that the rise in victimization in this group started earlier and lasted longer than the trend for white teen and young adult males, having a larger impact on African American males.

Teenage and young adult females' pattern of victimization also starts to resemble that of older adults. For young women, homicide by a friend or acquaintance is common (24%), but intimate-partner homicide becomes a slightly higher risk factor. Twenty-six percent of 14–24-year-old females from 1976–2002 were killed in intimate-partner homicides (Fox, 2005).

MIDDLE AGE

Historically in the United States, middle-aged adults have had the highest rates of homicide. As we moved into the 1980s, this began to change. Rates of homicide for people 25–64 started to decline (see Figure 1). In fact, prior to 1987, the rate of homicide for 25–34-year-olds was higher than other age groups. With the soaring rate of homicide among 18–24-year-olds in the late 1980s and early 1990s, as discussed earlier, middle-aged adults were outpaced as victims. The rate of victimization among 25–64-year-olds continued to decline, with the exception of victims in the 25–34-year-old age group, whose rate increased slightly between 2000 and 2002 (see Figure 1). The circumstances surrounding homicides of adults aged 25 to 65, like young adults, revolve around acquaintance homicides and intimate-partner homicides. The most notable differences in homicides in middle age are related to gender differences in the risk of intimate-partner homicide.

From 1976 to 2002 in the United States, 62.8% of all victims of intimate-partner homicide were female (Fox & Zawitz, 2004). Research finds that there was a steady decrease in intimate-partner homicides during the 1980s and 1990s (Blumstein et al., 2000; Puzone, Saltzman, Kresnow, Thompson, & Mercy, 2000; Wells & DeLeon-Granados, 2004). Interestingly, males benefited most from this decline, with fewer males being killed by female intimate partners than females being killed by male intimates. Of all intimate partners, African American male victims of intimate-partner homicide have declined the most (Blumstein et al., 2000; Wells & DeLeon-Granados, 2004). Indeed, in Blumstein, Rivara, and Rosenfeld's (2000) study of U.S. homicide rates from 1976 to 1996, African American male intimate-partner homicides decreased more than 80%. Much of this decline in intimate-partner homicide is attributed to increased availability of services for victims of domestic violence and declining rates of marriage (Puzone et al., 2000). These factors are thought to have prevented homicides by female victims of domestic violence who kill a male intimate partner while defending against a domestic assault. The lower marriage rate is related to the ability of women to escape troubled marriages before they result in a violent end.

Among women in middle age, intimate-partner homicide accounts for 38% of all homicides, greater than all other victim/offender-relationship categories (Fox, 2005). In addition to intimate-partner homicide, males are still disproportionately

142 / PERSPECTIVES ON VIOLENCE AND VIOLENT DEATH

at risk of victimization by their friends and acquaintances, as they are from middle childhood on. In the 25–64-year-old age range for males, 31% of homicides are committed by offenders such as friends, acquaintances, and co-workers (Fox, 2005).

THE ELDERLY

Eldercide, the killing of people aged 65 and older, occurs less frequently than homicide in other age groups, with the exception of those aged 14 and younger (see Figure 1). Among all homicides in the United States from 1976 to 2002, approximately 5% were eldercides (Fox & Zawitz, 2004). The risk of eldercide has declined steadily in the United States since the mid 1980s. U.S. eldercide victims are disproportionately white as compared with other homicide victims (68.9% white, 29.6% African American) (Fox & Zawitz, 2004). One characteristic of eldercide is that older victims are less likely to survive a felony criminal act such as a robbery, becoming homicide victims. In addition to the risk of surviving attacks during felonies, the elderly are also at risk of homicide that is the result of abuse, most often by their own children (Alvarez & Bachman, 2003).

SOCIOLOGICAL EXPLANATIONS OF HOMICIDE

Homicide, like other forms of outward aggression, such as aggravated assault or rape, is the outcome of the acting out of feelings of frustration and anger. Frequently, homicide is the result of an emotional outburst that escalated from a simple disagreement or an affront to one's character, to an explosion of physical aggression resulting in the death of one of the persons involved (Luckenbill, 1977). Aggression results in homicide when either physical or weapon superiority provides advantage to one of the parties involved. The decision to aggress outwardly is influenced by social factors relating to the environment in which the homicidal event occurs. The sociology of homicide has focused on two avenues of explanation for the variation in the rate and character of homicide: the influence of social structural factors, such as income inequality; and differences in cultural values among social groups.

Culture and Homicide

Much of the early homicide research set out to explain regional and racial differences in the rate of homicide through the examination of cultural and subcultural differences in homicide (Curtis, 1975; Hackney, 1979; Wolfgang & Ferracuti, 1967). One of the most influential works on the sociology of subcultures and homicide is *The Subculture of Violence* by Wolfgang and Ferracuti (1967).

CHARACTERISTICS OF HOMICIDE / 143

Their research provides one of the most comprehensive theoretical examinations of subcultures and homicide. The subculture-of-violence thesis suggests that a lot of deviant behavior is a reflection of normative support for deviant values by a subgroup within a culture. That is, violent behaviors are supported and encouraged by certain groups. Wolfgang and Ferracuti proposed that different subcultures within society would have higher rates of violent crime because violent behavior was used to protect one's self image in these subgroups. Their thesis contends that violent behavior is a necessary and accepted way of life among certain groups. The subculture passes on the attitudes and beliefs as to the accepted use of physical aggression as a problem-solving technique in certain situations. The choices in resolving a conflict situation are limited to culturally learned responses such as violence, especially when confronted with persons of similar upbringing.

According to the subculture-of-violence argument, situations are most likely to involve culturally accepted violence when an individual's character has been questioned, ridiculed, or insulted (Wolfgang & Ferracuti, 1967). Individuals use physical aggression to defend their character, which sometimes leads to death. A subculture of violence, according to Wolfgang and Ferracuti, tends to flourish when certain social conditions such as poverty, unemployment, and blocked legitimate opportunities are strongest. These structural conditions restrict alternatives to violence as recourse to an affront on one's character which might otherwise be available under more favorable conditions. Three social groups have been identified by Wolfgang and Ferracuti as most closely identified with a subculture of violence: young males, African Americans and other minorities, and persons of low socioeconomic status.

Curtis (1975) expanded on Wolfgang and Ferracuti's subculture-of-violence thesis, arguing that it was the economic, structural, and racial constraints of the South that created the violent subculture that exists today. The culture of black males, in particular, is seen as an extension of the traditions of masculinity, honor, and toughness that developed in the antebellum South. "What we observe is more likely the redirection of intact masculinity into exaggerations of certain allowable kinds of dominant-culture manliness displayed in the everyday transactions of the ghetto-slum" (1975, p. 30). Curtis found that his cultural/structural explanation better predicted rates of violence than the purely cultural thesis proposed by Wolfgang and Ferracuti. Since Wolfgang and Ferracuti's seminal work, additional research has lent support to their argument (e.g., Anderson, 1999). However, the challenge with cultural and subcultural explanations of homicide are related to concerns with imprecise measurement of culture and the use of proxy variables, such as the percentage of African Americans residing in a city, as a measure of a subculture of violence. The failure of researchers to operationalize a variety of measures of culture at aggregate levels of measurement such as cities, counties, and states has been problematic.

144 / PERSPECTIVES ON VIOLENCE AND VIOLENT DEATH

Social Structure and Homicide

Other researchers believe that social-structural factors best explain variance in the rate of homicide. Social-structural-homicide research has predominantly focused on inequalities and stratification based on socioeconomic status, race, and gender (e.g., Blau & Blau, 1982; Phillips, 2002). Examination of social-class stratification has been at the core of social-structural-homicide research. Researchers have argued that lack of access to necessary and desired social resources may pressure people to engage in homicide (Messner & Rosenfeld, 1999). In particular, much homicide research has focused on the relationship between poverty and homicide, examining either absolute poverty (e.g., Harer & Steffensmeier, 1992; Williams & Flewelling, 1988) or relative deprivation associated with conditions of poverty (e.g., Blau & Blau, 1982; Land, McCall, & Cohen, 1990). Messner and Rosenfeld (1999) note that research findings have been inconsistent for both absolute poverty and relative deprivation measures as well as homicide. However, models using sex- and race-specific rates of homicide have been better able to measure the relationship between socioeconomic status and homicide (Harer & Steffensmeier, 1992).

Homicide researchers have consistently reported an overrepresentation of minority groups in victimization and offending (Messner & Rosenfeld, 1999). Hawkins (1983, 1985) specifically argued that subcultural theories could not be substantiated for the African American population due to the institutional discrimination of African Americans in U. S. society. Hawkins identified the historical pattern of discrimination against African Americans in social, economic, and political institutions as the major cause of high rates of African American violence. Homicide can be viewed as a predictable outcome in the efforts by African Americans, particularly males, to gain control over their environment. The historical lack of law enforcement in predominantly African American neighborhoods represents an extension of societal attitudes toward the value of African American lives. The economic/conflict argument presented by Hawkins is a strong structural alternative to the subcultural explanation of the high rates of violence among the African American population.

Research by Phillips (2002) advances the structural inequality argument even further, suggesting that differences in the rate of homicide victimization for whites, African Americans, and Latinos are often correlated with structural conditions such as living in high crime neighborhoods that are segregated and disproportionately poor. Using data from 129 metropolitan statistical areas with populations over 100,000 and minimum minority populations of 10,000, she examines the effects of measured characteristics, such as family structure, poverty, income inequality, employment stability, and segregation, on rates of white, African American, and Latino homicide. Using the methodological technique of Oaxaca decomposition, Phillips determined that over *half* (57.9%) of the difference between the white and African American homicide rate is attributable

CHARACTERISTICS OF HOMICIDE / 145

to the composition of the social structure in which they live. For example, disadvantages related to family structure (divorce) and economic problems (poverty, lack of a college education) faced by many African Americans facilitate the high homicide rate in this group. Phillips finds that "if the Latino population were subject to the same set of structural characteristics as the white population, the Latino homicide rate would actually be lower than the current white rate" (2002, p. 366).

What the structural homicide research implies is that the importance of social conditions that are often beyond our control, such as poverty or lack of financial access to higher education, do affect the rate of homicide among different social groups.

Integrated Theory

Most recently, homicide researchers have developed integrated models that combine characteristics of social-structural and cultural explanations of homicide. Using measures of social support (culture), institutional anomie, and general strain (structure), Pratt and Godsey (2003) analyzed homicide rates from 46 developed nations around the world. Their research builds on earlier work such as Sampson and Groves' (1989) as well as Messner and Rosenfeld's (2001) work on community context, community/institutional structure, and crime. Pratt and Godsey found that an integrated theory is useful in explaining variation in the rate of homicide at the national level. They found that nations with low levels of social support and high economic inequality had higher rates of homicide; that there was an interaction effect between the two measures (Pratt & Godsey, 2003, p. 630). The integrated-theory research is important because their findings suggest that we can reduce levels of homicide that do not rely solely on sweeping changes to the social structure. The authors suggest that increasing levels of social support can insulate against the negative impact of economic inequality on homicide (p. 631). This finding is important as we discuss coping with loss from a homicide as well as prevention efforts related to homicide.

GRIEF, BEREAVEMENT, AND HOMICIDE

Beeghley (2003, p. 11) estimates that the number of people affected by homicide in the United States (e.g., friends, family, neighbors and co-workers) is about 150,000 people *every year*. What are the consequences of homicide for those left behind? Deborah Spungen (1998) identifies the family, friends, and others affected by homicide as covictims of homicide. The experiences of being notified of the death of a loved one by homicide and dealing with the criminal justice system, the media, and even one's community can be traumatic for covictims of homicide. Spungen (1998) describes what covictims experience as a combination of grief and trauma. The shock and horror of the notification is

146 / PERSPECTIVES ON VIOLENCE AND VIOLENT DEATH

extremely traumatic and outside the general life experiences of the average person, even if they have experienced the grief from other deaths. Different types of murder can cause varying reactions of grief and trauma; murder/suicides, vehicular homicides, and workplace homicides affect covictims in different ways based on their relational distance to the victim, gender, and cultural background.

Spungen (1998) argues that one of the most important things that those who are responsible for notifying and working with covictims of homicide can do is to be trained in homicide-death notification specifically. In addition, being sensitive to difficulties that covictims may face when having to identify victims or cleaning up a crime scene should be well-thought-out and part of a comprehensive model of homicide-death notification. The Office for Victims of Crime, part of the U.S. Department of Justice, provides excellent resources and guidelines on the process of death notification and other concerns for covictims of homicide (http://www.ojp.usdoj.gov/ovc/publications/infores/hv.htm).

In assisting covictims through the grief process, caregivers have a variety of intervention techniques at their disposal, such as posttrauma counseling, family therapy, and homicide-survivor support groups. Important to the bereavement process is assisting covictims with the complexities of navigating the criminal justice system. Unfortunately, covictims of homicide are often dismayed to find out that the U.S. criminal justice system is designed to address the needs of offenders, not victims. Maintaining support for covictims, particularly through the development of positive relationships with personnel throughout the criminal justice system, is crucial.

CONCLUSION

This chapter has explored the current state of homicide victimization across the life span in the United States. Homicide, regardless of age group, differs most noticeably by race and gender, with African American males suffering disproportionately and alarmingly high rates of death by homicide. Children are often the victim of fatal abuse, suffered at the hands of a parent or male caretaker. Teenagers and young adults are victims of their newfound freedom to associate outside the safety of their home; being killed in arguments with friends, sexual rivalries, and criminal activities. Middle-age male adults are killed most often by friends and acquaintances. Middle-age females are killed most often by intimate partners, often as the result of an escalation of ongoing situations of domestic assault. The elderly, while having low rates of homicide overall, are susceptible to homicides in the commission of another crime, such as a robbery homicide in the workplace, because they are less likely to survive an assault. Elders are also at risk of fatal-abuse homicide by caretaking relatives.

Sociologists and criminologists have sought to explain variation in the rate of homicide among social groups using both structural (inequality) and cultural

CHARACTERISTICS OF HOMICIDE / 147

(norms and values) theories. Cultural theories have been criticized for not effectively operationalizing constructs effectively that are used to measure the concept of culture. Social-structural explanations have been ineffective at explaining race- and gender-specific rates of homicide. Recent attempts to integrate cultural and structural theories look promising (Pratt & Godsey, 2003). Integrated theories contend that social-structural conditions may be mediated by the effects of social support. For example, higher levels of social support for young parents may increase parenting skills, thus reducing the incidence of fatal child abuse.

Given the theoretical and empirical research that was presented, what could we do to reduce the rate of homicide? Criminal-justice and public-health practitioners have used a variety of approaches to reduce rates of homicide among targeted populations. One of the best examples of effective intervention techniques is Boston's Operation Ceasefire, which targets the reduction of teen and young-adult homicides through problem-oriented policing and crackdowns on serious young offenders (Braga, Kennedy, Waring, & Piehl, 2001). Boston, like many other large cities in the United States in the 1990s, faced a staggering youth-homicide problem. Their intervention initiative was highly successful at reducing gun assaults and related problems, reducing their teen and young adult homicide rate significantly. The Ceasefire initiative involved active cooperation of local, state, and federal law-enforcement authorities—cracking down on gun trafficking, directly addressing violent behavior by gang members by communicating a zero-tolerance approach to gun violence, and by invoking the full force of the criminal-justice system when gun violence occurred (Braga et al., 2001, pp. 199-200). This program, with its work-group problem-solving approach, has been highly successful.

Similarly, public-health approaches that involve interagency teamwork and communication show promise at reducing homicide. One example is the development of child-fatality review teams (e.g., Ewigman, Kivalahan, & Land, 1993). Child-fatality review teams usually operate at the city or county level, bringing together doctors, social workers, and other professionals to review all deaths of children under the age of five. The review teams examine case files to determine whether or not deaths are being misclassified (e.g., homicide as SIDS) and to develop policies and practices that may reduce child deaths.

Both projects are examples of the steps that communities can take to address the problem of homicide. In addition, changes at the social-structural level may be difficult, but are nonetheless indicated by homicide research. Beeghley (2003) points out some of the most commonly cited: reduce the availability of guns, reduce the exposure to violence in the media and in person, reduce racial and ethnic discrimination, and reduce the dangers associated with illegal drug markets.

Beeghley and others do not necessarily advocate for the complete elimination of access to firearms in the United States, an unreasonable expectation given our culture, but advocate for controls on firearms such as gun locks, waiting periods, and cracking down on the illegal purchase and sale of firearms. He

148 / PERSPECTIVES ON VIOLENCE AND VIOLENT DEATH

advocates for harm reduction in dealing with drug users, such as readily available, long-term treatment rather than incarceration, along with strong social support and aftercare.

And, as Spungen suggests, we must have in place social support systems to assist those left behind when homicides occur. Doing so may reduce the impact of the ripple effect that the taking of a life has on all of us, helping covictims, and all of us in coping with homicide.

REFERENCES

Alder, C. M., & K. Polk. (2001). *Child victims of homicide*. Cambridge, UK: Cambridge University Press.

Alvarez, A., & Bachman, R. (2003). *Murder American style*. Belmont, CA: Wadsworth/Thompson Learning.

Anderson, E. (1999). *Code of the street: Decency, Violence, and the moral life of the inner city*. New York: W. W. Norton.

Beeghley, L. (2003). *Homicide: A sociological explanation*. Lanham, MD: Rowman & Littlefield.

Blau, J. R., & Blau, P. M. (1982). The cost of inequality: Metropolitan structure and violent crime. *American Sociological Review, 47*, 114-129.

Blumstein, A., Rivara, F. P., & Rosenfeld, R. (2000). The rise and decline of homicide—and why. *Annual Review of Public Health, 21*, 505-541.

Boudreaux, M. C., Lord, W. D., & Jarvis, J. P. (2001). Behavioral perspectives on child homicide: The role of access, vulnerability and routine activities theory. *Trauma, Violence & Abuse, 2*, 56-78.

Braga, A. A., Kennedy, D. M., Waring, E. J., & Piehl, A. M. (2001). Problem-oriented policing, deterrence, and youth violence: An evaluation of Boston's Operation Ceasefire. *Journal of Research in Crime and Delinquency, 38*, 195-225.

Christoffel, K. K., Anzinger, M. K., & Amari, M. (1983). Homicide in childhood: Distinguishable patterns of risk related to developmental levels of victims. *American Journal of Forensic Medicine and Pathology, 4*, 129-137.

Copeland, A. R. (1985). Homicide in childhood: The metro-Dade County experience from 1956 to 1982. *The American Journal of Forensic Medicine and Pathology, 6*, 21-24.

Crittenden, P. M., & Craig, S. E. (1990). Developmental trends in the nature of child homicide. *Journal of Interpersonal Violence, 5*, 202-216.

Curtis, L. A. (1975). *Violence, race, and culture*. Lexington, MA: Lexington Books.

Ewigman, B., Kivalahan, C., & Land, G. (1993). The Missouri child fatality study: Underreporting of maltreatment fatalities among children younger than five years of age, 1983 through 1986. *Pediatrics, 91*, 330-337.

Finkelhor, D. (1997). The homicides of children and youth: A developmental perspective. In G. K. Kantor & J. L. Jasinski (Eds.), *Out of the darkness: Contemporary research perspectives on family violence* (pp. 17-34). Thousand Oaks, CA: Sage.

Finkelhor, D., & Ormrod, R. (2001). *Homicides of children and youth*. Washington, DC: USDOJ, Juvenile Justice Bulletin # NCJ 187239.

Fox, J. A. (2005). *Uniform Crime Reports [United States]: Supplementary Homicide Reports, 1976-2002* [Computer File]. Compiled by Northeastern University, College of Criminal Justice. ICPSR (Ed.). Ann Arbor, MI: Inter-University Consortium for Political and Social Research [producer and distributor].

Fox, J. A., & Piquero, A. R. (2003). Deadly demographics: Population characteristics and forecasting homicide trends. *Crime & Delinquency, 49,* 339-359.

Fox, J. A., & Zawitz, M. W. (2004). *Homicide trends in the United States.* Washington, DC: U.S.D.O.J., Bureau of Justice Statistics. Accessed 2/21/2005. http://www.ojp.usdoj.gov/bjs/homicide/homtrnd.htm.

Hackney, S. (1979). Southern violence. In H. D. Graham & T. R. Gurr (Eds.), *Violence in America.* Beverly Hills, CA: Sage.

Harer, M. D., & Steffensmeier, D. (1992). The differing effects of economic inequality on Black and White rates of violence. *Social Forces, 70,* 1035-1054.

Hawkins, D. F. (1983). Black and white homicide differentials: Alternatives to an inadequate theory. *Criminal Justice and Behavior, 10,* 407-440.

Hawkins, D. F. (1985). Black homicide: The adequacy of existing research for devising prevention strategies. *Crime and Delinquency, 31,* 83-103.

Krug, E., Dahlberg, L. L, Mercy, J. A., Zwi, A. B., & Lozano, R. (Eds.). (2002). *World report on violence and health.* Geneva: World Health Organization. http://www.who.int/violence_injury_prevention/violence/world_report/wrvheng/en/.

Land, K. C., McCall, P. L., & Cohen, L. E. (1990). Structural covariates of homicide rates: Are there any invariances across time and social space? *American Journal of Sociology, 95,* 922-963.

Lord, W. D., Boudreaux, M. C., Jarvis, J. P., Waldvogel, J., & Weeks, H. (2002). Comparative patterns in life course victimization. *Homicide Studies, 6,* 325-347.

Luckenbill, D. F. (1977). Criminal homicide as a situated transaction. *Social Problems, 25,* 176-186.

Messner, S. F., & Rosenfeld, R. (1999). Social structure and homicide: Theory and research. In M. D. Smith & M. A. Zahn (Eds.), *Homicide: A sourcebook of social research* (pp. 27-41). Thousand Oaks, CA: Sage.

Messner, S. F., & Rosenfeld, R. (2001). *Crime and the American dream* (3rd ed.). Belmont, CA: Wadsworth.

National Center for Health Statistics. (1995). *Health, United States, 1994.* Hyattsville, MD: Public Health Service.

Phillips, J. A. (2002). White, Black, and Latino homicide rates: Why the difference? *Social Problems, 49,* 349-373.

Potter, L. (2001). Influence of homicide on racial disparity in life expectancy—United States, 1998. *Morbidity and Mortality Weekly Report, 50,* 780-783.

Pratt, T. C., & Godsey, T. W. (2003). Social support, inequality, and homicide: A cross-national test of an integrated theoretical model. *Criminology, 41,* 611-643.

Puzone, C. A., Saltzman, L. E., Kresnow, M., Thompson, M. P., & Mercy, J. A. (2000). National trends in intimate partner homicide: United States, 1976-1995. *Violence against Women, 6,* 409-426.

Sampson, R. J., & Groves, W. B. (1989). Community structure and crime: Testing social disorganization theory. *American Journal of Sociology, 94,* 774-802.

Smithey, M. (1998). Infant homicide: Victim/offender relationship and causes of death. *Journal of Family Violence, 13,* 285-297.

Spungen, D. (1998). *Homicide: The hidden victims. A guide for professionals.* Thousand Oaks, CA: Sage.

Vogt, K. A., & Block, C. R. (2003). Child homicide victimization in Chicago, 1965-1995. In C. R. Block & R. Block (Eds.), *Public health and criminal justice approaches to homicide research* (pp. 337-354). Proceedings of the Homicide Research Working Group annual meeting, Sacramento, CA, June 5-8.

Wells, W., & DeLeon-Granados, W. (2004). The intimate partner homicide decline: Disaggregated trends, theoretical explanations, and policy implications. *Criminal Justice Policy Review, 15,* 229-246.

Williams, K. R., & Flewelling, R. L. (1988). The social production of criminal homicide: A comparative study of disaggregated rates in American cities. *American Sociological Review, 53,* 421-31.

Wolfgang, M. E., & Ferracuti, F. (1967). *Subculture of violence.* London, UK: Travistock Press.

CHAPTER 11
Grief and Attachment Within the Context of Family Violence

Kimberly A. Rapoza
Kathleen Malley-Morrison

This chapter addresses the connections between attachment, interpersonal violence, loss, and grief. In particular, the chapter focuses on the ways in which attachment theory can add to our understanding of the role of grief in violence. For example, it shows how grief and the fear of loss of an attachment figure may be both a precursor to and outcome of family violence. In addition, it shows that an individual's attachment style may be related to the form of grief reaction (relatively simple versus more complicated or chronic) following traumatic experiences, such as the loss of a family member due to interpersonal violence.

Although the death of a loved one may be one of the more easily recognized sources of grief, other experiences and losses can also be significant sources of such emotional anguish. As this chapter reveals, grief can also result from the trauma and pain caused by child abuse and can have an impact on intimate relationships throughout the life span. Grief can also result from the pain and suffering associated with being in a relationship in which a loved one, who is expected to be a source of love and comfort, is in fact a source of threat, pain, humiliation, and fear. In the case of domestic violence, loss and grief may ensue not only from the loss of a family member to intimate homicide, but also from the loss of less tangible relationship benefits, such as feeling loved and protected from harm. The chapter begins with an overview of theories of attachment and grief. It then provides information on the links between child maltreatment and both insecure attachment systems and grief. The next sections address the relationship between attachment style and intimate violence as well as attachment styles and complicated grieving due to child or domestic homicide. The final section gives a brief overview of results from our own research program, which provides

152 / PERSPECTIVES ON VIOLENCE AND VIOLENT DEATH

empirical support for the proposed links among childhood maltreatment, attachment, grief reactions, and intimate violence.

THE ROOTS OF ATTACHMENT AND
ATTACHMENT THEORY

The bonds that form between children and their primary caretakers, and the influence of those early attachments on relationships through out the life span, are the major focus of attachment theory. Bowlby (e.g., 1969) viewed attachment as having biological roots and being activated by stress. In keeping with Darwin's evolutionary principles, Bowlby suggested that the formation of attachment bonds helps human beings survive as individuals and as a species, and consequently infants are genetically predisposed to form such bonds. These attachment bonds consist of a system of thoughts, feelings, and behaviors experienced or utilized by a child with the goal of keeping caregivers in close proximity and avoiding loss. Because humans have a long period of infant development, attachment behaviors (e.g., crying, clinging) help maintain parental proximity and protection, hence increasing infant survival. At the same time, early experiences teach the child the extent to which the primary caregiver can be relied upon as a source of security and protection. Bowlby proposed that "internal working models" of the self and others, formed during the early years, shape and guide interactions and relationships with others throughout the life span.

Bowlby's observations of institutionalized infants provided some early evidence of the link between attachment and grief. Bowlby noted that children over six months in age responded to prolonged separation from their primary caregivers with a predictable sequence of behaviors—protest, despair, and detachment.

- In the protest phase, children became acutely distressed (crying loudly, searching eagerly for any sign of the mother, throwing tantrums, and showing anger and hostility). This phase lasted a few hours to a week or more.
- In the despair phase, children were still preoccupied with the loss of their caregivers, but became increasingly withdrawn and inactive. In this phase, the children's crying was more muted and intermittent, and the children *appeared* "to be in a deep state of mourning" (Bowlby, 1980, p. 27).

In the final, detachment, phase, the children seemed more responsive to care from others, and able to take more interest in their surroundings. If reunited with the mother, these infants no longer sought proximity and contact and were often remote and apathetic towards her. Bowlby viewed such detachment as a defensive process that repressed and blocked attachment due to the continued failure of the prior behaviors to regain the caregiver.

It is clear that not all infants respond to separations from their caretakers in the same way. Some appear immediately to grieve strongly and actively over their loss; others appear more resigned and depressed. Building on Bowlby's attachment theory, Ainsworth, Blehar, Waters, and Wall (1978) identified three attachment "styles" used by infants in response to brief separation from their primary caregivers (the "Strange Situation"). Some children (labeled "securely attached") initially displayed mild distress but showed an ability to calm down in the face of the loss. Other children (labeled "anxious/ambivalent") showed intense distress after their mother's departure. Another group (labeled "anxious/ avoidant") showed little distress and seemed rather apathetic when their mother left them. Ainsworth and her colleagues found that when the mothers reunited with their youngsters, the securely attached children readily sought contact as well as comfort and seemed more easily placated. Anxious/ambivalent children reacted with mixed expressions of emotion, alternating between seeking proximity to the caregiver and reacting with anger or hostility. Finally, anxious/avoidant children responded with detachment and avoidance to reunion with the caregiver. Ainsworth (1973) viewed the development of secure, anxious/ambivalent, and anxious/avoidant patterns of attachment as linked to the caregiver's responsiveness to the infant. She suggested that the particular form of the attachment relationship evolved from the continual interactions between the infant and the primary caregiver and persisted over time.

Fraley and Shaver (1999) noted that the patterns found in children's reunion with the caregiver in the Strange Situation can be viewed as miniature versions of different types of mourning found in some clinical disorders. The anxious/ ambivalent infants, who seemed overly focused on the attachment figure, showed extreme distress, and yet were not able to be comforted by the caregiver, seemed to display a short-term version of *chronic mourning* (or *grieving*). Avoidant infants, who showed little outward distress at the loss of the caregiver and displayed little interest when she returned, appeared to be exhibiting a short-term version of what some clinicians refer to as *delayed* or *absent* grief (characterized by the absence of any outward sign of anger, anxiety, or emotional disturbance in the face of loss). Securely attached infants, who showed signs of distress and protest when the mother left, but were able to be comforted and to resolve the negative emotions that resulted from separation and loss when she returned, were the counterpart of adults who experience a more clinically normal course of grief and mourning.

Attachment theory, with its focus on the different experiences and expectations of those who develop secure or insecure attachment styles, has proved to be an extremely powerful framework for making sense out of problems in human relationships. Several researchers have proposed additional categories to encompass the different ways in which children and adults can be insecurely attached. For example, some children display a pattern of affect and behavior that seems best described as disorganized/disoriented (Main & Solomon, 1990). These

154 / PERSPECTIVES ON VIOLENCE AND VIOLENT DEATH

children are nearly overwhelmed with their ambivalence to an attachment figure, who may be simultaneously a potential refuge from and a source of tremendous anxiety. When the caretaker of disorganized/disoriented children returns after a brief separation, the children are typically unable to pursue a consistent strategy to deal with their stress and recover from their loss, often alternating between seeking proximity and avoiding contact—"freezing"—and showing symptoms of anxiety and depression. It is possible that the parents of these children are themselves the victims of unresolved grief stemming from childhood trauma such as child sexual abuse, and that they are both frightened and frightening in relation to their children (Alexander, 1992).

The serious clinical implications of insecure attachment have been recognized by the inclusion of attachment disorders (that is, persistent disturbances in social relatedness beginning before age five and extending across social situations in the DSM). The DSM-IV described two types of attachment disorder: (1) the emotionally withdrawn/inhibited type, characterizing children who rarely seek or respond to comfort and demonstrate no preference for any particular caregiver; and (2) the indiscriminate/disinhibited type, characterizing children who are oversociable and who seek comfort and affection nonselectively, even from unfamiliar adults (Zeanah et al., 2004).

Although Bowlby viewed the attachment system as somewhat flexible and therefore capable of modification over time based on experience, he and other attachment researchers generally assume considerable continuity between the attachment style developed in early childhood and the attachment styles of adults. Hazan and Shaver (1987) suggested that the qualitatively different childhood systems of secure, avoidant, and anxious/ambivalent attachment have parallels in patterns that characterize adults. Based on Hazan and Shaver's (1987) work, Bartholomew and Horowitz (1991) defined adult attachment patterns in relation to positive and negative representations of the self and others and developed a four-category model of attachment—secure, dismissive, preoccupied, and fearful. Adults who have developed a secure pattern have positive views of themselves and others; secure individuals are confident and comfortable with intimacy in their close relationships. Individuals who have developed the dismissing form of insecure attachment have a positive self-image, but negative views of others. These people maintain a positive self-image by defensively downplaying the importance of attachment needs and maintaining emotional distance in their relationships. The preoccupied style combines a negative view of the self (which is seen as unworthy of love) and a positive view of others. This combination leads to a preoccupation with maintaining the affections of others and using clinging behavior to hold onto them. The fearful attachment style is characterized by a negative sense of the self and a negative view of others, who are seen as unaccepting and unresponsive to the individuals' intimacy needs.

GRIEF

The origin, expression, and progression of grief have been conceptualized in a variety of ways in the clinical literature. Worden (1991) noted that one view, derived from Freudian theory, is that grief and mourning are like an illness. From this psychiatric view of loss and the grief that follows it, grief is seen as a threat to the healthy psyche, and mourning is the healing process that brings a person back into balance. Bowlby (1980), by contrast, looked at grief from an attachment perspective, arguing that cognitive, affective, and behavioral responses to loss could be expected. Bowlby posited that grieving responses, based on attachment and affectional bonds to others, can be considered part of the potential course of all mourning. From this perspective, individuals perceiving the loss of an attachment figure will move through a series of phases, and "any one individual may oscillate for a time back and forth between any two" (Bowlby, 1980, p. 85).

The first phase in response to loss, which may last from a few hours to a week, is numbness, characterized by difficulty or inability to accept the loss, feelings of shock, and intense anxiety or distress. The second phase is characterized by yearning and searching, and may last a few months to years. The grieved person in this phase may experience restlessness, intense longing, preoccupation with the lost person, and visual or auditory hallucinations (for example, hearing someone come up the stairs and believing it is the lost person coming home from work). The searching and yearning seen in this phase appears similar to the response of an infant who initially protests the loss of the caregiver and exhibits behaviors intended to regain them. The intense pain, restlessness, preoccupation, crying, and calling out for the missing person, often characterizing an adult in mourning, have parallels in the responses of infants who yearn, search for, and attempt to recover a lost attachment figure. According to Bowlby, while anger and hostility toward the lost attachment figure might be regarded as potentially pathological from a psychoanalytic perspective, anger and hostility toward the lost person, towards others who are attempting to console, and toward the self (if not excessive) can be seen as part of healthy mourning. In his view, anger is an emotional reaction experienced in response to unmet attachment needs. It functions as a potential mechanism to regain and reestablish contact with the caregiver. As already noted, although children typically may experience emotional pain and yearn for the return of missing caregivers, some infants, upon reunion with a missing caregiver, exhibit hostility, hitting, and tantrums. Indeed, Ainsworth (1973) noted that when anxious/ambivalent infants were reunited with their mothers following a separation, the reunions were marked by the distressed infants' anger, hostility, and resistance toward the caregiver. The anger that often accompanies adult grieving may be a similar type of response to the threat or loss of an attachment figure.

156 / PERSPECTIVES ON VIOLENCE AND VIOLENT DEATH

The third phase of mourning is disorganization and despair, characterized by the central task of reconciling the fact that reunion with the attachment figure is improbable with the urge to recover the lost person. Overwhelming sadness, apathy, loneliness, and depression may appear as bereft individuals come to realize that their behavior will in all probability not bring back the lost person. In the fourth phase, reorganization, individuals relinquish hope for regaining the lost person and make efforts to acquire or integrate the roles and skills that will be needed to live their lives in the absence of the lost person. This process may require a redefinition of the self (the griever is no longer a wife, but a widow) and of the current life situation (the tasks that the husband performed may need to be completed by the widow). The reorganization phase allows that some bond or attachment to the lost person may continue, and bereaved individuals may retain a strong feeling of the lost person as a continued presence in their life; however, by the final stage the intense negative affect present at the start of the loss has waned.

In consideration of the rejection of a phase or stage model of grieving and instead, conceptualizing the grieving process as consisting of tasks to be actively completed by the mourner, Worden (1991) developed a clinical model that also viewed grief as composed of more than just affective responses to loss. Worden noted that uncomplicated grief and normal grief reactions were varied, but in clinical practice were found to fall within four broad categories, which overlap with attachment-system-theory concepts of affect, cognition, and behavior.

- Category 1 consists of the feelings associated with normal grieving including emotional reactions such as sadness, anger, guilt and self reproach, anxiety, loneliness, feelings of fatigue, helplessness, shock, yearning, numbness, and emancipation and relief (in response to the loss of an overbearing person or someone who had been suffering during an illness).
- Category 2 consists of the cognitions surrounding the loss encompassing disbelief, confusion, preoccupation, a sense of the person's presence, and hallucinations.
- Category 3 consists of behaviors frequently associated with loss, such as sleep disturbances, appetite disturbances, absentmindedness, social withdrawal, dreams of the deceased, avoiding reminders of the deceased, searching for and calling out for the deceased, sighing and crying, restless overactivity, visiting places, carrying objects, or treasuring items that remind them of the deceased.
- Category 4 includes a constellation of physical sensations associated with grief, for example, hollowness in the stomach, tightness in the chest or throat, feeling short of breath, oversensitivity to noise, lack of energy, dry mouth, and a sense of depersonalization around the self and daily activities.

GRIEF AND ATTACHMENT / 157

CHILDHOOD MALTREATMENT AND ITS AFTERMATH:
INSECURE ATTACHMENT AND GRIEF

What kinds of experiences in the childhood family of origin lead to the development of secure or insecure attachment styles? An overwhelming amount of evidence links childhood maltreatment with insecure attachment. For example, Morton and Browne (1998) found that all but two of the relevant studies they reviewed revealed that, compared to control children, significantly more of the maltreated infants displayed insecure attachments. Aber and Allen (1987) found that maltreatment by mothers appeared to disrupt the construction of a secure attachment in infancy, to affect social/emotional development, and to disrupt the child's motivation to establish secure relationships with adults. Cicchetti and Barnett (1991) also found insecure attachment in infancy to be linked to abuse by the caregiver, with abused infants being more likely to show insecure attachment patterns and to maintain those insecure attachment patterns over time (6–18 months). Zeanah et al. (2004) found that both the inhibited and the socially indiscriminate types of reactive attachment disorder could be found in a group of maltreated toddlers. Lyons-Ruth, Connell, Grunebaum, and Botein (1990) also found in their sample of maltreated children that 55% were classifiable as disorganized/disoriented in attachment style.

Childhood maltreatment takes many forms. It is not only physical and sexual abuse, but also neglect that can contribute to the development of insecure attachment systems. In one sample of children who had been physically and emotionally neglected, 82% of the children were classified as exhibiting disorganized attachment (Carlson, Cicchetti, Barnett, & Braunwald, 1989). Another study revealed that although 57% of a sample of emotionally neglected children were securely attached at the age of 12 months, many of these children had become anxiously attached by 18 months of age (Egeland & Sroufe, 1981). Scarr (1992) found that when young children are emotionally neglected, their attachment problems can worsen over time.

Although the impact of direct maltreatment on children has received considerable attention, the possible negative effects of witnessing domestic violence were long overlooked (Diamond & Muller, 2004). It has recently become clear that witnessing violence between the parents can make unique and independent contributions to child and adolescent behavioral and psychological difficulties. For example, in a sample of over 300 women, Feerick and Haugaard (1999) found that when personal experiences of abuse were controlled for, witnessed violence was still associated with increased reports of PTSD symptoms. Diamond and Muller (2004) also found that individuals with a history of witnessing physical and major psychological domestic violence had higher levels of psychopathology (emotional and behavioral problems and trauma symptoms) than those not witnessing any parental violence (or witnessing only low levels of psychological abuse between the parents). In that sample, violence

158 / PERSPECTIVES ON VIOLENCE AND VIOLENT DEATH

perpetrated by the father seemed more influential in predicting PTSD symptoms and internalizing, whereas witnessed perpetration by the mother better predicted symptoms of externalizing.

Holden and Ritchie (1991) have proposed that violence occurring between the parents may result in inconsistent care or inadequate attention, due to the level of stress on the caretaker and the impact the violence has on a caretaker's ability to be available for the child. In a study examining the relationship between marital conflict and insecure attachment, Owen and Cox (1997) found infants of couples who were experiencing high levels of marital conflict to be at an increased risk for disorganized (insecure) attachment. The authors noted that marital conflict may create a climate wherein the child is exposed to frightening situations (or to parental behavior that is frightening) and may also lessen the parents' ability to provide sensitive caregiving.

In addition to evidence connecting child maltreatment with the development of insecure attachment, including a clinical diagnosis of disordered attachment, there is evidence linking childhood maltreatment with the development of symptoms of grief, such as depression and stress-related physical symptoms. There is considerable research indicating that some of the problems associated with child maltreatment are depression (e.g., Ethier, Lemelin, & Lacharite, 2004; Johnson et al., 2002; Saywitz, Mannarino, Berliner, & Cohen, 2000; Toth, Manly, & Cicchetti, 1992), PTSD symptoms (e.g., McLeer, Deblinger, Atkins, Foa, & Ralphe, 1988; Shea, Walsh, MacMillan, & Steiner, 2004; Swett & Halpert, 1993), and borderline personality disorder (Cohen, Mannarino, & Knudsen, 2005; Swett & Halpert, 1993). Grief has also been pinpointed specifically as an outcome of childhood abuse, especially sexual abuse (Courtois, 1988; Farber, Herbert, & Reviere, 1996; Tsun-Yin, 1998).

Interestingly, Lyons-Ruth and Jacobvitz (1999) noted that the intergenerational transmission of violence (abused children going on to abuse their own children) may in part be explained by the intergenerational transmission of attachment styles. For instance, studies have found that a parent's experiences of trauma or abuse as a child are associated with their infants displaying a disorganized attachment pattern. The parents, still trying to deal with maltreatment and loss experiences surrounding their own caregiver, may engage in frightening or abusive behavior with their own child. According to this perspective, a parent who suffered trauma, missed out on sensitive caregiving due to witnessing or experiencing family violence, or experienced a caregiver loss, will be more likely to have an insecure attachment style. The representational pattern becomes an inner working model of how to interact with others and guides interactions with their own children. Lyons-Ruth and Jacobvitz noted that disorganized attachment has been found at elevated levels in both victims and perpetrators of marital violence. They suggest that insecure attachment, particularly disorganized attachment, can be seen as a potential mediator between experiences in childhood and later perpetration of abuse as an adult.

ATTACHMENT, GRIEF, AND INTIMATE VIOLENCE

Many studies have demonstrated a link between the experience of child maltreatment and later involvement in child abuse and intimate violence. However, the data also show clearly that not everyone who grows up in a violent or abusive environment will become abusive with children or partners. Attachment styles appear to play an important role in the extent to which individuals who have been abused become abusers themselves. The extent to which children are unable to resolve the grief and loss associated with child maltreatment may also mediate the relationship between the negative early experiences and the tendency to use aggression in later relationships.

Lyons-Ruth and Jacobvitz (1999), in their stress-relational-diathesis model, propose that there is an interactive effect between childhood trauma and the quality of childhood attachment. While the child may display adequate social behavior most of the time, when stressed he or she will be more likely to evidence disorganization and maladaptive social behavior. In some ways, stress later in life (perhaps the real or imagined threat of being abandoned by the partner or being abused by the partner) may trigger earlier grief that has not been resolved. Lyons-Ruth and Jacobvitz note that, "In short, the more insecure the underlying attachment, the more difficult the mental resolution of a loss becomes" (p. 548).

When situations arise that threaten the adult attachment bond, such as when a partner is not seen as providing adequate responsiveness or accessibility, intense fear and anxiety over potential loss of the partner can trigger emotions, such as jealousy, that aim to reestablish affiliate contact with the attachment figure (Bowlby, 1988). Actual loss, however, is not necessary to trigger violent behavior towards a partner. This is because early lack of care, responsiveness, or abuse from the caregiver will have influenced the individuals' working models, such that they will have hypervigilance and increased sensitivity to cues regarding separation or loss of the attachment figure (Bowlby, 1980). Fraley and Shaver (1999) note that anxious/ambivalent adults seem to have organized their working model of attachment around the notion that the attachment figure will not be available or is not trustworthy. Hence, they are continually monitoring the attachment figure for signs of abandonment, potential loss, or unavailability. The behavioral expression of their attachment style, coinciding with an attempt to retain the attachment figure or prevent loss or rejection, can be clinginess, dependence, and jealousy.

Jealousy, like anger, can be viewed as a response to the perceived threat of abandonment and part of an attachment response designed to maintain and protect a relationship. Dutton, Saunders, Starzomski, and Bartholomew (1994) found the insecure patterns of both fearful and preoccupied attachment had a significant relationship to elevated levels of jealousy; conversely, the more securely attached the male was, the less jealousy he reported. Jealousy has also been thought to have both a contributing role (Barnett, Martinez, & Bluestein, 1995) and a precipitating role (Gagne & Lavoie, 1993) in expressions of adult relationship

160 / PERSPECTIVES ON VIOLENCE AND VIOLENT DEATH

violence. Maritally violent men have reported elevated levels of jealousy as compared with nonviolent controls (Barnett et al., 1995). However, the literature on dating and courtship violence seems to indicate that jealousy is a better predictor of committing dating violence for women than for men (Bookwala, Frieze, Smith, & Ryan, 1992; Stets & Pirog-Good, 1987).

Violence in an adult relationship can be viewed as a dysfunctional and maladaptive attempt to strengthen the bond with the partner, especially when the perpetrator perceives the relationship as being threatened (Bowlby, 1984). According to this perspective, individuals with insecure attachment styles may be more prone to utilize violence in their intimate relationships (Mayseless, 1991). A number of studies have provided evidence supporting this link between insecure attachment styles and relationship violence in adulthood. For example, in a study comparing a sample of violent males with matched controls, Dutton et al. (1994) found that fearful-attachment was the strongest predictor of the use of violence in a relationship. While similar trends were found for preoccupied attachment, fearful attachment style was more strongly associated with emotional abuse of the partner than were secure or dismissive attachment. Holtzworth-Monroe, Stuart, and Hutchinson (1997) similarly found that violent husbands evidenced significantly more insecure attachment, particularly more preoccupied and disorganized/insecure attachment, than did nonviolent husbands. Hudson and Ward (1997) examined the self-reported attachment styles of incarcerated child molesters, rapists, violent criminals not convicted of a sex crime, and a control group consisting of individuals convicted of nonviolent offenses. Overall, the incarcerated individuals generally reported insecure attachment styles. However, differences in type of insecure attachment were found among the different groups of offenders. For example, the child molesters reported more fearful or pre-occupied attachment and less dismissive attachment than the other groups. The rapists and violent offenders reported more dismissive attachment, while the nonviolent, non-sex-crime offenders reported more secure attachment than the other groups.

Research has also shown links between insecure attachment and psychological abuse in romantic relationships. Specifically, college women who are preoccupied in their attachment style tend to perpetrate more emotional abuse against their partners as well as experience more emotional abuse (O'Hearn & Davis, 1997). Preoccupied attachment also seems to contribute to the perpetration of emotional abuse by men (Dutton et al., 1994). Henderson, Bartholomew, and Dutton (1997) also examined the relationship between receiving abuse in a romantic relationship and insecure attachment. They assessed the attachment styles of 63 women who had recently left an abusive relationship. The physically abused participants were recruited through shelters, transition houses, or male partners in abuse treatment programs, while the psychologically abused participants were recruited through newspaper advertisements. Overall, the study found preoccupied and fearful attachment to be the predominant patterns reported by the women. However, the preoccupied and fearfully attached women differed in patterns of separation and reconciliation with their abusers. Women with the fearful style had sustained a longer relationship with the abuser and initially seemed to have more difficulty leaving him. However, once separated, the fearfully attached women were far less likely than preoccupied women to return to the abusive relationship. By contrast, women with a preoccupied-attachment style were characterized by more frequent separating from and returning to the abusive relationship, more involvement with the partner after separation, and more difficulty in separating emotionally from their abusive partner.

Grief can be viewed as an active process that attempts to reconcile the reality of how things are with the wishes and desires of the grieving person (Parkes, 1972). It is the process by which the person attempts to regain a sense of normalcy and stability following a loss. Grief can be seen as a way of coping with the loss (or what is perceived to be lost) and attempting to regain a sense of stability. Although death is a major loss, it is not the only one. The apparent loss of a loving relationship that is felt when a partner starts battering may also be a significant loss, and grief may be experienced by many battered women in response to that loss. Russell and Uhlemann (1994) noted that the grief experienced by battered women as a result of their experiences of violence has often been overlooked, perhaps because of the ambiguous nature of this type of loss. Unfortunately, the ambiguity of the loss also leaves battered women with few culturally sanctioned rituals that allow the processing of grief. Russell and Uhlemann attempted to identify some of the types of losses a woman experiences as a result of violence from an intimate. Many of the losses they identify echo Parkes' conceptualization of grief as being a change or assault on the woman's "assumptive world" (the world before the loss). For example, an abused woman's grief may stem from the loss of (a) expectations she has about herself and her relationship, (b) an idealized relationship, (c) the roles associated with relationship, and (d) economic security and shared parenting responsibilities. In keeping with literature on the normal grieving process, Russell and Uhlemann found that the grief process for battered women entailed physical, cognitive, and affective expression analogous to grieving other major losses. Among those expressions of grief were depression, guilt, blame, anxiety, fatigue, confusion and decision making difficulty, feelings of meaninglessness and a lack of control, and physical symptoms such as a lack of appetite, energy, and sleep.

ATTACHMENT STYLES AND COMPLICATED GRIEVING DUE TO CHILD OR DOMESTIC HOMICIDE

Recent trends noted by the Bureau of Justice Statistics report (Fox & Zawitz, 2002) for the years 1976 to 2002 indicate that domestic homicide and child homicide have been decreasing in the last decade. Nevertheless, when the murder

162 / PERSPECTIVES ON VIOLENCE AND VIOLENT DEATH

of a family member occurs, the most likely perpetrator continues to be someone in the family (or a close family acquaintance). A parent is the perpetrator in most homicides of children under the age of 5, with 31% of murdered children killed by the father, 30% killed by the mother, 23% killed by a male friend/acquaintance, and 6% killed by another relative. Only 3% of child homicides were attributable to a stranger. The risk for homicide seemed to be greatest for young children (under one year). The method of killing was often extremely brutal, with statistics from 1974 to 1994 indicating that 58% of murdered children were killed by beating with fists or blunt objects or by kicking.

Recent trends also indicate a decrease in intimate-partner homicide, with 11% of murder victims killed by an intimate from 1976 to 2002, and females disproportionably affected (one-third of female victims were killed by an intimate). In general, guns were most often used in intimate homicide, with over two-thirds of spouses and ex-spouses killed by guns (with knives being the next most common weapon use).

The nature of domestic homicide and child homicide then raises some issues regarding the impact of the loss on surviving victims. The traumatic instances surrounding the death of a loved one, the brutal nature of the crime, and the potential familial relationship and ties to the perpetrator may well precipitate chronic or traumatic grief reactions.

Based on a review of the literature on chronic grief, Bonanno et al. (2002) reported that individuals with chronic grief constitute between 10% and 20% of the sample in bereavement studies. Neimeyer, Prigerson, and Davis (2002) noted that traumatic deaths (such as homicides) and deaths violating the "natural order" of our conceptions of death (as when someone young dies) can be particularly challenging for the bereaved. Cohen, Mannarino, Greenberg, Padlo, and Shipley (2002) also noted that childhood traumatic grief can stem from a child losing a loved one under particularly traumatic circumstances, such as through interpersonal violence.

For both children and adults, traumatic symptomology may resemble PTSD symptoms. For instance, Cohen and her associates noted that traumatic grief reactions in children may involve intrusive thoughts and memories, extreme physiological arousal, and emotional numbing that interferes with a healthier grieving of the loss. Prigerson et al. (1997) argued that traumatic grief in adults is based on the presence of two underlying dimensions: traumatic distress and separation distress. Traumatic distress and accompanying symptoms are viewed as similar to PTSD, in that both syndromes encompass intrusive or vivid reexperiencing of the event, psychological avoidance, and numbness. Separation distress was described as emotional responses and behaviors such as yearning and searching for the partner, feelings of distrust and disbelief, anger, bitterness, severe feelings of emptiness and loneliness, and avoiding reminders of the deceased. To explain why grieving traumatic events may later engender PTSD-like symptoms, Neimeyer and associates (2002) proposed that the brain may respond differently to traumatic loss than to a devastating loss. Under conditions of a traumatic incident or sudden loss (perhaps due to the murder of a loved one by another family member), the brain floods with neurotransmitters, which increase the retention of vivid memories, sensations, and emotions stored in association with the event. This response can become problematic when events (which may or may not be directly related to the initial loss) continually result in hyperarousal of the limbic system (producing PTSD-like symptoms, such as disassociated images, intrusive memories, and emotional avoidance).

Neimeyer and his associates (2002) view tragic or traumatic loss as something that makes individuals call into question many of assumptions about the world, which can invalidate an individual's sense of security, trust, and optimism. The long-term effects of a traumatic loss, however, may be more intense and pose more challenges based on the attachment profile of the affected individual. A person's "internal working model" is thought to be a potential risk factor in the development of complicated grief responses. Based on attachment theory, Neimeyer and associates proposed that a bereaved person whose attachment profile is characterized by disorganization (high levels of both approach/ avoidance), compulsive caregiving, and excessive dependence would be at heightened risk for complicated grief.

Indeed, Moos and Schaefer (1986) have noted that life transitions can be stressful, and that to successfully cope with a life crisis (or to potentially experience positive growth from the experience), there are six factors to consider: background and personal characteristics, characteristics of the event, physical and social environmental factors, cognitive appraisal, adaptive tasks, and coping skills. While there is no precise formula available, the absence or presence of positive or negative factors can lead to resilience or increased risk for distress. Hence, when faced with a crisis, such as the death of a loved one due to family violence, personal/background factors such as an insecure attachment style, event-related factors such as traumatic circumstances surrounding the death of the loved one, the potential lack of support from the environment (wherein others may also be dealing with the devastating loss or the family unit has been strained and in distress for some time) may all increase an individual's risk for traumatic or complicated grieving.

Bowlby (1980) theorized that experiences in childhood that shape a person's working model of self and others can influence the propensity to experience a disordered variant in mourning as an adult. In collecting accounts of people's childhoods, Bowlby noted that individuals whose mourning was characterized as pathological reported being unwanted as children, having a stressful childhood, and experiencing separation or loss of the parent. People prone to disordered mourning appeared to have a certain constellation of personality traits stemming from their childhood attachment styles and could be divided into groups based on their reactions to loss. Anxious attachment appeared to be related to chronic

164 / PERSPECTIVES ON VIOLENCE AND VIOLENT DEATH

mourning, viewed as prolonged extensions of the protest (yearning and searching) and despair phases. Avoidant attachment appeared to be related to a prolonged absence of grief or conscious mourning, and perhaps a quick movement to the reorganization phase. Bowlby suggested that avoidant individuals might not overtly register their loss, but would be prone to physical and psychological maladies and a possible eruption of depression at a later date.

The anxious/ambivalent attachment style appears to be associated with chronic grieving at the end of a romantic relationship. It is also associated with an increased propensity to suffer from chronic mourning following the death of a loved one (Fraley & Shaver, 1999). Moreover, anxious/ambivalent attachment is associated with intense anxiety, prolonged yearning for the lost spouse, and extreme difficulty adjusting to the loss. The avoidant style, characterized by the suppression of emotion or at least the lack of overt display in the face of loss or separation, was originally thought by Bowlby to be at risk for psychological and physical ills. There is also evidence, however, that although avoidant individuals engage in the suppression of expressions of grief and may emotionally disassociate from experiences of loss, they do not necessarily have a complicated recovery from loss and may recover with relatively few difficulties (Fraley & Shaver, 1999). It is possible that avoidant individuals may not be highly emotionally attached to their partners and may not have their sense of self and security heavily invested in the relationship. Therefore, the absence of grief reactions or extended grief may be due to a minimal attachment to the partner and the compulsive self-reliance that characterizes this type of individual.

A follow-up study (Bonanno et al., 2002) of widowed persons (starting prior to the death and continuing 18 months after loss) revealed five main bereavement patterns: common grief, chronic grief, resilience, chronic depression, and depression improvement. Individuals suffering from chronic grief were distinct from those in the chronic-depression group (high levels of depression before loss), in that those with chronic grief had no distinct preloss depression or high levels of ambivalence toward the spouse. However, the chronic-grief group was characterized by excessive dependency on the spouse, which can be conceptually related to anxious attachment. The resilient group, whose symptoms seemed to begin decreasing after a shorter time (six months), seemed to consist of well-adjusted individuals with good coping skills and resources, which can be conceptually related to secure attachment. The depressed/ improved group, which had high levels of depression preloss, also showed improved functioning at six months, but were relatively maladjusted, self-absorbed, negative and ambivalent about their spouses, emotionally unstable, felt the world was unjust toward them, and had inadequate coping resources, which can be conceptually related to avoidant attachment. So, while quicker postloss adjustment for one group seemed to be indicative of psychological health and resilience (in keeping with a securely attached profile), quick adjustment could also indicate a more anxious/avoidant style of coping. A later study by Fraley and Bonanno (2004) revealed that emotional avoidance was not necessarily indicative of maladjustment to the loss of a loved one. While individuals characterized by a more anxious/avoidant style (fearful attachment) were likely to have difficulty adapting to the loss of a loved one, individuals characterized by dismissive attachment were able to adapt quite well to such a loss.

In summary then, it would seem that the loss of a loved one under particularity violent conditions, such as through domestic or child homicide, would constitute a risk factor for traumatic or chronic grieving. Based on the available evidence, it would seem that it is not merely insecure attachment that might increase susceptibility for complicated grief, but traits associated more with the anxious component of attachment. In certain ways, an anxious-attachment style can be viewed as a double-edged sword. Although experiences of abuse and neglect may increase a child's propensity for developing an anxious pattern of attachment, this same working model of the self and others may also leave an anxious individual at an increased risk for complicated and traumatic grieving from family violence as an adult.

Empirical Research Addressing the Model

In this section, we describe some of our own research addressing the conceptual model derived from the literature reviewed thus far. This conceptual model is summarized in Figure 1.

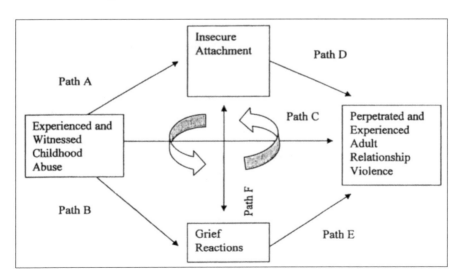

Figure 1. Conceptual model in which experiences of abuse within the family of origin temporally precedes insecure attachment and grief, with potential individual and interactive influences posited among these constructs on the perpetration and experience of adult relationship violence.

166 / PERSPECTIVES ON VIOLENCE AND VIOLENT DEATH

The respondents for the study being described here included 123 female and 77 male participants who completed an anonymous survey packet. The demographic profile of the sample was as follows: the age range was 17–60, with an average age of 21. The sample was 57% Caucasian, 6% African American, 20% Asian, 7% Latin, and 9% nonspecified. Most participants were single (94%), with 84% reporting the United States as their country of birth. Most participants had completed some college (72%) and most reported being middle (48%) or upper-middle class (38%). The average length of the current or most recent dating relationship was 17 months. The sample's religious affiliations were 48% Christian, 12% Jewish, 2% Muslin, 3% Hindu, 7% other, 21% no religion or agnostic, and 1% atheist.

The survey packets included measures of adult attachment styles, indicating the extent to which participants were secure, dismissive, preoccupied, or fearful in their orientation to the self and others (Bartholomew & Horowitz, 1991). Also included was (1) a shortened version of Straus's (1979) Conflict Tactics Scales, which provides scores for the amount of physical and psychological aggression participants received from and observed between their parents during childhood; and (2) another version of the Conflict Tactics Scale to measure perpetrated and received psychological and physical aggression in the respondents' current or most recent dating relationship.

This grief index included items addressing (1) the frequency and intensity with which the participant felt anger, directed anger toward others, and internalized and directed anger toward the self (Seigel, 1986); (2) measuring assessed feelings of jealousy associated with fear of losing the partner to someone else or being abandoned by the partner (Mathes, 1984); and (3) the frequency of somatic complaints related to grief. The items chosen described physical symptoms known to be correlates of grief reactions (for example, chest pain, shortness of breath, headaches, muscle tension, joint pain or back pain, acid indigestion, lack of appetite, etc.).

TESTING THE RELATIONSHIP PATHS
IN THE MODEL

The relationships predicted within the empirical model were tested initially by computing Person Product Moment Correlations (see Figure 1).

Path A

It hypothesized that experiences of physical and psychological abuse, as well as abuse witnessed between the parents, would be associated with higher scores on the insecure-attachment styles and lower scores on secure attachment. We found a direct correlation between the participant's scores on the fearful attachment style, and the reported levels of physical abuse from the father and the witnessing of psychological abuse from the father to the mother.

Path B

It was hypothesized that experiences of childhood abuse (both experienced and witnessed) would be positively related to scores on the grief index. Our correlational analyses provided considerable support for this hypothesis: the higher the scores on the grief index, the greater the level of psychological abuse witnessed between mothers and fathers, the more physical abuse experienced from mothers, and the more psychological abuse experienced from both mothers and fathers.

The model predicts that experiences of physical and psychological abuse as well as witnessed abuse between the parents **(Path C)**, insecure attachment **(Path D)**, and high scores on the grief index **(Path E)** all would be associated with an increased propensity to experience or perpetrate physical or psychological abuse in the dating relationship. We also examined the relationship between attachment styles and grief reactions **(Path F)**, predicting that insecure-attachment styles are associated with high scores on the grief index. The specific findings concerning these predicted connections are as follows:

Path C

Our analyses revealed that experiencing physical and psychological abuse from both the father and mother, witnessing physical abuse between the mother and the father, and witnessing psychological abuse by the father to the mother were positively associated with perpetrating physical abuse towards a partner. Also, witnessing psychological abuse from the mother to the father and experiencing physical and psychological abuse from both the father and the mother was positively associated with perpetrating psychological abuse toward the partner. Higher levels of reported abuse from the father were associated with experiencing physical abuse from the partner, and higher levels of psychological abuse from the mother were associated with reports of experiencing psychological abuse from the partner.

Path D

The higher the participants' scores on secure attachment, the less physical abuse they reported perpetrating. The higher their scores on fearful attachment, the more physical abuse they reported perpetrating toward the partner.

Path E

High scores on the grief index were associated with more reports of perpetrating physical and psychological abuse towards the partner.

Path F

As predicted, higher scores on preoccupied and fearful attachment were associated with higher scores on the grief index. Moreover, higher scores on secure attachment were associated with lower scores on the grief index.

168 / PERSPECTIVES ON VIOLENCE AND VIOLENT DEATH

THE RESULTS OF REGRESSION ANALYSES

Several hierarchical regression analyses were conducted (with males and females separately) to identify the strongest predictors of perpetrated and experienced physical and psychological abuse in the romantic relationship. These analyses allowed for the assessment of how much childhood experiences, insecure-attachment styles, and the grief index predicted the experience of or perpetration of adult-relationship violence. Predictor variables were entered in blocks, in keeping with the study's theoretical model. Experience of physical and psychological abuse was entered in the first block. Witnessed abuse between the mother and father was entered in the second block. The grief index and insecure-attachment styles were entered in the third block. To assess the possibility that grief and insecure attachment may interact with each other to produce a more potent effect than either of those variables alone, the regression equation also included three interaction terms based on the multiplication of the grief index with each of the insecure-attachment styles. These interaction terms were entered in the fourth block.

The major finding from these regression analyses was somewhat startling. The theoretical model was most robust for the female participants, particularly for the perpetration or experience of physical abuse. The model was not significant for predicting the male participants' experienced or perpetrated physical abuse nor was the model a significant predictor for experienced and perpetrated psychological abuse.

In the regression equation predicting perpetrated physical abuse for the female participants, the model accounted for about 60% of the variance in the women's physical aggression ($R^2 = .59$), which was highly significant $F(4, 71) = 4.53$, $p < .001$. An examination of the final beta statistics provided by the regression analyses revealed that witnessed physical abuse and psychological abuse from the father to the mother, preoccupied attachment, and the interaction between the grief index and fearful attachment were the most significant predictors of female perpetration of physical aggression against partners. A significant change in R^2 indicates a significant change in the percentage of variance accounted for by that variable when entered into the regression equation at that step. Hence, experiences of childhood abuse, witnessed parental violence, insecure attachment, and scores on the grief index all increased the model's predicative ability. Importantly, witnessed abuse by the father seemed to emerge as the most salient childhood abuse variable for the female participants. Moreover, the interaction between grief and fearful attachment was significant, indicating that the combination of these two characteristics provided even more predictive power than either of them alone.

In the regression analysis predicting physical abuse experienced by the female participants from their male partners, the model explained almost half of the variance ($R^2 = .47$), which was significant $F(4, 70) = 3.14$, $p < .05$. An examination of the final beta statistics revealed that experienced physical and psychological abuse from the father, witnessed physical abuse and psychological abuse from the father to the mother, preoccupied attachment, and the interaction between the grief index and preoccupied attachment scores were the most significant predictors. Hence, witnessed parental violence, insecure attachment, and scores on the grief index all increased the model's predicative ability and seemed to each be important independent contributors. Interestingly, with regard to physical abuse perpetrated by a relationship partner, direct experiences of physical and psychological abuse from the father, in addition to witnessed physical and psychological abuse by the father, seemed to emerge as the most salient childhood abuse variables. The interaction between grief and the insecure/preoccupied attachment style was significant in this equation, indicating again that the combination of these two characteristics provided even more predictive power than either of them alone.

CONCLUSION

A test of our conceptual model confirmed many of our predictions about how experiences of childhood abuse, grief reactions, and insecure attachment may be both independent contributors and interrelated precursors to intimate-partner violence. Our grief index measured the participant's experiences of anger, jealousy, and physical symptomology, all of which can be seen as reactions in keeping with Bowlby's model of grief. All are responses that might be expected in the initial phase of grieving the perceived loss of an attachment figure.

Previous research has indicated that insecure attachment (specifically anxious or disorganized attachment) is related to experiences of abuse in childhood as well as to increased risk for chronic grief or disordered mourning in the face of the potential or actual loss of an attachment figure. In testing our model, we found that fearful attachment was associated with experiencing physical abuse from the father as well as with witnessing psychological abuse from the father to the mother. Grief reactions, too, were related to abusive childhood experiences. Interestingly, it was not only experienced abuse, but also witnessed abuse that was related to increased reports of grief reactions. Witnessing both parents' psychological abuse towards each other, experiencing physical abuse from the mother, and psychological abuse from either parent were all related to reports of heightened grief reactions.

In developing our model, we viewed grief reactions as a way of coping with potential loss. The available literature seems to indicate that attachment characterized by anxiety is a risk factor for complicated grief responses or chronic grief in the face of loss, while avoidant attachment is not (Fraley & Shaver, 1999). Grief reactions in our sample appeared to be related more to an insecure working model of attachment characterized by anxiety than to one characterized by avoidance. Specifically, we found support for a relationship between grief reactions and

170 / PERSPECTIVES ON VIOLENCE AND VIOLENT DEATH

preoccupied and fearful attachment, but not avoidant attachment. Grief and insecure attachment were also related to perpetrating physical abuse, while grief alone was also related to perpetrating psychological abuse against the partner. Lyons-Ruth and Jacobvitz (1999), in their stress-relational-diathesis model, note that there may be an interactive effect between childhood trauma and childhood attachment, such that a stressful experience may trigger earlier grief and unresolved trauma, which will result in the display of maladaptive social behavior. While grief may be most readily thought of as a product of being abused, the results of our study also seem to indicate that it is characteristic of those who are abusing. Indeed, both insecure attachment and grief reactions were characteristic of intimate abusers in our sample.

The results of the regression analyses provided some interesting findings regarding the strongest predictors of perpetrated and experienced abuse in the romantic relationship. First, the regression model using childhood experiences of abuse, attachment style, and the grief index seems to be most robust for the female participants, particularly for the prediction of the experience and perpetration of physical violence. With regards to the specific variables that were most predictive of perpetrating and experiencing abuse in an intimate relationship, it seems that the female participants were most affected by their fathers' aggression. Witnessing physical and psychological abuse from the father to the mother emerged as a significant predictor for women's perpetration of physical abuse against the partner. Witnessed abuse from the father to the mother was also a significant predictor of being victimized by the partner, as was directly experiencing physical and psychological abuse from the father. The notion that witnessing or experiencing violence in the family of origin will increase an individual's risk of perpetrating or experiencing violence in an adult intimate relationship is not a new one. Over three decades ago, Straus, Gelles, and Steinmetz (1980) also found that young adults who had experienced or observed family violence in the home were twice as likely to engage in violence in their own relationships. Interestingly, it seems in our sample, the behavior of the father had traumatic and disruptive effects on the female participants, more so than the behavior of the mother. This finding is in keeping with other research findings. For instance Henning, Leitenberg, Coffey, Bennett, and Jankowski (1997) found that both male and female young adults who reported witnessing violence between the parents indicated experiencing higher levels of psychological distress than controls. However, witnessing the same-sex parent's victimization *increased* the negative impact on the individual. So for women, while distress was related to witnessed abuse from the father to the mother, abuse by the mother was not related to increased psychological distress. Kolbo (1996) also found that while domestic violence negatively affected both boys and girls, girls tended to evidence more behavioral problems than boys. Likewise, Forsstrom-Cohen and Rosenbaum (1985) found that both male and female witnesses of domestic violence suffered from increased anxiety; however, only females showed higher levels of aggression too.

It is also possible that for the female participants, the father's use of violence against the mother is also co-occurring with violence perpetrated against her, while this may not be the case for witnessed abuse by the mother. For instance, O'Keefe (1994), found an association between the amount of marital violence witnessed in the home and an increased likelihood of the father perpetrating abuse against the child, but this connection was not found for the mother. So, while the mother may have engaged in or been the victim of violence in the home, this did not coincide with increased use of violence against the child. In our sample, too, witnessing and experiencing violence, especially from the father, tended to predict both abusing the partner as well as being abused, indicating that for females, paternal aggressiveness is a more salient predictor both of their acting out aggressively as well as being vulnerable to victimization.

The grief index and the fearful-attachment style both independently predicted perpetrating physical abuse for the female participants; moreover, the interaction between these variables provided even more predictive power than either of them alone. Likewise, scores on the grief index and preoccupied attachment showed an interactive effect, wherein the predictive power of both combined was stronger for predicting the experience of physical abuse from the partner. Fraley and Shaver (1999) have noted that individuals with this combination of anxiety and ambivalence seem to have organized their working model of attachment around the notion that the attachment figure will not be available or is not trustworthy and are hypervigilant to signs of abandonment or potential loss of the attachment figure. Behavioral expressions that can be seen as an attempt to retain or prevent the loss of the attachment figure, such as jealousy, anger, and the use of violence, are all more characteristic of individuals with an internal model of attachment evidencing an anxious component. For instance, Davis, Shaver, and Vernon (2003) found that based on attachment styles, individuals had different physical, emotional, and behavioral reactions to the dissolution of a romantic relationship. Avoidant attachment was associated with less use of social resources, greater self-reliance, and avoiding the partner in response to the dissolution of a romantic relationship. Individuals who were high in attachment anxiety were more likely to seek support from others, but also to have stronger grief reactions, such as the use of drugs or alcohol as a dysfunctional coping strategy, to report greater physical and emotional distress over the loss and to report greater preoccupation with and desire for the lost partner. Paradoxically, anxious attachment was also related to greater anger, hostility, and vengeful behavior directed towards the partner. Although physical violence was found to occur at a low rate in the overall sample, reported attachment anxiety was higher among those who reported having physically hurt the partner than among those who did not engage in this behavior.

The results of our study seem to indicate that the combination of childhood experiences of violence, grief reactions, and insecure attachment all provide a viable model for predicting intimate relationship violence. In particular, the combination of grief reactions and anxious or fearful attachment seemed

172 / PERSPECTIVES ON VIOLENCE AND VIOLENT DEATH

particularly salient. However, care should be taken not to overinterpret these findings as evidence of a deterministic and inevitable path to violence for individuals who experienced childhood abuse, find themselves dealing with resulting grief, or possessing an insecure attachment style. The literature on dating violence has found that although young adults from abusive households report higher incidence of violence in their own dating relationships (and a greater likelihood of remaining in a violent relationship rather than ending it), in actuality only one in five who came from an abusive home reported dating violence in their own relationship (Smith & Williams, 1992). Likewise, Bonanno (2004) has noted that in the face of adversity and trauma, individuals are far more resilient and experience less disruption to functioning than what has been commonly believed by both lay people and clinicians. The model we investigated provided tentative evidence for a constellation of life experiences and reactions to those experiences that may increase susceptibility to perpetrating or being the victim of violence. However, the model does not contradict the reality that there is room for resiliency in many people's lives. Indeed, even for those who may need clinical intervention, healthy psychological and physical well-being and less violent ways of interacting are indeed possible.

REFERENCES

Aber, J. L., & Allen, J. P. (1987). Effects of maltreatment on young children's socioemotional development: An attachment theory perspective. *Developmental Psychology, 23,* 406-414.

Ainsworth, D. (1973). The development of infant mother attachment. In B. M. Caldwell & H. N. Ricciuti (Eds.), *Review of child development research* (Vol. 3., pp. 1-94), Chicago: University of Chicago Press.

Ainsworth, M. D. S., Blehar, M. C., Waters, E., & Wall, S. (1978). *Patterns of attachment: A psychological study of the strange situation.* Hillsdale, NJ: Erlbaum.

Alexander, P. C. (1992). Applications of attachment theory to the study of sexual abuse. *Journal of Consulting and Clinical Psychology, 60,* 185-195.

Barnett, O. W., Martinez, T., & Bluestein, B. W. (1995). Jealousy and romantic attachment in martially violent and non-violent men. *Journal of Interpersonal Violence, 10,* 473-486.

Bartholomew, K., & Horowitz, L. M. (1991). Attachment styles among young adults: A test of a four-category model. *Journal of Personality and Social Psychology, 61,* 226-244.

Bonanno, G. A. (2004). Loss, trauma, and human resilience. *American Psychologist, 59*(1), 20-28.

Bonanno, G. A., Wortman, C. B., Lehman, D. R., Tweed, R. G., Haring, M., Sonnega, J., Carr, D., & Nesse, R. M. (2002). Resilience to loss and chronic grief: A prospective study from preloss to 18 months postloss. *Journal of Personality and Social Psychology, 83*(5), 1150-1164.

Bookwalla, J., Frieze, I. H., Smith, C., & Ryan, K. (1992). Predictors of dating violence: A multivariate analysis. *Violence and Victims, 7*(4), 295-311.

Bowlby, J. (1969). *Attachment and loss. Vol. 1. Attachment.* New York: Basic Books.

Bowlby, J. (1980). *Attachment and loss: Vol. 3. Loss: Sadness and depression.* New York: Basic Books.

Bowlby, J. (1984). Violence in the family as a disorder of the attachment and caregiving systems. *American Journal of Psychiatry, 145*(1), 1-10.

Bowlby, J. (1988). *A secure base: Parent-child attachment and healthy human development.* New York: Basic Books.

Carlson, V., Cicchetti, D., Barnett, D., & Braunwald, K. G. (1989). Disorganized/disoriented attachment relationships in maltreated infants. *Developmental Psychology, 25,* 525-531.

Cicchetti, D., & Barnett, D. (1991). Attachment organization in maltreated preschoolers. *Development and Psychopathology, 3*(4), 397-411.

Cohen, J. A., Mannarino, A. P., Greenberg, T., Padlo, S., & Shipley, C. (2002). Childhood traumatic grief: Concepts and controversies. *Trauma, Violence, & Abuse, 3*(4), 307-327.

Cohen, J. A., Mannarino, A. P., & Knudsen, K. (2005). Treating sexually abused children: 1 year follow-up of a randomized controlled trial. *Child Abuse & Neglect, 29,* 135-145.

Courtois, C. A. (1988). *Healing the incest wound.* New York: W. W. Norton & Co.

Davis, D., Shaver, P. R., & Vernon, M. L. (2003). Physical, emotional, and behavioral reactions to breaking up: The roles of gender, age, emotional involvement, and attachment style. *Personality and Social Psychology Bulletin, 29*(7), 871-884.

Diamond, T., & Muller, R. T. (2004). The relationship between witnessing parental conflict during childhood and later psychological adjustment among university students: Disentangling confounding risk factor. *Canadian Journal of Behavioral Science, 36*(4), 295-309.

Dutton, D. G., Saunders, K., Starzomski, A. J., & Bartholomew, K. (1994). Intimacy-anger and insecure attachment as precursors of abuse in intimate relationships. *Journal of Applied Social Psychology, 24,* 1367-1386.

Egeland, B., & Sroufe, L. A. (1981). Attachment and early maltreatment. *Child Development, 52*(1), 44-52.

Ethier, L. S., Lemelin, J. P., & Lacharite, C. (2004). A longitudinal study of the effects of chronic maltreatment on children's behavioral and emotional problems. *Child Abuse & Neglect, 28,* 1265-1278.

Farber, E. W., Herbert, S. E., &. Reviere, S. L. (1996). Childhood abuse and suicidality in obstetrics patients in a hospital-based urban prenatal clinic. *General Hospital Psychiatry, 18,* 56-60.

Feerick, M. M., & Haugaard, J. J. (1999). Long-term effects of witnessing marital violence for women: The contribution of childhood physical and sexual abuse. *Journal of Family Violence, 14*(4), 377-398.

Forsstrom-Cohen, B., & Rosenbaum, A. (1985). The effects of parental martial violence on young adults: An exploratory investigation. *Journal of Marriage and the Family, 47,* 467-472.

Fox, J. A., & Zawitz, M. W. (2002). Homicide trends in the United States. *U.S. Department of Justice, Bureau of Justice Statistics.* Retrieved November 15, 2004, from www.ojp.usdoj.gov/bjs/homicide/homtrnd.htm

174 / PERSPECTIVES ON VIOLENCE AND VIOLENT DEATH

Fraley, R. C., & Bonanno, G. A. (2004). Attachment and loss: A test of three competing models on the association between attachment-related avoidance and adaptation to bereavement. *Personality and Social Psychology Bulletin, 30*(7), 878-890.

Fraley, R. C., & Shaver, P. R. (1999). Loss and bereavement: Attachment theory and recent controversies concerning "grief work" and the nature of detachment. In J. Cassidy & P. R. Shaver (Eds.), *Handbook of attachment: Theory, research and clinical practice* (pp. 735-759). New York: Guilford.

Gagne, M., & Lavoie, F. (1993). Young people's view on the causes of violence in adolescents' romantic relationships. *Canada's Mental Health, 41,* 11-15.

Hazan, C., & Shaver, P. R. (1987). Conceptualizing romantic love as an attachment process. *Journal of Personality and Social Psychology, 52,* 511-524.

Henderson, A. J. Z., Bartholomew, K., & Dutton, D. G. (1997). He loves me; He loves me not: Attachment and separation resolution of abused women. *Journal of Family Violence, 12,* 169-192.

Henning, K., Leitenberg, H., Coffey, P., Bennett, T., & Jankowski, M. K. (1997). Long-term psychological adjustment to witnessing interparental physical conflict during childhood. *Child Abuse and Neglect, 21*(6), 501-515.

Holden, G. W., & Ritchie, K. L. (1991). Linking extreme martial discord, childrearing, and child behavior problems: Evidence from battered women. *Child Development, 62,* 311-327.

Holtzworth-Monroe, A., Stuart, G., & Hutchinson, G. (1997). Violent versus nonviolent husbands: Differences in attachment patterns, dependency, and jealousy. *Journal of Family Psychology, 11*(3), 314-331.

Hudson, S. M., & Ward, T. (1997). Intimacy, loneliness, and attachment style in sexual offenders. *Journal of Interpersonal Violence, 12*(3), 323-339.

Johnson, R. M., Kotch, J. B., Catellier, D. J., Winsor, J. R., Dufort, V., Hunter, W., & Amaya-Jackson, L. (2002). Adverse behavioral and emotional outcomes from child abuse and witnessed violence. *Child Maltreatment, 7,* 179-186.

Kolbo, J. R. (1996). Risk and resilience among children exposed to family violence. *Violence and Victims, 11*(2), 113-128.

Lyons-Ruth, K., Connell, D. B., Grunebaum, H. U., & Botein, S. (1990). Infants at social risk: Maternal depression and family support services as mediators of infant development and security of attachment. *Child Development, 61*(1), 85-98.

Lyons-Ruth, K., & Jacobvitz, D. (1999). Attachment disorganization: Unresolved loss, relational violence, and lapses in behavioral and attentional strategies. In J. Cassidy & P. R. Shaver (Eds.), *Handbook of attachment: Theory, research and clinical practice* (pp. 735-759). New York: Guilford.

Main, M., & Solomon, J. (1990). Procedures for identifying infants as Disorganized/disoriented during the Ainsworth Strange Situation. In M. T. Greenburg, D. Cicchetti, & E. M. Cummings (Eds.), *Attachment in the preschool years: Theory, research and intervention* (pp. 121-160). Chicago: University of Chicago Press.

Mathes, E. W. (1984). Convergence among measures of interpersonal attraction. *Motivation and Emotion, 8,* 77-84.

Mayseless, O. (1991). Adult attachment patterns and courtship violence. *Family Relations, 40,* 21-28.

McLeer, S. V., Deblinger, E., Atkins, M. S., Foa, E. B., & Ralphe, D. L. (1988). Post-traumatic stress disorder in sexually abused children. *Journal of the American Academy of Child and Adolescent Psychiatry, 27,* 650-654.

Moos, R. H., & Schaefer, J. A. (1986). Life transitions and crises: A conceptual overview. In R. H. Moos & J. A. Schaefer (Eds.), *Coping with life crises: An integrated approach* (pp. 3-28). New York: Plenum Press.

Morton, N., & Browne, K. D. (1998). Theory and observation of attachment and its relation to child maltreatment: A review. *Child Neglect and Abuse, 22*(11), 1093-1104.

Neimeyer, R. A., Prigerson, H. G., & Davis, B. (2002). Mourning and meaning. *American Behavioral Scientist, 46*(2), 235-251.

O'Hearn, R. E., & Davis, K. E. (1997). Women's experiences of giving and receiving emotional abuse. *Journal of Interpersonal Violence, 12*(3), 375-381.

O'Keefe, M. (1994). Linking marital violence, mother-child/father-child aggression, and child behavior problems. *Journal of Family Violence, 9*(1), 63-75.

Owen, M. T., & Cox, M. J. (1997). Marital conflict and the development of infant-parent attachment relationships. *Journal of Family Psychology, 11*(2), 152-164.

Parkes, C. M. (1972). *Bereavement.* London: Tavistock.

Prigerson, H. G., Shear, M. K., Frank, E., Beery, L. C., Silberman, R., Prigerson, J., & Reynolds, C. F. (1997). Traumatic grief: A case of loss induced trauma. *American Journal of Psychiatry, 154*(7), 1003-1009.

Russell, B., & Uhlemann, M. R. (1994). Women surviving an abusive relationship: Grief and the process of change. *Journal of Counseling and Development, 72*(4), 362-368.

Saywitz, K., Mannarino, A. P., Berliner, L., & Cohen, J. A. (2000). Treatment for children who have been sexually abused, *American Psychologist, 55,* 1040-1049.

Scarr, S. (1992). Developmental theories for the 1990s: Development and individual differences. *Child Development, 63,* 119.

Seigel, J. M. (1986). The multidimensional anger inventory. *Journal of Personality and Social Psychology, 51,* 191-200.

Shea, A., Walsh, C., MacMillan, H., & Steiner, M. (2004). Child maltreatment and HPA axis dysregulation: Relationship to major depressive disorder and post traumatic stress disorder in females. *Psychoneuroendocrinology, 30,* 162-178.

Smith, J. P., & Williams, J. G. (1992). From abusive household to dating violence. *Journal of Family Violence, 7*(2), 153-165.

Stets, J. E., & Pirog-Good, M. A. (1987). Violence in dating relationships. *Social Psychology Quarterly, 50*(3), 237-246.

Straus, M. A. (1979). Measuring intrafamily conflict and violence: The Conflict Tactics Scale. *Journal of Marriage and the Family, 41,* 75-88.

Straus, M. A., Gelles, R., & Steinmetz, S. (1980). *Behind closed doors: Violence in American families.* New York: Doubleday.

Swett, C., & Halpert, M. (1993). Reported history of physical and sexual abuse in relation to dissociation and other symptomatology in women psychiatric inpatients. *Journal of Interpersonal Violence, 8,* 545-555.

Toth, S. L., Manly, J. T., & Cicchetti, D. (1992). Child maltreatment and vulnerability to depression. *Development and Psychopathology, 4,* 97-112.

176 / PERSPECTIVES ON VIOLENCE AND VIOLENT DEATH

Tsun-Yin, E. L. (1998). Sexual abuse trauma among Chinese survivors. *Child Abuse & Neglect, 22,* 1013–1026.

Worden, J. W. (1991). *Grief counseling & grief therapy: A handbook for the mental health practitioner* (2nd ed.). New York: Springer.

Zeanah, C. H., Scheeringa, M., Boris, N. W., Heller, S. S., Smyle, A. T., & Trapani, J. (2004). Reactive attachment disorder in maltreated toddlers. *Child Abuse and Neglect, 28*(8), 877-888.

CHAPTER 12

Bereavement Following Violent Death: An Assault on Life and Meaning

Joseph M. Currier
Jason M. Holland
Rachel A. Coleman
Robert A. Neimeyer

Central to understanding our lives as human beings is an understanding of how we deal with loss (Viorst, 1986). Whether we think of loss generally as a theme that weaves throughout our lives in innumerable situational and developmental changes, crises, and transitions, or narrow our focus to the death of family members, friends, colleagues, or acquaintances, few events in life are more devastating than the loss of a loved one to violent death (Davis, Wortman, Lehman, & Cohen Silver, 2000; Rynearson, 2001). Thus, identifying the specific factors that contribute to the challenges posed by bereavement following violent death has become a high priority for clinical researchers and practicing professionals alike.

Typically, violent death is characterized by one of three unnatural modes of dying: suicide, homicide, or accident (e.g., vehicle crash, drowning, natural disaster). Rynearson (1994, 2001) has offered a framework for identifying the defining features of such death, which he terms "The Three V's." First, the act of dying is *violent*; that is, a forceful, physically painful, and suddenly traumatic act, which frequently causes mutilating injuries. Second, the dying is commonly a *violation*; that is, a transgression that directly disregards the individual rights of the deceased and surviving loved ones. Finally, the dying can follow from *volition*; that is, an intentional or freely chosen act on the part of the perpetrator (in cases of murder) or victim (in instances of suicide).

It appears that violent deaths frequently invalidate the comforting belief among many people that there is protection from violence and inhumanity (Rynearson,

178 / PERSPECTIVES ON VIOLENCE AND VIOLENT DEATH

1986), an invalidation that can leave survivors at risk of greater psychological distress when compared with those losing a loved one to natural death (Davis et al., 2000; Dyregrov, Nordanger, & Dyregrov, 2003; Kaltman & Bonanno, 2003). Unfortunately, this heightened vulnerability to psychological trauma (Green, 2000; Neria & Litz, 2003) and complicated grief (Prigerson & Jacobs, 2001) is often reinforced by the community's reactions to the bereaved (Armour, 2003; Riches & Dawson, 1998), which can include stigmatization (Jordan, 2001), "social ineptitude" or lack of helpful responses from one's support network (Dyregrov, 2003), unempathic responses from friends and family members (Calhoun, Selby, & Abernathy, 1984; Neimeyer & Jordan, 2002), and the tendency of investigative and judicial institutions that pressure the bereaved to seek retribution (Riches & Dawson, 1998). In view of the multiple challenges facing those bereaved by violent means, the purpose of the current chapter is to (1) review the available literature on the intrapersonal and interpersonal implications of bereavement following violent death; (2) offer new data on factors associated with adaptation to violent death in a large sample of recently bereaved college students; and (3) conclude with a discussion of the clinical implications of our preliminary findings and other available evidence.

INTRAPERSONAL IMPLICATIONS OF VIOLENT DEATH

There is consensus that losing a loved one to violent death is associated with poor recovery for bereaved individuals (Rando 1992, 1996; Stroebe & Schut, 2001). From a trauma perspective, losses from violent deaths are likely to promote reactions resembling posttraumatic stress disorder (PTSD; Bonanno & Kaltman, 1999; Green, 2000). Some researchers suggest that psychological trauma involves a violation of basic assumptive worldviews connected with the individual's survival and that of the social group (Brewin, Dalgleish, & Joseph, 1996; Matthews & Marwit, 2004; Schwartzberg & Janoff-Bulman, 1991). Therefore, loss by suicide, homicide, or accident is commonly conceptualized as a traumatic event that can lead to PTSD, thereby causing profound complications in grieving and difficulties with meaning making (Neimeyer, 2002) that persist over time. In accordance with the recommendations of some researchers (e.g., Schut, De Keijser, Van Den Bout, & Dijkhuis, 1991), changes to the PTSD diagnosis in the Fourth Edition of the Diagnostic and Statistical Manual of Mental Disorders widened the scope of the stressor criterion from an "event outside the normal range of human experience" to include "learning about the unexpected or violent death . . . experienced by a family member or close associate" (DSM-IV, APA, 1994, p. 424), thereby providing a legitimate bridge into exploring this complex interface between trauma and complicated bereavement following violent death.

Historically, most of the evidence linking violent-death bereavement with PTSD has been found following deaths by homicide (Green et al., 2001; Rynearson, 1994). Yet it should be noted that contrary to studies of deaths by suicide or accident, studies of homicide survivors have focused more on the assessment of PTSD symptoms and have generally found symptoms to be heightened in survivors of this type of death, compared with other types of violent deaths (Murphy et al., 1999; Murphy, Johnson, Chung, & Beaton, 2003b; Thompson, Norris, & Ruback, 1998). Empirical studies of homicidal bereavement have found prolonged responses of grief mixed with intense responses of trauma (Green, 2000; Redmond, 1996; Rynearson, 2001). Psychological trauma is associated with the horrific events of the murder, as seen by recurrent experiences of intrusive reenactment and reexperiencing symptoms, avoidance, hyperarousal, grotesque death imagery, victimization, and despair (Rando, 1996; Redmond, 1996; Rynearson, 1986, 1994). Interestingly, this "post-traumatic imagery" (Rynearson, 2001), which can prove so disturbing in the immediate aftermath of the loss and over time, evidently does not require the survivor to have been present at the murder scene as an eyewitness (Green, 2000). Rather, it appears that the reliving of an unwitnessed death by homicide can prove so visual, kinesthetic, and overwhelming that the bereaved frequently suffer in silent estrangement from themselves and the larger world (Rynearson, 1994).

Numerous researchers suggest that *complicated grief* following violent death generally triggers two concurrent but distinct syndromes: (1) *separation distress* as a response to the lost relationship and (2) *traumatic distress* in reaction to the manner of the dying (Prigerson et al., 1999; Prigerson & Jacobs, 2001; Rynearson & Sinnema, 1999). Traumatic distress includes reenactment thoughts, feelings of fear, and behavioral avoidance. Separation distress includes thoughts of reunion, feelings of longing, and searching behaviors for the deceased. These two distress responses are often mixed in the course of complicated bereavement. Although the "loss as trauma" framework might fail to capture the unique experiences of those who suffer from complicated grief (Green, 2000; Green et al., 2001; Neria & Litz, 2003), it has been theorized that those persons who are bereaved by violent means will usually present with sustained trauma distress, which overshadows separation distress in its intensity (Rynearson & Sinnema, 1999).

Several empirical studies have provided support for the proposition that those who have lost a loved one to violent death frequently experience symptomology consistent with traumatic distress. For example, Murphy and her colleagues (1999) studied 171 parents during the first 2 years of bereavement following the violent deaths of their children. The proportions of mothers who met PTSD criteria increased from 5% to 14% over a 20-month period. When compared with the base rates of PTSD in the "normal" population (Breslau, 2002; Helzer, Robins, & McEvoy, 1987), it appears that these findings are likely due to the nature of the death, and they additionally highlight the enduring nature of traumatic distress associated with recovery from violent bereavement. Evidence for the

180 / PERSPECTIVES ON VIOLENCE AND VIOLENT DEATH

psychosocial impact of such bereavement has been reported by Hardison, Neimeyer, and Lichstein (2005), who found that loss of a loved one through accident, suicide, or homicide was more commonly associated with both complicated grief symptomatology and the diagnosis of insomnia than was loss through natural causes. Another study by Thompson et al. (1998) found that 26% of a sample of 150 family members who lost a loved one to homicide could be considered clinically distressed, based on their scoring at least two standard deviations above race- and gender-appropriate norms on measures of depression, anxiety, somatization, or hostility. Furthermore, contrary to traditional grief theory, with its emphasis on "working through" to the achievement of resolution or closure (Freud, 1957), these researchers did not find that time since homicide predicted posthomicide distress, instead indicating that distress did not dramatically lessen over time.

Several empirical studies have corroborated the finding that violent death is associated with long-term distress (i.e., more than six months), which might compromise numerous primary and secondary areas of psychosocial functioning (Dyregrov et al., 2003; Lehman, Lang, Wortman, & Sorenson, 1989). In one such study, Lehman and his associates (1987) conducted interviews with 39 individuals who had lost a spouse in a motor vehicle crash and 41 parents who had lost a child in a crash 4 to 7 years previously, evaluating such factors as depression, coping strategies, psychological well-being, and overall adjustment. The researchers then completed interviews with 80 controls. In comparing the bereaved with the control respondents, the researchers found significantly poorer functioning for the former group on all measures. Violent bereavement was also associated with an increased mortality rate, a drop in financial status, and a higher divorce rate among the bereaved parents. There was additional evidence in both parents and spouses that the loss continued to occupy their thoughts, as many of the bereaved continued to ruminate about the accident or what they might have done to prevent it, and they appeared unable to accept, resolve, or find any meaning in the loss.

Together, studies such as these indicate that violent deaths might not only promote the development of traumatic distress symptoms but also exacerbate the more general grief response, engendering prolonged primary and secondary difficulties with grieving and life readjustment. From a broadly constructivist standpoint, these heightened levels of distress following violent death can be understood as expressions of underlying struggles with meaning making (Neimeyer, 1998, 2001, 2005a, 2005b). That is, particularly disturbing events, such as the violent death of a loved one, can profoundly challenge or sometimes even shatter individuals' core assumptions about themselves, the surrounding world, and other people (Janoff-Bulman, 1992). Thus, in instances of violent death, a central process in adaptation to bereavement entails the survivor's struggle to consolidate his or her understanding of the loss into broader meaning structures. To the extent that survivors are able to integrate such tragic losses into an intact and predominantly positive "self narrative" or system of personal meaning, they are able to respond with resilience and comparatively limited and short-term symptomatology. Conversely, when they assimilate the trauma into a stable but predominantly negative meaning system, they risk exacerbating preexisting depressive or fatalistic adjustment to life events (Neimeyer, 2005c). Finally, when traumatic loss sunders a previously optimistic self narrative, it may set in motion a protracted struggle to accommodate the person's meaning system to new and harsh realities, eventuating in significant posttraumatic growth (Calhoun & Tedeschi, 2001) if such an effort is successful, or chronic and complicated grief (Neimeyer, Prigerson, & Davies, 2002) when it is not. Such a conceptualization is compatible with longitudinal research on various trajectories through bereavement (Bonanno, Wortman, & Nesse, 2004), as well as a good deal of other recent research on adaptive and maladaptive grief (Neimeyer, 2005c).

Unfortunately, the existing empirical literature suggests that the successful integration of losses associated with violent modes of dying eludes the majority of bereaved individuals (Armour, 2003; Davis et al., 2000; Matthews & Marwit, 2004; Murphy, Johnson, & Lohan, 2003a). Although evidence is not entirely consistent, when the loss occurs suddenly and without warning, it appears to pose grave obstacles to sense-making or comprehending the event and its implication for the survivor's life (Davis et al., 2000; Janoff-Bulman, 1992). Additionally, if the death occurred as a result of an intentional act, such as in instances of suicide and homicide, research shows that the loss will be more difficult to resolve than if the death were due to normal circumstances (Rynearson, 2001). Armour (2003, p. 519) powerfully describes the predicament of these violently bereaved individuals: "As their meaning systems implode, they enter into a netherworld where they fight to find footing in a world that no longer fits."

Successful adaptation in this "netherworld" of "shattered assumptions" depends upon somehow squaring the appraised meaning of the traumatic loss and long-standing global beliefs about life's order and purpose, including convictions about the world's benevolence, a sense of fairness and predictable order, and evaluations of one's self as worthy (Janoff-Bulman, 1992). Interestingly, this process of finding meaning can even prove difficult in instances of nonviolent loss or bereavement by natural means, especially in the immediate aftermath of the loss (Schwartzberg & Janoff-Bulman, 1991). Considering objectively traumatic stressors, such as death by suicide, homicide, or accident, it is therefore not surprising that violent death can challenge the global meaning system at its most fundamental level because beliefs about how and why things happen no longer seem plausible (Bonanno & Kaltman, 1999; Neimeyer, 2002). Thus, rather than simply "letting go" and "moving forward," the bereaved frequently face the arduous and perplexing task of reconstructing life's most basic meanings in the wake of a shattering experience.

Neimeyer and Anderson (2002) have proposed a framework for this process of meaning reconstruction that holds relevance for those dealing with violent death. They have theorized that this meaning-making process occurs along three

182 / PERSPECTIVES ON VIOLENCE AND VIOLENT DEATH

different paths: (1) sense-making; (2) benefit-finding; and (3) identity reconstruction. First, sense-making reflects the ability to find some sort of explanation for the seemingly inexplicable loss. Second, benefit-finding entails the paradoxical ability in the long term to find spiritual, existential, and personal benefits in the loss (e.g., "I feel closer to God after the loss," "I appreciate life more because of the loss.") Finally, identity reconstruction includes the reorganization of one's identity at social as well as individual levels following the experience of fragmentation associated with the loss. Taken together, these three contexts of meaning making help the bereaved endure and synthesize the painful feelings of distress and sometimes even grow as a result of the traumatic loss (Calhoun & Tedeschi, 2001).

INTERPERSONAL IMPLICATIONS OF VIOLENT DEATH

Neimeyer and Anderson (2002) additionally emphasize that this process of meaning making is not simply negotiated as an intrapersonal process. Rather, particularly for individuals in great distress, the reconstruction of meaning in the wake of loss is inherently shared with others. Therefore, the ability to find meaning by constructing a coherent narrative of bereavement may be largely dependent on a supportive and validating social network. Nevertheless, in instances of violent death, it is sadly the case that the potential restorative functions of the bereaved person's social network are often obscured and undermined by the catastrophic nature of the loss itself.

Although bereavement following violent death is commonly characterized by enduring complications in grieving and profound difficulties with meaning making, survivors rarely receive consistent affirmation and support by their social networks (Allen, Calhoun, Cann, & Tedeschi, 1993; Calhoun & Allen, 1991; Dyregrov et al., 2003). In instances of bereavement, social support usually refers to the emotional, economic, and practical help or information provided to the bereaved by family, friends, neighbors, colleagues, and other members of the community (Dyregrov, 2003). Not surprisingly, research has clearly shown that social support can prove particularly helpful to those recovering from bereavement. It is suggested by some researchers that social support is an important mediating variable for healthy bereavement outcomes (Barlow & Coleman, 2003). Similarly, cognitive-stress theory supposes that high levels of social support are thought to protect the bereaved individual against the harmful impact of stress on health and promote long-term loss accommodation. Although this "buffering model" has not received consistent empirical support (Stroebe, Stroebe, Schut, & Abakoumkin, 1996), the consensus among researchers and most survivors appears to reinforce the supposition that friends and family members can be a great help to bereaved individuals. For example, Stroebe and his colleagues (1996) conducted a longitudinal study of a matched sample of 60 recently widowed and 60 married persons and found that respondents who perceived the social support available to them as high reported less depressive and somatic symptoms than individuals who perceived the availability of social support as low. Also, Ott (2003) has reported that those bereaved persons who experienced less social support were especially likely to struggle with symptoms of complicated grief over an 18-month period.

Tragically, despite the frequent involvement of outside parties following violent death, it seems that persons bereaved by suicide, murder, or accident are at increased risk of experiencing *disenfranchised grief* (Doka, 1989). In other words, especially with the cultural presuppositions attached to suicide and murder, these persons might experience a loss that is not or cannot be openly acknowledged, publicly mourned, or socially supported. It is a paradox that the very nature of disenfranchised grief can create additional complications to bereavement recovery from violent death, while simultaneously removing or minimizing sources of social and emotional support. For example, consider bereavement following the murder of an urban adolescent with a known history of involvement with a street gang, truancy, deviance, and potential violent behaviors. In instances such as these, the expression of grief on the part of some bereaved family members might be met with "empathic failure" (Neimeyer & Jordan, 2002) by members of the broader community and possibly even some in the kinship network itself, due to ascriptions of blame and feelings of anger toward the victim for his antisocial lifestyle.

In an effort to shed some light on this trend, research in the area of criminal justice has demonstrated that criminal offending increases a person's risk for lethal victimization (Dobrin, 2001). Explanations for this relationship between delinquency and homicide victimization in particular include a higher frequency of interactions with other criminals, inability to rely on legal authorities for protection, and the increased likelihood of becoming the object of retaliatory behavior (Dobrin, 2001). Considering the potential perceptions attached to the role of personal responsibility in circumstances leading to violent death, it is not surprising that the cause of death (violent or natural) has been found to affect the social experience of the bereaved (Calhoun & Allen, 1991; Dannemiller, 2002; Dyregrov, 2003), as survivors often need to provide explanations regarding the nature of the death (Range & Calhoun, 1990) and harbor more intense feelings of guilt when compared with persons dealing with deaths from natural causes (Allen, Calhoun, Cann, & Tedeschi, 1993).

One common explanation that researchers have offered for the phenomenon of disenfranchised grief following violent death involves a lack of clear societal guidelines for interacting with these survivors in our culture (Calhoun & Allen, 1991; Rando, 1996). For example, in an effort to explore the reasons why the social support system so often fails survivors of traumatic deaths, Dyregrov (2003) conducted a qualitative study with 69 parents who lost their offspring to suicide,

184 / PERSPECTIVES ON VIOLENCE AND VIOLENT DEATH

SIDS, or accident. She found that despite some positive experiences with social supports, the majority of survivors also experienced the "social ineptitude" of family, friends, neighbors, and co-workers, defined in terms of the "difficulty a social network encounters in responding to and supporting those bereaved by traumatic deaths in a manner that is appreciated by the bereaved" (p. 31). Interestingly, the survivors did not attribute their experience of social ineptitude to indifference or lack of concern on the parts of social supports; rather, they explained it in terms of the lack of norms to guide this uncommon type of social encounter.

Coupled with this dearth of social norms, the distress arising from violent death is increased by the stigma commonly attached to the suicide, murder, or accident (Calhoun & Allen, 1991; Dannemiller, 2002; Jordan, 2001) and by criminal proceedings that sometimes eclipse the anguish of bereaved family members (Riches & Dawson, 1998). Common themes expressed by the bereaved include outrage and a sense of unique loneliness arising from the horror of the death itself, in addition to frustration arising from inadequacies of the criminal justice system. In another study, Dyregrov and her colleagues (2003) found that social isolation of the bereaved following loss by suicide, SIDS, or accident was the best predictor of psychosocial distress. Although these results do not provide a clear causal explanation for such loneliness, they add support to studies that have demonstrated that survivors of violent death frequently become more isolated and distressed than other bereaved groups (Armour, 2003; Seguin, Lesage, & Kiely, 1995). Furthermore, for many violent deaths, news media reports might produce notoriety for the victim and their families, especially if the victim is linked with deviant behaviors or the lifestyle of the perpetrator(s) of the violent act (Barlow & Coleman, 2003; Riches & Dawson, 1998). Thus, because the journey of healing for survivors of violent death typically takes place in the public eye, the central process of meaning reconstruction inevitably becomes both an intrapersonal and interpersonal event (Armour, 2003).

Although disagreement persists as to whether suicidal bereavement should be viewed as more distressing when compared with bereavement following homicide or accidental death (Ellenbogen & Gratton, 2001; Jordan, 2001; McIntosh, 1993; Murphy, Johnson, & Lohan, 2003b), there appears to be consensus in the literature that social interactions between suicide survivors and others are problematic (Calhoun, Selby, & Abernathy, 1984; Clark, 2001; Hawton & Simkin, 2003). It has been argued that suicide is perceived by potentially supportive others as a more difficult type of death with which to cope, and that interactions with survivors of suicidal death are seen as more stressful for these persons (Calhoun, Selby, & Abernathy, 1984). Also, it is suggested that finding meaning in these circumstances can prove a daunting task for the bereaved, who might harbor intense feelings of guilt, responsibility, rejection, anger, and shame (Allen et al., 1993; Hawton & Simkin, 2003; Jordan, 2001; Range & Calhoun, 1990), as well as questioning their own value system (Clark, 2001), though these themes can be seen in bereavement following homicide (Rynearson, 2001) and accident (Davis et al., 2000; Lehman et al., 1987) as well.

Regarding the interpersonal implications of suicidal bereavement, it is suggested that these survivors feel more isolated and stigmatized than other mourners and may in fact be viewed more negatively by others in their social networks and by themselves. The greater isolation and stigmatization of the suicidally bereaved was reported by Calhoun and Allen (1991), who found that they seemed to absorb the negative stigma attached to the suicidal act and were in fact viewed by others as more psychologically disturbed, less likable, more blameworthy, more ashamed, more in need of professional mental-health care, and more likely to remain sad and evaluated negatively by others. Furthermore, some have argued that suicide might prove especially difficult for the family unit, leading to breakdowns in family interaction patterns and heightened risk for future suicide among surviving family members (Clark, 2001).

As highlighted earlier with regard to the explicit focus on the assessment of PTSD symptoms in studies of homicidal bereavement, the outcomes being considered in studies of suicidal bereavement are also important to consider. In light of claims that death by suicide, particularly when the loss involves a child, results in the worst bereavement outcomes, Murphy, Johnson, and Lohan (2003b) caution that empirical study of the effect of deaths by suicide on survivors has a thirty-year history, whereas the effect of deaths by homicide has a very brief history, suggesting that more comparative research is required to evaluate the unique challenges associated with each. Beyond the sheer intensity of distress, it could be hypothesized that persons bereaved by different modes of violent death experience different symptom profiles.

STUDY AIMS

In light of this review of the available literature on bereavement related to violent death, the following questions arise: Do survivors of violent death experience greater levels of psychological distress and complicated grief symptoms when compared with persons bereaved by natural means? How do survivors of different modes of violent death compare with one another on these same outcomes? What groups are most likely to confront significant struggles with the process of meaning making in the three contexts of sense-making, benefit-finding, and identity reconstruction? Are the interpersonal ramifications (e.g., for social support) similar or different for individuals bereaved by various forms of violent and nonviolent deaths? To answer these questions, the present empirical study explores the differences in (1) psychological distress, (2) meaning reconstruction, and (3) psychosocial responses of survivors of violent and nonviolent deaths in a large and diverse cohort of college students contending with the loss of a wide range of significant others.

186 / PERSPECTIVES ON VIOLENCE AND VIOLENT DEATH

METHODS

Participants

Seventeen hundred twenty-three participants from undergraduate psychology courses from a large southern urban university were recruited. Participants met the following two criteria for eligibility in this study: (1) each was at least eighteen years in age; and (2) each reported the death of a friend or loved one within the past two years. The basis for this latter requisite stems from past research that suggests that significant bereavement phenomena can be observed over 24 months, or longer in some cases (Prigerson & Jacobs, 2001).

The current sample ranged in age from 18 to 60 years with a mean of 20.71 years. Women made up 74% of the sample, and 26% were men. In addition, 56% of the participants were Caucasian, 39.3% African American, 1.5% Asian American, and roughly 5% were of another ethnicity, reflecting the undergraduate distribution of ethnicities at the urban research institution. Approximately 28% of the reported losses in the current sample were due to homicide ($n = 100$), suicide ($n = 78$), or accident ($n = 303$). The remaining 72% of the losses reported by participants were due to either natural anticipated causes, such as deaths from cancer and other progressive diseases ($n = 748$); natural sudden causes, such as heart failure ($n = 359$); or other causes ($n = 66$), such as perinatal or unexplained death. Table 1 presents other demographic characteristics and further information regarding the nature of the losses.

Procedure

These data were collected in a series of 4 waves, from Fall 1999 to Spring 2002. For each wave, eligible participants completed a single-session grief questionnaire that included the *Inventory of Complicated Grief* (ICG; Prigerson et al., 1995), *Core Bereavement Items* (CBI; Burnett, Middleton, Raphael, & Martinek, 1997), questions pertaining to meaning reconstruction, questions concerning demographic information, and questions regarding the circumstances surrounding the loss (e.g., *How did the death occur? What was the decedent's relationship to you? How long ago did the death occur?*). It should be noted that some waves of the data collection used different measures and omitted others. Therefore, in the individual analyses that follow, only the portion of the sample that filled out the particular measure will be included.

Measures

Inventory of Complicated Grief (ICG; Prigerson et al., 1995)

Of the 1774 research participants, 961 forms of the most recent version of the ICG were fully completed and usable for analysis. The ICG is composed of 28 declarative statements, such as *I feel bitter over this person's death* and *Ever since*

BEREAVEMENT FOLLOWING VIOLENT DEATH / 187

Table 1. Demographics and Other Bereavement-Specific Information

Variable	Mean (*SD*)	Range
Age of deceased	52.67 yrs (26.33)	0 to 102
Time since loss	12.08 mos. (12.23)	0 to 24
Time spent talking about the loss	2.18 (1.12)	0 to 4
CBI	14.91 (10.49)	0 to 68
ICG	48.08 (17.84)	23 to 137

Relationship of decedent to bereaved	Frequency	
Parent	82 (4.6%)	
Sibling	27 (1.5%)	
Child	78 (4.4%)	
Partner/spouse	66 (3.7%)	
Grandparent	447 (25%)	
Aunt/uncle/cousin	512 (29%)	
Friend	351 (20%)	

s/he died, I feel like I have lost the ability to care about other people or I feel distant from other people I care about, to which responses are made on a five-point Likert-type scale describing the frequency of symptoms from 1 = *never* to 5 = *always*. In addition to the 28 declarative statements, the ICG has 3 questions concerning the duration of time the respondent has experienced the symptoms and 1 open-ended question asking the respondent to describe how feelings of grief have changed over time.

The first 19-item version of the ICG has shown strong psychometric properties in a number of studies (Chen et al., 1999; Neimeyer & Hogan, 2001; Prigerson et al., 1999). Previous versions of the ICG have exhibited high internal consistency ($\alpha = .94$), a 6-month test/retest reliability of $r = .80$, and good concurrent validity with the Texas Revised Inventory of Grief (TRIG; Prigerson et al., 1995). The more recent version of the ICG, which was used in the present study, has also been tested in the Netherlands, where a Dutch translation displayed high internal consistency ($\alpha = .94$) and good temporal stability (.92) over a period ranging from 9 to 28 days (Boelen, Van Den Bout, De Keijser, & Hoitjink, 2003). The scale has been demonstrated to predict a broad range of serious long-term health and mental-health consequences of bereavement, justifying its interpretation as a measure of complicated grief symptomatology (Prigerson et al., 1999; Prigerson & Jacobs, 2001; Ott, 2003).

188 / PERSPECTIVES ON VIOLENCE AND VIOLENT DEATH

Core Bereavement Items (CBI)

Of the 1774 participants, 1286 fully completed the CBI forms. The CBI is a self-report measure composed of 17 items whose content focuses on the personal, cognitive, and emotional elements of grief currently experienced by the bereaved (Burnett et al., 1997). Each item is presented as a question such as, *Do you find yourself preoccupied with images or memories of* _____? or *Do you find yourself thinking of a reunion with* _____? Responses are given on a four-point Likert-type scale based on *how often* the respondent experiences that item. The respondent may choose *never, a little bit of the time, quite a bit of the time*, or *always*. Responses are scored 0, 1, 2, and 3, respectively, with the overall score being determined by the sum of the individual items.

The authors report high internal consistency for the CBI ($\alpha = .92$) with a sample of 158 bereaved adults under the age of 70 (Burnett et al., 1997). Evidence for its construct validity is that the CBI successfully discriminated between different intensities of grief in this sample of bereaved spouses and adult children, which included differentiating between expected and unexpected losses. The CBI is generally construed as a measure of normative, rather than pathological grief symptomatology (Burnett et al., 1997; Neimeyer & Hogan, 2001).

Meaning Reconstruction

Meaning reconstruction was assessed by four separate items that evaluated sense-making, benefit-finding, and identity reconstruction, three "contexts of meaning" described by Neimeyer and Anderson (2002). The first item assessed sense-making by having participants respond to the question, *How much sense would you say you have made of the loss?*, from 1 being *no sense of my loss* to 4 being *a good deal of sense*. The second item measured benefit-finding by asking the respondents, *Despite the loss, have you been able to find any benefit from your experience of the loss?*, from 1 being *no benefit* to 5 being *great benefit*. The final two items addressed the extent to which respondents felt that their *sense of identity has changed as a result of this loss* (1 being *no different* to 5 being *very different*) and if that particular change *was mostly for the better, mixed*, or *mostly for the worse*. It should be noted that each of these four items was used as a separate variable in the analysis.

Other Variables

Basic demographic information was gathered for each participant. This information included age, sex, and ethnicity. Participants additionally provided information regarding the circumstances surrounding their loss. This information included the cause of death, relationship to the deceased (e.g., father, cousin, spouse, friend), the age of the deceased when he or she died, the amount of time the participant had spent talking about the loss, and whether or not the participants felt that there was a person with whom they could talk to about the loss or upon whom they could rely for support through the experience.

Data Analysis

We used one-way analysis of variance tests to examine differences between mode of death (natural anticipated, natural sudden, accident, suicide, and homicide) on eight outcome measures, which included two grief measures, four meaning-making items, level of social support, and amount of time spent talking about the loss. When significant differences were found, specific comparisons were made using a Tukey's post-hoc test. In addition to computing an F ratio, an effect size was calculated for each dependent variable using Cohen's (1977) d, so statements could easily be made about the relative impact of violent versus nonviolent losses on the various measures. Cohen's d is defined as

$$d = \frac{m_1 - m_2}{s}$$

where m_1 and m_2 represent means for participants bereaved by violent (accident, suicide, homicide) and nonviolent (unexpected and anticipated natural death) causes, and s is the pooled-within-groups standard deviation. The mean of the nonviolently bereaved group was always subtracted from the mean of the violently bereaved group. In some cases, high scores on a measure indicated greater recovery (e.g., sense-making, benefit-finding); whereas, for other measures, low scores indicated greater recovery (e.g., the ICG, CBI). When lower scores on a measure were considered to be signs of recovery, the positive or negative valence of the effect size was adjusted in such a way that a negative d always denoted poorer outcomes for the violently bereaved.

RESULTS

Grief Measures

A one-way analysis of variance was first performed using mode of death as the independent variable and scores on the ICG as the dependent variable. As can be seen in Table 2, individuals significantly varied in their ICG scores based on the type of loss they experienced, $F(4, 946) = 16.34, p < .001$. An examination of the means in Table 3 reveals that, in general, violent losses tended to produce higher scores on the ICG compared to nonviolent losses, with homicide being the most complicating type of loss ($M = 59.41$). However, post-hoc analyses did not detect any significant differences between accident, suicide, and homicide on the ICG, meaning that chance alone cannot confidently be ruled out as an explanation for the observed differences among the different types of violent losses. It is worth noting that on average, individuals grieving any of the three types of violent loss had significantly higher scores on the ICG compared with participants bereaved by natural *anticipated* deaths, but only homicide and accidents produced significantly

190 / PERSPECTIVES ON VIOLENCE AND VIOLENT DEATH

Table 2. One-Way Analyses of Variance for Effects of Mode of
Death on Dependent Variables

Variable and sources	df	SS	MS	F
CBI				
Between groups	4	4609.87	1152.47	10.62**
Within groups	1275	138359.59	108.52	
ICG				
Between groups	4	19802.92	4950.73	16.34**
Within groups	946	286650.25	303.01	
Meaning reconstruction				
Sense-making				
Between groups	4	134.07	33.52	44.82**
Within groups	972	726.86	.748	
Benefit-finding				
Between groups	4	24.25	6.06	3.70*
Within groups	991	1625.08	1.64	
Identity change				
Between groups	4	9.36	2.34	1.44
Within groups	993	1617.43	1.63	
Direction of identity change				
Between groups	4	17.06	4.23	6.26**
Within groups	878	598.47	.682	
Support				
Perceived support				
Between groups	4	.423	.106	.947
Within groups	977	109.17	.112	
Time spent talking about loss				
Between groups	4	33.98	8.49	6.98**
Within groups	981	1194.31	1.22	

$*p < .01$, two-tailed. $**p < .001$, two-tailed.

higher scores on the ICG compared with natural *sudden* deaths. Overall, violently bereaved participants' ICG scores were .54 standard deviations above those who had lost someone to natural causes (see Table 4).

A similar pattern of results were found when the CBI was used as the dependent variable. As Table 3 shows, CBI scores significantly differed for participants

Table 3. Means and Standard Deviations: Five Modes of Death and Eight Dependent Variables

Variable	Natural anticipated		Natural sudden		Accident		Suicide		Homicide	
	M	SD	M	SD	M	SD	M	SD	M	SD
CBI**	13.34_a	9.77	14.66_{ab}	10.52	17.11_{bc}	10.49	18.09_{bc}	11.56	18.87_c	13.13
ICG**	44.62_a	16.47	46.95_{ab}	15.91	53.42_{bc}	18.40	54.41_c	18.51	59.41_c	24.74
Meaning reconstruction										
Sense-making**	3.52_c	.82	3.40_c	.79	3.04_b	.94	2.34_a	1.01	2.36_a	1.09
Benefit-finding**	2.79_b	1.29	2.77_{ab}	1.26	2.60_{ab}	1.31	2.33_{ab}	1.27	2.29_a	1.23
Identity change	2.29_a	1.26	2.31_a	1.29	2.52_a	1.29	2.43_a	1.19	2.49_a	1.32
Direction of identity change**	1.68_a	.82	1.79_{ab}	.96	1.89_{abc}	.73	2.15_c	.66	2.02_{bc}	.60
Support										
Perceived support	1.11_a	.32	1.15_a	.36	1.11_a	.32	1.09_a	.36	1.17_a	.38
Time spent talking about the loss**	2.04_a	1.08	2.14_{ab}	1.08	2.52_b	1.16	2.36_{ab}	1.09	2.33_{ab}	1.18

Note: a, b, c denote homogenous subsets or statistically equivalent groups of means.
*$p < .05$, two-tailed. **$p < .01$, two-tailed.

192 / PERSPECTIVES ON VIOLENCE AND VIOLENT DEATH

Table 4. Effect Sizes for Violent versus
Nonviolent Death on Eight
Dependent Variables

Variable	d
CBI	−.37
ICG	−.54
Meaning reconstruction	
Sense-making	−.79
Benefit-finding	−.23
Identity change	.16
Direction of identity change	−.36
Support	
Perceived support	−.01
Time spent talking about the loss	.35

based on the mode of death, $F(4, 1275) = 10.62, p < .001$. Again, violent losses tended to produce higher grief scores, with homicide being the most distressing type of loss ($M = 18.87$). Post-hoc tests also revealed that participants bereaved by the three violent causes of death did not differ significantly from each other, but had significantly higher scores on the CBI compared with those bereaved by anticipated natural causes. In addition, only those bereaved by homicide had significantly higher scores than those grieving sudden natural deaths. However, the CBI was not as sensitive to differences between violently and nonviolently bereaved participants, in that there was only a .37 standard deviation difference between those who experienced a violent loss and those who experienced a loss by natural causes.

Meaning-Making Items

As Table 2 shows, participants significantly differed in the degree to which they were able to make sense out of their experiences of loss, depending on the mode of death, $F(4, 972) = 44.82, p < .001$; and in general the results followed a trend similar to the two grief outcomes. Specifically, post-hoc tests indicated that among the three modes of violent death, those who lost a loved one to accident were more likely to make sense out of their experience than those bereaved by suicide or homicide. When compared to anticipated natural deaths, however, all three violently bereaved groups were less likely to have made sense out of the loss. Also, those bereaved by accident, suicide, and homicide had significantly lower scores on the sense-making measure relative to those who had lost a loved one to sudden natural causes. On average, violently bereaved participants reported levels of sense-making that were .79 standard deviations lower than their naturally bereaved counterparts.

In terms of benefit-finding, participants also differed based on the cause of death, $F(4, 991) = 3.70, p = .005$. Although a Tukey's post-hoc analysis detected only one significant difference with respect to natural anticipated and homicidal death, an examination of the means reveals a trend similar to that of sense-making, where those bereaved by suicide and homicide have the lowest scores followed by accident, sudden/anticipated, and natural/anticipated losses in ascending order (see Table 3). Overall, those bereaved by violent means reported less benefit-finding than those bereaved by natural causes by .23 standard deviation units.

Cause of death did not account for a significant portion of the variability in the degree of identity change experienced by participants, $F(4, 993) = 1.44, p = .22$. In general, there was a slight trend for violently bereaved participants to experience more of an identity change, but this difference was quite small, $d = .16$. However, participants did differ significantly on whether they felt like their identity had changed mostly for the better or mostly for the worse based on the cause of death, $F(4, 878) = 6.26, p < .001$, with those bereaved by suicide and homicide perceiving the most negative directions of change. Also, this dimension followed a trend similar to that of sense-making and benefit-finding, with violently bereaved groups experiencing worse outcomes compared with non-violently bereaved groups, $d = -.36$.

Interpersonal Factors

Participants bereaved by violent and nonviolent means responded in nearly an identical fashion when asked if there were people on whom they could rely for support, $F (4, 977) = .947, p = .436$. In fact, only a .01 standard deviation difference existed between those who had lost a loved one violently and those who had lost a loved one to natural causes. There was, however, a significant difference in the amount of time spent talking about the loss, depending on the cause of death, $F(4, 981) = 6.98, p < .001$. In general, those who had experienced a violent loss tended to talk more about the loss compared with those who had lost a loved one to natural causes, $d = .35$. However, post-hoc analyses revealed that the only significant differences that existed were between those bereaved by accidents and those bereaved by either sudden or anticipated natural deaths, with those bereaved by accidents spending more time talking about the loss.

DISCUSSION

The purpose of this empirical study was to compare potential differences in psychological distress, meaning reconstruction, and interpersonal complications

194 / PERSPECTIVES ON VIOLENCE AND VIOLENT DEATH

among a large sample of college students bereaved by recent experiences of violent and nonviolent deaths. The results support previous findings that violent death appears to intensify psychological suffering and complicated grief, in addition to increasing the risk of having problems in the ensuing search for meaning. Additionally, the results showed that those individuals bereaved by violent means spent greater periods of time talking about their losses, which supports previous findings that the amount of social sharing may further reflect a symptom of elevated distress (Stroebe, Stroebe, Schut, Van Den Bout, & Zech, 2002). However, diverging from the findings of prior studies on the social complications following violent death (Calhoun et al., 1984; Dyregrov, 2003; Jordan, 2001; Stroebe & Schut, 2001), the results of the current study indicate that students bereaved by natural and violent deaths each experience similar feelings of social support and have access to reliable friends or family members. Potential interpretations of these findings will be addressed below.

Compared with individuals who had lost a loved one to natural causes, those who were grieving a loss by accident, suicide, or homicide tended to experience higher levels of grief. Specifically, both the ICG and CBI produced the same patterns of results, in that homicide was the most perturbing cause of death for the bereaved followed in descending order by suicide, accidents, natural-sudden, and natural-anticipated deaths. These results are consistent with other literature on the immensely difficult nature of homicidal bereavement (Murphy et al., 2003a; Rynearson, 1994; Thompson et al., 1998) and how situational factors such as the suddenness of loss can increase vulnerability to poor bereavement outcomes (Rando, 1996; Stroebe & Schut, 2001). Although accidental, suicidal, and homicidal loss were each shown to exceed the overall level of psychological distress associated with natural-anticipated death, only grief following homicide was shown to differ significantly from sudden natural death on both of the grief measures, a finding which would run counter to the commonly shared perspective that individuals bereaved by suicide suffer worse bereavement outcomes (Allen et al., 1993; Ellenbogen & Gratton, 2001; Jordan 2001). However, the means show a different trend, with the individuals bereaved by suicide exhibiting higher levels of grief compared with all other groups, with the exception of homicide. This lack of significant findings for the suicidally bereaved is likely attributable to limited statistical power due to the relatively low frequency of suicide as a cause of death in the sample.

The results also suggest that both the ICG and CBI are effective measures that can successfully differentiate between violently and nonviolently bereaved groups. As noted above, both grief measures produced the same rank ordering for each of the different causes of death. However, the ICG seemed much more sensitive in detecting the unique impact of violent bereavement, as indicated by a .54 standard deviation difference between the violently and nonviolently bereaved groups on this measure, compared with a difference of only .37 standard deviations on the CBI. Thus, these results might add support to the claim that the

ICG taps into a traumatic component of complicated grief, whereas the CBI measures more "typical" grief symptoms (Neimeyer & Hogan, 2001).

Considering the growing consensus about the importance of finding meaning in successful adaptation to bereavement (Davis & Noelen-Hoeksema, 2001; Janoff-Bulman, 1992; Neimeyer, 1998, 2001), it is not surprising that the pattern of results on the meaning-making measures looked remarkably similar to those found on the ICG and CBI. For example, making sense of the loss proved to be considerably more difficult for those bereaved by violent death (i.e., accident, suicide, and homicide) compared with individuals who had lost a loved one to natural causes, as shown by a difference between the groups of .79 standard deviation units on the sense-making dimension. Specifically, the sense-making process proved to be most problematic for those grieving death by homicide and suicide, and on average, it seems that these individuals had still made *very little sense* of their losses an average of 12 months later. Significantly, sense-making yielded by far the largest effect size in the study (.79), buttressing the claim that meaning reconstruction is a centrally relevant process in traumatic bereavement (Neimeyer, 2002, 2005b).

The same trend in the results extended to the measure of benefit-finding across the five modes of death, with suicide and homicide survivors discerning the least amount of benefit. However, for benefit-finding, the disparity between the students bereaved by violent and nonviolent means did not prove as striking. This finding might be explained by literature that suggests that sense-making usually assumes prominence during the early period of traumatic bereavement, as the individual works to reestablish a sense of cohesion and resiliency, with the discovery of practical, spiritual, or relational benefits playing out more gradually over time (Neimeyer & Anderson, 2002). Since all participants in this study were bereaved within the last two years, it follows that problems with sense-making, rather than benefit-finding, might be a more prominent distinguishing feature of the violently bereaved. Considering the dimension of identity reconstruction, the majority of the students felt that they either *did not change* or *somewhat changed* because of their losses at the time of the study. Yet, for those violently bereaved individuals who reported experiencing a change in their identity, the results indicated that on average they did not judge this alteration to be for the better compared with those bereaved by natural causes.

As mentioned above, students bereaved by violent and nonviolent deaths reported equal levels of perceived social support. At first glance, this finding seems to contradict claims from earlier research studies (Dyregrov, 2003; Jordan, 2001; Riches & Dawson, 1998). However, the majority of these previous investigations focused specifically on spousal and parental bereavement. It is important to note that the current sample has a broad representation of relationships to the deceased, with the loss of a grandparent, friend, and other familial relative (e.g., uncle, aunt, or cousin) being the most frequent types of losses.

196 / PERSPECTIVES ON VIOLENCE AND VIOLENT DEATH

One interpretation of this finding is that the period of college provides students with an intact social network that remains largely distinct from family and other prominent relationships. In the aftermath of a potentially traumatic loss, a surrogate family of sorts might then already surround bereaved students, and one that could be resilient to the disruption of support that may characterize systems composed largely of other bereaved family members. Moreover, this lack of a shared history might have enabled those students bereaved by violent deaths to exercise more control over the way they offered explanations and drew upon their support systems. Furthermore, considering their ability to attend college, it might be that these students possessed strong internal resources from the beginning, which would increase the likelihood of healthy relational functioning, while simultaneously decreasing the students' needs to excessively depend on others. In addition, there was some indication that bereaved students would be most likely to seek someone to talk with about the experience if the death were sudden, although this difference achieved statistical significance only in the comparison of accidental death and natural-anticipated death. It is possible that discussion of more stigmatizing losses by suicide or homicide was suppressed by shame or fear of censure, but this hypothesis cannot be tested using the current data.

Clinical Implications

As we have discussed, bereavement following violent death often involves a blend of grief, trauma, and depressive symptoms. From an assessment perspective, this study suggests that both the ICG and CBI are useful screening instruments for measuring the unique impact of bereavement following violent death. Nevertheless, the ICG might prove especially helpful in detecting possible symptoms of complicated grief, which could precipitate a referral for therapy. Additionally, the results indicate that bereaved college students might have unique resources in terms of social support, a strength that clinicians would do well to recognize as a potential buffering agent that might help clients move more smoothly through the difficult process of adaptation and life readjustment.

A further implication of our study is that the processes of sense-making and benefit-finding remained elusive for many of the violently bereaved students in this study. On average, the students bereaved by violent means still reported making *very little sense* of their loss and had found limited benefits in their experience at the time of the study. The fact that so few of the violently bereaved participants in this study made sense of their loss is reason for concern. Past research suggests that bereaved persons who find a measure of meaning in the experience seem to fare better on grief outcomes, whereas for those who pursue meaning and find none, the loss can prove especially excruciating (Davis et al., 2000). Thus, it appears that therapists would be well-advised to help a client struggling to find significance in the loss by facilitating and supporting a process of meaning making (Neimeyer, 1998). Nevertheless, research suggests that therapists should exercise discretion in working with bereaved persons in treatment (Neimeyer, 2000). It would be naïve to approach these bereaved individuals with the belief that psychotherapy is necessary to help them find a sense of meaning, inasmuch as many bereaved follow a resilient trajectory through grief with only fleeting distress (Bonanno, Wortman, & Nesse, 2004), and current evidence seriously questions the utility of grief therapy for the majority of bereaved persons (Jordan & Neimeyer, 2003). Instead, depending on the level of distress, some clinical researchers have suggested (e.g., Rynearson, 2001) that the initial focus of working with violently bereaved individuals might be one of crisis resolution, which should focus on helping the bereaved to reestablish a sense of stability and cohesion. This might then be coupled with some provision for longer-term follow-up, offering services to only those whose debilitating symptoms persist over an extended period (e.g., beyond six months; Neimeyer, 2002).

Limitations and Future Directions

In summary, the results of the present study partially replicate and extend previous research findings, while also raising questions regarding the distinctive social implications of violent death among younger adults. However, there are some limitations to this study. First, although the use of a college sample allowed the examination of an understudied population in this area, it also presents obstacles to the generalization of the findings to other groups. Although college student bereavement is extensive, potentially disenfranchised, and linked to deleterious outcomes (Balk, 2001; Hardison et al., 2005), it is nonetheless likely that other bereaved populations (e.g., those experiencing spousal or child loss by violent means) are at (still) greater risk for complication. Second, meaning reconstruction was measured by only four items, which does not likely reflect the many ways people find meaning in their loss. Despite the impressive results obtained with this simple assessment, it is likely that the development of better measures of these phenomena with strong psychometric properties would improve the precision and quality of future studies. Additionally, considering the cross-sectional design of the study, it is difficult to know if it was the violent nature of the death that produced higher grief scores, or if other factors were at play. Therefore, no strong causal inferences can be drawn based on this study alone. However, considering the findings of other researchers using longitudinal designs (e.g., Kaltman & Bonanno, 2003; Lehman et al., 1987; Murphy et al., 2003b), it seems likely that violent death is in fact a precipitating factor that increases the likelihood of problematic grief responses.

Despite the aforementioned limitations, these results support the emerging consensus among researchers and theorists regarding the complicating nature of violent bereavement, setting in motion a struggle both for meaning and for relief from debilitating grief symptoms. However, the nature of the relationship between

198 / PERSPECTIVES ON VIOLENCE AND VIOLENT DEATH

grief and meaning making remains ambiguous. Particularly in instances of catastrophic losses, it appears reasonable to suggest that meaning making will prove more difficult, as more modification of basic assumptions will be required of the bereaved individual. Future work in this area might benefit from empirically examining the mediational properties of meaning making with respect to the process of healing and life readjustment. In this way, clinical researchers and practitioners could better understand both the dynamics and potential limits in the process of meaning reconstruction in the wake of potentially traumatizing loss.

REFERENCES

Allen, B. G., Calhoun, L. G., Cann, A., & Tedeschi, R. G. (1993). The effects of cause of death on responses to the bereaved: Suicide compared to accident and natural causes. *Omega, 28*(1), 39-48.

American Psychiatric Association. (1994). *Diagnostic and statistical manual of mental disorders* (4th ed.). Washington, DC: Author.

Armour, M. (2003). Meaning making in the aftermath of homicide. *Death Studies, 27,* 519-540.

Balk, D. E. (2001). College student bereavement, scholarship, and the university: A call for university engagement. *Death Studies, 25,* 67-84.

Barlow, C. A., & Coleman, H. (2003). The healing alliance: How families use social support after a suicide? *Omega, 47*(3), 187-201.

Boelen, P. A., Van Den Bout, J., De Keijser, J., & Hoitjink, H. (2003). Reliability and validity of the Dutch version of the Inventory of Traumatic Grief (ITG). *Death Studies, 27,* 227-247.

Bonanno, G. A., & Kaltman, S. (1999). Toward an integrative perspective on bereavement. *Psychological Bulletin, 126*(6), 760-776.

Bonanno, G. A., Wortman, C. B., & Nesse, R. M. (2004). Prospective patterns of resilience and maladjustment during widowhood. *Psychology and Aging, 19*, 260-271.

Breslau, N. (2002). Epidemiologic studies of trauma, posttraumatic stress disorder, and other psychiatric disorders. *Canadian Journal of Psychiatry, 47*(10), 923-929.

Brewin, C. R., Dalgleish, T., & Joseph, S. (1996). A dual representation of posttraumatic stress disorder. *Psychological Review, 103,* 670-686.

Burnett, P., Middleton, W., Raphael, B., & Martinek, N. (1997). Measuring core bereavement phenomena. *Psychological Medicine, 27,* 49-57.

Calhoun, L. G., & Allen, B. G. (1991). Social reactions to the survivor of a suicide in the family: A review of the literature. *Omega, 23*(2), 95-107.

Calhoun, L. G., Selby, J. W., & Abernathy, C. B. (1984). Suicidal death: Social reactions to bereaved survivors. *Journal of Psychology, 116,* 255-261.

Calhoun, L. C., & Tedeschi, R. O. (2001). Posttraumatic growth: The positive lessons of loss. In R. A. Neimeyer (Ed.), *Meaning reconstruction and the experience of loss* (pp. 157-172) Washington, DC: American Psychological Association.

Chen, H. J., Bierhals, A. J., Prigerson, H. G., Kasl, S. V., Mazure, C. M., Reynolds, C. F., Shear, M. K., Day, N., & Jacobs, S. C. (1999). Gender differences in the effects of bereavement-related psychological distress in health outcomes. *Psychological Medicine, 29,* 367-380.

BEREAVEMENT FOLLOWING VIOLENT DEATH / 199

Clark, S. (2001). Bereavement after suicide—How far have we come and where do we go from here? *Crisis, 3,* 102-108.

Cohen, J. (1977). *Statistical power analysis for the behavioral sciences* (rev. ed.). New York: Academic Press.

Dannemiller, H. C. (2002). The parent's response to a child's murder. *Omega, 45*(1), 1-21.

Davis, C. G., & Nolen-Hoeksema, S. (2001). Loss and meaning: How do people make sense of loss? *American Behavioral Scientist, 44*(5), 726-741.

Davis, C., Wortman, C. B., Lehman, D. R., & Cohen Silver, R. (2000). Searching for meaning in loss: Are clinical assumptions correct? *Death Studies, 24*(6), 497-540.

Dobrin, A. (2001). The risk of offending of homicide victimization: A case control study. *Journal of Research in Crime and Delinquency, 38*(2), 154-173.

Doka, K. (Ed.). (1989). *Disenfranchised grief. Recognizing hidden sorrow.* Lexington, MA: Lexington Books.

Dyregrov, K. (2003). Micro-sociological analysis of social support following traumatic bereavement: Unhelpful and avoidant responses from the community. *Omega, 48*(1), 23-44.

Dyregrov, K., Nordanger, D., & Dyregrov, A. (2003). Predictors of psychosocial distress after suicide, SIDS, and accidents. *Death Studies, 27,* 143-165.

Ellenbogen, S., & Gratton, F. (2001). Do they suffer more? Reflections on research comparing suicide survivors to other survivors. *Suicide and Life-Threatening Behavior, 31*(1), 83-90.

Freud, S. (1957). Mourning and melancholia. In J. Strachey (Ed.), *The standard edition of the complete works of Sigmund Freud.* London: Hogarth Press.

Green, B. L. (2000). Traumatic loss: Conceptual and empirical links between trauma and bereavement. *Journal of Personal and Interpersonal Loss, 5*(1), 1-17.

Green, B. L., Krupnick, J. L., Stockton, P., Goodman, L., Corcoran, C., & Petty, R. (2001). Psychological outcomes associated with traumatic loss in a sample of young women. *American Behavioral Scientist, 44*(5), 817-837.

Hardison, H. G., Neimeyer, R. A., & Lichstein, K. L. (2005). Insomnia and complicated grief symptoms in bereaved college students. *Behavioral Sleep Medicine, 3,* 99-111.

Hawton, K., & Simkin, S. (2003). Helping people bereaved by suicide. *British Medical Journal, 327,* 177-178.

Helzer, J. E., Robins, L. N., & McEvoy, L. (1987). Post-traumatic stress disorder in the general population. *New England Journal of Medicine, 317,* 1630-1634.

Janoff-Bulman, R. (1992). *Shattered assumptions: Toward a new psychology of trauma.* New York: Free Press.

Jordan, J. R. (2001). Is suicide bereavement different? A reassessment of the literature. *Suicide and Life-Threatening Behavior, 31*(1), 91-102.

Jordan, J. R., & Neimeyer, R. A. (2003). Does grief counseling work? *Death Studies, 27,* 765-786.

Kaltman, S., & Bonanno, G. A. (2003). Trauma and bereavement: Examining the impact of sudden and violent deaths. *Anxiety Disorders, 17,* 131-147.

Lehman, D. R., Lang, E. L., Wortman, C. B., & Sorenson, S. B. (1989). Long-term effects of sudden bereavement: Marital and parent-child relationships and children's reactions. *Journal of Family Psychology, 2*(3), 344-367.

200 / PERSPECTIVES ON VIOLENCE AND VIOLENT DEATH

Lehman, D. R., Wortman, C. B., & Williams, A. F. (1987). Long-term effects of losing a spouse or child in a motor vehicle crash. *Journal of Personality and Social Psychology, 52*(1), 218-231.

Matthews, L. T., & Marwit, S. J. (2004). Examining the assumptive world views of parents bereaved by accident, murder, and illness. *Omega, 48*(2), 115-136.

McIntosh, J. L. (1993). Control group studies of suicide survivors: A review and critique. *Suicide and Life-Threatening Behavior, 23*(2), 146-161.

Murphy, S. A., Braun, T., Tillery, L., Cain, K. C., Johnson, C. L., & Beaton, R. D. (1999). PTSD among bereaved parents following the violent deaths of their 12- to 28-year-old children: A longitudinal prospective analysis. *Journal of Traumatic Stress, 12*(2), 273-291.

Murphy, S. A., Johnson, L. C., Wu, L., Fan, J. J., & Lohan, J. (2003a). Bereaved parents' outcomes 4 to 60 months after their children's deaths by accident, suicide, or homicide: A comparative study demonstrating differences. *Death Studies, 27,* 39-61.

Murphy, S. A., Johnson, C. L., Chung, I. J., & Beaton, R. D. (2003b). The prevalence of PTSD following the violent death of a child and predictors of change 5 years later. *Journal of Traumatic Stress, 16,* 17-25.

Murphy, S. A., Johnson, L. C., & Lohan, J. (2003a). Finding meaning in a child's violent death: A five-year prospective analysis of parents' personal narratives and empirical data. *Death Studies, 27,* 381-404.

Murphy, S. A., Johnson, L. C., & Lohan, J. (2003b). Challenging the myths about parent's adjustment after the sudden, violent death of a child. *Journal of Nursing Scholarship, 35*(4), 359-364.

Neimeyer, R. A. (1998). *Lessons of loss: A guide to coping.* New York: McGraw-Hill.

Neimeyer, R. A. (2000). Searching for the meaning of meaning: Grief therapy and the process of reconstruction. *Death Studies, 24*(6), 17-28.

Neimeyer, R. A. (Ed.). (2001). *Meaning reconstruction and the experience of loss.* Washington, DC: American Psychological Association.

Neimeyer, R. A. (2002). Traumatic loss and the reconstruction of meaning. *Journal of Palliative Medicine, 5*(6), 935-942.

Neimeyer, R. A. (2005a). Re-storying loss: Fostering growth in the posttraumatic narrative. In L. Calhoun & R. Tedeschi (Eds.), *Handbook of posttraumatic growth: Research and practice.* Mahwah, NJ: Lawrence Erlbaum.

Neimeyer, R. A. (2005b). Growing through grief: Constructing coherence in narratives of loss. In D. Winter & L. Viney (Eds.), *Advances in personal construct psychotherapy.* London: Whurr.

Neimeyer, R. A. (2005c). Widowhood, grief and the quest for meaning: A narrative perspective on resilience. In D. Carr, R. M. Nesse, & C. B. Wortman (Eds.), *Late life widowhood in the United States.* New York: Springer.

Neimeyer, R. A., & Anderson, A. (2002). Meaning reconstruction theory. In N. Thompson (Ed.), *Loss and grief* (pp. 45-64). London: Palgrave.

Neimeyer, R. A., & Hogan, N. S. (2001). Quantitative or qualitative? Measurement issues in the study of grief. In M. S. Stroebe, W. Stroebe, & R. O. Hansson (Eds.), *Handbook of bereavement research* (pp. 89-118). Washington, DC: American Psychological Association.

Neimeyer, R. A., & Jordan, J. R. (2002). Disenfranchisement as empathic failure. In K. Doka (Ed.), *Disenfranchised grief* (pp. 95-117). Champaign, IL: Research Press.

Neimeyer, R. A., Prigerson, H., & Davies, B. (2002). Mourning and meaning. *American Behavioral Scientist, 46,* 235-251.

Neria, Y., & Litz, B. T. (2003). Bereavement by traumatic means: the complex synergy of trauma and grief. *Journal of Loss and Trauma, 9,* 73-87.

Ott, C. H. (2003). The impact of complicated grief on mental and physical health at various points in the bereavement process. *Death Studies, 27,* 249-272.

Prigerson, H. G., & Jacobs, S. C. (2001). Traumatic grief as a distinct disorder: A rationale, consensus criteria, and a preliminary empirical test. In M. S. Stroebe, W. Stroebe, & R. O. Hansson (Eds.), *Handbook of bereavement research* (pp. 613-645). Washington, DC: American Psychological Association.

Prigerson, H. G., Maciejewski, P., Reynolds, C., Bierhals, A. Newsom, J. Fasiczka, A. Frank, E., Doman, J., & Miller, M. (1995). Inventory of complicated grief. *Psychiatry Research, 59,* 65-79.

Prigerson, H. G., Shear, M. K., Jacobs, S. C., Reynolds, C. F., Maciejewski, P. D., Davidson, J. R. T., Rosenheck, R., Pilkonis, P. A., Wortman, C. B., Williams, J. B. W., Widiger, T. A., Frank, E., Kupfer, D. J., & Zistook, S. (1999). Consensus criteria for traumatic grief. *British Journal of Psychiatry, 174,* 67-73.

Rando, T. A. (1992). The increasing prevalence of complicated mourning: The onslaught is just beginning. *Omega, 26*(1), 43-59.

Rando, T. A. (1996). Complications in mourning traumatic death. In K. J. Doka (Ed.), *Living with grief after sudden loss: Suicide, homicide, accident, heart attack, stroke* (pp. 139-159). Washington, DC: Hospice Foundation of America.

Range, L. M., & Calhoun, L. G. (1990). Responses following suicide and other types of death: The perspective of the bereaved. *Omega, 21*(4), 311-320.

Redmond, L. M. (1996). Sudden violent death. In K. J. Doka (Ed.), *Living with grief after sudden loss: Suicide, homicide, accident, heart attack, stroke* (pp. 53-71). Washington, DC: Hospice Foundation of America.

Riches, G., & Dawson, P. (1998). Spoiled memories: problems of grief resolution in families bereaved through murder. *Mortality, 3*(2), 143-159.

Rynearson, E. K. (1986). Effects of unnatural dying on bereavement. *Psychiatric Annals, 16*(5), 272-275.

Rynearson, E. K. (1994). Psychotherapy of bereavement after homicide. *Journal of Psychotherapy Practice and Research, 3*(4), 341-347.

Rynearson, E. K. (2001). *Retelling violent death.* Philadelphia, PA: Brunner-Routledge.

Rynearson, E. K., & Sinnema, C. S. (1999). Supportive group therapy for bereavement after homicide. In D. Blake & B. Young (Eds.), *Group treatments for post-traumatic stress disorder* (pp. 137-147). Philadelphia, PA: Brunner/Mazel.

Schut, H., De Keijser, J., Van Den Bout, J., & Dijkhuis, J. H. (1991). Post-traumatic stress symptoms in the first years of conjugal bereavement. *Anxiety Research, 4,* 225-234.

Schwartzberg, S. S., & Janoff-Bulman, R. (1991). Grief and the search for meaning: Exploring the assumptive worlds of bereaved college students. *Journal of Social and Clinical Psychology, 10*(3), 270-288.

Seguin, M., Lesage, A., & Kiely, M. C. (1995). Parental bereavement after suicide and accident: A comparative study. *Suicide and Life-Threatening Behavior, 25,* 489-490.

202 / PERSPECTIVES ON VIOLENCE AND VIOLENT DEATH

Stroebe, W., & Schut, H. (2001). Risk factors in bereavement outcome: A methodological and empirical review. In R. O. Hansson, M. S. Stroebe, W. Stroebe, & H. Schut (Eds.), *Handbook of bereavement research* (pp. 349-372). Washington, DC: American Psychological Association.

Stroebe, W., Stroebe, M., Schut, H., & Abakoumkim, G. (1996). The role of loneliness and social support in adjustment to loss: A test of attachment versus stress theory. *Journal of Personality and Social Psychology, 70*(6), 1241-1249.

Stroebe, W., Stroebe, M., Schut, H., Van Den Bout, J., & Zech, E. (2002). Does disclosure of emotions facilitate recovery from bereavement? Evidence from two prospective studies. *Journal of Consulting and Clinical Psychology, 70*(1), 169-178.

Thompson, M. P., Norris, F. H., & Ruback, R. B. (1998). Comparative distress levels of inner-city family members of homicide victims. *Journal of Traumatic Stress, 11*(2), 223-242.

Viorst, J. (1986). *Necessary losses.* New York: Simon and Schuster.

CHAPTER 13

Violence In Our Own Backyard: September 11th Revisited

Barbara Melamed

> . . . I remember the morning of September 11, 2001 as if it were yesterday. After I prayed however, I did feel peace inside me. . . . Watching people jump out of windows and fall to their death was more horrifying than anything Hollywood could create. I know like many others, I will never be the same again. I have always valued and appreciated my family and close friends. Now I have an even greater appreciation for them. We don't let a day go by without saying "I love you."
>
> Words of a graduate student at
> Mercy College on September 11, 2003

The disaster of September 11, 2001 changed the way we deal with our lives on an everyday basis. The wars in Vietnam and the Gulf existed and were painful for those who lost family or returnees from these wars. We have become desensitized to the horrors of the killings in Iraq. Unfortunately, news recedes quickly when occurrences take place outside of our borders.

As school children, we learned of the history of Nazi genocide. Today we see newspaper pictures of children dying in Rwanda. But it wasn't supposed to happen right here in the United States of America on a sunny, cloudless day as we went to work or began the school year.

We do not tend to relive the 1993 World Trade Center bombing on a daily basis. Was it that not enough people died? It was just a television show, except for those involved in the dangerous situation. This time the event and the subsequent threats of acts of biological, chemical, and nuclear warfare created a looming specter of another sudden terrorist assault. The resultant effects have changed our beliefs about our level of safety and security. In contrast to a natural disaster, such as the tsunami in the Indian Ocean that killed many more people, terrorist attacks are deliberate, and the suddenness and loss of life was traumatic in a different way.

204 / PERSPECTIVES ON VIOLENCE AND VIOLENT DEATH

Each individual responded in his or her own way; it has changed with each day since then. Some of us responded with disbelief, shock, helplessness, anger, and insecurity. Much like the stages of bereavement when you lose a loved one, whether through illness or unexpected accident, there is no definite endpoint.

The lack of human remains made it difficult for family members to accept and go through the predictable stages of bereavement and recovery. It has been said that after the tragedies of September 11, Americans seemed to reconnect; in New York City, almost all citizens displayed American flags and showed a willingness to contribute blood, money, and time to helping the victims and their families. There must be some meaning and recovery and growth from such a horror.

At Mercy College, where I was a brand new faculty member with a PhD in psychology, I was supposed to, and needed to, do something. I had worked with survivors of the Bosnian-Croatian War, I had previously studied the reactions of students and foreigners in Jerusalem after bus bombings, and measured with my fancy instruments how the assassination of Itzhak Rabin further demoralized the inhabitants of a country used to killings. I have held hands with dying patients and comforted families that were left behind.

However, this time I was not prepared for my own response. In a conversation on the phone with my tax accountant, he said, "Turn on the television. The World Trade Center is on fire." It was happening before my very eyes: a shadow of a second airplane moved slowly across my television screen, much like a computer graphic in a Hollywood horror film. The crumbling of the buildings neatly down upon themselves is a vision I will never forget. I had never really liked the structures that were not part of my Brooklyn childhood, but I was totally stunned. People were being burned alive. The CBS newscasters were on the scene to cover the events in their usual manner, maybe a little less calmly. After making phone contact with my husband, I checked with my 7-year-old son's school and offered to come right over and give help. They had it under control. Only the teachers watched the televised events as they unfolded. In my quiet Westchester suburb, some children would not be having their mothers or fathers pick them up. Their parents were employed by Cantor Fitzgerald, the large financial firm on the 88th floor of the North Tower.

I went to the Mercy campus needing to do something. Some of our students were still staring in disbelief from our Hudson River campus watching the smoldering. I set up an immediate crisis center in the student cafeteria to help our students and staff deal with their shock, loss of a sense of invulnerability, and worry about the fate of those they knew who were missing and likely dead.

I sat with Maria, one of our veterinarian technicians, who spent almost ten hours of her day at the bombed-out site to offer pain relief to the dogs who were seeking out bodies and possible survivors. She applied salves to their burns and swathed their feet and assisted in their breathing. We don't know what these animals were feeling, but I could sense what Maria was experiencing. She needed to do something. She was reacting—not processing what she was doing. She was visibly exhausted, on the verge of tears, but unable even to talk. I asked her who she had at home. She remarked that she was primary caregiver for her five sisters and brothers. I encouraged her to go home without feeling guilty about abandoning what she felt was her role. In fact she needed permission to return to her family.

Another student, himself already limping off balance due to a debilitating muscular disease, walked around numbly. Every once in a while he would share that his cousin was missing, but he was sure that he had survived. Later the many photographs of downtown and Grand Central Terminal also illustrated the lack of reality in the devastation of human life. Disbelief gave rise to false hopes of survival.

Many teachers brought their classes through, as much to give them a task. Most of the students did not share their thoughts, and several expressed resentment at being forced to "*shake hands*" with the tragedy by going through a psychological service. I posted a large oil painting that I had bought in the Bowery from a homeless man, many months before this day. It was the World Trade Center towers in all their glory standing prominently in their city. This encouraged over 400 students and staff to walk through the doors of our "temporary headquarters." Many walked away. But each had a response.

The purpose of the present chapter is to understand this individual variability in coping and what it means for recovery. Both human stories told from the heart and empirical data derived from questionnaires are incorporated to make this point. Perhaps for me, it is also a catharsis for my own anxiety and grief. The oil painting described above is now kept on a shelf in my closet, faced upside down.

Despite the fact that we have a large empirical database and clinical studies on providing services, it was unclear whether posttraumatic stress disorder (PTSD) would occur in reaction to this unprecedented event. The clinicians disagreed as to whether individuals should be treated with debriefing (known in the psychology world as Critical Incident Debriefing), allowing the individual to face the event with cathartic responses. In different circumstances this has been shown to put their personal violation (rape, burglary, and assault) in perspective allowing them to reassess their "safety" with regards to their vulnerability in potential future incidents. We have been bombarded by our government with the notion that this situation has a high probability of reoccurring. Both 2004 presidential candidates agreed that it was not "if" but "when" would it happen again. We are given color-coded warnings, but these offer little in the way of action to take at different levels of alarm. We are told to give our children potassium chloride in order to diminish the effects of radiation poisoning with the result that the pharmacies were out of the recommended medicine within three days. The assumption of the invulnerability of the strongest nation in the world was shattered.

Attacks on foreigners and our own soldiers continue to occur in other countries. The fact that the horrifying events of 9/11 (not an accidental numerical choice in

206 / PERSPECTIVES ON VIOLENCE AND VIOLENT DEATH

my opinion) were witnessed "live" on television by millions of individuals around the globe gives some uniqueness to the process of recovery.

This chapter presents the empirical measures of distress as they appeared in the population over time. The objectives were to inform the college administration and the general public about what the psychological sequela would be. The second objective was to look at recovery in the first year after these tragedies. The population who volunteered to fill out some questionnaires was selected at random through classroom surveys. The data was collected during the week following the tragedy, one month later, three months later, and eight months later. We present the original word segments and thoughts of students who were asked on September 11, 2003 to respond to a question on how the events of 9/11 continued to influence.

The research questions posed during the first year of the study were:

1. What types of coping responses were reported to occur and how do they change over a period of several months following the attack?
2. To what extent did reaction to continued threats of terrorist attacks co-occur with depressive symptoms and depressive disorders?
3. To what extent did reaction to continued threats of terrorist attacks co-occur with posttraumatic stress symptoms and disorders?
4. Did the distance from the site of the World Trade Center influence the reactions?

We have more descriptive data from responses to the following questions:

5. How does repeated exposure to reruns of the original incident effect a population repeatedly viewing the collapse of the towers and human beings jumping to their death?
6. Can we pinpoint specific subgroups who are more at risk for developing trauma-related and depressive disorders that are likely to impair their functioning for years to come?
7. How do immediate family and other support networks (e.g., friends, church congregants) of those killed and injured influence the nature of the reactions?

REVIEW OF THE LITERATURE

In New York City, participants of a study (Galea, Ahern, Resnick, Kilpatrick, Bucuvalus, Gold, & Vhalov, 2002) were evaluated by a random-digital dialing system to contact 1008 adults (53% females and 72% white) living south of 110th Street in Manhattan. This area was closest to the World Trade Center. The interview involved a structured set of questions regarding demographics and where they were during the attacks. It also looked at social support, life stressors, and involvement in the attacks with regard to job loss and being hurt. Standard assessment tools were used to show whether participants showed the symptoms of PTSD or depression. The study revealed that 7.5% met the criteria for PTSD, and 9.7% met the criteria for depression. It was estimated that approximately 67,000 people had PTSD and 87,000 had depression at the time of the study. This showed that the prevalence of PTSD and depression was considerably higher than the national average. A multivariate model found that predictors of PTSD were Hispanic ethnicity, two or more prior stressors, a panic attack during or shortly after the events, residence south of Canal Street, and loss of possessions due to the events. Predictors of depression were Hispanic ethnicity, two or more prior stressors, a panic attack, a low level of social support, the death of a friend or relative during the attacks, and loss of a job due to the attacks.

In another study (Melnick, 2002), the psychological and emotional effects were studied in New York, New Jersey, and Connecticut. Again, a random-digit dialing telephone methodology was used, tapping responses from 1774 people in Connecticut, and 638 in New York. The study showed that women were more likely to attend religious services and seek help after the attack than men. They were more likely to smoke cigarettes. Men were more likely to abuse alcohol. Terrorism reactions were measured by 17 questions regarding how they dealt with the attack. There was a direct effect of television exposure, which exceeded that of the demographics.

Silver, Holman, McIntosh, Poulin, and Gil-Rivas (2002) examined the degree to which demographic factors, mental and physical history, lifetime exposure to stressful events, September 11 experiences, and coping strategies used after the attacks predict psychological outcomes over time. They looked at a national probability sample of 3496 adults who received a Web-based survey. The survey was completed by 78% of these individuals between 9 and 23 days following the terrorist attacks. Random samples of 1069 panelists who live outside of New York City were drawn from the original sample of 2729 individuals. They received a second survey, which was completed by 87% within 2 months after the attacks. A third survey was completed by 787 people after 6 months following the attacks. Outcome measures were 9/11-related symptoms of acute stress, posttraumatic stress, and global distress. Silver concluded that 17% of the U.S. population outside New York City reported symptoms of posttraumatic stress 2 months following the attack, and 5.3% did at 6 months. They found that high levels of posttraumatic-stress symptoms were associated with female gender, marital separation, pre-September 11 physician-diagnosed depression or anxiety disorders or physical illness, severity of exposure to the attacks, and early disengagement from coping efforts (e.g., giving up, denial, and self-distraction). They concluded that the psychological effects of a major national trauma are not limited to those who directly experience it, and that the degree of response is not predicted simply by objective measures to loss from the trauma. They found instead that the use of specific coping strategies shortly following an event is associated with symptoms over time, in particular, that disengaging from the

208 / PERSPECTIVES ON VIOLENCE AND VIOLENT DEATH

coping efforts could signal the likelihood of psychological difficulties up to six months following a trauma.

Schlenger, Caddell, Ebert, Jordan, Rourke, and Wilson (2002) assessed psychological symptom levels in the United States following the events of September 11. They examined the association between postattack symptoms and a variety of indices of exposure to the events. They used a Web-based epidemiological survey of a nationally representative cross-sectional sample using the Posttraumatic Stress Disorder Checklist and the Brief Symptom Inventory. These were administered one to two months following the attacks. They sampled 2273 adults, including individuals in New York City and the Washington, D.C. metropolitan areas. Outcome measures were self-reports of symptoms of PTSD and of clinically significant, nonspecific psychological distress. They found that the prevalence of probable PTSD was significantly higher in the New York City metropolitan area (11.2%) than in Washington, D.C. (2.7%), other major metropolitan areas (3.6%), and the rest of the country (4.0%). However, a broader measure of clinically significant psychological distress suggested that overall distress levels across the country were within expected ranges for a general community sample. In multivariate models, gender, the number of hours of television coverage viewed, and an index of the content of that coverage were associated with the broader distress measure. More that 60% of adults in New York City households with children reported that 1 or more children were upset by the attacks. Schlenger et al. (2002) concluded that one to two months following the attack, the PTSD was associated with direct exposure to the attack among adults. The prevalence in New York City was substantially higher than elsewhere in the country. However, overall distress levels in the country were within normal ranges.

Brandes, Ben-Schachar, Gilboa, Bonne, Freedman, and Shalev (2002) found that trauma survivors with high levels of PTSD symptoms showed impaired attention and immediate recall for figural information as well as lower intellectual function with no impairment of verbal recall and learning. Yehuda (2002) pointed out that factors that contribute to the intensity of the response to a psychologically traumatic experience include the degree of controllability, predictability, and perceived threat; the relative success of attempts to minimize injury to oneself or others; and actual loss. Ursano (2002) reports that PTSD is not the only trauma-related disorder or, perhaps, even the one most commonly seen by primary-care physicians. After a traumatic event, pathologic forms of grief, unexplained somatic symptoms, depression, sleep disturbance, and increased use of alcohol and cigarettes, as well as family conflict and family violence are not uncommon; but in each case, the role of the traumatic event may be easily overlooked (Ursano, 2002).

Sheehan and Zimmerman (2002) found that the Posttraumatic Diagnostic Scale performed as well in a general psychiatric setting as it did in original trauma-focused validation studies as a primary versus secondary reason for presenting.

Two other disasters can be compared to the events of September 11, 2001 insofar as television exposure of the actual event. These are the Oklahoma City bombing and the Challenger Space Shuttle tragedy. In the case of Oklahoma City, millions of people viewed the aftereffects of the building collapse. Images of half the Murrah Federal Building collapsed on the ground were observed on television by millions. Children in the daycare center were killed. The subsequent cleanup of the area after the bombing was also televised for many to see. This continual coverage as well as speculation about who did it and whether or not it would happen again filtered through the airwaves as well. These two factors added to the possibility of people developing mental illnesses such as depression due to intense exposure. One study (North, Nixon, Shariat, Mallonee, McMillen, Spitznagel, & Smith, 1999) found that one-third of a sample of 182 persons directly exposed (i.e., who saw the event in person or lost someone in the blast) had symptoms that are consistent with the criteria for depression and PTSD 6 months after the incident. This study shows that demographics (how close the person is to the trauma) could be an important factor in identifying people who are most at risk for developing mental illnesses.

Another study related to the Oklahoma City bombing compared random telephone interviews in Oklahoma City and Indianapolis, Indiana. The study was conducted 3 to 4 months after the bombing and found that 43% of those living in Oklahoma City reported 4 or more stress symptoms compared with 11% of those living in Indianapolis, Indiana (Smith, Christianson, Vincent, & Hann, 1999). Increased stress symptoms can lead to a variety of mental illnesses such as depression and PTSD. It also shows that distance from the actual event was important, because there was such a discrepancy between the random phone call responses from Oklahoma compared with the Indianapolis, Indiana.

The Challenger Space Shuttle disaster occurred only minutes after takeoff on January 28, 1986. There was already fanfare for this mission because a schoolteacher was a member of the Challenger crew. For that reason, a lot more people (especially children) wanted to witness this historic event. Several thousand people saw Challenger explode live on television, and millions more saw it replayed over and over again throughout the days to come. It was believed that this tragedy would have far-reaching negative effects around the country. Instead (for the most part) people had a renewed respect and admiration for the space program not seen since the 1960s (NASA.com). This national tragedy led to the restructuring of the space program, which led to even more safety precautions, so that there wouldn't be a similar incident. The Challenger disaster demonstrates that it is possible for good things to come out of a bad situation. At that time, it was very possible that the whole space program might have been shut down because it was deemed too dangerous to continue. According to NASA, the Challenger disaster actually rejuvenated the Space Program. It was the hope of many that the events of September 11th would bring a similar rejuvenation to the country.

210 / PERSPECTIVES ON VIOLENCE AND VIOLENT DEATH

MERCY PROJECT

Our study was unique in that we assessed individual's reactions in person and did it within 7 days of the 9/11 attacks. We recorded responses at several Mercy College campuses. We obtained responses from students at our campuses in Manhattan (at W. 33rd Street, where debris and suffocating odors were apparent); Dobbs Ferry (on the Hudson River, where the smoldering buildings could be directly observed); and at the Bronx Campus (where many of our students have previously experienced violence and disaster in their own communities). We were also able to measure reactions over time, up until two years later.

METHODOLOGY

Participant Characteristics

The impact of events was studied in a population of 389 Mercy College students, who voluntarily responded to several questionnaires. We had an equal distribution of Black, Hispanic and White students. More than one-third of our students had lost a relative or immediate-family member in this disaster. While very few of the students were present within the zone (now known as Ground Zero) of the actual attack, the views from the Dobbs Ferry and Manhattan campuses evoked great anxiety and long-lasting effects. Our sample consisted of more females than males (79/5). The majority of our sample was below the age of 45, with 45% less than 25-years-old.

The elements of comparison between segments of this population include gender, racial, religious, and socioeconomic differences. We also had data on the participants' distance from the World Trade Center. While the study is an attempt to look at differences over time, it is limited in that, because of the anonymity of the respondents, the number of the same students who were assessed at each interval since the attack is unknown. Another limitation is that the voluntary nature of the participation may indicate a subjective bias in those willing to report on affective experiences.

Procedure

The study involved the distribution of almost 1000 questionnaires. Only 432 of those returned met our initial requirements of English-speaking, college-educated students, who completely filled out the questionnaires.

Measures and Definitions of Variables

Posttraumatic Stress Symptoms—The DSM-IV describes the setting event for PTSD as exposure to a traumatic event during which one feels fear, helplessness, or horror. Afterwards, victims reexperience the event through memories and nightmares. When memories occur very suddenly, and the victims find themselves reliving the event, they are having flashbacks. Victims may also avoid anything that reminds them of trauma. They display a characteristic restriction or blunting of emotional responsiveness, which may be very disruptive to interpersonal relationships. Individuals who use this "blunting" approach may be hesitant to experience intense emotions as they might retrigger the events. Victims of trauma who develop PTSD are typically chronically overaroused, easily startled, and quick to anger (Barlow & Durand, 2005).

Two measures were used in this study to look at the outcomes in this category:

1. Foa, Cashman, Jaycox, and Perry (1997) is a 17-item scale that includes items that, when answered in a certain direction, are highly related to other scales and consistent with the requirement for PTSD on the DSM-IV criteria.
2. The Impact of Events (Horowitz, Wilner, & Alvarez, 1979) correlated highly with the above. It measures the degree of avoidance, reexperiencing, and arousal.

Clinical Depression—Diagnosable clinical depression is defined by the *DSM-IV* (American Psychiatric Association, 1994) as

1. Depressed mood (or irritable, especially in children)
2. Anhedonia (no longer able to experience pleasure)
3. Appetite or weight change (gain or loss)
4. Sleep change (more or less than normal)
5. Psychomotor agitation or retardation
6. Fatigue
7. Feelings of worthlessness or inappropriate guilt
8. Poor concentration
9. Suicidal ideation or attempt, recurrent thoughts of death and dying

Five of these symptoms are needed for a diagnosis of clinical depression. It is also important to note that all five symptoms must present during the *same two-week period.* Distress or disability must be found to be *clinically significant.* Mental illnesses are considered clinically significant when they cause significant disability or distress to the individual in a given case.

In this study, it was expected that all individuals experienced bereavement reactions to some extent, whether for losses in their own families or vicariously in reaction to others losses. We therefore expected to see varying degrees of sadness and looked not primarily for the disorder itself but those symptoms that occurred at lower levels.

Measures

The Center for Epidemiological Depression Scale (CESD; Radloff, 1977) is a 21-item questionnaire, which allows the respondent to indicate to what extent

212 / PERSPECTIVES ON VIOLENCE AND VIOLENT DEATH

(4-point scale) they have been experiencing symptoms of depression, insomnia, and somatic problems in the past week. The use of this scale determines mild to severe symptoms, but does not diagnose a major clinical depression syndrome.

In order to share the main findings, a description of the measures discussed will be followed by the method and results found. The various measures reflect how individuals coped. The posttraumatic-stress measure reflected the intrusion of thoughts, flashbacks, and feelings of unrealness. The depression measures revealed, not only those who could be classified as clinically depressed, but those showing lack of ability to enjoy previous activities, difficulty sleeping, eating, and in general a lack of ability to make certain decisions.

Assessment Intervals

We sampled a broad population of our students in Manhattan, Dobbs Ferry, the Bronx, and White Plains and looked at how their responses differed. The responses were sampled across time periods following the tragic events (within a week; one month, three months, and eight months). Due to the anonymous responses, it was difficult to judge how many of the same individuals were sampled more than once. We were interested in comparing our findings with our review of how others looked upon the initial responses. Seventy-five of the participants were male, and three hundred and fourteen were females; 36% had some college or an Associates degree; 17% had a Bachelor's degree; 6% had some graduate level of education; 7% had a Master's degree, 2% had a PhD or medical degree; 34% were African American; 20% were Caucasian; 34% were Hispanic; and 9% of the participants were other.

RESULTS

Results showed that in the 398 participants assessed at one week, one month, two months, and eight months, the following symptoms were demonstrated using Chi-square analyses.

Coping

The Brief Cope subscaled into three factors: active coping, disengagement, external coping, which included the use of alcohol and lack of religious orientation. These factors in the literature have been predicted to have different outcomes with responses to trauma; active coping being correlated positively with lower depression and the disengagement and use of alcohol being correlated with greater depression. In the results of this study, both of these factors predicted depression. It may be that any attempt at coping reflected the degree of depression experienced. The avoidance coping related to higher depression. With avoidance coping predominant, there is a sevenfold probability of depression. Blacks reported more avoidance-coping tendencies than other nonwhites.

Passive coping was eight times more likely to predict depression. Denial was eight times more likely to predict the probability of depression. In the report of the Impact of Events Scale, intrusive thoughts were six times more likely to predict depression. Intrusive thoughts and reported use of passive coping were highly correlated.

Depression

Clinical depression was reduced over time, however there was still an over 40% rate of depression 8 months after the WTC disaster. Those who knew someone who died (relative or acquaintance) reported a higher percentage of depression (60%) as compared with those who did not know anyone personally. These individuals also experienced a greater degree of intrusive thoughts (see Figures 1 and 2).

A finding that was unexpected but quite interesting showed that those who initially reported not experiencing symptoms of depression actually increased their reports of symptoms over the eight-month period of time. This would suggest that delayed depression was in fact an issue to be dealt with (see Figure 3).

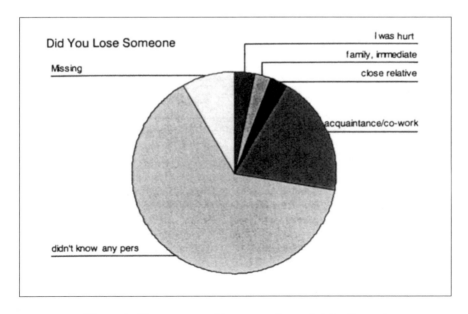

Figure 1. The sources of loss experienced at the time of the World Trade Center disaster.

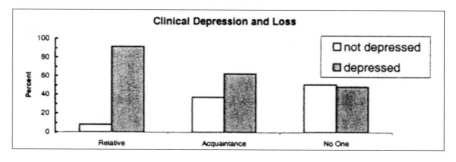

Figure 2. The relationship between depression and the loss of a relative, acquaintance or, no specific person that they knew.

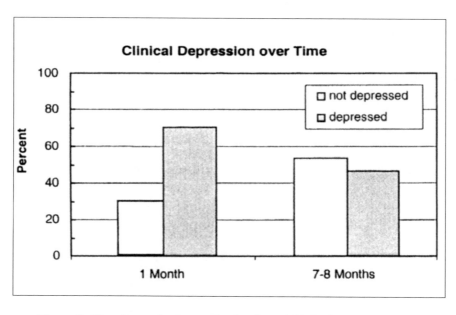

Figure 3. The change in depression for those initially depressed versus those who did not report significant depressive disorders.

Posttraumatic Stress Disorder

There were no significant diagnosable cases of PTSD reported at any time periods, although the percentage of severity and frequency of PTSD symptoms were similar to those reported in other studies. Using ethnic minority New Yorkers, 13% had severe symptoms, with a frequency of 16%. Those individuals who were highest in PTSD frequency after the attacks tended to continue to avoid subways and travel. There is also a positive relationship between worry about anthrax and total PTSD frequency.

Distance

Those who were closest to the site tended to drink alcohol and had the most intrusive thoughts; although there was a counterintuitive finding of a higher rate of depression in those furthest from the attack. This suggests that the destruction as viewed on television or seen from a distance was more significant.

Loss of Life

Those who lost someone were more likely to report engaging in substance abuse and report more intrusive memories.

Repeated Exposure

There were no significant differences in depression in those who viewed the actual events and those who saw the television replay.

Subgroups

- a. Thirty-seven percent of women reported clinical depression compared with 16% of males (chi, 2, 254 = 6.60; p < .04).
- b. Hispanics had higher rates of depression and posttraumatic stress symptoms at all times, but there were no clear distinctions when compared to Whites and Blacks.

DISCUSSION

One reason why this sample of students did not show the same levels of PTSD reported in the telephone survey might be that they had a greater degree of previous trauma. The results documented that those individuals reporting the use of active coping and passive coping in their past way of dealing with stress indicated more depression. However, those reportedly using avoidance strategies were less successful in this effort to deal with events, thus showing greater depression and more symptoms of PTSD.

The full impact of the September 11th tragedy has still to be determined. Some researchers still expect to see high rates of depression and posttraumatic stress disorder as well as other mood and anxiety disorders in the near future. At this point, it is still unclear which individuals are most likely to suffer from delayed, long-term affects. It is still important for mental-health workers to identify the individuals who are in need of help.

216 / PERSPECTIVES ON VIOLENCE AND VIOLENT DEATH

Depression could be the biggest problem to develop after September 11th. Everyone, at some point, may feel depressed, but it generally goes away. When it doesn't go away, the individual has a problem that can require the help of a mental-health professional. With any medically diagnosed case of depression, there is significant loss. This loss could be a literal loss of a loved one or a more abstract loss (the loss of feelings of safety) or a symbolic loss (such as the death of a major personality to whom an individual feels a connection). The thinking pattern that an individual has when depressed tends to keep the person in a rut that becomes self-perpetuating and is hard to cope with effectively.

TWO YEARS LATER: 2003

A recent study (Holmes, Grey, & Young, 2005) of emotional imagery and the reexperiencing of "hot spots" of trauma memories found that individuals who relived their peak emotional distress during the event were more likely to report intrusive images. Their intrusive recollections are thought to be predominantly visual (Ehlers, Hackmann, Steil, Clohessy, Wenninger, & Winter, 2002). Those who reported a lingering sense of helplessness, fear, and anger were most likely to have flashbacks. These are described as taking the form of "film clips" of part of the trauma. They are thought to function as a "warning signal," thus, the intrusions serve a sense of serious concern. The individuals who have only a verbal narrative are less likely to relive this experience voluntarily.

To comprehend the lingering effects of this disaster, it was necessary to understand the memories of Mercy College graduate students from the perspective of September 11, 2003, as written in response to the question, "Can you tell me how your personal behavior has changed in any recognizable form since September 11, 2001?" These responses are coded to reflect types of coping strategies still in use. Italics are used to demonstrate the content that reflects various coping categories.

Intrusive

"I think about how so many victims suffered in the final moments of their lives. How they died in a manner that most of us, prior to 9-11, only dreamed of in our nightmares. I try to comprehend what would have caused so many people to jump to their death, but I cannot. *The image of a man in a black suit falling from the north tower with his arms rapidly rotating in a futile manner to gain leverage as he fell remains vividly stuck in my memory.*"

(A retired police officer.) "Bright sunny mornings cause me to fear that something terrible might happen. I initially surmised that the plane struck the tower by accident. . . . I was grossly in error. Then the news that a jetliner struck the Pentagon compounded my confusion and fears causing profound emotions of sadness to erupt within my mind. I thought, what the hell is going on and why? I was with the New York City SWAT team and I knew many of my former coworkers from the emergency service unit were among the hundreds of rescue workers . . . in the process of responding to it. I wanted to do what I loved to do the most helping others. Then my world came crashing in. I was in total shock . . . as the television media announcer stated that the tower had collapsed. I was paralyzed, both mentally and physically. This was further exacerbated by the collapse of the north tower. In a state I would characterize as zombie, I walked to the basement where I cried like a baby. I had intended to go to the WTC somewhere between work and home, for reasons I still cannot determine, I redirected myself and picked up my kids from school and took them home. I felt scared and vulnerable, not knowing what was next to occurring or who was next to be killed or injured. I still feel that way two years later. I am terrified by bright sunny days. *The peace and serenity I once knew to be part of my life has been forever shattered by this event. I experience emotions about what occurred from time to time, not just on the anniversary of the event. I will never be the same person I was before 8:45 AM on September 11th.*"

"The newspapers (September 11, 2003) . . . all the memories of that day came rushing back. You could hear people screaming outside for their family members. People began frantically calling the friends and family . . . tears fill my eyes . . . that same nervous feeling returned . . . *even two years have past the terror of not knowing what will happen or will something like this happen. My friends cringe when they hear a plane fly overhead.*"

Passive Coping

"I smoke a hell of a lot more, eat more especially comfort foods, I stopped yelling at the kids so much about keeping their room tidy—life is too short . . . if I can see the floor, that's good enough for now. I took my husband back, although I know he is still a lying cheating bastard, he's a warm cuddly lying cheating bastard. . . . I don't go to Orchard Street any more, I turned down a job on Exchange place I don't want to be in the middle of the reconstruction."

Anger

"One aspect of September 11 and the war that I found ironic is that we are attempting to free people of fear, but yet we are living in fear."

"I do not agree with the fact that the mayor and builders want to re-build the World Trade Center, I feel that they should just leave it alone and make a monument. By building over that dirt and that spot is like trying to erase what happened, and I don't think anyone will ever forget that day."

"I asked her if she had any family or friends down the city during 911. She said she wasn't concerned because none of her loved ones were down there. She was however, shocked by the number of deaths and how people were dying. When asked now she feels today about the 911 events she said "nobody is the same after this, there is a residue of depression. The world has lost some of its value.""

218 / PERSPECTIVES ON VIOLENCE AND VIOLENT DEATH

Active Coping
(Positive Reattribution of the Event)

"I decided to continue my education . . . time is a precious commodity and we each have chosen to invest it in ways that increase our happiness and fulfill our desires for ourselves, our families, and country. It was the day the war came home. We have since re-defined ourselves and what makes us happy or afraid."

"Visiting Ground Zero two years later . . . I see the thick layer of dust and dirt. I watched the towers fall on television, but now visiting the area I could not find a word to describe my feeling. At the same time I was horrified and sad for those who lost someone. Yet, I felt happy for my friends who escaped. *I became more open to people. Also I could discuss my feeling more freely. This incident made me realize that each day should be taken to the fullest because you truly do not know what could happen in the next second. Not only has it positively influenced me by making me appreciate things more,* but it has had a negative influence as well. I now continuously check over my shoulder, double check who's around me and become nervous when I travel. One of the most positive things I witness was people from many different races, ethnicities and cultural backgrounds uniting to console and aid each other. *It reminded me that good things can be birthed out of bad situations.*"

Avoidance

"Perhaps my way of coping is the chicken route, but I choose to avoid as much as possible the memory of that horrific day. I am usually a person who rarely deals with fear . . . now I deal with fear on more than one occasion."

"My daughter acts as if she felt as though trees were going to fall on her. Every time we walked near trees she would take off running to a place on the street where she felt secure. After explaining to her numerous times that that was something that could never happen she sounded satisfied. The next day she would proceed to ask me the same questions. . . . A few months later I asked her did she still think the trees were going to fall and she remarked, 'of course I do, but since it makes you upset when I say that I have decided not to mention it.' *Time she spoke about the tree issue it reminded me of that day and I would be filled with so much anger. The terrorists have destroyed not only the lives of the people that died but also severely affected the people who had to move on.*"

"Since September 11, I only travel to Manhattan when it is necessary. While I was on the subway, I saw a man of Middle Eastern descent reading his book of prayers and praying. In one hand he had a little book containing prayers and in the other hand he held a metal object that he was hiding so no one could see it. Immediately I started praying. I was standing directly in front of this man and fear engulfed me. . . . I didn't know if he was just a faithful believer and praying or if he was a terrorist waiting for another chance to attack. My heart was beating so fast as I tried to look at the circular-metal object to see if I was really in danger. *I didn't allow fear to control me. I am glad that I did stay on the train because it turns out that the small metal object the man was carrying was nothing more that a counter.* He was simply counting the number of prayers he was saying. But because of past events I found myself fearing ordinary situations. . . . *Time would not permit me to tell of other events which have caused me to avoid the September 11th issue. I do not watch documentaries; news broadcasts, or go to prayer vigils. I try to do my best to forget it ever happened, not to absolve the terrorists, but to survive its effects.*"

Religiosity

"It was like you were watching a movie. I just turned to my fiancée and grabbed him and hugged him, because he was supposed to go to work early that day, and he would have been in that building when the plane came crashing out. A lot of people have told him that he is lucky, *but I tell him that he is blessed, because an angel was definitely on his side.*"

"*I remember the morning of September 11, 2001 as if it were yesterday. After I prayed however, I did feel peace inside me.* . . . Watching people jump out of windows and fall to their death was more horrifying than anything Hollywood could create. I know like many others, I will never be the same again. I have always valued and appreciated my family and close friends. Now I have an even greater appreciation for them. We don't let a day go by without saying 'I love you.'"

These paragraphs demonstrate the continued efforts of individuals to cope with an event that was unpredictable and horrific. As seen in our data results, those individuals reporting denial or avoidance strategies do not seem ready to go on with their lives. The events of September 2001 will be studied for years to come. Despite all of the theories projecting recovery and reattribution, the full emotional impact of that day and its aftermath is still not known and the "first awareness" of the personal impact of September 11, 2001 is still being felt by many.

REFERENCES

American Psychiatric Association. (1994). *Diagnostic and statistical manual of mental disorders* (4th ed.). Washington, DC: American Psychiatric Association.

Barlow, D., & Durand, V. M.(2005). *Abnormal psychology*. Belmont, CA: Wadsworth.

Brandes, D., Ben-Schachar, G., Gilboa, A., Bonne, O., Freedman, S., & Shalev, A. (2002). SD Symptoms and cognitive performance in recent trauma survivors. *Psychiatry Research, 110,* 231-238.

Foa, E. B., Cashman, L., Jaycox, L., & Perry, K. (1997). The validation of self-report measure of posttraumatic stress disorder: The PTSD scale. *Psychological Assessment, 9,* 445-451.

Ehlers, A., Hackmann, A., Steil, R., Clohessy, S., Wenninger, K., & Winter, H. (2002). The nature of intrusive memories after trauma: The warning signal hypothesis. *Behavioral Research Therapy, 40*(9): 995-1002.

220 / PERSPECTIVES ON VIOLENCE AND VIOLENT DEATH

Galea, S., Ahern, J., Resnick, H., Lilpatric, D., Buculuvas, M., Gold, J., & Valhov, D. (2002). Psychological sequelae of the September 11 terrorist attacks in New York City. *New England Journal of Medicine, 346,* 982-987.

Holmes, E. A., Grey, N., & Young, K. A. D. (2005). Intrusive images and "hotspots" of traumatic memories in posttraumatic stress disorder. *Journal of Behavior Therapy and Experimental Psychiatry, 36,* 3-17.

Horowitz, M., Wilner, N., & Alvarez, W. (1979). Impact of Event Scale: A measure of subjective stress. *Psychosomatic Medicine, 41,* 209-218.

Manne, S., Du Hamel, K., Galleli, K., Sorgen, K., & Redd, W. (1998). Posttraumatic stress disorder among mothers of pediatric cancer survivors: Diagnosis, comorbidity, and utility of the PTSD checklist as a screening instrument. *Journal of Pediatric Psychology, 23,* 357-366.

Melnick, T. A., Baker, C. T., Adams, M. L., O'Dowd, Mokdad, A. H., Brown, D., Murphy, W., Giles, W., & Bales, M. P. (2002). Psychological and emotional effects of the September 11 attacks on the World Trade Center Connecticut, New Jersey and New York, 2001, *CDC Weekly, 51*(35), 784-786.

North, C. S., Nixon, S. J., Shariat, S., Mallonee, S., McMillen, J. C., Spitznagel, E. L., & Smith, E. M. (1999). Psychiatric disorders among survivors of the Oklahoma City bombing. *Journal of the American Medical Association, 282,* 755-762.

Radloff, L. (1977). The CES-D Scale: A self report depression scale for research in the general population. *Applied Psychological Measurement, 1,* 365-401.

Schlenger, W., Caddell, J., Ebert, L., Jordan, B., Rourke, K., & Wilson, D. (2002). Psychological reactions to terrorist attacks: Findings from the National Study of Americans' Reactions to September 11. *Journal of the American Medical Association, 288,* 581-588.

Schuster, M., Stein, B., Jaycox, L., et al. (2001). A national survey of stress reactions after the September 11, 2001 terrorist attacks. *New England Journal of Medicine, 345,* 1507-1512.

Sheehan, T., & Zimmerman, M. (2002). Screening for posttraumatic stress disorder in a general psychiatric outpatient setting. *Journal of Consultant Clinical Psychology, 70,* 961-966.

Silver, R., Holman, E., McIntosh, D., Poulin, M., & Gil-Rivas, V. (2002). Nationwide Longitudinal Study of Psychological Responses to September 11. *Journal of the American Medical Association, 288,* 1235-1244.

Smith, D., Christianson, E., Vincent, R., & Hann, N. (1999). Population effects of the bombing of Oklahoma City. *Journal of Oklahoma State Medical Association, 92,* 193-198.

Ursano, R. (2002) Post-traumatic stress disorder. *New England Journal of Medicine, 346,* 130-131.

Vlahov, D., Galea, S., Resnick, H., et al. (2002). Increased use of cigarettes, alcohol, and marijuana among Manhattan, New York, residents after the September 11th terrorist attacks. *American Journal of Epidemiological Research, 155,* 988-996.

Yehuda, R. (2002). Posttraumatic stress disorder. *New England Journal of Medicine, 346,* 108-114.

PART IV

Alternatives to Violence/Coping with Violence

CHAPTER 14

Making and Breaking Cycles of Violence

Colin Murray Parkes

Some of the most harmful consequences of violence arise when a cycle of violence becomes established. In order to break cycles of violence, we need to analyze the causes of such cycles. Yet violence evokes such strong emotions that it clouds our thinking and inhibits analytic thought. Indeed there is something "calculating" about the very exercise in which we are engaged in this chapter. Like the anatomists who first dissected the human body, we need to find a way to touch the untouchable, to think clearly about the unthinkable, to inhibit our own revulsion from so dangerous a task.

Everyone has their own solution to the problem of violence, which usually consists of identifying an enemy and defeating it. Another is the idea that the best way to break cycles of violence is to forbid violence; yet how can we enforce that prohibition if we are not willing to use violence itself? Police forces may need to use violence to apprehend a serial killer and "peacekeeping" forces may need to use violence to protect themselves and to bring peace. Each discipline tends to develop its own model. Soldiers seek military solutions, clergy seek religious solutions, politicians seek political solutions, and economists seek economic solutions. Some of these solutions sometimes work, but none of them provides a comprehensive or integrated view; all are, to some extent, simplistic; they attempt a simple solution to complex problems. And, as we shall see, some simplistic models do more harm than good.

In this chapter, a model will be described, which explains many, but not all, of the cycles of violence and illustrates how they can and have been broken. The examples are either derived from actual cases or from systematic research. They show that, although the causes may be complex, they are often comprehensible, and although solutions may not be easy, they are often possible.

224 / PERSPECTIVES ON VIOLENCE AND VIOLENT DEATH

We look first at the way cycles of violence arise at each level of social unit, from the individual to the international. We then look for continuities across different levels, asking what we can learn from each level that may aid our understanding at another level.

INDIVIDUAL LEVEL

A person finds him or herself compelled to repeated acts of violence irrespective of outside influence. At first sight, this may seem unlikely since violence is itself an interactive event. However, there are some situations in which a strong propensity to violence can arise repeatedly, with little or no outside influence. Examples include rare cases of premenstrual tension, organic brain conditions producing extreme irritability, and rare types of paranoid schizophrenia. The underlying causes of these cycles are often endocrine or structural brain damage to the areas of the brain concerned with impulse control. In each case, recurrent feelings of rage can be assuaged only by violent acts. In paranoid schizophrenia, the motivation is not clear but usually includes a delusion that the sufferer is being attacked and must retaliate.

Such cycles of violence are not unbreakable. Given proper care, premenstrual tension can be alleviated and the emotional disorder caused by brain damage and paranoid schizophrenia controlled. Indeed, with proper treatment, the risk of violence in severely ill psychiatric patients is less than that in the nonpsychiatric population (Torrey, 1994).

FAMILY AND INTERPERSONAL LEVEL

Two or more individuals perpetuate or repeat acts of violence or abuse. These often involve circular "traps" in which short-term relief from rising tension leads to perpetuation of conflict; for example, marital tensions leading to alcohol abuse leading to repeated violence, or sadomasochistic sexual relationships. Although at the outset, such cycles usually involve two individuals, others are soon drawn in to take sides.

SMALL GROUP/COMMUNITY LEVEL

In many species, cyclical changes in hormone levels trigger aggression against conspecifics at certain times each year; these lead to combats that come to an end as soon as one of the combatants submits or runs away; they seldom end fatally, witness the rutting of stags in the spring. In humans, it is reasonable to assume that similar hormonal changes predispose young people, particularly males, to engage in aggressive, challenging behavior. Young females may encourage conflict by favoring winners.

MAKING AND BREAKING CYCLES OF VIOLENCE / 225

A large difference between humans and other species is, of course, the opportunity to achieve status by means other than combat. Psychological battles usually take the place of physical conflict, and the takeovers, feuds, and "broken hearts" that result are seldom fatal.

Although few societies in which a small scale of clan or tribal organization is established still exist, they were, over the long period of human evolution, the main unit of social organization. Most societies lived in peace much of the time, but sooner or later conflicts over territory, food, or available mates would arise. Repeated battles against neighboring tribes met the purpose of extending or maintaining territory; they also widened the gene pool by enabling the victors to claim mates from another tribe. Young males, who did most of the fighting, were also rewarded with "warrior" status. This enabled some tribes to survive while less martial tribes perished. Thus, in evolutionary terms, the cost to the community of the death of some warriors was balanced by the survival of the clan/tribe.

There were, and still are, some tribes in which most deaths are assumed to be the consequence of human acts or witchcraft. These then place upon the survivors an obligation to revenge, which may give rise to a cycle of violence (Rosenblatt, 1997).

Large scale societies attempt to forbid or limit internecine feuds at the small group level with varying success. Within many societies, subcultures see themselves as outside the law, outlaws or gangs, which resemble the clan or tribe. They are particularly likely to arise when central government breaks down or the rewards of obedience to higher authority—wealth, jobs, security, etc.—are denied, as in the poor areas of major cities with high levels of unemployment and little hope for the future. Gangs often use drugs or alcohol to reduce fear or increase excitement; this in turn reduces inhibitions against violence, which is usually directed against other gangs or supposed enemies who may then become victims.

NATIONAL LEVEL

Coups and revolutions occur when a powerful group within a large scale society attempts to wrest power from the leaders. If the conflict is not soon resolved, cycles of violence may become established, and we have a civil war. Even when the conflict is resolved, the seeds of future violence may have been sown. Since the emergent power is likely to enact severe penalties against future revolt, the defeated parties may become outlaws as described above. For a revolution to become a civil war, two things are needed: (1) a balance of power between the contending parties such that neither can win a decisive victory, and (2) the contending parties need to be unwilling or unable to find a way to share power.

INTERNATIONAL LEVEL

When a powerful large-scale society attacks a weak or small-scale society, the conflict is soon over, although as above, the seeds of future conflict may have been sown and, acts of resistance or terrorism may continue. Wars occur when two or more powerful countries use violence against each other and, as in civil wars, the contenders cannot reach agreement to share power.

Although at first glance, the differences between wars and smaller-scale conflict seem great, they become less so when we consider the important roles played by leaders and young males. At all levels of analysis, except the individual, it is a small number of leaders who have the power to stop the conflict or to allow it to continue. Likewise, at all levels of analysis, it is young males who do most of the fighting.

A MODEL OF THE CYCLE THAT CROSSES LEVELS OF SOCIAL UNIT

With this in mind, members of *the International Work Group on Death, Dying, and Bereavement* (IWG) have developed a common model of cycles of violence (see Figure 1) capable of shedding light on all levels above the individual. The model also suggests points at which intervention may break the cycle.

The IWG is a group of clinicians, researchers, and educators from many countries, who develop research and practice dealing with death, dying, and bereavement. Our work brings us face to face with the consequences of cycles of violence. It is this involvement that motivates IWG to find ways to understand and find solutions to the problem. A more detailed account of the model to be described here has been published in *Death Studies* (International Work Group on Death, Dying, and Bereavement, 2005).

Although the circumstances listed in the cycle tend to occur in sequence, each influences all the others. Possible interventions are shown in bold.

Violent Behavior

Violent behavior seldom occurs out of the blue. It is usually preceded by a period of rising tension, during which preventive intervention is possible. Here are some examples:

> Mothers who serially abuse their children are often themselves under stress. Only when she "gets to the end of her tether" does a mother, who may genuinely love her child, suddenly find herself losing her temper and hitting the child against a wall. Social workers may be able to form a relationship of trust such that, whenever the mother becomes aware that her level of tension is rising, she will contact the social worker for immediate support and guidance.

> At an international level, the United Nations has appointed a Special Advisor on the Prevention of Genocide, whose role is to ensure that the

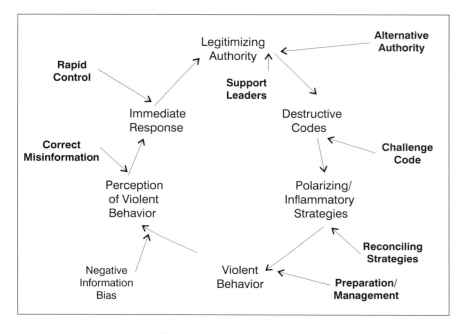

Figure 1. Cycle of violence.

Security Council is informed fully about threats of genocide, which also represent threats to international peace and security.

Violence is most likely to lead to retaliation and the initiation of a cycle if it is excessive, disproportionate, cruel, or inhumane. When violence is threatened, it may be possible to persuade or train those who are to carry it out to keep it to a minimum, consistent with their aims. This is particularly the case when the violence is planned in advance. Rules of punishment and rules of engagement may authorize violence, but they also allow for opportunities for minimizing it, as in:

> The abolition of corporal punishment in schools or the use of nonlethal methods of crowd control, such as "foam baton rounds" in place of conventional ammunition.

Those who carry out acts of violence need to monitor the consequences of their acts if they are to keep their violence to a minimum. This is easier in face-to-face combat than in conflicts that, with modern weapons, can be carried out without ever seeing the "enemy." In these circumstances, the temptation to "over kill" in order to be sure of success regularly leads to death and injuries to noncombatants. Agreements can forbid or limit the use of weapons likely to give rise to excessive consequences. Such agreements can take the form of:

228 / PERSPECTIVES ON VIOLENCE AND VIOLENT DEATH

Legislation against the right of ordinary citizens to own or carry lethal weapons, or international agreements against development, ownership, and use of weapons of mass destruction.

Perception of Violent Behavior

It is the perception of an act that determines the response. Following acts of violence, the magnitude of the impact and interpretation of the event is influenced by witnesses and how information is communicated to others. Thus, child abuse is often perpetuated because the abused child is afraid to reveal the abuse, or because it is disbelieved. On the other hand, some children exaggerate or imagine abuse that has not happened (False Memory Syndrome). This can lead to "witch hunts" that drag on and lead to more injustice. Clearly accurate and impartial reporting as well as open-minded listening are essential if communication is to succeed and an appropriate response to be made. In psychiatric circles, this is referred to as "reality testing" and involves very much more than the communication of factual information.

Similar failure of communication can take place at other levels, as when newspaper reporters play down or, conversely, exaggerate the magnitude of an event and the dangers associated with it or when prejudice clouds our interpretation of the information we receive.

But accurate reporting does not necessarily solve the problem. While modern weaponry may make it hard for combatants to witness the consequences of their actions, modern media of communication have the opposite effect. On September 11, 2001, hijacked airliners crashed into nearly every home in the world in possession of a television set. Although the total number of deaths was about one-hundredth of the number who died in the genocide in Rwanda, and no greater than the number who die on the roads every week in the United States, the perception of the outrage was much greater after 9/11 and its impact and consequences quite disproportionate. We cannot blame the mass media for showing these pictures, but a great deal more could have been done to put them in perspective. In a few months the acts of a handful of religious extremists started a succession of wars, which are still not over.

Judges, whose experience of the adversarial system trains them to see both sides of every case; statisticians, who are trained to weigh the significance of large numbers; historians, who are trained to see events in their historical context; and psychotherapists, who are trained to take a family history and hear what is not being said as well as what is may be better placed than others to get such things in proportion. Journalists have so much influence, that a high standard of training and performance should be required and monitored outside of political and other partisan influence. Schools should teach children how to read, understand, and evaluate news. The following examples illustrate the power of an unbiased perspective:

MAKING AND BREAKING CYCLES OF VIOLENCE / 229

After the murder of his wife by a drug addict, John Robelli roamed the streets with a loaded revolver in search of the killer. He had no doubt that, had he found the man, he would have killed him. Fortunately the police arrested the murderer before John got to him. When referred for psychiatric help, John was still very angry. In the course of psychotherapy, he realized that, "If I had killed that man, I would have been doing to his daughter just what he did to mine." He might also have triggered retaliation by the killer's associates. Gangland wars are sometimes initiated in this way. Three years later, John appeared on a television debate and spoke out against capital punishment for murder.

In 1966, an avalanche, caused by the collapse of a spoil heap from the local coal mine in the village of Aberfan in South Wales, resulted in the death of 116 children. In the weeks that followed, anger was spilling in all directions, and three public meetings broke up in fistfights. Reporters from the *Merthyr Gazette* worked closely with the Disaster Response Team to scotch rumors and to provide distressed people with accurate information and opportunities to express their feelings in ways that would not add to their problems (e.g., in a poetry column). Subsequently, the newspaper received a well-earned award for the quality of its support to the community. Many villagers attended the Board of Inquiry and found that the impartial exam-ining of witnesses changed their perception of what had happened. Even when blame was attributed, they could now acknowledge that those respon-sible were fallible human beings, not outright monsters (Parkes, 1976).

Immediate Responses to Violence

Fear and rage are natural responses to threat, along with a tendency to seek out others in mutual defense. Throughout evolution, such behavior often enabled people to survive, and even today this is sometimes the case. Unfortunately, misperception of the situation, pressure to take immediate action for fear of worse to come, and the escalation of fear that may infect crowds or other groups of people may lead to intemperate responses that aggravate the situation and lead to a cycle of violence. Vilification and immediate retaliatory acts against a supposed enemy, triumphalist behavior by victors, and attributions of martyrdom to victims may all contribute to escalate the violence.

It is of crucial importance that those responsible for keeping the peace take immediate action to advertise their presence and to take control of the situation, prevent further violence, and give emotional support to those affected. This may include neighbors and others not directly under threat.

Murders are often carried out by family members. This sometimes makes investigating police officers suspicious and uncommunicative in their handling of bereaved families and aggravates bitterness and anger. In

230 / PERSPECTIVES ON VIOLENCE AND VIOLENT DEATH

the United Kingdom, special training is now provided to Police Family Liaison teams who are expected to provide emotional support at the same time as carrying out their investigative roles. One such team worked closely with bereavement volunteers from Cruse Bereavement Care to provide "psychological first aid" to traumatized families from the United Kingdom who were flown to New York in the wake of 9/11.

Legitimizing Authorities

Cycles of violence seldom persist without the support of an authority or authorities who legitimize further violence. These may include parents, political leaders, religious leaders, military authorities, cult leaders, insurgent leaders, and gang leaders. They may perpetuate the violence by direct command of military or other forces by exaggerating the danger in order to obtain popular support for retaliation, by reminding people of past wrongs and humiliations, and by "monsterizing the enemy." These acts may be necessary responses to real dangers, but they may also be unnecessary or disproportionate responses to minimal dangers.

Unnecessary or disproportionate responses are likely to occur if the leader seeks to buttress an insecure power by uniting others behind himself and against a common enemy. It then becomes unpatriotic to oppose the leader.

At times of violence, parents and other leaders are often themselves traumatized and their ability to make wise decisions impaired. Some are more vulnerable than others: they may have personal problems, have suffered trauma in the past, or lack emotional support. Only too often, those at the top of the tree are supposed to support people below them and to have no need for support for themselves. Having, in a crisis, adopted a particular stance, it may then be difficult or politically disastrous for them to change their minds. It follows that every effort should be made to give psychological support to leaders following violent events and to dissuade them from drastic actions that may exacerbate the problems they face.

To varying degrees, all leaders are subject to pressures and influence from power groups and from others. At times of violence, such pressures are often in the direction of retaliation, and leaders who temporize are seen as weak. Opposition groups may vie with the leader for public support for aggressive action, each group adopting more extreme positions. Military leaders and political leaders who find their main support from the military are particularly likely to seek military solutions to their problems.

Other groups are likely to oppose violence and to offer alternatives to retaliation. Indeed, some are themselves alternative authorities with the role of limiting the power of the parents or other leaders. These include legislative authorities such as social workers, religious leaders, judges, peacekeeping forces, arbitrators (who are authorized to make decisions about disputed issues) and mediators (who facilitate negotiation in the hope that contenders will reach agreement). All of these bodies can, at times, break cycles of violence, as in these 3 examples:

> After the death of his wife, a caring but insecure father found it hard to cope with a nine-year-old son whose grief was reflected in rebellious behavior. He exerted his authority by the only means he knew, beating the boy. His son responded by becoming increasingly bitter and by bullying other children. When a school teacher informed the social services, the son was placed on the "at risk" register and the father was induced, by the threat of judicial action, to accept the guidance of a social worker. He subsequently learned to obtain his son's cooperation by rewarding good behavior in preference to coercion. The cycle of violence was broken, the relationship between son and father improved, and the child's bullying ceased.

> In Britain, the monarch, unlike her Ministers, is relatively free of pressure from the electorate and often acts as a close advisor to her Prime Minister. In December 1861, at the height of the American Civil War, Britain's aged, gout-crippled Prime Minister, Lord Palmerston, learned that a British ship, the *Trent*, had been intercepted by an American Union warship and two Confederate envoys, Mason and Slidell, taken into custody. Reaction in the press to this insult to the British flag was strong and, under pressure from his Foreign Secretary (John Russell), Palmerston showed the Queen a draft of a belligerent letter to the American Secretary of State. This would probably have led to extension of the war, with Britain taking the side of the Confederates and France drawn in to support the Union. Queen Victoria and Prince Albert, who was already suffering from typhoid fever, which would kill him two weeks later, persuaded Palmerston to accept a redraft of the letter, which provided the Americans with an opportunity to deny hostile intent and avoid an escalation of the war (Weintraub,1987).

> Although the United Nations was criticized for its failure to prevent the genocide in Rwanda, the subsequent presence of small numbers of UN peacekeeping officers, who moved rapidly to trouble spots in the wake of the genocide, probably helped to break the cycle of violence that had smouldered on for over 25 years.

Acts of legitimizing authorities that may increase the risk of cycles of violence include concealment of relevant information or plans, misrepresentation of dangers, and adoption of double standards. Leaders who act covertly often encourage others to do the same; trust is undermined, and all sides tend to expect the worst. Conversely, open awareness reduces suspicion and the paranoid assumptions that encourage further violence, as in these examples:

> After their daughter died, George and Mary each responded in their own ways: Mary, by crying and seeking attention, and George, by refusing to

232 / PERSPECTIVES ON VIOLENCE AND VIOLENT DEATH

speak about his daughter, going to the pub and getting drunk. Mary accused George of not caring, and George, who felt helpless and threatened by his wife's clinging, continued to distance himself from her. The affection that they had previously felt for each other seemed to dissolve. As time went by, the tension between them increased, and they took out their bitterness by abusing each other verbally and, at times, physically. Eventually, Mary sought the help of a psychiatrist, and her husband agreed to attend with her. The psychiatrist reminded them that anger is a natural reaction to bereavement and invited each of them to reveal how they felt about their daughter's death. Once George realized that he was not under attack or being blamed for his daughter's death, he confessed that he felt a failure as both husband and parent. He had backed away from his wife because he did not know how to help her. His frankness had an immediate effect on his wife who realized that, in his own way, her husband cared just as much as she.

Recently revealed documents about the Cuban Missile Crisis (Chang & Kornbluh, 2004) show how the danger of a nuclear war was greatly increased by the fact that both sides kept their intentions secret and deliberately set out to mislead the other. This led to each side assuming the worst and making plans for preemptive strikes against each other. Only when Kennedy and Khrushchev spoke directly and corrected these misperceptions of each other's intentions could trust be established and a basis for agreement reached. Even then, both sides continued to conceal their negotiations from their followers in order to take credit for the outcome.

Destructive Codes

Our brain is an organ, one of whose main functions is to take in a huge amount of information and simplify it to the point at which we can comprehend the world around us and cope with it successfully. One way of doing that is to adopt shorthand "codes" to represent complex aspects of reality. Most of them we take for granted; they become axioms that form the basis of our assumptive worlds, the world that we assume to exist. Among these codes, are assumptions about friends and enemies, good and bad, and right and wrong. Friends we can trust; we can count on their loyalty at times of trouble, they will help to defend us from our enemies. On the whole, we assume that friends are good and right. When they are not, we forgive them their failings, tending to idealize them. Enemies, on the other hand, are not to be trusted; they will harm our allies and us; they are bad and in the wrong. When they are not, we ignore the discrepancy, tending to monsterize them.

Although these codes are always simplifications of reality, there is nothing wrong with having them, indeed we could not survive without them. Even so, it is important to recognize that they can never be anything more than approximations of reality, the best we can manage. And there are times when they become destructive and contribute to cycles of violence. Cycles of violence are likely to

MAKING AND BREAKING CYCLES OF VIOLENCE / 233

persist if maintained by the belief that my side is right, just, and good; while the enemy is wrong, unjust, and bad. Strangers and foreigners are often assumed to be dangerous and easily come to be seen as enemies. When we treat them as enemies, it is not surprising if they do the same to us, thereby confirming and perpetuating our belief system (hence the saw, "Give a dog a bad name and it will bite you").

Codes of justice range from concepts of fairness in personal relationships to more general belief in a rule of law based on human rights and assumed to be maintained by the ruling power. Codes of morality distinguish good from bad. Codes of honor guide assessment of worth and esteem. Codes of propriety define what is proper, decent, and correct. These codes, though all concerned with value, may conflict or compete with each other. Thus, the code of honor among young men may value bravery and pride above moral codes of gentleness and humanity. Indeed there are times when ruthlessness and cruelty to an enemy is seen as right by one side and monstrous by the other. At a family level, codes that perpetuate cycles of violence include family myths such as "spare the rod and spoil the child," "children are wicked by nature and the sin must be beaten out of them for the sake of their immortal souls."

Cycles of violence are most likely to persist if buttressed by strongly held, inflexible, belief in codes that permit or encourage violence. Destructive codes include:

- Codes, such as "An eye for an eye," which encourages retaliation,
- Codes that are exclusive, the "only true faith," and denigrate other faiths,
- Codes that foster a belief in the superiority of a person or group; that makes them entitled to special privileges.
- Codes that permit, reward, or encourage cruelty, killing, suicide, or martyrdom.

It follows that anything that persuades people to question, abandon, or modify destructive codes will reduce the chances of violence becoming cyclical. Tolerance of people different from oneself may not come easily, but can be taught; so can respect for the positive codes of others and the establishment of new codes that foster humility and tolerance while discouraging extremism and violence. This is easier said than done, for it is our codes that give us our identity. Question them and you devalue us. Even so, some remarkable successes can be cited.

Mahatma Ghandi developed his code of nonviolence in South Africa. He wrote:

> It is necessary to revive the eternal law of answering anger by love and of violence by non-violence; "Hate the sin and not the sinner" is a precept which, though easy enough to understand, is rarely practised, and that is why the poison of hatred spreads in the world. . . . It is quite proper to resist and attack a system, but to resist and attack its author is tantamount to resisting and attacking oneself. . . . It is the acid test of non-violence that, in a non-violent conflict, there is no rancour left behind, and in the end the enemies are

234 / PERSPECTIVES ON VIOLENCE AND VIOLENT DEATH

> converted into friends. That was my experience in South Africa, with General Smuts. He started with being my bitterest opponent and critic. Today he is my warmest friend (Prabhu & Rao, 1945).

The application of Ghandi's policy of passive resistance to British domination of India became a nondestructive code that succeeded in producing major social change in India and eventual independence. There was very little violence on either side, and the change has left a legacy of mutual respect between the two nations.

> The Roman Emperor Constantine, in 313 CE, pronounced the "Edict of Milan," declaring that "complete toleration" should be given by the State to anyone who had "given up his mind to the Christians" or any other cult. This brought an end to a long cycle of persecution of Christians (Johnson, 1976).

When codes are written down, or *codified*, they become more rigid, reduce ambiguity, and simplify decision making. Most religions codify both moral codes and codes of propriety. Believers then have a simple guide to what is right. Unfortunately, different religions adopt different codes, and even within the major religions there is considerable variation from fundamentalists to liberals in the flexibility with which the codes are applied. Codes of justice and human rights are codified as laws, and these are usually assumed to apply to leaders as well as followers. This said, leaders often have the power to change laws. Cycles of violence may be created or broken by changing the law.

> Marriage guidance counsellors often make use of a "contract" which both sides can agree to and, if kept, will reduce the chance of further conflict. Most civilized countries now acknowledge such human rights as the right of people accused of an offense to hear the evidence against them and to be entitled to legal defense in a court of law. Even so, following 9/11, the British government introduced legislation allowing the indefinite detention, without such trial, of foreign nationals who are thought to support terrorism. Although this attempt to deprive foreigners of their human rights was intended to break the cycle of terrorist violence, it may have had the opposite effect. By undermining Britain's ethical position, it supported the destructive code of some Muslims that Britain is a corrupt country ruled by Satan. The British legislation has recently been successfully challenged in the European court of human rights.

Polarizing, Inflammatory Strategies

All of the foregoing factors influence the formation of strategies that sometimes inflame the situation and establish or perpetuate a cycle of violence. Perpetuation is particularly likely if the strategies result from an assumption that there is *no alternative to a violent response*. This is likely to be associated with scapegoating;

MAKING AND BREAKING CYCLES OF VIOLENCE / 235

that is, focusing on a *single assumed source* (e.g., Arabs, Jews, religious extremists) who can be defined as monsters or enemies and defeated.

A cycle of violence is most likely to be established if either the balance of power is such that neither side can be defeated or having demonstrated their superior power by threatening or defeating the enemy, the powerful then
• attempt to humiliate, punish, or take revenge, or
• fail to deal with underlying causes of the conflict (e.g., injustice, poverty, or exploitation).

By depriving the weaker side of any chance of an acceptable existence, hatred is generated, destructive codes established, and the probability of future violence increased. Conversely, anything that allows all parties to live an acceptable existence, respects their worldview, and attempts to put right the underlying causes of conflict will reduce the chance of further conflict.

The film *One Flew over the Cuckoo's Nest* demonstrated how the abuse of power by the staff of a mental hospital could lead to resentment and eventual retaliation by the patients in their care. Although fictional, the film explains why the removal of physical methods of restraint, the unlocking of doors, and the creation of "therapeutic communities" in such institutions during the 1950s and '60s, contrary to the expectations of older staff (who were locked into a destructive code), led to a reduction in violence and improvement in symptoms and relationships between staff and patients (Jones 1982).

After World War I, the humiliation of Germany sowed the seeds of bitterness and, in the end, led to World War II. Two years after the end of World War II, on June 5, 1947, Secretary of State George C. Marshall spoke at Harvard University.

> I need not tell you gentlemen that the world situation is very serious . . . the United States should do whatever it is able to do to assist in the return of normal economic health in the world, without which there can be no political stability and no assured peace. Our policy is directed, not against any country or doctrine, but against hunger, poverty, desperation, and chaos. Its purpose should be the revival of working economy in the world so as to permit the emergence of political and social conditions in which free institutions can exist (Department of State, 1947).

The Marshall Plan provided Germany with opportunities for economic recovery and broke the cycle of violence.

When violence starts, it usually involves only a small number of people. They may be extremists or people who misperceive a situation as exceedingly dangerous. For the reasons given above, violence evokes violent responses, and before long others are likely to be drawn in to take sides. This *polarization* is usually a gradual process, but it may be accelerated by the magnitude of the

236 / PERSPECTIVES ON VIOLENCE AND VIOLENT DEATH

perceived threat and by group or individual pressures. Leaders who insist that "All who are not for us are against us" are attempting to force people out of the middle ground. Consequently, those who advocate peaceful alternatives may be framed as less committed to the group's welfare, as appeasers, disloyal, naïve, or cowards. Such behaviors increase polarization and may foster cycles of violence. On the other hand, those who resist such pressures or oppose extremism may help to break a cycle of violence. If polarization is the centrifugal force driving people toward the poles, then centrism is the centripetal force that pulls them together. Those who insist on maintaining a middle ground can encourage centrism.

In the case of George and Mary, previously cited, their surviving children sided with Mary, and George felt increasingly isolated and bitter as a result. He had now lost not only his daughter but his entire family. Their psychiatrist, on the other hand, refused to take sides or to judge either party. By holding to the middle ground, he implied that it was possible for George and Mary to do the same. Instead of justifying their positions by attacking each other, they each tried to understand the other's point of view. Once the door to honest communication was open, each parent realized the extent to which their grief had driven them to defend themselves and set up a cycle of distrust. They came to understand that they were needed by and had something to give to the other.

In May 1986 Nelson Mandela, who had been in prison for 23 years, received a visit from a group of Commonwealth leaders. His account of this meeting illustrates that it is possible for a leader, who had been seen as an extremist, to demonstrate a moderate or centrist position without betraying his cause:

> I told them . . . that I was firmly committed to a non-racial society. I told them I believed in the Freedom Charter, that the Charter embodied principles of democracy and human rights, and that it was not a blue-print for socialism. I spoke of my concern that the white minority should feel a sense of security in any new South Africa. I told them I thought that many of our problems were a result of lack of communication between the government and the ANC [African National Congress], and that some of these could be resolved through actual talks. They questioned me extensively on the issue of violence, and while I was not yet willing to renounce violence, I affirmed in the strongest possible terms that violence could never be the ultimate solution to the situation in South Africa (Mandela, 1994).

The meeting marked a turning point in the negotiations that were to lead to the abandonment of apartheid in South Africa, Mandela's emergence as the first black South African president, and the first man to govern a democratic, multiracial South African society.

CONCLUSIONS

Some have claimed that is it the "animal" nature of man that explains both the occurrence of violence and its perpetuation. Yet, as we have seen, aggression between nonhuman animals of the same species is rarely fatal. Furthermore, all social animals share with human beings the tendency to make attachments to parents, children, and in most cases, peers. This inhibits aggression and facilitates social intercourse. Hence, it can be argued that it is our animal capacity for love that provides us with a natural tendency to abhor violence. Viewed in this way, cycles of violence are an aberration. They are certainly not inevitable and should be preventable. Mankind is not doomed by his animal nature; we may treat strangers with suspicion, but they need not remain strangers for long. Indeed, as Ghandi maintained, it is natural to turn strangers, and even enemies, to friends.

Over the years we have developed systems of justice and social organization that have reduced violence at family and community levels in many parts of the world. When this is not the case this often reflects social injustice and "structural violence" that leave the disempowered no perceived alternatives to violence. The wholehearted adoption of international law and justice, the universal establishment of codes of human rights and the fostering of "internationalism" as an alternative to "nationalism" would all tend to break the cycles of violence that destroy the peace of the world.

Scientific and technical developments have resulted in most of us living in a world that is largely manmade. Thanks to these developments, we are now, in theory, capable of eliminating poverty and creating a society in which human rights can be guaranteed. We can even use our hard-won knowledge to solve the problems caused by technology. For instance, the development of methods of transport has improved the distribution of food but has also created another cause of death, the road traffic accident. As a consequence, much time, research, and legislation has improved road safety, and despite an enormous increase in the number of vehicles on the roads, the death rate from motor-vehicle accidents in England and Wales dropped by 53% between 1971 and 2002 (National Statistics Online).

Given the global danger of cycles of violence in an age when weapons of mass destruction are available, it is surprising that similar attention has not been paid to the study and legislation that are necessary if we are to eliminate these cycles. Part of the difficulty may lie in the fact that there is no one scientific discipline that covers the field. The model developed here integrates knowledge from several different disciplines. This is a field in which psychologists, sociologists, political scientists, historians, economists, journalists, theologians, ethicists, military scholars, and many others need to learn to work together. If they will take the trouble to reach out beyond the limits of their own restricted vision, they may discover that cycles of violence are neither inevitable nor irreversible.

238 / PERSPECTIVES ON VIOLENCE AND VIOLENT DEATH

REFERENCES

Chang, L., & Kornbluh, P. (Eds.). (2004). *The Cuban missile crisis.* National Security Archive, Washington University published on the Web at http://www2.gwu.edu/~nsarchiv/nsa/cuba_mis_cri/.

Department of State Bulletin. (1947, June 15)., XVI, No. 415, pp. 1159-1160.

International Work Group on Death, Dying, and Bereavement. (2005). Breaking cycles of violence. *Death Studies, 29*(2), 585-600.

Johnson, P. (1976). *A history of Christianity* (p. 67). Harmondsworth: Penguin Books.

Jones, M. (1982). *The process of change.* London: Routledge & Kegan Paul.

Mandela, N. (1994). *Long walk to freedom: The autobiography of Nelson Mandela* (pp. 629-630). London: Abacus.

Parkes, C. M. (1976). Preface and postscript to *In the Wake of the Flood* by Kai T Erikson. London/Boston/Sydney: Allen & Unwin.

Prabhu, R. K., & Rao, U. R. (1945). *The mind of Mahatma Ghandi.* Ahemadabad: Mudranalaya.

Rosenblatt, P. C. (1997). Grief in small scale societies. In C. M. Parkes, P. Laungani, & B. Young (Eds.), *Death and bereavement across cultures* (Ch. 3). London/New York: Routledge.

Torrey, E. F. (1994). Violent behavior by individuals with serious mental illness. *Hospital and Community Psychiatry, 45,* 7.

Weintraub, S. (1987). *Victoria* (pp. 294-295). London: John Murray.

CHAPTER 15

Coping with Violent Death: The Role of Spirituality

Gerry R. Cox

All deaths are difficult. Perhaps the most difficult death is violent death, especially death that could have been avoided. Managing violent death is extremely difficult. The pain and the hurt can be deep and so severe as to cripple a person emotionally and even physically. To cope with such a tragedy requires skills that few are equipped to master. As an educator and sociologist rather than as a therapist, I offer some possible ways to help manage violent death.

The death of a loved one or even a stranger by violent death presents a unique challenge to our ability to cope. Violent death is unlike any other death. Often, the death does not make sense. It is not only senseless, but may have also been caused by another loved one or a friend, which means an even greater loss. If a man kills his wife, not only is the wife lost, but so is the husband who commits the murder. If the death was caused by a stranger, then countless hours are spent trying to understand why the stranger chose to kill your loved one. If the death was a violent accident, then countless hours are spent trying to reconstruct what occurred and how it might have been prevented. While many possible scenarios exist, the point is that all possible scenarios lead to great angst for the griever.

If the police, prosecutors, court system, and correctional system are involved, then countless hours, days, months, and years of dealing with bureaucracies, questions of justice, fairness, appeals, punishment, and so forth rage. Our loved one cannot be brought back, but the trial, appeal, sentencing, punishment, and so forth are constant reminders of the tragic loss and senselessness of their death. While we often seek and desire revenge, the constant concerns for the discretionary potential of our criminal justice system only increase our anxiety and do not aid our coping with our loss. Being in court every day during the trial may seem to be a way to support our lost loved one, but it does not make it easier for us to cope with our loss. While we may still have our hatred of the person who

240 / PERSPECTIVES ON VIOLENCE AND VIOLENT DEATH

caused the death and still have the desire for revenge, we need to place our focus on our own life and survival. We cannot let the violent act destroy our life even more than the violence already has.

BONDING AND RELATIONSHIPS

With each person, our relationship is unique. Each of us allows others to become a part of ourselves. We give meaning to our lives through our relationships. Any parent would acknowledge that when the child was born, their life changed forever. Friends become part of our hopes and dreams as well. With the death of a loved one, not only do we lose the person, but we also lose our hopes and dreams that were connected with them as well. We also generally seem to think that we will die before the other person. Perhaps we want them to grieve for us rather than have us grieve for them. The closer one bonds with the person who died a violent death, the greater the sense of loss. When these relationships are severed, we flounder.

We have many bonds in our lives. We may bond with the doorperson in our apartment building, with the mail carrier, with the person who serves us coffee at the coffee shop, with co-workers, with celebrities, with strangers who offer us a smile, and with thousands of others who become part of our lives. We also choose to bond at an even stronger level with friends, partners, children, parents, siblings, and others. The loss of several classmates to violent death in school, the death of a childhood friend's father to a drunk driver, the loss of family members in childhood, the loss of a trusted friend in a helicopter crash in Vietnam, the loss of a cousin in a car crash, and countless others still haunt me years later. Every year of my life, someone close to me has died. Some were closer than others. Some died violent deaths. While all deaths give hurt, violent deaths seem to give more hurt.

With each of the significant people in my life who have died, I chose to bond with them. With some people, we bond before we even know them: the person who gave you a smile that turned your heart and later became your spouse and best friend, the person that stood tall and erect in the face of danger who became your commanding officer, the person who gave the sermon that changed your life who became your parish priest, and the child in the womb who became the love of your life. Others became part of your heart because you were thrust together in war, the Peace Corps, work, sports, or other important parts of your life. These and many more became a part of your life because you chose to allow them into your heart.

As we bond and choose to bond with others who become part of our life, we also must know deeply in our hearts that everyone that we love will eventually die. While knowing this may give us anxiety, it may also allow us to appreciate our relationships before they are lost. We marry, make friends, have children, and become attached to strangers knowing that all relationships end. If we knew that the person next to us in the airplane would never be seen again, would we bare our soul to them? Or do we bare our soul because we know that we will not ever see them again? Is the choice to bond with another time bound? Would we say no to the relationship if we knew that it would end in twenty years? Five years? A month? A day? At what point would we decide that to bond and suffer the grief of loss is too great a cost? If parents knew that their baby would live only a day or die at birth, would they take the baby anyway? If the baby lived for sixty years, would that be enough? When we choose to have babies, marry, make friends, and so forth, we make that agreement. Is your life better for having bonded with another person if only for a few hours? We simply do not know how long we will have our relationships. Time is not the issue. The real issue is the quality of the relationship.

GRIEF AND VIOLENT DEATH

To lose a quality relationship to the needlessness of a violent death is devastating. It is an unnecessary loss. The grief that results can be crippling. While each of us grieves differently—we also grieve differently for each person who dies—we can develop patterns of coping. Others around us do not grieve the way that we do. Others may observe our behavior and actions, but they cannot feel what we feel. Others may experience the same loss that we have, but our response is not the same as theirs. They may in kindness say to us, "I know how you feel," but they do not know. Sometimes we do not even know "how we feel." Grief is private and cannot be easily shared. Sometimes the person who died is the only one with whom we can share our grief. We may talk to them, visit with them at the funeral home or cemetery, or imagine them being with us. Perhaps they are with us. Each of us is a product of what we have experienced in our lives. They are part of our experiences; they are a part of who we are. They give us meaning and help us continue to make meaning even when they die.

The terribly intense grief will eventually subside, but it will return. Grief may be like an ocean. Sometimes the seas are calm, and sometimes they rage. Our grief is sometimes manageable, and sometimes, it is out of control. One does not return to normal after suffering the loss of a loved one in a violent death. Perhaps we should examine what normal really is and who might actually be normal. Life is full of both blessings and burdens. Perhaps those of us who suffer losses are more normal than those who do not.

No matter what you feel or emotion that you experience, it is okay. Feelings are not the problem. We cannot help it if we have blame, hate, fear, or whatever, but we can help how we choose to respond to those feelings. Others around us may seem to not hurt as much as we are hurting. We may choose to mistreat them because they are not grieving as much as we think they should. We may choose to

242 / PERSPECTIVES ON VIOLENCE AND VIOLENT DEATH

ignore or avoid others around us because we have so much pain that we cannot give them the love we would usually offer to and receive from them. We do not all grieve the same way, nor do we grieve the same way for the many deaths that occur in our own lives. While we grieve differently, we also grieve in similar ways. We may cry with tears, avoid tears, we may play or work to avoid thinking about the death, we may go into seclusion, we may immerse ourselves with people, we may choose to play a tennis match after the murder of a sibling, we may spend our time praying, and a host of other options.

No way of grieving is wrong. Some are just more effective than others. Each of us has our own style of coping with loss. We learned our coping techniques from those around us. Some of those styles were effective and some were harmful. We may think that others are not grieving because they seem not to be showing any emotion. Everybody has their own style of coping with grief. Each of us needs to be free to not only live our own life, but also to find our own style of coping. In a family, the one who returns to work first if both work is generally the one who seems to be coping the best. For some, work is like therapy. It allows them to deal with stresses and to better think about things. For others, it is a way to avoid managing or coping with one's grief. Work becomes a distraction that then delays the intense grief. Work associates may compound the problem by not knowing what to say or do. It is like the loss never occurred when one is at work and such a great loss when one returns home. No size fits all. Each of us has to learn what style works best for us. As Alcoholic's Anonymous is quite helpful for some, it fails many others. No one therapy, approach, or style of coping works for all.

COPING WITH VIOLENT DEATH

Friends, family, caregivers, clergy, social workers, physicians, and loved ones often compound our efforts to cope by their own discomforts and attempts to be helpful. The lack of coping skills of those around us can further compound our own efforts to cope. A friend who lost two teenage children in a devastating car wreck was told, "at least you have another child." This is not helpful, but given as a well-meaning statement. At the same time, those who have developed positive coping skills can be of great help to us when a loved one dies a violent death.

Coping skills are needed to help us mange all kinds of problems in life. Each of us faces losses everyday in our lives. Crises are a part of life. Change always bring loss, even when change is welcomed. Going to school for first time may have been a greatly anticipated event for both the child and the parents; yet both parent and child suffer loss when the event takes place. Few children dread graduation. Many cannot wait for graduation to occur; yet, when it happens, they experience loss whether it is from kindergarten, elementary school, high

COPING WITH VIOLENT DEATH / 243

school, or college. We leave home to go to kindergarten with anticipation, yet dread of leaving our safe home with our mother. We graduate from high school and lose our place among our childhood friends, and yet we eagerly anticipate what will happen in our lives. With loss comes growth. People move, lose jobs, retire, and they die. The skills that allow us to manage life's burdens can be changed into life's blessings. Coping skills are needed to manage divorce, widowhood, aging, and other crises in the cycle of one's life. Such skills can help us better manage when a loved one dies a violent death.

For most of us, the biggest obstacle to coping is that we focus on what we lost rather than on what we had in the relationship with the deceased. In every relationship, there are good times and bad. The bad times may not have kept us from loving them in life. This bad event does not end our love nor our relationship with them in life. They are still a part of us and still affect what we say, do, and think. Their death ended the relationship as it previously existed. We can still keep them as a part of who we are and what we are. We can be enriched that they were a part of our life. Remember the good times and accept the bad.

To cope with violent death, we must remember that others do not cope in the same way that we do. Do not be impatient with your spouse who seems to not grieve as much or at least as openly as you do. Do not break off your relationship with friends or family members who seem to minimize your loss. They, too, are grieving and are usually trying to help you in their stumbling efforts. Your mother may put away the pictures of your husband who died violently. It is not that she does not care, but rather that she does care about you and is trying to take your pain away. We cannot take away the pain of loss from others, but we can help them to face it and to cope with it. It is helplessness rather than heartlessness that causes those around us to say and do the wrong things.

To cope, one needs to recognize that there will be good days and that there will be bad days. Like the ocean, our ability to cope with grief ebbs and flows. Holidays, anniversaries, birthdays, and so forth will be faced with dread and a desire to avoid anything to do with them. Coping will require that we make our loved one a part of these days. Perhaps you might buy a present for their birthday, Christmas, or whatever and donate it to someone else of their age after having a ritual in honor of the person who died a violent death. Their death does not remove them from your life. You can find many creative ways to continue to include them in your daily life. Bad days may occur also for seemingly no reason. Time goes by, and you think that things are better. Then suddenly, you have a bad day. That is normal. It is normal to experience pain and all sorts of feelings when one is grieving. Time is not a healer. Feelings are not bad. The emotion itself is blameless. To have a momentary feeling of hatred is not wrong. To kill the drunk driver is. To cope, eventually, we must come to accept what life has given to us and go on. The pain of grief does not go away, but rather, we learn to live with the pain. One approach to managing violent death is spirituality.

244 / PERSPECTIVES ON VIOLENCE AND VIOLENT DEATH

SPIRITUAL GROWTH AS A MEANS OF COPING
WITH VIOLENT DEATH

Spiritual growth is a journey. Most of us grow from our childhood view of the spiritual world to a more rational view that we call adult. Perhaps the child's view is more comforting and satisfying. For each of us, the journey is different. Our experiences cause our view of spirituality to be different. All of us face losses. One's spirituality can be an important component in that learning process.

The pattern of the universe is such that for life to continue, there will need to be loss and death. Losses are constant. No one lives in this world without loss and its hurt. Friends move away; people die; songs are forgotten; graduations occur; teachers change jobs, schools, or move away; toys get broken; and imaginary friends cease to exist. The world of each of us is filled with beauty and goodness. But we will see only the beauty and goodness if they have the eyes to behold the beauty and goodness that surrounds us. How can we learn to see ourselves or to teach others to see the beauty of an old, wrinkled face, the pains, or even the slums? Beauty is not just what Hollywood portrays. Beauty is what we see spiritually.

For most, unless the loss is a painful event or an ecstatic event, it is given little thought. For those experiencing the violent death of a loved one, it is a forced thought. Yet loss may lead to growth. Loss and growth, death and life are as much a part of our lives as food and drink. Each person must learn that loss and growth are partners. One cannot experience growth without loss. In marriages, couples need some conflict to experience growth. The person who is grieving a loss may ask others questions that are painful and confronting when they are in pain. We need to listen to the pain of our loved ones without judging or lecturing on the rightness or wrongness of their reactions (McKissock, 1998, pp. 111-112). After suffering a loss to a violent act, we may suffer dramatically over the loss of a favorite toy, a pet, or the loss of our house to a fire or other disaster and show little emotion over the death of a loved one. Our public reaction to the loss does not necessarily reflect the magnitude of the loss. Our grief for the toy or pet or even our grief for a person who was distant from us may be an outlet for other losses that occurred long ago (Gilbert, 1999, p. 89). When grieving the loss of a loved one to a violent death, the loss of a pet may be more than we can handle. Little losses become big losses.

Not all losses are of the same magnitude; some losses are barely noticeable while others are overwhelming. One can observe the loss of the limy greenness of an aspen leaf as it makes way for the shimmering gold of a brilliant fall. A caterpillar goes into the darkness and silence of the cocoon and ceases to be a caterpillar and becomes instead a brilliant butterfly that will offer beauty to others. Fields are plowed under to allow the growth of new crops. Our own bodies are constantly repairing and recreating themselves. Cuts and bruises repair themselves. New cells constantly replace dead cells. Even within our bodies, one can observe loss and growth, life and death. Our bodies also age. With that aging comes losses of shape, hair, youth, smoothness of skin, and much more.

We may or may not understand this process, but we need to try to understand the process of loss and growth to be able to cope with violent death.

LOSS AND GROWTH AND THE
SEASONS OF LIFE

James E. Miller, in *Winter Grief, Summer Grace: Returning to Life After a Loved One Dies* (1995), uses the seasons of life to describe the grief process. Loss and growth accompany each season of our lives. Our first loss may occur when we pass out of the protection of the womb into the world. Other losses occur when we venture into the tumult of school, when we leave the simplicity of the world of our family, in doing lessons, performances, and getting along with people who were previously strangers to us. As we gain in experiences and learning, we leave childhood and enter into adolescence, wherein people begin to expect us to act more grown-up. Our bodies begin to change. Our child's body grows and changes. As the child is being lost, we vacillate between our childhood dependence and our demand for adult independence. We begin to expand our intellectual and emotional experience. This process continues throughout our life. As we get older, we develop a perspective on loss. As we lose objects, persons, dreams, positions, we learn that each experience is never the same as the previous loss. Each loss is unique. When we grieve, the loss of the object is not the same as what the object meant to us. Humans engage in meaning making to make sense out of their lives and the events that occur in one's life. Janice Winchester Nadeau (1998, p. 3) indicates that reality is always experienced through the meaning that we give it. For the individual, each loss is unique because as one connects with people, objects, ideas, wishes, values, images, and roles, the person will give them great power. One's identity is formed through these connections that are made. Objects, people, images, values, roles, ideas, and wishes are invested with meaning and symbolic importance. If one loses any of these connections, they lose not only the thing itself or person, but also what it represented to the person and the meaning that he or she invested in it. If a person loses a job, he or she may grieve profoundly over the loss of not just a job, but also the income, prestige, the reason to get up in the morning. Few realize how much they have invested in something until they lose it. The unexpected, sudden loss through violent death presents an even greater shock of loss than many other losses. The way in which our loved one died affects our attempts to give meaning to their life. A war death loses meaning if the war is opposed or thought to have been thrown away by a lack of commitment by the country or the government. To give one's life for family, country, faith, or to save another can provide a basis for giving meaning to the death.

246 / PERSPECTIVES ON VIOLENCE AND VIOLENT DEATH

RESPONSE TO LOSS

Just as our losses are unique to each of us, so are our ways of coping with loss. As children, we often imitated our parent's ways of grieving. Over time, each of us learned a particular way of coping. Each time we use a pattern of coping, it becomes more deeply ingrained in our pattern of responding to loss. Over time, we come to believe that we do not have a choice in how we respond. Yet, we made choices that got us to where we are now. We need to learn to make choices that lead to healthy coping.

As we are humans, we are also imperfect people. Our parents, grandparents, siblings, and teachers, also being imperfect, may have taught us and rewarded us for ways of behaving that later did not work well for us. Our adult task is to examine what we have learned, hold on to what is healthy, and discard what is not.

Many unhealthy ways of coping begin with such messages as, "Boys don't cry," "Don't be a sissy," "Be my little man." Some ways of coping seem to be fairly common. Consider how your coping styles play in your own life, and then consider how they would play in the lives of children. There are many patterns of coping that we may use. A few examples follow.

Denial or disbelief is a common reaction to loss. I have trouble accepting a death until I see the body. A friend who died in Vietnam was not recovered. I hoped for years, without cause, that he had somehow been captured. The crash and explosion made that unlikely. Perhaps seeing the body gives time to accept the reality of the loss and to adjust to the change. This is not necessarily all bad, but if one stays in denial or disbelief, it may not be such a good coping style.

Anger is also a common reaction when faced with our own inability to control forces in our life. Anger often happens when it seems that we need control for our own happiness and well-being. If something occurs that seems to threaten our happiness and well-being, we often react with anger. When a violent death occurs, we may legitimately blame others for our pain or misfortune. Blame may be attributed to someone who was not involved. Anger, as any emotion, can be quite healthy for us. A little rage can make one feel a lot better quicker than most coping techniques. Directed anger can be harmful. We can be angry at God, the physician, the person who died, or whomever. The person who is angry often takes his or her anger out on others. We need to use anger constructively. Many positive coping styles exist. Some, like former President Ronald Reagan, chop firewood. I run. Others hit a punching bag.

Guilt is another common method of coping. All of us, and especially children, are prone to guilt. Children have great imaginations. Adults also have excellent imaginations, but generally they suppress them. Magical thinking can easily make a child think they caused the illness or death: "I wanted her bedroom," "Mom said I would be the death of her yet." Even if you were negligent and another person died, it is important to remember, (1) you did not intend for the death to occur, (2) you would have changed the situation if you could have done so, and (3) the person who died made decisions as well. You cannot control what others do. Of course, if you deliberately caused the other person's death, then guilt is appropriate.

Sadness is also a common style of coping. Whenever life takes away or asks us to let go of something that we have recognized as part of us, we can expect sadness.

Unfortunately, no magic formula or scientific scale can tell us how a person will react when something is lost from their life. There are many other reactions that may rage within us, including fear, confusion, despair, and loneliness.

We must be careful when judging the value of someone else's loss. An ex-spouse may cause us to have grief that is surprising to others. We must also be careful when judging the techniques of coping used by another. Whatever method we use is not necessarily better than ones used by others. We also cannot see the heart of another. A loss that on the surface should be devastating may not be, while a loss than seems trivial may devastate. Broken hearts cannot be seen with an MRI.

Each of us needs to ask ourselves a number of questions:

1. How were you taught to cope with losses?
2. When you were a child, what did your parents or significant others tell you about showing your emotions?
3. What are the losses in your own life that you are having trouble releasing?
4. Are you willing to see the treasure of your own life and that your life is filled with opportunities for growth through the losses that you have experienced?

EACH LOSS IS AN OPPORTUNITY

Response to loss is a sign that life is happening through everything that we experience. Our own life history is filled with loss and opportunities for growth, for wholeness, and for holiness. Each life is filled with burdens and blessings. We cannot minimize the burdens and blessings that we experience. Losses are opportunities for us to grow. No one can control the losses in one's life, but each person can control how he or she reacts to them. The parable of the wheat grain indicates that one must die to grow. One must experience loss to grow. Would you want to remain as you were in the womb? Would you want to remain a two-year-old child? Stay in elementary school until you retire?

HOW DO WE GROW THROUGH LOSS?

In each experience of loss, one can move toward life or death. Yet most of us do not see that we have choices. All of us need to be made aware of our choices. Most of us want to believe, at least secretly, that losses are unnecessary. We want to believe that our lives will never change; yet, change always occurs whether we like

248 / PERSPECTIVES ON VIOLENCE AND VIOLENT DEATH

it or not. We often focus our attention on the positive aspects of our life and thus avoid facing losses, or perhaps we view the loss as an aberration. We hear of the losses of others and pretend that they will not happen to us, but they will. No one teaches us that the only way to new growth is through loss. No one tells us that loss is normal and natural. No one tells us that the only time that change ends is the end of our life. And no one shows us how to cope with loss in any organized, useful manner. Did anyone tell you about the trials and tribulations of dating and courtship before you began dating? Did anyone tell you the rules of using the car in your family before you got your driver's license? Did anyone tell you about bullies and friendship and users and givers before you started making friends? We all need to be aware of life's blessing and burdens.

As tragic, untimely, dreaded, and feared as loss and death may be, none of us will ever be able to avoid them. No matter how much we try to avoid loss and death, we cannot stop them from occurring. We can begin to acknowledge the losses in our own lives and to live and grow through them. Then we can better help others with their losses. By choosing to grow through small losses, we can then make better choices when big losses occur. All of us grow with the same process. Life is the continuous process of choice making.

Every choice that one makes is another choice not made. If I buy a new car, the cost of the car is not the payment, but the trips, vacations, clothes, gifts, and so forth that I cannot purchase because I am making a car payment. Each choice that we make affects future choices as well. If I choose to begin to smoke at thirteen, I may later experience shortness of breath or illnesses because of my earlier choice. We must all learn that choices have consequences. To truly make a choice, one must be aware of those consequences both good and bad. To begin to smoke without an awareness of consequences is not really a choice. Others model our behavior. We should know the consequences and help others make better choices by providing good role models.

WAYS TO HELP OTHERS DEVELOP STYLES OF HEALTHY GRIEVING

1. Grieving begins when we openly acknowledge what has been lost.

2. Healthy grieving begins when we express whatever feelings and emotions that are called forth when we acknowledge the loss. No emotion is wrong. What we do with emotions is more important.

3. If we are healthy in our grieving, we need to choose to change our relationship with the person who died a violent death. Our relationships do not end with death. Is the person you love most in life with you right now? If they are not, does your relationship with them end? We do not need people to be present for them to be a part of our lives. They can continue to be a part of who we are, what we are, and how we relate to the world. It is not unhealthy to continue to be

with them even if they are not present. We do have to accept that they cannot be with us in the same way that they were when they were alive. Those that I have loved continue to make me a better person and to be able to face each day. They are with me in spirit.

THINGS TO DO WITH THOSE WHO EXPERIENCE LOSS

There are many things that we can do to aid those who experience loss through a violent death. The same model can be applied to coping with any significant loss.

1. Create a sacred place. This can be a memory room or a spot in a room or hall. It can be a place to keep items of value to you in a visible, open place.

2. Journaling or storytelling is another technique to manage loss. Write a journal of your journey through grief. If the grieving person is too young to write or developmentally disabled, chronicle through drawings or other art forms. Drawing or writing can be a process of discovery. If you draw or write for any length of time, you will probably state what is in your heart and your mind. You will unearth much that you may not recognize about your own grief for your losses.

3. Humor is an excellent coping mechanism. Laughter helps us find inner peace. Humorous stories, particularly about ourselves, are perhaps the easiest form of humor to aid the grieving or the dying. Humor is not the absence of sadness; it allows us to view our situations with a different lens, to not take our selves and our lives so seriously. Laughter helps us find inner peace. This is not laughing at other people, but laughing with other people.

4. Music, like other art forms, heals. The particular style of music to be used with a person depends upon that person. Your favorite music may not help them manage their loss, but it could help you manage yours. Each of us tends to find most satisfying the kind of music that we enjoyed while growing up. The heartbeat of the universe may be expressed with the beat of music. It can speak to us in ways that can reach our inner existence. It can mirror our own heartbeat.

5. Art, drama, clay, drawing, painting, and other forms of expression, like journaling, may aid our attempts to cope with loss.

6. Friendship is a powerful form of coping. People may be the best source of help. Friends share their joys and their sorrows. Few of us have lives that we would want to trade with others.

7. Acceptance is also a coping tool. We must learn to accept each person as he or she is, trust his or her judgment while recognizing that each person, like us, will make mistakes. When your daughter or son chooses a spouse, do not second guess their choice. It is their choice. If you show acceptance and trust, your relationship will be strong. If you question their choice, you will strain your relationship.

250 / PERSPECTIVES ON VIOLENCE AND VIOLENT DEATH

8. Balance may also help. Life is a series of blessings and burdens. One must find balance in one's own life. This can mean that one should find the place in life, the job, or vocation that one is called to serve. If one focuses upon making money, one may miss the career that would have offered joy and purpose to one's life.

9. Love is another tool to help manage loss. People need each other. We cannot survive without one another. Family, friends, and spiritual friends give life meaning and purpose. Knowing that friends and family will be there for you is a valuable lesson for children. Love is freely given in spite of mistakes. None of us is perfect. Children are loved in spite of their errors. Learning our heritage is part of this sharing of love. Stories about the great-grandmother who died when you were an infant may show the love that she felt for you even though you do not remember her. The quilt that she made, or some other treasure, may be a visible sign of her love. Our loved ones do not have to be here with us for us to know that they still love us.

10. Harmony and security is necessary for the person experiencing loss. One needs to be secure in home, school, work, play, and life.

11. Facing reality as it is can also help us to know what things can be changed and what things cannot. To accept what cannot be changed and to have the courage to change what can is described in the Serenity Prayer of St. Francis.

12. Rituals can allow each person to express spirituality. Family rituals may be a remembrance of the deceased family members or friends offered on special days. Such rituals may also include simply keeping family treasures because they belonged to deceased love ones. It can be making a basket, weaving a rug, a sand painting, or whatever. Rituals support belief and give purpose to faith.

13. Work is a major method of coping. Play is a child's work. Just as our jobs can add meaning and purpose to our lives, so too can a child's play add meaning and purpose to his or her life. Children can experience unrestrained joy in play. Perhaps we still feel that kind of joy in our work. Work and play are both spiritual and a source of spiritual growth. Play differs from sport in that it lacks rules. As adults, we impose rules on children and destroy their ability to play effectively.

14. Another useful tool is prayer. Life itself can be a prayer. One can pray for the animal or plant that gave its life to feed us, for the opportunity to have a job to support one's family, for one's family, for the earth that provides all that is needed for life, for the universe, for everything in life. Prayers can be ritualized, take place in religious settings, be memorized, or simply lived.

15. People can also use forgiveness as a coping tool. Each of us has wronged others and been wronged by others. Our spiritual growth also includes moments of forgiving and being forgiven. A soldier who was driving in a crash that killed his best friend was forgiven and made part of the family by the friend's parents. True forgiveness. They accepted that their own son was at fault as well for drinking and allowing his friend to drive, and that he would have wanted his friend to go on with his life.

COPING WITH VIOLENT DEATH / 251

16. Each life must also have hope. Life is full of awe and wonder for the child and hopefully for adults as well, but it is also full of pain and suffering. From the cutting of the first tooth, to earaches, to death, life is full of pain and suffering. Hope does not come from sweetness and protecting us from poverty, racism, hate crimes, violence, death, and even the suffering of innocents. Hope comes from seeing the goodness in the hearts of people in spite of the suffering and pain that life offers. To sugarcoat life leads to cynicism and despair rather than hope. How could one face mobs in peace marches; Nazi's, as Ann Frank did; the poor, as Mother Teresa did; or any other act of courage without hope? Each of us has shortcomings, failings, and makes mistakes, yet life can still be full of hope, dreams, and fulfillment. Perhaps you can save your soda cans to give to a homeless person. The joy in the face of the homeless person may allow you to learn about hope.

17. We all need to be taught sharing and caring. As adults, we can experience joy when we share. The child who offers you a lick of his sucker or ice cream can feel real joy in watching you oblige the offer. Spirituality needs to include sharing and caring for others as well as the usual "me first" ethic of the U.S. culture.

18. Those experiencing loss need to know that we are actually listening to them. Listening, both verbally and nonverbally, will help others cope. We must actually listen. Put down your paper, turn off the television, and give the person your true attention. True listening shows that you really care. Perhaps you may remember being read stories as a child. It may be the last time that you had the undivided attention of your parents.

19. Spirituality itself is a coping tool. I am not sure if we can teach others about spirituality. Children may be the best teachers. It seems that they are better teachers for us. A Hopi child understood the conflict with the Navajo tribe better than most adults. She indicated that the battle was over the land. She said that the Navajo wanted to cut up the land, to farm it, which in her view of spirituality meant to harm the land. To divide the land was to hurt the land. The land deserved its freedom and a chance to live. In her spiritual orientation, she felt that the Hopi must protect the spirit and well-being of the land because the land can feel the difference. A Navajo child indicated that the white people who try to amass property and things have a problem. Their problem is that they have so much that they cannot choose what to love or need and are lost because they have no homeland, just houses and things. Another Navajo child facing the impending death of her grandmother saw no reason to pray for her to live. She saw that death is not bad. She saw that her grandmother was suffering in life. She prayed for her grandmother to have a peaceful death, rather than praying that she suffer by living longer.

20. Encouragement may also help others to cope. Offer encouragement rather than praising, saying that the person is pretty or whatever. Encourage them by focusing upon the process rather than the outcome. Loss in athletics, school, or whatever is not failure. Failing to try is failure. Rather than allowing the other

252 / PERSPECTIVES ON VIOLENCE AND VIOLENT DEATH

person to say that he or she cannot do something, encourage them to try. Real courage comes from the scars that result from trying to do the seemingly impossible. Have you ever clapped for a Special Olympics participant that you did not even know? Perhaps, tears came to your eyes. Sharing is part of encouragement. As part of my training in an Outward Bound program, my feet were tied together, my hands tied behind my back, and I was tossed into the ocean for an hour. Being somewhat afraid of drowning, I was sure that I could not survive, but I did survive. In the process of training for the event, I received encouragement to try. I was told that I would be rescued if I needed to be. Life is a journey. We must all be encouraged to do the seemingly impossible. The struggle together adds much meaning and purpose to life.

21. We all need to be taught to try to live our dreams. We need to be aware of the power of dreams to help give meaning and purpose to life. Each day is a blessing. Each day should be better than yesterday and tomorrow better than today. We foster pessimism, cynicism, and doom by living in the past rather than living in the present. We must try to live our dreams and strive to accomplish them. Everyone needs something to look forward to each day to have a reason to get up in the morning. Remember the excitement of your own childhood when an anticipated event that so excited your sense of life kept you from sleeping the night before? Hopefully, you will eventually capture that excitement in your life again. Dreams can help us do that even in severe grief.

22. We need to be taught the power of miracles. Saints tend to live ordinary lives and do ordinary things extraordinarily well. Instead of looking for great miracles in one's life, look for the little ones that make each day what it is. When you have no money for bills or whatever, a friend pays you what is owed or a painting is sold or whatever. When you are tired and nearly falling asleep while driving, something occurs to cause you to awaken fully; the beauty of the face of a homeless woman; the singing voice of a developmentally disabled child; the miracle of birth or even death; the first word that your child speaks; the cry when the light shocks them as they leave the womb. What are your life's miracles? They need not be what provides the fodder for books or movies, and yet, maybe they are. Perhaps the greatest miracle is our life; that every human and animal has something to offer, and that every life is precious.

CONCLUSIONS

Spirituality can aid the grieving of those coping with violent death by allowing them to be open to the power of grieving. We all need to open ourselves to the power of grieving. Let the spirit awaken within you. Live each day for today, and tomorrow will follow with flourish!

There is no magic formula for coping with violent death, but we are not helpless. We can enter a new journey in our lives as a person who grows from the blessings and burdens that the victim of violent death has given to us. They are still part of our lives. They still help make us the person that we are. We can try to be the person that they would want us to be. Our spiritual journey is one approach to becoming that person.

Spiritual journeys have paths that each must develop and follow as we go through our lives. Each journey is special and different. We must accept both the blessings and burdens that life has to offer. Each journey is unique. We cannot make the journey for others. We can, at best, be spiritual guides. Let the journey begin!

REFERENCES

Gilbert, R. (1999). *Finding your way after your parent dies*. Notre Dame, IN: Ave Maria Press.

McKissock, D. (1998). *The grief of our children*. Sydney, Australia: Australian Broadcasting Company.

Miller, J. E. (1995). *Winter grief, summer grace: Returning to life after a loved one dies*. Minneapolis, MN: Augsburg Press.

Nadeau, J. W. (1998). *Families making sense of death*. Thousand Oaks, CA: Sage Publications.

CHAPTER 16

From Violence to Peace: Posthomicide Memorials

Inge B. Corless
Phyllis R. Silverman

> We had to decide if we were going to be part of the problem or part of the solution.
>
> Louis Brown's parents after he was murdered

This chapter is about how families find solace and comfort after the violent death of a family member. It is about how families memorialize those who died and how these same families' actions may prevent further violence. Perpetrated in war, violence may also be a concomitant of environmental phenomena such as earthquakes, fire, or flood. This chapter, however, focuses on violence that occurs in domestic and community situations when the death is the result of an act of violence, and the victim may have simply been in the wrong place at the wrong time. In such cases, there is a perpetrator who may need to be identified. The mourners' grief is more public as they are often involved with the police, the courts, and the media. How do the survivors make sense of a senseless act of violence? The pain of the loss is real. Some think that when the perpetrator is caught, the family can find "closure." The case may be closed for the police, or for the courts, but the survivors must go on with their lives, with a new configuration of relationships. How do survivors deal with their grief, with their pain, and having lost a sense of safety in the world?

WAYS OF REMEMBERING

What is it that we know about all mourners that helps us understand survivors of this type of violence? We know that mourners do not recover from their grief. They do not "get over it." In general, most mourners cannot put the past

256 / PERSPECTIVES ON VIOLENCE AND VIOLENT DEATH

behind them (Silverman & Klass, 1996). For family members, the concept of closure has little meaning. They generally seek ways of keeping the presence and the spirit of the deceased alive. They find that this provides them with some comfort and solace as they cope with their pain and the loss in their lives. Depending on their talent and resources, they find various ways of honoring their dead, so that they do not live in the past, but the past becomes a part of their present lives. We know that in ways that are often quite profound, they are changed by the experience, in the sense of who they are and how they live their lives.

There are a variety of ways that mourners find to connect to the deceased and from which survivors of community violence have taken examples as they seek ways of remembering and maintaining a connection. S. Silverman (2000) describes how composers use music to express their own feelings about death, to memorialize lost friends, and sometimes their loss of community as well. Through their music they find meaning. The deceased live as long as the music is listened to.

Cemeteries in the mid-nineteenth century, such as Gettysburg in Pennsylvania and Mt. Auburn in Boston, were designed as parks, inviting people to mingle with the dead and to remember them (Gothein, 1979). Most religious traditions provide rituals on a regular basis to remember and honor the dead. These rituals help the living to maintain a bond with their deceased loved one (Gillman, 1998).

A new ritual was created with the production of AIDS quilt panels. Imagination and dedication are emphasized in the quilt panels, which have been made by people mourning someone who had died of AIDS. Each quilt panel represents a person who died of AIDS and is the result of the creativity of their families and friends (Corless, 1997). Each panel is sewn together with other panels to form a whole, reminding us of the larger impact of the epidemic while honoring each deceased person. While the deaths are not the result of an act of violence, these quilts have served as models for remembering deaths from many causes.

As we explore the directions that families take in coming to terms with an individual loss through violence, we need also look at the ways in which society has dealt with violence on a different scale, such as during or after war. Often there is the hope that this war will lead to peace, so some memorials are dedicated to this goal. Peace symbols adorn the memorials to lend meaning to the life sacrifices made by so many.

After World War I, the agreements that ended the war were so unsatisfactory that instead of leading to a lasting peace, the Versailles Peace Conference pro- duced terms that actually sowed the seeds of the next war. After World War II, the approaches to the vanquished resulted in a new and more effective rapproche- ment between nations. However, society still has not found an effective way of solving problems between countries or people peacefully.

For soldiers, violence is expected. And for the citizens caught up in these conflicts, violence becomes part and parcel of the conflict on an almost daily basis. Individuals caught up in the Holocaust were targeted for violence based on religious, ethnic, and other characteristics. Although there has been a cessation of violence for 60 years among the countries involved as the chief combatants in World War II, for those with memories of the war, and of the Holocaust in particular, there is a constant energy to find new ways of remembering. Lest we forget (Shalev & Avraham, 2005; Young, 1994). Similarly, the continuing genocide in Africa has left behind many mourners for whom peace is elusive.

Memorials have traditionally been one way of honoring those who died in war. These sculptures usually depict individuals, whether generals or foot soldiers. The Vietnam War Memorial in Washington, D.C. ushered in a new era. In that sculpture, the names of Americans who died in that war are listed. Those who have visited the site are struck by the reverent silence that pervades the area and affects all who come there.

Another way of remembering is through the creation of a Garden of Peace. There are a number of such gardens, serving as memorials to people or events. In their very name, they celebrate society's aspirations for peace. Like the Vietnam Memorial, they serve as a reminder of what occurred there with the hope that it will not happen again.

Some memorials celebrate the lives of individuals, many of whom are famous military leaders. At the National Museum of the Pacific War in Fredericksburg, Texas, the Japanese Garden of Peace honors Fleet Admiral Chester W. Nimitz and is a gift from the military leaders of Japan to the people of the United States. Peace Gardens have also been dedicated to inspirational leaders. Fresno State University developed such a garden to serve as a site for a statue of Mahatma Gandhi, a leader dedicated to nonviolent change.

Other sites for a Garden of Peace mark events or organizations. These include Paris, where the *Jardins de l'Unesco* is located, and on the grounds of the Imperial War Museum in London, where the Tibetan Peace Garden is situated. Peace Parks can be found in Hiroshima and Nagasaki, both of which were the sites of the dropping of atomic bombs. Perhaps less well known in Japan are Kuriyama Peace Park and Goremba Peace Park in Hakone National Park. There are numerous other peace parks, including Gallipoli Peace Park near the site of the famous battle in Turkey and also My Lai Peace Park in Vietnam.

Peace parks also honor the friendship between nations. The International Peace Garden is situated on the border of the United States and Canada between North Dakota and Manitoba. Covering 2300 acres, the International Peace Garden serves as a monument to peace and international cooperation. Another such international garden, on the border between Nicaragua and Costa Rico, is *Si-A-Paz,* or Yes to Peace.

Spanning both the dedication to the cause of peace and the remembrance of special people in each of our lives (whether the victims of violence or not) is the Garden of Peace and Remembrance developed by the Brooklyn Society for Ethical Culture. The Society members who helped to create it state, "Any garden lends the visitor a sense of peace and serenity, but the Garden of Peace and

258 / PERSPECTIVES ON VIOLENCE AND VIOLENT DEATH

Remembrance was mindfully planned to represent the oneness and equality of all human beings, and our coming together in a circle of peace" (Brooklyn Society of Ethical Culture, 2004).

One of the most well-known peace gardens is dedicated to the life of an individual who died as a result of violence. In Central Park in New York City, Strawberry Fields commemorates the life and death of John Lennon. One of the Beatles, he was dedicated to the cause of peace and sang the song *Give Peace a Chance.* It provides a place of peace for many in the midst of the frenetic pace of New York. In the spirit of Strawberry Fields, the Garden of Peace in Boston is one way the violence perpetrated against individuals is being remembered. The Boston Garden of Peace, and those who took the initiative to develop this site, are the focus of the remainder of this chapter.

THE GARDEN OF PEACE (BOSTON, MA)

The Garden of Peace, which is approximately 7000 square feet, resulted from the activities of families who experienced the violent death of one of their family members. This Garden of Peace now contains the names of more than 400 individuals who died as a consequence of homicide.

On the Web site of the Garden of Peace, this purpose is noted: "The Garden of peace is a memorial commemorating victims of homicide and a living reminder of the impact of violence. It is a visual testament to the need for eliminating violence. The Garden is a symbol of hope for peace and renewal in our lives, our community, and the world" (Garden of Peace Memorial: About Us: 2002–2005).

The members of the Garden of Peace Memorial organization eloquently address the need for such a memorial when they state, "Losing a loved one through violence is a wrenching experience for the victim's family and friends. Immediate survivors discover firsthand the importance of paying homage, seeking solace and hope, and working for peace. In the absence of acknowledgement, the human tendency for denial will prevail and recognition of the negative impact of violence will be suppressed" (Garden of Peace Memorial: About Us: Why This Memorial is Important).

The design of the Garden of Peace encompasses a dry stream bed where smooth river stones, each with the name of a homicide victim and dates of birth and death, are placed. The stones, although similar in size, are nonetheless as unique as the individuals to whom they are dedicated. Each of the stones represents an individual, whether the victim or survivor, who has ties to Massachusetts. In addition to the commemorative river stones, the garden contains two other special features.

One of these is "Tragic Density." It is "a huge circular black granite stone . . . which symbolizes the enormous weight of sadness and grief" (Garden of Peace Memorial: Garden Design). Tragic Density is described further: "The surface is the only part visible of the huge stone of sadness and grief buried in the hearts of those who have lost a loved one" (Garden of Peace Memorial: Garden Design: Garden Design Map). The streambed moves forward from this granite stone. A cascade of water serves as a reminder "that life is an ongoing process" with a pool of water symbolizing "the possibilities that still exist" (Garden of Peace Memorial: Garden Design: Garden Design Map).

The other notable feature is placed at the end of the streambed. "The streambed moves through the Garden and culminates with a trickle of water into a pool out of which rises "Ibis Ascending," a skyward sculpture representing hope" (Garden of Peace Memorial: About Us). Ibis Ascending is further described as, "a burst of life, springing from the pool, three ibises rise to the sky transcending pain, anger, and grief" (Garden of Peace Memorial: Garden Design: Garden Design Map).

The site contains birch trees, yew trees, and native ground cover with seat walls throughout. The description of the trees is poetic. The River Birch is described thusly: "Its bark changes, mahogany in its first season then salmon and gold as it matures, and back to deepest brown at its fragile edges. It grows best in groups, each tree drawing strength from the others, stems leaning and clacking against each other in the strongest winds" (Garden of Peace Memorial: Garden Design: Garden Design Map). The yew trees are "limited in height, straight, evergreen, unchanging in all seasons, providing shelter from winter winds, evergreen, ever young" (Garden of Peace Memorial: Garden Design: Garden Design Map).

The thought, creativity, and symbolism in this (and other) Gardens of Peace are self-evident. What the creators of the Garden of Peace, located in Government Center, Boston, have attempted to do is to remove the isolation and solitary nature of each homicide death by bringing them together into a collectivity of individuals and families affected by violence. The Web site of this garden provides another way of knowing who died and of remembering them by telling the personal stories of some of those honored in the Garden of Peace. There are stories that contain information about the legal treatment of the perpetrators. The sorrow (and anger) at the leniency with which some of those convicted of the homicides were treated is reflected in the personal stories available on the Web site.

A stone is in some ways an impersonal memorial. What is special here, though, is the strength survivors gather from being with others who have suffered the same grievous losses. It is the coming together with others that may be most critical to their finding a way of living with and through their pain and to finding some satisfaction in the direction their lives now take (Silverman, 2000, 2004). They no longer feel isolated and different. There is a community that can sustain them, and in helping each other, they can find new satisfaction.

MAKING CHANGE HAPPEN

Over time, most mourners find new meaning and consider anew the place of death in the human experience (Frankl, 1984; Neimeyer, 2001). They talk about

260 / PERSPECTIVES ON VIOLENCE AND VIOLENT DEATH

new selves, new ways of living in the world with a new perspective and appreciation of life and of others around them (Silverman, 2000, 2004). This growth is often reflected in the changed focus of the surviving families' lives or in the immediate community in which the mourners live (Silverman, 2000). One survivor of loss stated, "Yes, I experienced a growth that would not have been possible before if I had continued to be a 'submissive' partner. . . . This does not mean that I felt liberated in losing a partner but this is what happened as a result" (Silverman, 2004, p. 56). For most survivors, there is no public declaration of change, although it does occur.

This exemplifies how something good can happen even with the death of a loved one. We see this process when death comes from old age, from illness, from an accident. But what change occurs when the deceased was murdered? How do people find anything positive in the experience of violent death that can honor these who died? There seem to be several choices. Some of these can be seen in parents' reactions after the murders of their children at Columbine High School in Littleton, Colorado.

There were parents who focused on the event and what they lost. When their children died, as with all of the parents, they lost part of who they were, part of their future. However, some parents believed that unless the perpetrators also suffered a major loss, they could never move on with their own lives. They would not allow any mention of the perpetrators, focusing on how their memories must be obliterated. The perpetrators were no longer children with any other identity except that of murderers. This is exemplified by the response of a mother who reacted to a recent Supreme Court ruling forbidding the execution of adolescent murderers. She expressed her view that as long as the murderer of her son lived she could not rest. This mother seemed unable to step back from the murder and find other ways of living in the world; ways that would encompass new directions and new meanings; ways that have brought new meaning and comfort to others.

Others have sought to make a difference in the world around them. This has led some survivors in directions that resonate in their communities in ways they could never have imagined. They talk about the death not having "been in vain." To that end, one Columbine parent has taken up the fight for gun control that might have made guns less accessible to potential perpetrators. Still others seek change from something that takes place inside themselves: "I was always very shy, and now I have a passion that drives me to make a difference." The difference they make is in the society around them, and in this way they honor the memory of those who were murdered.

Mother's Against Drunk Driving is a good example of a mutual help organization, with a national constituency, designed to help parents support and care for each other. Not only do members provide support for each other, but they focus on education, legislation, and social change as well. They are strong advocates raising the public's awareness of the dangers of drinking and driving. They lobby state legislatures to pass laws to punish impaired drivers and to keep

FROM VIOLENCE TO PEACE / 261

them off the roads. They are involved in roles that they could not have imagined for themselves prior to the tragedy that took the life of their child.

Louis Brown's parents, Tina and Joseph Chery, describe how his death turned them into community activists. Their son was an innocent bystander, caught in the crossfire of a gang gun battle. Whenever there is a murder victim in their Boston community, they reach out and involve these family members in various activities to provide support and care. They help them with their pain and grief, so that they do not grieve alone. Many of these children are memorialized in the Peace Garden. A key part of their activism is their focus on crime prevention, keeping the public's awareness of the problem alive as a way of honoring the memory of their children. The Cherys took their initiative one step further in collaboration with the Boston Public Schools:

> We heard so many families blaming themselves or trying to convince themselves that their children were killed because of the color of their skin. You feel helpless because you could not prevent it. We could have become part of the problem or part of the solution. We looked at his friends and we knew we had to do something. We weren't going to be trapped in helplessness and we wanted to show them there were other ways. So we created a way of being part of the solution. We raised money with bake sales, from returning deposit bottles as well as soliciting Foundations. We worked with the Boston School Department and they developed the Louis Brown Peace Curriculum for 10th grade students, now taught in several high schools. The focus is on prevention. Students learn new ways of solving personal problems by controlling feelings and thinking about alternatives to violence before they act (Silverman, 2000, pp. 211-212).

Students in this peace program, as part of their final assignment, write essays that are published in small books at the end of the year. What is the lesson these students teach us?

> I learned that in order to make peace you need to stay away from trouble and be your own person. I deal with my conflicts by ignoring insults; walking away from fights and not letting people take advantage of me. . . . The support and help I needed were the voices inside my head. They would tell me not to fight and to do the right things (Green, 1997, pp. 45-46).

Parental grief leads to changes, not only in themselves, but in those around them as well, as they honor their children's memory. With these changes, there is a kind of peace for those who experience the death of a loved one through violence. And hopefully, they will stimulate others to find new ways to avert violence. When this is achieved, no additional stones will be needed for the Garden of Peace, and peace will encompass the environment for all of us.

262 / PERSPECTIVES ON VIOLENCE AND VIOLENT DEATH

WE REMEMBER THEM

Four of these personal stories as written on the Garden of Peace Web site are quoted in their entirety. Remembering them seems a fitting way to end this chapter.

Anne Elizabeth Borghesani 1967–1990
Daughter of Garden of Peace Board Member, Betty Borghesani

Anne, a child of Massachusetts, grew up in Lexington and graduated from Tufts University in 1989, where she majored in International Relations. She was an intelligent young woman filled with enthusiasm for life, curiosity, warmth and humor. A great communicator, she brought people together from different religions and cultures and was an active participant in her community. Anne consistently exhibited love, compassion, honesty and loyalty to others and was committed to the importance of personal dignity, equal opportunity, freedom of choice and justice.

After college Anne worked as a legal assistant in Washington, D.C. She hoped to attend law school and talked of being a public defender. She was walking from her apartment to the Metro early on a Saturday evening when she was attacked and violently murdered by a stranger in Arlington, Virginia. Anne was on her way to her own 23rd birthday party. (Garden of Peace Memorial, 2002–2205, Personal Stories: Anne Elizabeth Borghesani)

Louis David Brown 1978–1993
Son of Garden of Peace Board Member, Clementina M. Chery

Louis David Brown was 15 and a tenth grader at West Roxbury High School in the fall of 1993. College was high on his agenda, then graduate school, where he intended to earn a doctoral degree in aerodynamic engineering. But his long-term goal, the one he talked about a lot with his family, friends and teachers was to become the first black—and youngest— President of the United States.

But big as his dreams were, and as hard as he pursued them, his dreams were shattered just as he was starting to firm them up. On December 20, 1993, on his way to the Christmas party of the group, Teens Against Gang Violence, Louis was shot and killed. He was caught in a gunfight just as he was about to enter the subway ramp in Fields Corner Station. It was in the middle of the afternoon, five days before Christmas. (Garden of Peace Memorial, 2002–2205, Personal Stories: Louis David Brown)

Kathleen Mary Dempsey 1961–1992
Daughter of Garden of Peace Board Member, Evelyn Tobin

Kathy Dempsey was 31 when she was murdered. She was a freelance graphic designer about to enter graduate school to obtain a Master's in education so that she could teach art to young children.

She was the oldest of three children and her parents' only daughter. Kathy had many talents, but the greatest was her ability to bring people together and

FROM VIOLENCE TO PEACE / 263

to nurture her many relationships. She loved her friends and family. She loved the earth and every living thing on it. And she loved life.

During the early morning hours of August 23, 1992, while asleep in her home in Lexington, MA, Kathy was stabbed by an intruder. She dialed 911 for help, but through a series of tragic errors by the telephone operator and the emergency dispatcher, help never came and she bled to death. Her attacker has not been apprehended. (Garden of Peace Memorial, 2002–2205, Personal Stories: Kathleen Mary Dempsey)

Jesse Simon McKie 1969–1990
Son of Garden of Peace Sculptor, Judy Kensley McKie

Jesse McKie was a talented artist, performer and musician. He was a graceful athlete and a real good dancer. Jesse had a unique sense of humor and a pile of friends of all colors. In his first year at Emerson College he was the host of a popular rap music program. He was devoted to urban culture. And fly fishing.

On January 25th, 1990, a few days after his 21st birthday, Jesse was walking home from a friend's house in Cambridge. He was surrounded by six young men. They demanded his leather jacket. He gave it to them. Then they kicked and beat and stabbed him to death.

Three of his assailants are serving life sentences. Another was convicted as an accessory and served a short sentence. The fifth person testified for the prosecution. The sixth attacker was acquitted. Also serving life sentences: Jesse's parents, relatives, and friends. (Garden of Peace Memorial, 2002–2005, Personal Stories: Jesse Simon McKie)

As is evidenced from these statements, there is no easy way to put the past behind. There is no closure. A memorial does not prevent mindless killing. It is a way, however, for survivors to work together and to find creative solutions. It is as we offer friendship and care to these families that they find hope for the future. They perceive the power of the passion that emanates from their pain; they find new directions for change, for hope, and for a new way of building community. If it is not peace, it is at least an ability to live with what happened and to work together to try to prevent this kind of violence from happening again. Such efforts memorialize the dead, and give rise to the hope that from violence there will come peace.

REFERENCES

Brooklyn Society of Ethical Culture. (2004). Garden of Peace and Remembrance Dedication: May 16th, 2004. Retrieved 2/1/05.
http://www.bsec.org/news/peacegarden040516.html.

Corless, I. B. (1997). Modulated mourning: The grief and mourning of those infected and affected by HIV/AIDS. In K. J. Doka with J. Davidson (Eds.), *Living with grief: When illness is prolonged* (pp. 105-118). Washington, DC: Taylor & Francis.

264 / PERSPECTIVES ON VIOLENCE AND VIOLENT DEATH

Frankl, V. E. (1984). *Man's search for meaning: An introduction to logotherapy.* New York: Simon & Schuster.

Garden of Peace Memorial. (2002-2005). About Us. Retrieved 2/1/05. http://www.gardenofpeacememorial.org/about/index.html.

Garden of Peace Memorial. (2002-2005). About Us: Why this Memorial is Important. Retrieved 2/1/05. http://www.gardenofpeacememorial.org/about/whyimpor.html.

Garden of Peace Memorial. (2002-2005). Garden Design. Retrieved 2/1/05. http://www.gardenofpeacememorial.org/garden_design/index/html.

Garden of Peace Memorial. (2002-2005). Garden Design: Garden Design Map. Retrieved 2/1/05. http://www.gardenofpeacememorial.org/garden_design/gardendesign.html.

Garden of Peace Memorial. (2002-2005). Personal Stories: Anne Elizabeth Borghesani. Retrieved 2/1/05. http://www.gardenofpeacememorial.org/personal/vic_annelisabor.html.

Garden of Peace Memorial. (2002-2005). Personal Stories: Louis David Brown Retrieved 2/1/05. http://www.gardenofpeacememorial.org/personal/vic_louisbrown.html.

Garden of Peace Memorial. (2002-2005). Personal Stories: Kathleen Mary Dempsey. Retrieved 2/1/05. http://www.gardenofpeacememorial.org/personal/vic_kathdemsy.html

Garden of Peace Memorial. (2002-2205). Personal Stories: Jesse Simon McKie. Retrieved 2/1/05. http://www.gardenofpeacememorial.org/personal/vic_jessemckie.html

Gillman, N. (1998). *The death of death: Resurrection and immortality in Jewish thought.* Woodstock, VT: Jewish Lights Publishing.

Gothein, M. L. (1979). *A history of garden art.* In W. P. Wright (Ed.), translated from the German by Mrs. Archer-Hind. New York: Hacker Art Books.

Green, S. (1997). My life . . . my mission. In J. W. Chery & B. Shackelton (Eds.), *Boston's book of peace* (Vol. 3, pp. 45-46). Dorchester, MA: Louis D. Brown Social Development Corporation.

Mt. Auburn Cemetery. Retrieved March 15, 2005. www.mountauburn.org.

Neimeyer, R. (2001). *Meaning construction and experience of loss.* Washington, DC: American Psychological Association.

Silverman, P. R. (2000). *Never too young to know: Death in children's lives.* New York: Oxford University Press.

Silverman, P. R. (2004). *Widow-to-widow: How the bereaved help one another.* New York: Bruner Routledge.

Silverman, P. R., & Klass, D. (1996). Introduction: What's the problem. In D. Klass, P. R. Silverman, & S. L. Nickman (Eds.), *Continuing bonds: New understandings of grief* (pp. 73-86). Washington, DC: Taylor and Francis.

Silverman, S. M. (2000). Expressing death and loss through music. In J. D. Morgan (Ed.), *Meeting the needs of our clients creatively: The impact of art and culture on caregiving* (pp. 27-36). Amityville, NY: Baywood.

Shalev, A., & Avraham, A. (2005). *"Unto every person there is a name" in materials on the memorial to the murdered Jews of Europe* (pp. 128-137). Berlin, Germany: The Foundation for the Memorial to the Murdered Jews of Europe.

Young, J. (1994). *The texture of memory: Holocaust memorials and meaning.* New Haven: Yale University Press.

CHAPTER 17

Talk it Out! Walk it Out! Wait it Out! Take Ten: An Intercultural Approach to Creating Safer Schools

Kim Overdyck
Jay Caponigro

> Many who live with violence day in and day out assume that it is an intrinsic part of the human condition. But this is not so. Violence can be prevented.
>
> Nelson Mandela

On December 7, 2004, a handful of African American pastors gathered together in South Bend, Indiana, to hold a press conference decrying the effects of violence in their community. In a scene played out all too often in the inner city, the homicide of a young black man by another young black man had stirred various community leaders to do something—commit to mentor a child, confront drug dealers, or police; to pray; or to start social service programs to address the consequences of poverty, substance abuse, or respect for family. However, in this press conference, as in so many, few resources had been identified, and the vision was not cohesive. The problem seems clear: young men are killing and hurting each other and innocents. The solutions confound. Start with personal interventions with the individual? The family? Or organize publicly to confront forces in the media? Bullying in the schools? Institutionalized violence in the prisons? One can easily become overwhelmed with the enormity of the proposition.

But one idea building momentum in the Midwest is starting with the basics, and challenging all those that have come to accept that violence is the norm. Take Ten, an initiative created by Anne Parry, now the Director of Violence Prevention for the Chicago Department of Public Health, starts with a firm foundation—a Violence-Free Zone. While children can promote or enforce this, adults need to create a violence-free zone, as they have authority in almost all

266 / PERSPECTIVES ON VIOLENCE AND VIOLENT DEATH

main institutions children visit regularly. Within a well-established violence-free zone with clear consequences for violent behavior, every student is expected to practice the lessons of nonviolence that are taught to the children—and so are the adults. For clearly if adults are not committed to acting without violence in their daily interactions with each other or the children, then there is no sense teaching children to choose to "Talk it out, Walk it out or Wait it out" rather than fighting.

Fighting. Probably the most clearly identified form of violence that children will name when queried. But here, too, Take Ten starts from the basics. In each school, the children's definition of violence may vary somewhat, but it ultimately reduces to the following:

> Violence is any act that harms oneself or another living being, place, or thing.

This inclusive definition often contradicts the children's learned understanding of violence that focuses on the physical violence that has become so common. But relational violence abounds, with painful stories of bullying, exclusion, and internet-based attacks that use pictures, rumor, e-mail, and instant messaging to defame, distort, and destroy the reputations of classmates. Children (and adults) are surprised at the number of violent acts they commit per day when they reflect on this definition; how their words have inflicted harm upon another, or their jokes; an e-mail sent that they cannot retract; or perhaps a look; the writing of a name on another's property; breaking a window. Wherever there is a victim harmed in an interaction, suffering is the result of a conflict resolved through violence because other tools were not known or accessible. Take Ten says a new norm can be established, and in fact, the children prefer it to the pattern of victimization and bullying that occurs on a daily basis. So Take Ten shouts out loud: "Let our youth LEAD themselves!"

Children are powerful examples to one another, and if youth leaders declare Take Ten cool, hip, in, or straight, then the adults can step back and support their young leaders through the maintenance of the violence-free zone. When children teach, they also learn. They "are aware that they continue to learn from each other and from the struggles they see in other young people their own age" (Lantieri & Patti, 1996, p. 158). And that is the strategy to be discussed in the remainder of this work. But the question to be posited is this: can Take Ten operate across various cultures? Can Take Ten, while indicating measures of success in inner city midwestern United States, cross an ocean and replicate its impact in other cultures. To consider this possibility, the comments of volunteers, principals, evaluators, and staff will be woven throughout this document. Employing a participant/observer approach, the authors have assembled observations of students participating in community-based learning courses, active principals and faculty, as well as evaluators who have recorded their perspectives along the way. While a research-based study is underway with surveys, pre- and post-tests, and analysis, this treatment seeks to use narrative and critical reflection to describe the impact of Take Ten among the children and communities where it is being practiced with consistency and care. These authors will argue that transfer to a foreign environment is possible, though some conditions must be in place culturally before Take Ten can take root.

POWER AND THE LEARNING ENVIRONMENT

Parker Palmer (1998, p. 20), in *The Courage to Teach,* quotes Václav Havel, poet and former president of the Czech Republic, regarding the insight he discerned after the fall of totalitarianism in his country:

> The salvation of this human world lies nowhere else than in the human heart, in the human power to reflect, in human meekness and in human responsibility. Without a global revolution in . . . human consciousness, nothing will change for the better . . .

Palmer expounds on the point, suggesting that like the Czechs, we are "not the victims of external forces, but persons possessed of an inner power that cannot be taken from us, though we can and do give it away" (1998, p. 20). Take Ten calls for just such a reawakening of consciousness. Understanding that one has choices, and the power to choose is central to its foundation. Yet, this cannot be achieved by individuals in isolation, particularly in the organization of the school.

David Nyberg (1981, p. 43), in a treatment on power in education, argues in *Power Over Power* that "every organization is a matter of at least two people (but there is no maximum number), and at least one idea for action." He continues, "where there is organization, there is power; where there is power, there is organization. If organization is inevitable in social life, then it is also true that power is inevitable in all social relations." Usually, within an organization there is some type of ordering or rank—a hierarchy—either formal or informal. Certainly this can describe a school environment wherein administrators and teachers are charged with certain responsibilities or authority. But for effective learning (the "action" of this organization), there must be consent from those governed by the authorities. As Take Ten assists individual learners to experience their own sense of power by understanding their choices and the consequences of actions (self-consciousness), authority will want to nurture positive choices in a cooperative environment. If Take Ten does not operate in such an atmosphere, the opposite effect may result as Nyberg (1981, p. 46) explains: "Authority that is based on forced acquiescence is tenuous, for it is extremely vulnerable to the withdrawal of consent which can destroy it. Refusal to respect authority is the power over power that is present in the minds of all persons."

Rather than reducing the level of respect in a classroom, Take Ten seeks a classroom environment wherein teachers and administrators share power with students. This concept, termed "Relational Power" by Bernard Loomer (1976, p. 19) and championed by Palmer, seeks the consent of the student through informed judgment; that is, an understanding of the student's interests,

268 / PERSPECTIVES ON VIOLENCE AND VIOLENT DEATH

experiences, and desires to act that will be met in relation to the authorities in the school. In the right environment, consent is given freely, and power is delegated widely. This leads to successful learning and students who are enabled to make positive choices for themselves, providing hope that Havel's "change for the better" might one day become reality.

> For academic learning to take place, you have to first provide a safe environment. . . . The children need to feel comfortable and safe and then they will put effort into their education.
>
> Mr. James Kapsa, Principal
> Jefferson Intermediate Center

CONDITIONS NECESSARY FOR LEARNING: WHY IS TAKE TEN IMPORTANT?

Conflict Resolution Education (CRE) has been in our schools in some form since the 1960s. According to the Association for Conflict Resolution (Jones, 2003, p. 19), CRE models and teaches, in culturally meaningful ways, a variety of processes, practices, and skills that help address individual, interpersonal, and institutional conflicts, as well as create safe and welcoming communities. These processes, practices, and skills help individuals understand conflict processes and empower them to use communication and creative thinking to build relationships and manage and resolve conflicts fairly and peacefully.

CRE presents itself in a number of different programs though not all programs are alike; but they have a number of common elements (Jones, 2003, pp. 19-20). The programs focus on developing critical skills and abilities and provide children with a basic understanding of conflict. This awareness of the nature of conflict helps the children appreciate the variety of ways that people can respond to conflict; they are then able to explore the different conflict styles and consider the advantages and disadvantages of both. Children are taught basic problem-solving skills, effective listening skills, perspective taking, emotional awareness, emotional control and so on. All the CRE programs emphasize that violent response is almost never an appropriate response to a conflict.

As the programs are not alike, neither are their goals (Jones, 2003, pp. 21-25). The four most common goals are

- to create a safe learning environment,
- to create a constructive learning environment,
- to enhance students' social and emotional development and
- to create a constructive-conflict community.

The question, then, is whether or not CRE has an impact on schools and if it does, what is that impact? Research conducted by the WT Grant Consortium on the School-Based Promotion of Social Competence (Lantieri & Patti, 1996, p. 15)

TALK IT OUT! WALK IT OUT! WAIT IT OUT! / 269

shows that CRE does have an impact on the school. Learning prosocial skills—those skills taught by CRE programs—not only helps children with their attitudes toward school, but they are able to better interact with fellow students and teachers. And the result is that they find school a comfortable place to be, and this results in higher academic achievements. In addition to all the valuable skills that the children learn, which assist them not only with dealing with conflict but also with their academic work, CRE has proven to decrease aggressiveness, discipline referrals, dropout rates, social withdrawal, suspension rates, victimized behavior, and violence. There is also considerable evidence that it has a strong positive impact on the school and classroom climate (Jones, 2003, p. 31).

TAKE TEN: THE HISTORY

Back in 1994 someone challenged Anne Parry, the architect of Take Ten, to create a social-justice marketing-campaign idea that would have the potential for reducing and preventing violence; something that people would like, understand, and remember. The approach that Anne took was to use a positive message, setting aside the general "don't/stop/end" approach to prevention. Take Ten had to be "doable." So, as Anne tells the story, at 5:30 one morning in Chicago, over a cup of coffee and meditation before driving her children to school, Take Ten: Talk it out! Walk it out! Wait it out! officially became an idea.

Take Ten is an action plan for teaching nonviolent alternatives for solving problems and handling conflicts. For example, "Take Ten deep breaths . . ." before you say something that hurts. Or "Take Ten steps back . . ." before getting involved in a fight. "Take Ten seconds to think . . ." about what you are doing before using something as a weapon. The Brazilian educator Paulo Freire believed that in order to change society, we need individuals to both THINK and ACT, which Take Ten models. It provides individuals with options to consider before they act, building their capacity to make more informed choices when faced with a conflict. Take Ten recognizes that we face conflict on a daily basis, and that disagreements and arguments are part of our journey through life. But it is how we deal with these disagreements and arguments that matters in the end. The philosophy of Take Ten is that there are more constructive ways to solve problems and resolve conflicts; that there are better ways for us as individuals to say that we are angry, frustrated, or hurt; that there are better ways than violence.

The majority of work done with Take Ten has been with school children. Today, children are being exposed to violence on a constant basis: violence within their communities, violence in the media and in games that they play, gang violence, firearm/gun violence, family violence, and interpersonal violence. The greatest tragedy is that children are being exposed to violence at home and at school, the two places where they should feel safe. Because of this exposure,

270 / PERSPECTIVES ON VIOLENCE AND VIOLENT DEATH

the violence-free zones that adults create are critical; areas where there are no weapons, where violence is not tolerated, expected, or accepted, and where children can feel safe. Take Ten is based on the belief that when you are in a safe place, violence is not necessary, should not be tolerated or accepted, and everyone is responsible for maintaining safety. According to Mr. James Kapsa (personal communication, January 26, 2005), a veteran Take Ten principal who started programming at two different schools, "Take Ten provides strategies to deal with conflict and therefore provides a safe environment."

Adults—parents, teachers and members of the community—play a fundamental role in creating violence-free zones and in the success of Take Ten. Not only are the adults involved with Take Ten as role models, and therefore have to "practice what they preach," but they also have to be honest in the process of creating violence-free zones. They acknowledge that there are areas in the community where violence-free zones do not exist. To ensure the safety of the children initially, we expect the children to practice Take Ten only in the designated violence-free zones. Adults often need to acknowledge that violence is a learned behavior and is sometimes enjoyed by adults and children alike. When adults take on this honest role with the children, they build genuine trust. This is critical, because in situations where Take Ten does not work, children are encouraged to get an adult's help, and they will not do so if they do not trust in the adults who can make a difference.

Take Ten: The Ground Rules

Along with the violence-free zones and the positive message of Talk it out! Walk it out! Wait it out!, Take Ten comes with certain ground rules and principles. The ground rules deal with how we as individuals are going to treat each other:

- Everyone has the right to speak, but no one has to speak
- Everyone must listen, but there is to be no put downs or name calling
- We can disagree on issues, but we cannot attack the individuals with whom we disagree
- We can agree to disagree
- Keep a sense of humor at all times.

Take Ten: The Principles

The following are 10 Take Ten Principles, as originally designed by Anne Parry. These principles, while not meant to be static or authoritarian, help a school to establish a nonviolence zone:

- Every individual has the right to safe and violence-free places
- Schools should be violence-free zones
- Disagreements are normal and to be expected

- Everyone has the right to feel however they feel
- No one has the right to hurt someone or destroy something because of how they feel
- Weapons have no place in solving conflicts in schools
- Every individual has the right to choose how they will solve problems and express themselves
- Talk it out! Walk it out! Wait it out! and knowing when to get help can work in a violence-free zone
- Individuals have the power to decide if a place is going to be a violence-free zone
- There is a connection between respect, personal power, and self-esteem.

Take Ten is also based on the belief that young people are effective teachers of younger children, and that people of all ages should be seen as partners in choosing nonviolence. Richard Cohen, founder and director of School Mediation Associates, says that children bring a unique strength to mediation as they "understand their peers and know the pressures, the attitude and language of the time. They know what their peers think and why. . . . Students also command a tacit and unique sort of respect from their peers" (2003, p. 114).

Take Ten "Ambassadors," as originally conceived, are individuals (adults, teenagers, or their peers) whom the children could count on to remind them, support them, and sometimes teach them the alternatives to violence. In South Bend, the ambassadors tend to be older children in a school, who are charged with interacting with younger children in constructive, nonviolent ways on a day-to-day basis. Through role modeling and other activities, the children are taught skills for solving problems and handling conflicts nonviolently by other children in their building.

Take Ten schools can be found in Chicago, Indiana, Florida, and Michigan. In Chicago, for example, the Southwest Organizing Project (SWOP), a nonprofit organization of churches and schools, implemented a neighborhoodwide Take Ten Campaign in the 1996–97 academic year to deal with a rash of violence in the community. More than twenty schools participated under the direction of a Lutheran Volunteer Corps member on SWOP's staff. Anne Parry trained key school personnel, as well as counselors from a local agency. Significantly, Take Ten was integrated into both the public and parochial schools of the community, though in a variety of ways. In one example, Lee Chicago Public Elementary School joined with St. Mary's Star of the Sea Catholic School each October for the national Pledge Against Gun Violence Day. This event would bring together nearly 2,000 children and adults from both school communities. In other schools, a counselor would work with children to identify issues of violence in the school, and troubleshoot hot spots using Take Ten principles. Another school's librarian used literature to explore issues of nonviolence with children during their weekly library class.

272 / PERSPECTIVES ON VIOLENCE AND VIOLENT DEATH

While interpersonal violence was addressed at various levels using Take Ten, as an organization, SWOP promoted the initiative to address structural issues especially. One school, St. Gall, was experiencing a rise in shootings and gang-related violence in its neighborhood. Its Take Ten Ambassadors, upon witnessing the erection of a blue jeans advertisement claiming that "our models can beat up there models," organized a petition drive to remove the sign. With parent and administration support, over 3,000 signatures were obtained in two weeks, and these were sent to the company's president. By week three, the company's marketing director contacted the Ambassadors stating that the billboard campaign had been discontinued—a cause for great celebration!

Take Ten youth regularly entered floats in local parades (Wedam, 2000, p. 129), spoke at meetings with parents and community leaders, started a small rap group with Take Ten songs, and even developed a following among local police. An evaluation, conducted by Nancy Mathews (1999) of Northeastern Illinois University, suggested that heightened awareness of nonviolence was indeed occurring on the southwest side of Chicago. However, she rightly observed that the challenge for Take Ten was to move to the next phase of a deep implementation of the initiative; that is, truly transforming aggressive attitudes and violent behavioral patterns among youth.

TAKE TEN ARRIVES IN SOUTH BEND

Take Ten was brought to South Bend, Indiana in 1999 by Jay Caponigro, who had been the Director of SWOP in Chicago. Taking the approach that young adults are naturally effective teachers of younger children, Caponigro decided to initiate a different strategy with Take Ten in 2000 in the hopes of deepening its impact with youth. While at the Center for Social Concerns of the University of Notre Dame, he started recruiting college students to work with children in the schools and community centers. With an average of 85% of students participating in some service before graduation, Notre Dame was a fertile ground in which to find volunteers. Seven students participated in the original training in the fall of 1999, and visited their first school, St. Adalbert Catholic School, in spring of 2000. That very morning, while grades 5–8 were in training, a first grade student was showing his classmates the gun he had brought to school. While volunteers thought their training was disappointing to the principal, who left the room midsession, they soon came to realize how important their presence truly would become in fostering a more peaceful school.

Caponigro is currently the Director of the Robinson Community Learning Center (RCLC), a four-year-old initiative of the University of Notre Dame in partnership with its neighbors in the Northeast Neighborhood of South Bend. Initiated in 2001 by Rev. Edward "Monk" Malloy, C.S.C., the RCLC provides educational programming to all ages, including tutoring, computer courses, exercise, career counseling, and music awareness. The RCLC relies upon the support of hundreds of volunteers per semester, most coming from the University with the exception of the Youth Justice Project, a juvenile court diversion program, which, like Take Ten, operates in the wider community. Having Take Ten based in such a center of learning and community activity increased its visibility and partnership opportunities. It also opened the door to new financial resources to expand Take Ten's reach.

In fall, 2000, we began working with children as part of the after-school programming in the public schools and various community centers. The two parochial schools decided to carry Take Ten one step further and provided student volunteers with an opportunity to work with the children in the classroom during the school day. So, in 2002 we began working with every single child from prekindergarten to the eighth grade in the first of these institutions, Saint Adalbert Catholic School.

Early Insights in South Bend

Many lessons were gleaned in the first couple of semesters about the student volunteers' effectiveness teaching Take Ten. An original student volunteer, Anne Moriarty, recounted in a report she prepared in May, 2000:

> Perhaps the greatest area in need of improvement in the South Bend Take Ten initiative is the defining and limiting of the role of the ND [Notre Dame] Take Ten team members . . . St. Adalbert's students initially saw us as *the* Take Ten leaders of *their* school. This set-up does not encourage the students within a school to take the initiative, to the greatest extent possible, in solving the problem of violence in their classroom.

Still others have noted other concerns regarding the use of student volunteers to provide this training. A founding school principal stated, "The disadvantage is their schedules and that we do not have enough of them to send to the school." Student leaders acknowledge limitations as well, such as cultural differences, the varying degree of industriousness among volunteers, and the lack of continuity from year-to-year. Another key principal concurs with these observations, but counters, "The message coming from the volunteers, it means a lot to the children, and it is better. Take Ten brings in 'high class' volunteers who are intelligent and committed to education and they are committed to community service." According to Morgan Monte (personal communication, January 2005), a three-year volunteer who sees these advantages, "Student volunteers are an integral part of the Take Ten Program. Because we are closer in age to the students than many of their teachers . . . the students have a greater respect and a heightened attention toward the college volunteers."

Assessment of successful schools clearly demonstrated that the most effective Ambassadors are children with leadership skills, children whose peers look up to and respect them. Teachers and administrators are encouraged to think beyond the

274 / PERSPECTIVES ON VIOLENCE AND VIOLENT DEATH

teacher's favorite, or the valedictorian students, toward children who will take ownership of Take Ten, support their peers in practicing Take Ten, be positive role models, and spread the philosophy of Take Ten throughout the school. This may require taking the risk that a student may fail, but in many cases it has also become a means for leadership development and transformation of negative behaviors in that student. Volunteer Brigid Curry (personal communication, 2001) knew that she would not be meeting with the most well-behaved children when she met after school:

> In our ambassador meetings, I would find myself reminding students not to harass each other or engage in violent behavior, but for every discouraging action there were always moments when I realized the students genuinely cared about promoting nonviolence. They were excited to share their ideas about issues ranging from gun violence to world peace. Several times the students expressed their belief that it was important to be positive role models . . .

Other lessons pointed to the need for regular communication with teachers and Take Ten leadership, as well as cooperation from administrators. Weekly volunteer planning sessions have also been identified as central to successful encounters with the children. Over the first couple of years, these lessons all became important components of volunteer training and the school's commitment when introducing Take Ten into the classroom environment.

BUILDING COMMUNITY SUPPORT

In the years to follow, Take Ten has developed community support through various efforts: presentations at schools, churches, and local conferences; luncheons sponsored by students on campus; through the children themselves and the messages that they take home; various press accounts surrounding Take Ten activities; and events open to the public. These public events include award ceremonies for the Take Ten poster and bookmark competitions and the Annual Take Ten Festival.

The South Bend community has demonstrated support of Take Ten in multiple venues. There is the moral support provided by parents, teachers, and other advocates promoting Take Ten within the community, and encouraging various institutions that work with children to bring the Take Ten philosophy into their buildings. One local church has included Take Ten in the Sunday homilies. There have been financial resources from local hospitals and banks, and "in-kind" donations from other local businesses and governmental entities.

The backing of the community was also evident during the *Take Ten Week without Violence* that was held in October, 2004, which focused on the issue of bullying in our schools. School personnel attended a Take Ten workshop on bullying, and 150 community members attended a town hall meeting that was held to discuss potential solutions to the bullying issue. Partners included the Mayor of South Bend; the South Bend Tribune; the YWCA; and 22 WSBT, a local television station. At the end of the week, 27 Take Ten Ambassadors were treated to a Notre Dame vs. Boston College football game and were featured over the public address system to an audience of 80,000! To further encourage the involvement of the community, Take Ten now actively recruits students from other local universities and colleges—Indiana University of South Bend (I.U.S.B), St. Mary's College, and Bethel College—to broaden and deepen the work with children in the community schools.

To take advantage of the community's interest in supporting the children, we formed a Take Ten Advisory Board to provide direction and insight for programming. Now composed of church volunteers, teachers, principals, and university staff, the team realized that the consistent amount of time that the student volunteers worked with the children each week would provide the opportunity to teach the children the skills to practice Take Ten and thereby deepen their commitment to Take Ten. These skills include basic conflict resolution, anger management, listening and communication skills, and to begin nurturing within themselves a respect for diversity. We could now move Take Ten from being a campaign idea to an opportunity to teach children the skills necessary to Talk it out! Walk it out! Wait it out! This decision to teach children skills moved Take Ten into the arena of conflict resolution education.

At the time of this writing, Take Ten is part of programming at 10 community schools ranging from primary centers to high schools (8 public and 2 parochial schools), local community centers, and the Boys and Girls Clubs of St. Joseph County. Approximately 452 children are Take Ten Ambassadors, reaching over 5,700 in their schools and programs. Of the participating schools, 90% have seen rates of suspension decrease by the second year of Take Ten activity (South Bend Tribune, January 28, 2005). Asked if Take Ten was having an impact on the culture of her school, Sr. Dian Majsterek (personal communication, January 13, 2005), flatly replied "Yes, the hardest month of the year is the very first month of the school year as the new children who come to join the school do not know about Take Ten."

HOW TAKE TEN WORKS IN 2005

Before the student volunteers begin working at their assigned school, they undergo training by Take Ten staff, current volunteers, and other educators. This training covers the fundamentals of Take Ten and the practical concerns of mentoring children. Specifically, training includes the use of consistent language with regard to conflict and nonviolence; teaching skills to develop and use lesson plans; modeling teaching through role play or storytelling; and the basics skills of discipline and classroom management to keep the children engaged. The

276 / PERSPECTIVES ON VIOLENCE AND VIOLENT DEATH

issue of mandatory reporting in suspected cases of child abuse under Indiana law is also covered with the student volunteers.

Once the student volunteers have completed the training, they are assigned to a team. The size of each team varies, depending on the number of children in the group and the number of student volunteers available to volunteer at that time. Each team has a team leader, who receives additional training in the resource materials, and whose role it is to ensure that the team comes prepared to work with their group of children. The teams spend approximately 10 weeks per academic semester with the children, meeting with the same group of children on a weekly basis. On average, the student volunteers meet with the children, who participate in after-school programming for approximately 75 minutes per week. In the parochial schools, the student volunteers meet with the children in their classrooms anywhere from 30 to 40 minutes per week, depending on the grade of the group of children. Asked about the advantages of college students teaching the children conflict resolution skills, volunteer Stephanie Downham (personal communication, January 7, 2005), a senior at Bethel College, replied:

> Students sees us as friends and confidants. We're not the teacher, so the students don't see us as a person that they have to see every day, hour after hour. It's a treat for them to see us in their school.

Take Ten Toolkit: Curriculum and Activities

> Take Ten is definitely a concrete program. It is designed to have a lifetime impact on the students. . . . Violence is expected in the neighborhood where I work with these children. We're trying to teach that it's not only unacceptable, but there is a different option. TakeTen is not a program that disregards violence that has already occurred . . . it's a program that's making a change on the streets in our neighborhood (Downham, personal communication, January 7, 2005).

The move from a marketing campaign to a campaign that also teaches children the skills required to practice Take Ten necessitated the development of the "Take Ten Toolkit." The toolkit is divided into two parts: the first part is the curriculum for grades prekindergarten to eighth grade; and the second part is a wide selection of activities to assist the children in spreading the Take Ten philosophy to the rest of the school or community center. The foundation of the curriculum was developed by two psychologists, and these foundations were further developed by a teacher, a mediator, and the coordinator (coauthor Kim Overdyck) of Take Ten.

The curriculum provides lesson plans on the various skills required to Talk it out! Walk it out! Wait it out!, and the common thread throughout this curriculum is respect for diversity. The children learn that what makes us a diverse community is not only the color of our skin, our ethnic background, or our gender, but diversity also includes our age, class, communication styles, country of origin, learning styles, looks, mannerisms, mental ability, physical ability, religion, sexual orientation, and privilege (Chappelle & Bigman, 1998, p. 377). While Take Ten nurtures a respect for diversity and the fact that we are all unique, it also fosters a sense of connectedness among the children. We may have qualities that make us diverse and unique, but we all experience similar feelings, and once we realize that, it becomes more difficult to cause harm to one another. The ability to see another's perspective reduces the barriers behind which we could hide and cause harm and reveals how we are all connected. Katelyn O'Reilly (personal communication, April 2004), a participant in a one-credit Take Ten Seminar offered through the Center for Social Concerns at Notre Dame, stated it this way:

> What I quickly discovered was that although I did not have any firsthand experience with violence, or many of the other problems these kids faced, such as broken homes and exposure to drugs, I did have something valuable to offer them. I remember what it is like to be a 10 to 14-year-old—the struggles that you go through when you are in between being a child and a young adult, the awkwardness, the desire to fit in and be cool, the need to feel as though you matter. As I remembered how much children that age are looking for recognition and encouragement, I realized that one of the most important things I could do for the students at Brown (Intermediate Center) was to listen to them.

The lesson plans in the curriculum are a guide for the student volunteers and provides consistency in the way that Take Ten is taught within the community. We also encourage the student volunteers to use their individual creativity and that of the children to ensure the success of the lesson. The length of each lesson plan is 40 minutes, but they have been written in such a way that they can be split and used over two meetings. The student volunteers are also encouraged to diverge from the lesson plan, when necessary, and use a teachable moment when it arises.

Before the student volunteers begin working with the children on the curriculum or on getting the Take Ten philosophy across to the rest of the school, they become acquainted with the children and establish ground rules for their meetings. These are amended as necessary and agreed upon by both the children and the volunteers. Student volunteers are encouraged to establish beforehand if there are existing ground rules that apply to the children and to use those, together with the Take Ten ground rules and principles, in establishing the environment that nurtures respect for self, others, and place. By giving the children input on the ground rules, they have increased ownership of these rules and are more inclined to follow them.

The following sections describe activities and instruction found within the Take Ten Toolkit. This instrument is in its final stage of development, having been tested by volunteers and educators over the fall, 2004 and spring, 2005. To reiterate, the Toolkit is meant to be a fluid tool that allows for addition and

278 / PERSPECTIVES ON VIOLENCE AND VIOLENT DEATH

innovation, depending on the creativity and charisma of volunteers and children. Core themes give the handbook its structure, and these are explained below.

Theme 1: Conflict and Violence

Once the ground rules have been established and the student volunteers and the children have gotten to know one another, work on the curriculum and getting the Take Ten message out to the school begins. The first issues that are addressed in the curriculum are those of conflict and violence and introducing Take Ten to the children. As important as it is to establish ground rules for meeting times, it is just as important to establish a working definition of violence for the group. As stated earlier, many children see violence as kicking, hitting, biting, pushing, scratching, punching, and slapping, but they do not include name calling, spreading rumors, teasing, or social exclusion in their definition of violence. The impact of these more subtle forms of violence are often more traumatic and have a longer lasting impact on the victim than physical violence. Take Ten defines violence as "anything that harms oneself or another living being, place, or thing." The operative word in this definition is "harm," and includes self-destructive behavior, destruction of property, and harming animals. The reason for focusing on harm was to take the standard definition of violence beyond the mere physical and include emotional violence, thereby giving the children a wider definition of violence to work with.

The children learn what conflict is; that it is not always to be viewed as something negative, but rather that it is to be seen as an opportunity to bring about positive change. The children learn that who we are, our life experiences, where we come from, and the communities to which we belong all have an impact on how we deal with conflict. If their experiences and responses to conflict have been negative and violent, it becomes even more important to ensure that they are provided the necessary skills to choose how to respond to conflict; to choose a positive, nonviolent approach such as Talk it Out! Walk it Out! Wait it Out! These are important lessons for the student volunteers as well as the children, according to Jessica Collado (personal communication, January 25, 2005), a Notre Dame junior.

> I have learned more about what a conflict actually is and how to respond to it, by teaching and learning from my fourth graders, than I have in any other context I've experienced at Notre Dame. You have to get right down to the point with 9 and 10 year olds, so there's no dancing around the subject and hiding behind words like conflict transformation or non-violent conflict resolution. Presenting the material to them on constructive emotions and anger especially, as well as listening to what they had to say on what conflict means to them, . . . has changed my outlook and reactions towards conflict.

Theme 2: Values and Principles

The Toolkit goes on to deal with values and principles. Understanding our values and principles is important as they define who we are as individuals and how we react to and deal with conflict. Our values are our internal standards of behavior, and our principles are our foundation for belief or action in day-to-day life. Take Ten does not prescribe a standard set of values and principles that the children should believe or follow, but rather explores differences among beliefs and values among the children. Importantly, it teaches them that being different is okay, stressing that diversity is beneficial.

Some of the questions that are addressed involve whether people who like different things or believe in different things can get along with each other. And if they have any friends who like things that they don't, is this okay? Why is it important to have things to believe in or things we think are important or that we value? Some of these questions are suggested in the book *Odd Velvet* (Whitcomb & King, 1998), a story about a girl who is different, and whom no one wants to be like. Used in a lesson plan, the children are shown that even though Velvet seems different, once her classmates spend some time with her, they discover that she really is not so different after all.

Theme 3: Fair and Assertive Behavior

From values and principles, children are encouraged to understand the benefits of fair and assertive behavior. Student volunteers can choose from a number of resources, including "The Green Boots," a story from *Chicken Soup for the Kid's Soul* (Rosenberg, 1998, p. 142). In this work, the author is reprimanded unfairly by her teacher, and she has to choose between standing up for herself and risking her teacher's reaction, or not defending herself and compromising her values. The goal of working with the children on fair and assertive behavior is for them to understand the purpose of fairness in a conflict and to act on this fairness by behaving assertively, as opposed to aggressively. Children are encouraged to appreciate the value of standing up for oneself and others, to deal with put-downs, and to pursue one's needs in a conflict situation, as well as how to appreciate the value of respecting other people involved in the conflict and their needs.

We also explore the spectrum of behavior that could arise in a conflict, behavior ranging from soft and passive to mean and aggressive. The children are reminded that by being fair and assertive, Take Ten is not requiring them to be submissive, but rather it is encouraging them to stand up for themselves and to do so by talking it out, walking it out, waiting it out. Resources also illustrate different forms of behavior that are violent, such as bullying and discrimination, and provides the students with the opportunity to identify their own personal conflict styles. Morgan Monte (personal communication, January 2005), a junior at Notre Dame, reflects on her own transformation:

280 / PERSPECTIVES ON VIOLENCE AND VIOLENT DEATH

Take Ten has definitely altered my actions and thought processes. I find myself confronting people by whom I am offended instead of keeping it inside. Sometimes I find that the person meant no harm; it was simply my poor interpretation.

Theme 4: Anger Management

Aristotle said that "anybody can become angry, this is easy; but to be angry with the right person, and to the right degree, and at the right time, and for the right purpose, and in the right way, that is not within everybody's power, that is not easy." Anger-management materials assist children in learning to recognize behaviors that can escalate a conflict, behaviors that contribute to personal feelings of anger, and techniques on how to manage these behaviors in such a way so that they do not express their anger violently, escalating the conflict. The children are reminded of two important Take Ten principles: (1) everyone has the right to feel however they feel, (2) no one has the right to hurt someone or destroy something because of the way that they feel. The techniques that the children are taught provide them with the skills to take 10 deep breaths before saying something that hurts; to take 10 steps back before getting involved in a fight; and to take 10 seconds to think before using something as a weapon.

Theme 5: Effective Communication

All conflict resolution involves communication—not more communication, but rather better communication. Ernest Hemingway said that when people talk, we need to listen, as most people never listen. The two most important elements of communication are talking—the experience of being genuinely heard—and listening—the ability to understand the speaker's perspective and being interested in what the speaker is saying. In order to be a good communicator, we need to use our ears, eyes, mind, attention, and heart to assist us in being more knowledgeable of the person with whom we are having a conflict. The children learn that the more aware we are and the better understanding we have of the communities to which an adversary belongs, the better equipped we will be to communicate, and therefore resolve the conflict.

There are various filters that have an impact on our observations, our perceptions being one of them. What we observe has an impact on how we deal with conflict. From the story *Mr. Peabody's Apples* (Madonna & Long, 2003), the children learn that their observations may not always be correct as they observe the unfolding of a tale in which an incorrect observation can result in a vicious rumor. A young boy sees *Mr. Peabody,* his baseball coach and a man who he thought was "the greatest," take an apple from a fruit vendor without paying for it. The young boy believes that *Mr. Peabody* is a thief and quickly rushes off to tell his friends what he saw. The result of this rumor is that no one comes to play on *Mr. Peabody's* baseball team, and everyone in the town thinks that he is a thief.

What the young boy did not know was that *Mr. Peabody* had already paid for his apple. In the end, *Mr. Peabody* teaches the young boy that just as it is impossible to collect a pillow full of feathers released in the wind, it is just as impossible to undo the harm done by spreading a rumor.

One of the most common activities used to teach communication skills is the *I* statement. Phrasing a sentence using an *I* statement prevents the accusatory you statement, which often results in a defensive reaction. Instead, the *I* statement simply expresses how the speaker feels in relation to the other party's actions. The general formula for an *I* statement is "I feel (the emotion that the person is feeling) when you (state action causing feeling) because (state reason)." As this formula is such a commonly taught tactic, student volunteers role-play using language that is common to the children in order to make it most effective. For example, "Hey Andrew, I'm starting to get angry, and I don't like it when you call me wire teeth—it's making me embarrassed. Can we talk about why you are dissin' me?" When the children feel more comfortable using their own language in the formula, they will be more inclined to use an *I* statement to prevent potential conflicts.

One of the most popular activities to reinforce the understanding of effective communication is called *Two Villages*. The group is broken up into two, and each group is given characteristics that are completely opposite to that of the other group. One group is loud, enjoys physical contact, is outgoing and very gregarious. They consider themselves one big family, and they greet each other with a roaring chant. For this group, socializing and trade are core traits, and it is considered an insult not to trade.

The second group is idealistic and meditative, and they have taken a vow of silence. They do not like their personal space invaded, and they see themselves as autonomous units. Once the groups have gotten into character, ambassadors are sent from each group to make friends with the other group, to meet a culture totally different from theirs. Once we have finished the activity, we ask the children what it was like to encounter a group of individuals whose culture was completely opposite to theirs, and we ask them two important questions: if they had known more about this culture, would communication have been easier? And what could they have done to better understand this culture that is so different from theirs?

Theme 6: Problem Solving

There are many resources available to promote problem-solving techniques with children. Student volunteers often use cooperative games to define the problem, find a solution, choose the solution, and then act. Another of the techniques that we use to teach these skills is to take a story or well-known fairy tale and have the children work together in rewriting the ending with a solution that is appropriate to the Take Ten message. Dr. Martin Luther King Jr. is a role model used to teach the children strategies in dealing with problems by

282 / PERSPECTIVES ON VIOLENCE AND VIOLENT DEATH

reflecting on issues he faced and how he solved them peacefully. To bring a little reality to the issue of problem solving, we assist the children in identifying conflict in their personal lives and how to plan effective nonviolent solutions.

One of the stories used to promote problem-solving techniques is that of *The Crayon Box that Talked* (DeRolf & Letzig, 1997). This is a story about a box of crayons that just could not get along, until a little girl takes them home and starts coloring with them, creating a picture. The crayons then realize that the big picture that they make together is more exciting and varied than the small picture that each makes alone; together they make a complete picture. After reading the story to the children, the volunteers ask each child to choose only one crayon out of a box, and as a group, they work together like the crayons in the story to create a mural.

Theme 7: Trading Perspectives

When deciding which skills to teach children so that they could practice Take Ten most effectively, and to keep our commitment to nurturing a respect for diversity, we felt that trading perspectives was a core part of Take Ten and deserved more emphasis in the Toolkit. Thus, volunteers work with the children on the importance and impact of understanding another person's point of view in a conflict. For children to be able to practice Take Ten, they need to understand the value of another individual's experience and to practice putting themselves in another person's position. Diversity is approached by showing that people come in different packages, and we revisit the impact that diversity has on communication and conflict resolution. We also teach the children skills for discussing and negotiating needs so that conflicts can be resolved nonviolently. The focus of the conflict is moved from the problem to possible solutions; agreeing to disagree, compromise, apologies, restitution or putting things right, and asking the other person what he or she wants you to do.

Once again, literature is used to suggest the message. Children are introduced to two characters in the story *Hey Little Ant* (Hoose, Hoose, & Tilley, 1998). One is a boy who wants to squish an ant, and the other is the ant. The boy tells the ant why he should squish him, and the ant in turn, tells the boy why he should not be squished. The shoe is placed on the other foot in this story, with the ant asking "if you were me and I were you, what would you want me to do?" The story ends with the authors asking the readers if the ant should be squished or not. By being placed in the situation of the ant, the children are far less eager to squish the ant than when they were in the position of the little boy.

Opportunities are provided to practice negotiation skills and create an understanding of the positions (what is outwardly expressed in response to a conflict), interests (what a person would really like to see happen), needs (what it takes for us to feel happy and content), and the role that they play in a conflict. The children also identify conflict in their lives and analyze it from the perspective of each party involved in the conflict. They learn how to use open-ended requests to gain information, such as "Describe your feelings when the conflict began . . ." as a way to improve communication.

Theme 8: Knowing When to Walk Away

On the final page of the book *The Spider and the Fly* (Howitt & DiTerlizzi, 2002), the Spider addresses a letter to his "Dear Sweet Creatures" wondering why the readers may be surprised by the "little tragedy" that took place in the story when the story is after all about a spider and a fly. The Spider reminds us that even with all our knowledge about spiders and their crafty carnivorous ways, not a day passes without "a hapless bug or two stopping by." The reader may wonder what traps and spiders have to do with them. But the Spider reminds the reader that spiders are not the only hunters, and bugs are not the only victims and warns the reader not to get caught in some schemers web, with sweet words being spoken by those who hide their not-so-sweet intentions. Knowing when to walk away from a conflict is one of the most important skills to teach children, and it is also one of the hardest. The Spider warns us about those who use sweet words to hide their not-so-sweet intentions, but few of us heed this warning as we (children and adults alike) find it easier to stay in a conflict and face the consequences of our actions, than to deal with the verbal taunting of walking away and finding help.

Upon the commemoration of the sixtieth anniversary of the liberation of Auschwitz, New York Times commentator Roger Cohen (New York Times, January 30, 2005) recalled the words of Fritz Stern, a great German historian. Stern recently appealed for recognition of individuals who attempted to ease suffering and oppose the evil of the Nazi's genocide. He pleaded, "I wish these people would be given a proper European memorial not to appease our conscience, but to summon the courage of future generations." Through Take Ten, we remind children that courage comes in different forms, such as helping a victim in the face of overwhelming intimidation; being the new kid on the block and introducing yourself to the neighborhood kids; suddenly remembering a silly joke when you absolutely cannot laugh; and walking away from a fight when it is the smart and right thing to do.

Children who walk away from a fight feel that there is a stigma attached and that they will be "dissed" by their peers for doing so and be excluded. It is therefore important that we develop constructive, nonviolent attitudes about walking away from a conflict, to understand that it is the smartest thing to do if personal safety and nonviolent goals are more important than proving we can fight; to realize that fighting because someone else taunts us is lowering ourselves to the level of the person whose behavior we do not respect; to appreciate that leaving sometimes takes more courage than fighting.

The question of when and how to walk away is important, and we remind them that walking away is not backing down, especially if they are in danger; it is

284 / PERSPECTIVES ON VIOLENCE AND VIOLENT DEATH

an assertion of their personal power that stops the situation from deteriorating into violence. The children are taught that in a violence-free zone, they should walk away when it is impossible to do anything constructive with the other person in the conflict; when everything that they have been taught is not working; or when finding an adult's help is the smarter thing to do. They learn that by fighting with someone, you do not improve that person's behavior. Student volunteers introduce the concept that if you are able to walk away from a conflict, you have overcome the other individual and have taken control of the situation; by refusing to fight, you have prevented the violence that the threatening person was trying to make happen. This is perhaps the most difficult concept for new volunteers to understand, accept, and teach effectively. One student volunteer, Leigh Moreno (personal communication, December 2001) struggled with this question, despite an overall effectiveness working with the youth:

> Sadly our society does not allow these students to retain the idealism and simplicity that we ought to protect for them. . . . While nonviolence may become their *ideal*, they live in the *real* world where the dynamic of in-school violence cannot be entirely divorced from the dynamic of the neighborhood in which they live after 2:30 PM. So long as they have no alternative to participation in that world, they will never be able to completely stand for nonviolence in school, since reputation in some ways is their best defense.

The question then is how do you walk away from a conflict and not diminish the reputation that protects you "on the street"? Through honest relationships with Take Ten student volunteers, children ask the hard questions and are faced with hard answers. Making good decisions when faced with a conflict takes courage and power, but it also takes adults who are committed to walking alongside a stumbling child, encouraging him/her to try again "the Take Ten way." It takes administrators enforcing violence-free zones inside our institutions, but also striving with the children to make the "real" world safer as well. Through Take Ten, we all learn about choices, but how we choose is affected by the relationships with those around us who demonstrate consistency and care for our growth and development.

THE NEXT STAGE

This is why the press conference at the Church is so relevant. Take Ten offers concrete Conflict Resolution Education, in places that can be declared Violence-Free Zones, taught by people who are energetic role models. But Take Ten needs the churches, mosques, synagogues, and other local institutions to truly affect cultural change in our communities. More Violence-Free Communities are needed, and moral leadership and proactive relationship building are a necessary and powerful combination to influence government officials, violent offenders, and youth alike. Examples such as the St. Gall petition drive demonstrate the connection between nonviolence education and concrete organizing that can positively affect youth in a community. And the required resources to keep that effort in focus, and Take Ten thriving in other communities, can be delivered through faithful, organized people declaring the priorities of their members to their representatives at various levels.

The purpose of this is not to create a manual for the organizing of communities, which has been done elsewhere. Instead, the present exercise has one final task: to apply the lessons learned about Take Ten in the midwestern United States, and to explore, albeit briefly, whether the Take Ten model could motivate youth and adult partners to change cultures far beyond United States borders.

ASSESSING THE SCALE OF VIOLENCE AND CONDITIONS FOR CHANGE

Much has been written about conditions of schools in America: economic inequality between urban and suburban districts, lagging performance in inner city public schools, discrepancies between male and female performance, violence, and many other factors. A recent Web site document developed by the U.S. Center for Disease Control (January 31, 2005) illustrates research demonstrating the interrelated factors that determine levels of violence among youth, primarily in urban areas.

There are a number of community characteristics that increase the probability of youth violence. Crime and violence tend to be high in areas in which at least 20% of the residents are poor (Lamison-White, 1996). These areas are often characterized by

- high concentrations of poverty and unemployment,
- high levels of residential instability,
- family disruption,
- crowded housing,
- drug-distribution networks, and
- low community participation (Sampson & Lauritsen, 1994).

In addition to their demographic characteristics, economically poor neighborhoods differ from more affluent neighborhoods in a number of ways. Poor neighborhoods tend to be characterized by disorganization or a lack of neighborhood cohesion, and as a result, frequently lack effective social controls (Elliot et al., 1996; Sampson, Raudenbush, & Earls, 1997).

South African media reports and academic research yield similar observations, even though the sociopolitical contexts differ in degree and development from the United States experience. Youth gangs certainly existed before apartheid, but at present these gangs are formed and maintained by complex economic and political forces, with poverty and unemployment playing major roles. Studies

286 / PERSPECTIVES ON VIOLENCE AND VIOLENT DEATH

also point to family dynamics, pressures of status and masculinity, as well as the availability of guns, among other complex factors (McEvoy-Levy, 2005). One research project claims go even further. Its authors suggest that "from newspaper reports one can deduce that a culture of crime and violence prevails in South African education" and that "Street justice is the order of the day in South African education" (De Wet, 2003, pp. 118-119).

Differences in geography, race, and history between South Africa and the midwestern United States abound. Resources will not look the same. Buildings will be built for different climates. Youth will be in school for different lengths of time per day, with varying interests and subject material. Lunch may be served indoors or not at all, financed by the government or through the hard work of a family member, but these authors nevertheless are struck by the similarities of concern and perspective on educational dynamics voiced by researchers, but specifically educational leaders. For a South African voice, we turn to Mr. Shafiq Abrahams, the Manager (Principal) at Phoenix High School in Mannenberg, Cape Town, South Africa.

Consistent with research conducted about violence in South African schools and referred to above, Mr. Abrahams' (personal communication, January 17, 2005) affirms the danger for youth, particularly in Mannenberg, where he has taught for the last 25 years. Even though the South African Department of Education has a subdepartment whose role is to create safer schools, they believe that in order to make the schools safe, they have to put fences around the building, ". . . instead of introducing programming that can change the culture of the school." Abrahams' frustration is evident when he suggests that "The children see the fences as prisons or places of safety, not as a place to come and learn."

But this has not prevented Mr. Abrahams from inviting the community into the school. Social-work students from the University of Western Cape, a local university, come to the school during the day, and the children know that if they have a problem, they can go and speak with one of these students. Mr. Abrahams has witnessed the positive interaction, similar to the dynamic in the United States, wherein the children are able to work with the university students in his building. He even went so far as to experiment with and test the impact of outsiders on his children. Recently, he went into one of his classrooms and gave his children certain information. A little while later, he sent a foreigner into the same class to give the children the same information. Mr. Abrahams went into the class about a week later and asked his children about the information that they were given by both him and the foreigner, and the children were excited about the information given to them by the foreigner! Abrahams says that "The children see the role of the teachers as people who are supposed to tell them what is righteous and know that there are things that teachers should tell them." Moreover, as in South Bend, "When they [the children] see the students who are coming from the University of Cape Town, they see that they are fairly successful and that they were able to get into university. Having outsiders come into the school is beneficial for the children." But is there a culture for campus-community involvement in South Africa?

STUDENTS HEALTH AND WELFARE CENTRES
ORGANISATION (SHAWCO)

From its Web site, SHAWCO (January, 31, 2005) answers the question of student interest and engagement in the community from halfway across the world. This year SHAWCO celebrates 60 years of service to underprivileged communities in Cape Town. What started as a one-man initiative grew into one of the largest student volunteer organizations, attracting around 500 UCT students, close to 100 foreign students, as well as about 20 community volunteers every year, all of whom give of their time and energy for the same goal of building a better future.

Youth development is already a core concern for these South African students, who are involved in running multipurpose community centers with skills training and recreation projects. In fact, student volunteers from SHAWCO already come into Mr. Abrahams' building and do art with the children every Thursday. Student groups like this can be found around the world, and can be powerful agents for teaching younger children in their surrounding communities about the alternatives to interpersonal and structural violence.

Our small sampling of administrators suggest that they understand the importance of their role, summarized succinctly by Sr. Dian Majsterck, "The commitment of the administration is very important, if the commitment is not there, Take Ten will not work." This sentiment is echoed by Mr. Abrahams: "Support for the program by the school's management is very important. It will also be easier to implement if the whole staff supports the program."

CONCLUSION

Obvious need, a culture of student volunteerism, committed administrators, and supportive educators—these factors are clearly in place in the South African context. Take Ten brings flexible resources reflecting diversity and technical skills. Assembling these elements in a cohesive strategy has been successful at the local school level in the midwestern United States system, where individual administrators ensure an environment that values the power of self-awareness, courage, and leadership. In like fashion, these authors conclude after this inquiry that Take Ten could flourish in individual South African schools, but only where administrators have latitude and creativity rather than relying solely on system-driven or simplistic answers such as building fences. Success with Take Ten happens in the heart through relationships, not through walls and security. But akin to the United States experience, Take Ten must broaden beyond

288 / PERSPECTIVES ON VIOLENCE AND VIOLENT DEATH

the school and engage other stakeholders. We are encouraged by Mr. Abrahams' attitude: "We also need to reach out into the community and involve the community. The school belongs to the community and by getting the community involved it will give them ownership in the school."

Take Ten has already been translated by a Colombian into Spanish, brought into Chile, and introduced in Honduras as student volunteers, now college graduates, have taken their experiences to new teaching positions. Perhaps it is now time to move Take Ten into the next hemisphere and find partners to globalize nonviolence.

POST-SCRIPT

As of May 2006, 16 schools in the South Bend community had incorporated Take Ten into their school environment plans, up from 10 when this chapter was first submitted. Take Ten staff and volunteers worked weekly with an average of 645 Take Ten Ambassadors this past academic year. Through various activities throughout the week, Ambassadors then shared the Take Ten philosophy and skills with approximately 8,320 of their peers. To support this volume, Take Ten staff recruited a record 161 volunteers to assist in the schools, the majority from college campuses in the area.

Take Ten staff also finalized the Pre-K to 8th Grade curriculum, which now consists of 126 lesson plans. A final version of the high school curriculum is also near completion. Staff and volunteers expanded work into three high schools, in a variation of the model described in the chapter. In high schools, volunteers meet weekly with designated peer mentors during a class period. Mentors, in turn, meet with the freshmen and deliver lessons based on what they have learned.

Significantly, Take Ten is now firmly incorporated into course requirements of a number of undergraduate courses at the University of Notre Dame. The Joan B. Kroc Institute for International Peace Studies, the Political Science Department, and the Center for Social Concerns all offer Take Ten in certain course requirements to encourage community-based learning among their students. Other project-based partnerships have unfolded, such as a business plan for Take Ten intended to aid in its expansion and sustainability, generated by graduate students from Notre Dame's College of Business.

Finally, as Take Ten has gained recognition locally, the Associate Director of Prevention Programs has provided training and engaged in discussions on the model with other professionals across the country. As a result, work has begun with the staff and students at the Santa Fe Indian School, New Mexico, who have incorporated Take Ten into the programming at their boarding school for 7th and 8th grade students. It is with great interest that these authors look to that experience to judge the potential impact of Take Ten outside of its current environment.

REFERENCES

Chappelle, S., & Bigman, L. (1998). *Diversity in action*. Project Adventure Inc.

Cohen, R. (2003). Students helping students: Peer mediation. In T. S. Jones & R. Compton (Eds.), *Kids working it out* (pp. 109-128). San Francisco: Jossey-Bass.

Cohen, R. (2005, January 30). One clear conscience 60 years after Auschwitz. *The New York Times*, p. 3.

Department of Health and Human Services: Centers for Disease Control and Prevention, Youth Violence Prevention through Community-Level Change. Retrieved January 31, 2005, from http://www.cdc.gov/od/pgo/funding/05020.htm.

DeRolf, S. & Letzig, M. (1997). *The crayon box that talked*. New York: Random House, Inc.

De Wet, C. (2003). Midsaad in die Suid-Afrikaanse onderwys soos wieerspieël in die gedrukte media. *South African Journal of Education, 23*(2), 113-121.

Elliott, D., Wilson, W. J., Huizinga, D., Sampson, R., Elliott, A., & Rankin, B. (1996). The effects of neighborhood and disadvantage on adolescent development. *Journal of Research in Crime and Delinquency, 33*(4), 389-426.

Hoose, P., Hoose, H., & Tilley, D. (1998). *Hey little Ant*. Berkeley: Tricycle Press.

Howitt, M., & DiTerlizzi, T. (2002). *The spider and the fly*. New York: Simon and Schuster Books for Young Readers.

Jones, T. S. (2003). An introduction to conflict resolution education. In T. S. Jones & R. Compton (Eds.), *Kids working it out* (pp. 17-34). San Francisco: Jossey-Bass.

Lamison-White, L. (1992). *Income, poverty, and wealth in the United States: A chart book*. United States: Bureau of the Census, Housing and Household Economic Statistics Division.

Lantieri, L., & Patti, J. (1996). *Waging peace in our schools*. Boston: Beacon Press.

Loomer, B. (Ed.). (1976). *Two conceptions of power, criterion*. Chicago: University of Chicago Press.

Madonna, & Long, L. (2003). *Mr. Peabody's apple*. New York: Callaway.

Matthews, N. A. (1999). *"It gets people talking" An evaluation of Take Ten Chicago!* (unpublished evaluation).

McEvoy-Levy, S. (2005). Introduction. In S. McEvoy-Levy (Ed.), *Post conflict peace-building*. (unpublished and submitted for publication)

Moriarty, A. (2000). *Take Ten as a concluding peace studies project*. (unpublished term paper, University of Notre Dame).

Nyberg, D. (1981). *Power over power*. Ithaca: Cornell University Press.

Palmer, P. J. (1998). *The courage to teach*. San Francisco: Jossey-Bass.

Rosenberg, L. (1998). The green boots. In J. Canfield, M. V. Hansen, P. Hansen, & I. Dunlap (Ed.), *Chicken soup for the kid's soul: 101 stories of hope, courage and laughter* (pp. 142-144). Deerfield Beach, FL: Health Communications, Inc.

Sampson, R., & Lauritsen, J. L. (1994). Violent victimization and offending: Individual and community-level risk factors. In A. Reiss & J. Roth (Eds.), *Understanding and preventing violence: Volume 3, Social influences* (pp. 1-114). Washington, DC: National Academy Press.

Sampson, R. J., Raudenbush, S. W., & Earls, F. (1997). Neighborhoods and violent crime: A multilevel study of collective efficacy. *Science, 277*(15), 918-924.

South Bend Tribune, The 2003-2004 Annual School Performance Report. (2005, January 28). pp. 1-10.

290 / PERSPECTIVES ON VIOLENCE AND VIOLENT DEATH

Students' Health and Welfare Centres Organisation. 60 years and still serving. Retrieved January 31, 2005 from http://www.shawco.org/.

Wedam, E. (2000). "God doesn't ask what language I pray in" community and culture on Chicago's southwest side. In L. Livezey (Ed.), *Public religion and urban transformation*. New York: New York University Press.

Whitcomb, M. E., & King, T. C. (1998). *Odd velvet*. Vancouver: Raincoast Books.

APPENDIX A

Violence: A Statement of Assumptions and Principles

Prepared by members of
The International Work Group On Death,
Dying, and Bereavement

At IWG Meetings from 1993 to 1996

Committee Members
Robert G. Stevenson, Chairperson

Leslie Balmer
Ronald Barrett
Jeanne Quint Benoliel
Miriam Blumenthal-Barby
David Bolton
Yael Danieli
Herman DeMonnink
Herman Feifel
Dick Gilbert
Earl Grollman
Stan B. Henan
Isa Jaramillo
William Lamers
Marcia Lattanzi-Licht
William Lee

Susan Lennox
Mal McKissock
John D. Morgan
Mary Ann Morgan
Miriam Moss
Patrice O'Connor
Colin Murray Parkes
Barbara Reyes
Brian Rock
Albert Lee Strickland
Harold Ter Blanche
Judith van Heerden
Hannelore Wass
Laurens P. White

292 / PERSPECTIVES ON VIOLENCE AND VIOLENT DEATH

GOALS

This document is designed to examine:

1. The relationship of violence to death, dying, and bereavement.
2. The ways in which survivors and others accommodate to these relationships.
3. Outcomes and implications of the above goals.

DEFINITIONS

Violence: the exertion by an agent of any force or action that injures or abuses whether physically, psychologically, emotionally or spiritually.

Violent Loss: traumatic death and/or other major loss(es) as an outcome of violence, either intentional or accidental.

Threat: communication of what will be done to hurt or punish someone

Bereavement: the state following the loss of someone or something held to be precious.

Traumatic Bereavement: the situation following a death or other major loss(es) as an outcome of violence.

Grief: the highly personal response to loss.

Grief Work: the process of accommodating to bereavement.

Response: something said, done, felt or thought in reaction to a stimulus.

Assumption: a statement accepted as fact on the basis of commonly observed experience. (IWG, 1992)

Principle: a collective judgment as to the proper response to an assumption. (IWG, 1992)

PREAMBLE

Violence takes place in particular contexts.

Violence exists on many levels: individual, familial, social, political, cultural and institutional.

Violence may be transmitted from person to person, from parent to child, from generation to generation.

Violence may be structural in that it may be developed within, or amplified by, systems.

Violence may be overt or covert, acute or chronic.

Violence may be intentional or unintentional.

APPENDIX A / 293

Violence may be spontaneous or premeditated.

Violence may be delivered with malicious, neutral or benevolent intent.

Violence may be inflicted on self or others.

Violence may be the result of action or of failure to act.

Violence affects an individual in ways which may be physical, psychological, social, emotional and spiritual.

Violence involves us all, whether or not we act in response to it.

Responses to violence may contribute to further violence.

Responses to violence may reduce the likelihood of further violence.

Perpetrators of violence may have been victims of violence.

Identifying the reasons for violent behavior does not necessarily excuse the action or exonerate the perpetrator.

The cycle of violence can be broken.

STATEMENTS

Violence

1. The perceived need to survive is a biological imperative which can lead to aggressive or violent behavior.
2. Understanding the causes of violence may provide insights into factors which promote violent behavior.
3. Understanding the causes of violent behavior may provide a basis for preventing violence.
4. Alcohol, drugs, addiction and affective disorders can be factors in causing violent behavior and continuing the cycle of violence.
5. Violence may be an outcome of contradictory values espoused by social and political systems, structures or institutions.
6. Violence may be a reaction to victimization.
7. Violence may be an expression of grief.
8. The reaction of those who are directly involved in violence or those who witness violence may differ from those who learn of it indirectly.
9. The ease in obtaining firearms is an important factor in the prevalence of violence.

Violent Death

10. Individuals exposed to violence, especially violent deaths, either directly or indirectly, may be impaired in their capacity to make judgments, to plan appropriate action, or to act wisely.
11. Violent death may result in grief that differs from grief that follows nonviolent death.
12. Individual responses to violent death take place in a social context that may or may not be supportive.
13. Individuals grieving violent death may be confronted with multiple, complex tasks relating both to the deceased and to the perpetrator of the violence.
14. The reactions of those affected by violent death may be influenced by a number of factors, including:
    - the nature and circumstances of the event,
    - any physical or mental trauma sustained by the survivor(s),
    - the degree of displacement from homes, networks and communities,
    - the developmental level of the survivor(s),
    - trauma and violence in the social and political milieu,
    - identification with the dead person(s) and/or the perpetrator(s),
    - the nature and quality of the relationship between the survivor(s) and the deceased,
    - the nature and quality of the relationship between the perpetrator(s) and the deceased,
    - the interaction among survivors,
    - the interaction between the survivor(s) and society,
    - previous and concurrent losses and their resolution,
    - the number of losses incurred,
    - previous and concurrent victimization and its resolution,
    - internal strengths (e.g., spiritual beliefs, psychological health),
    - external supports (e.g., family, community, society, economic resources),
    - the perceived impact of the loss,
    - perceived responsibility for the death,
    - availability of the body or other reminders of the deceased,
    - physical condition of the dead body,
    - the nature of the funeral and other rituals,
    - the persistence of threat,
    - the recurrence of loss.
15. The reactions of those involved in violence (whether as perpetrators, victims, or observers) reflect the meaning(s) they attribute to the experience.

ASSUMPTIONS AND PRINCIPLES REGARDING VIOLENCE

ASSUMPTIONS	PRINCIPLES
Violence is pervasive in society.	Violence must be addressed.
Regardless of the level of violence in any society, it is the individual who will perpetrate the act and has the choice of acting in a violent or nonviolent manner.	All individuals contemplating violence need to be made aware that nonviolent alternatives may exist.
Violence occurs at many levels.	Violence should be addressed at the levels of individual, family, institution, and society.
Violence occurs in many forms.	Response to violence should be multidimensional.
Violence has many causes.	Attention should be paid to the physical, spiritual, social, and psychological dimensions of violence.
Explaining the reason(s) for violent behavior does not necessarily excuse the action or exonerate the perpetrator.	Awareness of the difference between understanding and behavioral outcomes should be promoted.
Violence is contextual.	To understand violent actions or events, one must view them in the larger context and not in isolation.

Effects of Violence

Among other things, violence can cause physical, psychological, and spiritual damage to people and their environment.	It is important to provide for the physical, psychological, and spiritual needs of people affected by violence.
Violence begets violence.	It is important to recognize and, where possible, interrupt the cycle of violence.
Early exposure to violence predisposes to later violent behavior.	Interventions should be implemented early in life, involving all sources that influence children as well as the children themselves.

296 / PERSPECTIVES ON VIOLENCE AND VIOLENT DEATH

ASSUMPTIONS	PRINCIPLES
The impact of violent death on the survivors may be different from, and will often be greater than, the impact of nonviolent death.	The intervention process needs to be modified according to the context in which this death occurred.
Later reactions following violent death may differ from later reactions following nonviolent death.	Supportive resources should be offered to all affected individuals.
Survivors of violent loss are vulnerable to subsequent victimization.[1]	Caregivers need to identify and help prevent such victimization.
Caregivers and responders may suffer vicarious victimization.	The needs of caregivers and responders for support should be recognized and met.

Threats of Violence

Violence is usually preceded by threats of violence.	Threats of violence should be recognized and responded to appropriately.
Responses to threat may include: counter-threat, passivity, fight, flight, or an increase in group coherence.	Faced with a threat of violence individuals and groups can choose how to respond.
The response to threat is influenced by the anticipated outcome and presence or absence of an escape route.	When attempting to mediate violence, alternatives and escape routes should be sought.
In some circumstances, notably when individuals or groups feel insecure, threats of violence may be exaggerated or otherwise misinterpreted.	It is important to understand the circumstances under which people may over-react to threat(s).
The tendency to misperceive threat and to react violently is increase in a) those who have experienced abuse, especially in childhood, b) those who have been rewarded for aggressive behavior or c) those who have suffered rejection, frustration, or injustice.	Every effort should be made to reduce the level of abuse in our society and to mitigate its effects.

APPENDIX A / 297

ASSUMPTIONS	PRINCIPLES
In the face of a threat there is a tendency to identify all who are perceived as supporting the aggressor as "the enemy," and to treat them as a single entity.	All involved in responding to threatening situations should be aware of the dangers of over-generalizing and simplistic thinking.

Acceptance of Violence

Ideally, all human exchange would be nonviolent.	Individuals and societies should strive to find ways to resolve conflicts and address threats through nonviolent means.
In the absence of nonviolent alternatives, certain types of violence may be accepted as inevitable, justified, or necessary.	Even when accepted as inevitable, justified, or necessary, violence should be used only as a last resort and must be kept to a minimum.
Different societies establish difference levels of acceptable violence.	Where societies grant authority to use force, any violent use of such force, whether by an individual or nation state, should be open to review by an impartial third party.
Acceptance of violence may vary according to a number of factors.	To understand the acceptance of violence, one must examine factors such as:

  attitudes   history
  censorship repeated exposure
  tolerance   social context
  proximity   scale of violence
  perceived relevance
  government sanction or prohibition
  cultural myths/ heroic stories
  violent language

298 / PERSPECTIVES ON VIOLENCE AND VIOLENT DEATH

ASSUMPTIONS	PRINCIPLES

Violence and Society

Violence may engender conflicting responses on the part of society. For example: • fear/sympathy (which may cause mixed, ambivalent and unpredictable reactions.) • need to take action against the perpetrator/sympathy and support or the perpetrator or survivors • empathy with victims/the need to be impartial in judging those accused of the violence.	Ways should be found to recognize and to reconcile such conflicts.
An understanding of the dynamics of violence is essential for effective intervention.	Interventions to reduce the incidence and intensity of violence must be based on an understanding of the dynamics of violence.
Acts of violence often violent formally agreed upon human rights.	Information about their human rights should be made available and taught to all persons so that human rights are safeguarded.
All societies have cultural and/or religious traditions which govern their perception of basic human rights.	The effect of cultural and religious traditions on the perception of human rights must be acknowledged.
Social structure can be altered or destroyed by violence.	Restoration of social structure is integral to the healing process.

Power and Leadership

Much violence arises out of attempts to gain or maintain power.	People at every level of society, from families to nation states, have a responsibility to build, maintain, and encourage systems of shared power or collaboration.

APPENDIX A / 299

ASSUMPTIONS	PRINCIPLES
Persons in power are under pressure from various sources to make decisions which may lead to violence.	Persons in power often need counsel and support to enable them to bear this pressure and to make wise decisions.
Persons in power may themselves be victims.	The assistance available to those traumatized by violence should be made available to persons in power as well.
The most insidious, destructive, intractable forms of violence are those initiated, supported, and/or perpetuated by persons in power.	Persons in power should be role models in constructive behavior, conflict management, and nonviolent solutions to problems.
It is difficult to detect, monitor, and eradicate violence that is sanctioned by a government.	There is a need for an independent, external, impartial third party to monitor, document, and disseminate information about such violence, who has authority to take effective action.
Monitoring violence deters further violence.	Mechanisms for monitoring violence should be set up, preferably before violence occurs.

Education

Education is a means of preventing violence.	Education about violence should include the following: • identifying the cause(s) of violence, • teaching alternatives to violence, • using methodology appropriate to age, developmental level, and culture, • including ongoing methods of evaluation, • teaching conflict resolution, • teaching mediation, • raising awareness of the violent nature of acceptable language and promoting nonviolent communication, • incorporating supportive resources to enable individuals to confront and work through their own relationship to violence (as victim, perpetrator or observer).

300 / PERSPECTIVES ON VIOLENCE AND VIOLENT DEATH

ASSUMPTIONS	PRINCIPLES
Education may occur at a variety of levels.	Education about violence can occur at a familial, communal, societal, national, or international level.
Education about traumatic bereavement can benefit emergency responders.	Such education should include topics such as: • effects of violence, • post-traumatic stress disorders and responses, • critical incident stress-debriefing, and • grief responses to traumatic death/loss.

Intervention

Violent loss calls for a positive, timely response.	Following exposure to a violent loss, intervention should be available and offered immediately.
The damaging effects of traumatic bereavements can be mitigated by support[2] given by people (both volunteers and professionals) who have been appropriately selected and trained for the purpose. It is reasonable to believe that similar intervention will mitigate the effects of other major psychological violence.	The responses should include: • an infrastructure which initiates and coordinates appropriate support, • identification and proactive offers of assistance to all individuals and groups affected by the violence and its aftermath, • support by appropriate selected and trained individuals for persons experiencing violence and traumatic bereavement, • education of individuals and the community about the consequences of violent loss and the resources available to help.
Some of those who are bereaved or otherwise affected by violence value the help of mutual support (self-help) groups. These function best if provided with back-up from appropriately trained support staff.	Mutual support groups should be encouraged and provided with the back-up of properly trained supporters.

ASSUMPTIONS	PRINCIPLES
When people affected by violence develop psychiatric disorders specialist help is needed.	Facilities for the identification, assessment, and treatment of psychiatric disorder should be available to all who need them regardless of their ability to pay.
Interventions may be positive or negative.	Intervention protocols should identify the following: • why this intervention is necessary, • when response should take place, • what individuals or groups should respond, • how individuals and groups should respond, • when additional follow-up will be necessary.
Attempts to cope with violence can have mixed effects.	Caregivers should be trained to recognize and to differentiate among these effects.

Public Communication

Public communication about violence is often sensational, exploitative, or inaccurate.	Public communication needs to be responsible and to differentiate between the need to disseminate information and the sensational exploitation of violence.
Media coverage can have an impact on those affected by violence and can influence the levels of violence.	Training of all people who disseminate public information is needed concerning the impact of how influence is conveyed.

Justice

The response of the justice system to perpetrators and victims of violence can have effects on the victims which may be beneficial or harmful. Delays and insensitivity cause harm.	Training of people in the justice system should insure sensitivity to, and respect for, the rights of both victims and perpetrators, including as speedy a process as possible.
The response of the justice system to acts of violence potentiates the escalation or de-escalation of the violence.	Members of the justice system carry the responsibility to signal society's rejection of violence through speedy and appropriate processing of perpetrators.

302 / PERSPECTIVES ON VIOLENCE AND VIOLENT DEATH

ASSUMPTIONS	PRINCIPLES
All human systems, including those set up to obtain or maintain justice, are capable of perpetuating violence or protecting perpetrators.	There is a need to train and monitor many people in these systems and to provide advocacy and support for victims.
Systems that interface with victims of violence may revictimize the victims.	There is a need to train all relevant caregivers, monitor their activities, and provide advocacy for victims.
Violence can destroy the systems that maintain human rights and may impair legal systems.	It may be necessary to restore systems that maintain human rights, including the legal system.

Restitution

Victims of violence may be stigmatized, losing value, power, esteem, and dignity. This stigmatization may lead to or be associated with their separation from society.	Commemoration, memorials to heroism, empowerment, and education may relieve the stigmatization and separation. Compensation, restitution, and rehabilitation serve to re-establish the victim's status and esteem in society.
Programs of education and restitution with or without confrontation between perpetrators and victims are desirable.	Following the cessation of group violence, minimum interventions include: • securing public records • prosecution • apology • education

ENDNOTES

1. INDIVIDUAL RESPONSES to violent death may include:
   *1. Numbness, blunting, disbelief, denial, avoidance of reminders.
   *2. High levels of anxiety, hyper-vigilance, arousal of the sympathetic nervous system and inhibition of the parasympathetic nervous system with all the physiological consequences of these.
   *3. Panic attacks or episodes of distress prompted by the reminders of loss.
   *4. Nightmares reflecting the events of the loss.
   5. Intense anger directed against the perceived perpetrator of the violence and all associated with him/her.
   6. Feelings of self-reproach for any real or imaginary contribution to the death.
   7. Need to punish or seek retribution.

APPENDIX A / 303

8. Loss of confidence in protective sources—self, parents/family, police, law, government, God.
[* numbers 1 through 4 above constitute the syndrome known as Post-Traumatic Stress Disorder, P.T.S.D.]

COMMUNAL/SOCIETAL RESPONSES to violent death may include:
1. Intense interest, curiosity, fascination, excitement and, sometimes, prurience or intrusiveness.
2. Fear, horror, disgust, distress, revulsion and apprehension, sometimes leading to avoidance, withdrawal or loss of support.
3. Sympathy, pity, identification with the victim(s) or survivor(s), sometimes leading to cohesive support.
4. Loss of sympathy for, or desire for retribution, vengeance or punishment of the assumed perpetrator of the violence, leading to a search for the perpetrator and hostility toward those deemed responsible.
5. A communal/societal need for: protection, justice, support for survivors (including police, civil leaders, family, and friends of the dead person and survivors), and accurate public information.

2. The term "counselor" is sometimes used for individuals who have been selected and trained to provide support under supervision for people who have experienced bereavement or other trauma. Controversy exists regarding two issues
a) the use of the term by volunteers, however well trained, and
b) the amount of training and the criteria for selection necessary. For this reason we have chosen to use the term "supporter" rather than "counselor." A random-allocation study by Colin Murray Parkes demonstrated the beneficial effects of support to high-risk bereaved people given by supporters who have been carefully selected and supervised but whose training would not meet the criteria adopted by most programs of training in "counseling"(Parkes, C. M. (1981). Evaluation of a bereavement service. *Journal of Preventive Psychiatry, 1,* 179-188).

APPENDIX B

Summary of Guidelines, Protocols, and Procedures

The following are summaries of guidelines provided in this book. Each is explained in greater detail in one of the chapters. The name of the author of the chapter that contains the full text is shown in parentheses.

Guidelines for Coping with Violence in Schools (Stevenson)

♦ Create a sense of "connection" between students and staff
  Four exercises that can help a school community to move in that direction.
  o Safety-Net Awareness
  o Peer Leaders
  o Memorials
  o Symbols of Safety
♦ Identify all members of the school community with a visible school symbol.
♦ Develop a zero tolerance for violence.
♦ Train and maintain security personnel.
♦ Reexamine the curriculum.
♦ Educate people about violence.
♦ Teach the life cycle of crisis response.
♦ Use principles of critical-incident stress debriefing.

Questions for Gathering Information After a Violent Event (Stevenson)

♦ What was the *level* of the violence in this particular incident?
♦ What *exactly* happened?
♦ What do we know about the perpetrator(s) of the violence?
♦ What was the immediate "trigger" of this violence?
♦ What responses followed the violent episode?
♦ How have the survivors of the violence reacted?
♦ Have the survivors had an opportunity to process/give meaning to their experiences?

306 / PERSPECTIVES ON VIOLENCE AND VIOLENT DEATH

Guidelines for "Moving On" After a Violent Death (Stevenson)

- Accept the grief.
- Talk about the death when, and if, you can.
- Be patient with misstatements by yourself and others.
- Keep busy, but not too busy.
- Take care of yourself; eat well; exercise.
- Be aware of your surroundings and remain alert to any possible threat.
- Externalize you grief (symbols, journals, share with others).
- Deal with the guilt (real or imagined).
- Accept your understanding of the death.
- Draw on your spiritual background.
- Understand (but do not ignore) negative coping by yourself and others.

Guidelines for Clergy (Gilbert)

- Accept the reality that domestic violence exists, it exists in larger numbers and it exists in your congregation or place of ministry.
- Know your boundaries, but don't be afraid to stretch them.
- Help explore the deeper spiritual issues in a safe and informed way.
- Symbolic presence of another "word" or perspective
- Linkage to religious communities, traditions and values
- Administers sacraments and rituals as requested by the victim
- Represents sanctuary or safety
- Integrates spirituality into the individual's journey as an option and gift as well as in his/her approach to the team
- Advocacy, including advocacy before and to God
- Don't be surprised if you meet resistance.

Protocol for Use with Hispanic Families After Mass Casualties (Cabrera)

- Meet Privately
- Set the Rules
- Meet with a Team
- Establish the following Goals:
  - o Focus on the rapid reduction of intense reactions,
  - o Keep affected family members functioning,
  - o Help family members share information, responses and feelings about the incident,
  - o Supply information and skills to help with the coping process,
  - o Reaffirm that they are valued and important,

APPENDIX B / 307

- o Instill confidence in the ability of the family member(s) to handle their reactions to this event, and
- o Access additional support resources: chaplains/clergy, law enforcement official(s), ethnic team members, interpreters.
- ♦ Invitation to a Food Court
- ♦ Hear each Family Member's Story
- ♦ Follow up
- ♦ Debrief the Debriefer(s)

Workplace Conflict Risk Assessment (Thompson)

To begin to take on the challenge of conflict/violence in the workplace, answer the following questions:

- ♦ How likely is it that this conflict will escalate (or even combust)?
- ♦ If it does, what is at stake? How much harm is it likely to do?
- ♦ What is the worst case scenario?
- ♦ How likely is this to come about?
- ♦ Can you afford to risk this happening?
- ♦ What steps can you take to deal with this conflict?
- ♦ In terms of investing resources in such activities, how does this compare with the costs of the harm that can arise from the conflict being allowed to develop further?

Guidelines for Developing a Conflict/Violence Protocol for the Workplace (Thompson)

- ♦ Invest in developing interpersonal
- ♦ Base understanding on the dialectic of subjectivity and objectivity
- ♦ Develop the skills involved in managing contingency
- ♦ Respect individual identity

Coping With Loss Through Spirituality (Cox)

- ♦ Create a sacred place.
- ♦ Keep a journal or write a story.
- ♦ Find and use humor.
- ♦ Use music to aid healing. Art, drama, clay, drawing, painting, and other forms of expression can also aid coping with loss.
- ♦ Remember the power of Friendship and share with friends.
- ♦ Find a new sense of Balance in life.
- ♦ Draw strength and support from family and friends.
- ♦ Build (or rebuild) feelings of harmony and security.
- ♦ Face reality as it is.

308 / PERSPECTIVES ON VIOLENCE AND VIOLENT DEATH

- Develop rituals to mark important changes, express spirituality, support belief and give purpose to faith.
- Allow grieving children to play. Work is a major method of coping. Play is a child's version of work.
- If it part of personal belief or traditions, use prayer.
- Use forgiveness as a coping tool.
- Maintain hope. Hope comes from seeing the goodness in the hearts of people in spite of the suffering and pain that life offers.
- Practice sharing and caring, to help others and ourselves.
- Use Active Listening
- Accept and offer encouragement.

APPENDIX C

Bibliography:
Perspectives on Violence

Compiled by Reverend Richard B. Gilbert, PhD, CT

This bibliography is provided by The World Pastoral Care Center as part of its commitment to connecting you with resources. There is an annual supplement, as well as over 20 bibliographies, which are updated quarterly. All of them are available free, including quarterly updates, via e-mail, at dick.gilbert@yahoo.com. Feel free to contact them for information or an order form. This has been prepared for *Reflections on Violence,* Baywood Publishing, 2007, edited by Rob Stevenson, Ed.D. and Gerry Cox, PhD. We appreciate their commitment to extensive resource information.

The Rev'd. Richard B. Gilbert, PhD, CT

Adams, C. (1994). *Women-battering.* Minneapolis: Augsburg.
Adams, C., & Fortune, M. (1995). *Violence against women and children: A Christian theological sourcebook.* New York: Continuum.
Adelizzi, J. (1997). *Shades of trauma: The impact of psychological trauma on learning and functioning in women.* Plymouth, MA: Jones River Press.
Alcoholics Anonymous. *Alcoholics anonymous* (current ed.). New York: Alcoholics Anonymous World Services.
Alexander, D. (1999). *Children changed by trauma: A healing guide.* Oakland: New Harbinger.
Arbuckle, G. (2003). *Confronting the demon: A gospel response to adult bullying.* Collegeville, MN: St. Paul.
Arbuckle, G. (2004). *Violence, society and the church: A cultural approach.* Collegeville, MN: The Liturgical Press.
Arnold, J. (2002). *Escape routes for people who feel trapped in life's hells.* Maryknoll: Orbis.
Augsburger, D. (2004). *Hate-work: Working through the pain and pleasures of hate.* Louisville/London: Westminster John Knox Press.

309

310 / PERSPECTIVES ON VIOLENCE AND VIOLENT DEATH

Bachman, R., & Saltzman, L. (1995). *Violence against women: Estimates from the redesigned survey.* Washington: Office of Justice Programs.

Barkley, R., Edwards, G., & Robin, A. (1999). *Defiant teens: A clinician's manual for assessment and family intervention.* New York: Guilford.

Balsam, K. (Ed.). (2003). *Trauma, stress and resilience among sexual minority women: Rising like the phoenix.* Binghamton, NY: Harrington Park (Haworth Press).

Barnard, P., Moreland, I., & Nagy, J. (1999). *Children, bereavement and trauma: Nursing resilience.* New York: Taylor & Francis.

Barnett, O., Miller-Perrin, C., & Perrin, R. (1997/2004). *Family violence across the lifespan: An introduction* (2nd ed.). Thousand Oaks, CA: Sage.

Barton, A. (1970). *Communities in disaster: A sociological analysis of collective stress situations.* Garden City: Doubleday.

Bass, E., & David, L. (1988). *The courage to heal.* San Francisco: Harper & Row.

Bean, C. (1992). *Women murdered by the men they loved.* Binghamton, NY: Haworth Press.

Benedict, J. (1998). *Athletes and acquaintance rape.* Thousand Oaks, CA: Sage.

Benvenga, N. (1996). *Healing the wounds of emotional abuse: The journey worth the risk.* Mineola: Resurrection.

Betancourt, M. (1997). *What to do when love turns violent: A practical resource for women in abusive relationships.* New York: HarperCollins.

Bloomquist, M., & Schnell, S. (2002). *Helping children with aggression and conduct problems: Best practices for intervention.* New York: Guilford.

Cassiday-Shaw, A. (2002). *Aimee: Family abuse and the Bible (The scriptural perspective).* Binghamton, NY: Haworth Press.

Chu, J., & Bowman, E. (Eds.). (2003). *Trauma and sexuality: The effects of childhood sexual, physical, and emotional abuse on sexual identity and behavior.* Binghamton, NY: Haworth Press.

Constans, G. (1997). *Picking up the pieces: A program about violent death for use with middle school students.* Westminster, PA: Mar-co.

Cook, P. (1997). *Abused men: The hidden side of domestic violence.* Westport, CT: Praeger.

Cooper-White, P. (1995). *The cry of Tamar: Violence against women and the church's response.* Minneapolis: Augsburg Fortress.

Copeland, M., & Harris, M. (2000). *Healing the trauma of abuse: A women's workbook (A gentle step-by-step guide).* Oakland: New Harbinger.

Cox, G., Bendiksen, R., & Stevenson, R. (Eds.). (2002). *Complicated grieving and bereavement.* Amityville: Baywood.

Daher, D. (2003). *And the passenger was death: The drama and trauma of losing a child.* Amityville: Baywood.

Dale, P. (1999). *Adults abused as children: Experiences of counseling and psychotherapy.* Thousand Oaks, CA: Sage.

Davidson, J., & Doka, K. (Eds.). (1999). *Living with grief at work, at school, at worship.* New York: Taylor & Francis.

Davis, C. (2003). *Children who kill: Profiles of pre-teen and teenager killers.* London, UK: Allison & Busby.

Davis, D. (2004). *Your angry child: A guide for parents.* Binghamton, NY: Haworth Press.

Deaton, W., & Hertica, M. (2001). *A therapist's guide to growing free: A manual for survivors of domestic violence.* Binghamton, NY: Haworth Press.

APPENDIX C / 311

Decalmer, P., & Glendenning, F. (1997). *The mistreatment of elderly people.* Thousand Oaks, CA: Sage.

DeJong, J. (Ed.). (2002). *Trauma, war, and violence: Public mental health in socio-cultural context.* New York: Kluwer Academic.

Deskin, G., & Steckler, G. (1997). *When nothing makes sense: Disaster, crisis and their effects on children.* Minneapolis: Fairview.

Dobash, E., & Dobash, R. (1979). *Violence against wives.* New York: Free Press.

Doherty, W. (2000). *Take back your kids: Confident parenting in turbulent times.* Notre Dame: Sorin.

Doka, K. (Ed.). (1989). *Disenfranchised grief: Recognizing hidden sorrow.* Lexington, MA: Lexington.

Doka, K. (Ed.). (2002). *Disenfranchised grief: New directions, challenges, and strategies for practice.* Champaign: Research Press.

Doka, K., & Morgan, J. (1993). *Death & spirituality.* Amityville: Baywood.

Dutton, D. (1998). *The abusive personality: Violence and control in intimate relationships.* New York: Guilford.

Dutton, D., & Sonkin, D. (Eds.). (2002). *Intimate violence: Contemporary treatment innovations.* Binghamton, NY: Haworth Press.

Eugene, T., & Poling, J. (1998). *Balm for Gilead: Pastoral care for African American families experiencing abuse.* Nashville: Abingdon.

Fall, K. et al. (1999, 2004). *Alternatives to domestic violence: A homework manual for battering intervention groups* (2nd ed.). New York: Brunner-Routledge.

Family Violence Prevention Fund. (1999). *Report card on health care laws.* San Francisco: Family Violence Prevention Fund.

Farley, M. (Ed.). (2003). *Prostitution, trafficking, and traumatic stress.* Binghamton, NY: Haworth Press.

Figley, C. (Ed.). (1995). *Compassion fatigue: Coping with secondary traumatic stress disorder in those who treat the traumatized.* Philadelphia: Brunner/Mazel.

Figley, C. (Ed.). (1999). *Traumatology of grieving: Conceptual, theoretical, and treatment foundations.* New York: Brunner/Mazel.

Figley, C., Bride, D., & Mazza, N. (Eds.). (1997). *Death and trauma: The traumatology of grieving.* New York: Taylor & Francis.

Fitzgerald, H. (1992, 2003). *The grieving child: A parent's guide* (2nd ed.). New York: Fireside.

Flowers, R. (2002). *Kids who commit adult crimes: Serious criminality by juvenile offenders.* Binghamton, NY: Haworth Press.

Floyd, M. (1993). *Don't shoot: My life is valuable.* Phoenix: Escualdun.

Foa, E. (2000). *Effective treatments for PTSD.* New York: Guilford.

Fogarty, J. (2000). *The magical thoughts of grieving children.* Amityville: Baywood.

Fortune, M. (1983). *Sexual violence: The unmentionable sin—An ethical and pastoral perspective.* Cleveland: Pilgrim Press.

Fortune, M. (1991). *Violence in the family: A workshop curriculum for clergy and other helpers.* Cleveland: Pilgrim Press.

Fortune, M. (1995). *Keeping the faith: Guidance for Christian women facing abuse.* San Francisco: HarperCollins.

Fortune, M., & Longwood, W. M. (Eds.). (2003). *Sexual abuse in the Catholic Church: Trusting the clergy?* Binghamton, NY: Haworth Press.

312 / PERSPECTIVES ON VIOLENCE AND VIOLENT DEATH

Fortune, M., & Marshall, J. (Eds.). (2002). *Forgiveness and abuse: Jewish and Christian reflections.* Binghamton, NY: Haworth Press.

Furlong, M., Morrison, G., Skiba, R., & Cornell, D. (Eds.). (2004). *Issues in school violence research.* Binghamton, NY: Haworth Press.

Gaddis, P. (1996). *Battered but not broken: Help for abused wives and their church families.* Valley Forge, PA: Judson.

Geffner, R. et al. (Eds.). (2001). *Bullying behavior: Current issues, research and interventions.* Binghamton, NY: Haworth Press.

Geffner, R., Igelman, R., & Zellner, J. (Eds.). (2004). *The effects of intimate partner violence on children.* Binghamton, NY: Haworth Press.

Geffner, R., & Rosenbaum, A. (Eds.). (2002). *Domestic violence offenders: Current interventions, research, and implications for policies and standards.* Binghamton, NY: Haworth Press..

Gerler, E., Jr. (Ed.). (2004). *Handbook of school violence.* Binghamton, NY: Haworth Press.

Gilbert, R. (1999). *Finding your way after your parent dies: Hope for adults.* Indiana: Notre Dame.

Gilbert, R. (Ed.). (2002). *Healthcare & spirituality: Listening, assessing, caring.* Amityville: Baywood.

Gist, R., & Lubin, B. (1999). *Response to disaster: Psychosocial, community, and ecological approaches.* New York: Brunner/Mazel.

Gold, S. (2000). *Not trauma alone: Therapy for child abuse survivors in family and social context.* New York: Brunner-Routledge.

Goldman, L. (2001). *Breaking the silence: A guide to helping children with complicated grief—Suicide, homicide, AIDS, violence and abuse.* New York: Taylor & Francis.

Goldman, L. (2005). *Raising our children to be resilient: A guide to helping children cope with trauma in the world.* New York: Brunner-Routledge.

Gordon, N. et al. (1999). *Children & disasters.* New York: Brunner/Mazel.

Greenwald, R. (Ed.). (2002). *Trauma and juvenile delinquency: Theory, research, and interventions.* Binghamton, NY: Haworth Press.

Greider, K. (1997). *Reckoning with aggression, theology, violence, and vitality.* Louisville: Westminster John Knox Press.

Griffith, L. (2002). *The war on terrorism and the terror of God.* Grand Rapids/Cambridge, UK: Eerdmans.

Grossoehme, D. (2000). *The pastoral care of children.* Binghamton, NY: Haworth Press.

Gullota, T., & McElhany, S. (Eds.). (1999). *Violence in homes and communities: Prevention, intervention and treatment.* Thousand Oaks, CA: Sage.

Hackett, D., & Violanti, J. (2003). *Policy suicide.* Springfield: Charles C. Thomas.

Hampton, R. et al. (1998). *Substance abuse, family violence & child welfare: Building bridges.* Thousand Oaks, CA: Sage.

Hankins, G., & Hankins, C. (1993). *Prescription for anger.* New York: Warner.

Harris-Hendriks, J., Black, D., & Kaplan, T. (1993, 2000). *When father kills mother: Guiding children through trauma and grief* (2nd ed.). New York: Routledge.

Harteau, J., & Keegel, H. (1998). *A woman's guide to personal safety.* Minneapolis: Fairview.

Harvey, J. (2000). *Loss & trauma: General and close relationship perspectives.* New York: Brunner-Routledge.

APPENDIX C / 313

Harvey, J. (2001). *Give sorrow words: Perspectives on loss and trauma: Perspectives on loss and trauma.* New York: Brunner/Mazel.

Hatty, S. (2000). *Masculinities, violence and culture.* Thousand Oaks, CA: Sage.

Hazler, R. (1996). *Breaking the cycle of violence: Interventions for bullying and victimization.* New York: Taylor & Francis (Accelerated Development).

Heegard, M. (2003a). *Drawing together to learn about feelings.* Minneapolis: Fairview.

Heegard, M. (2003b). *Drawing together to manager anger: To be illustrated by children to help families communicate and learn together.* Minneapolis: Fairview.

Heide, K. (1999). *Young killers: The challenge of juvenile homicide.* Thousand Oaks, CA: Sage.

Hendricks, J. (1995). *When father kills mother: Guiding children through grief.* New York: Routledge.

Henggeler, S. et al. (2002). *Serious emotional disturbance in children and adolescents: Multisystematic therapy.* New York: Guilford.

Henry, V. (2004). *Death work: Police, trauma and the psychology of survival.* New York: Oxford University Press.

Herman, J. (1992). *Trauma and recovery: The aftermath of violence—From domestic violence to political terror.* San Francisco: Basic Books.

Holtkamp, S. (2002). *Wrapped in trauma: The gift of life and organ donor family trauma.* New York: Brunner-Routledge.

Hyer, L., & Sohnle, S. (2001). *Trauma among older people: Issues and treatment.* New York: Brunner-Routledge.

Island, D., & Letellier, P. (1991). *Men who beat the men who love them.* Binghamton, NY: Haworth Press.

Jacobs, S. (1999). *Traumatic grief: Diagnosis, treatment and prevention.* New York: Bruner/Mazel.

Jacobsen, N., & Gottman, J. (1998). *When men batter women: New insights into ending abusive relationships.* New York: Simon & Schuster.

James, T. (2003). *Domestic violence: The 12 things you aren't supposed to know.* San Diego: Aventine.

Janoff-Bulman, R. (1992). *Shattered assumptions: Towards a new psychology of trauma.* New York: Free Press.

Jenkins, B. (2001). *What to do when the police leave: A guide to the first days after a traumatic loss.* Richmond, VA: WBJ Press.

Jenkins, W. H. (1995). *Hard work journal: A guided workbook for coping with homicidal loss and grief.* Omaha: Centering.

Kagan, R. (2004). *Rebuilding attachments with traumatized children: Healing from losses, violence, abuse and neglect.* Binghamton, NY: Haworth Press.

Kalmanowitz, D., & Lloyd, B. (Eds.). (2005). *Art therapy & political violence.* New York: Brunner-Routledge.

Kaschak, E. (Ed.). (2001). *Intimate betrayal: Domestic violence in lesbian relationships.* Binghamton, NY: Haworth Press.

Kaufman, J. (Ed.). (2002). *Loss of the assumptive world: A theory of traumatic loss.* New York: Brunner-Routledge.

Kennedy, E. (2002). *9-11: Meditations at the center of the world.* Maryknoll: Orbis.

Kipnis, A. (1999). *Angry young men: How parents, teachers, and counselors can help "bad boys" become good men.* San Francisco: Jossey-Bass.

314 / PERSPECTIVES ON VIOLENCE AND VIOLENT DEATH

Kirschman, E. (1997). *I love a cop: What police families need to know.* New York: Guilford.

Klicker, R. (2000). *A student dies, a school mourns: Dealing with death and loss in the school community.* New York: Accelerated Development.

Knight, R. (2002). *A man's recovery from traumatic childhood abuse: The insiders.* Binghamton, NY: Haworth Press.

Koenig, H., & Weaver, A. (1997). *Counseling troubled older adults.* Nashville: Abingdon.

Kolski, T., Avriette, M., & Jongsma, A. Jr. (2001). *The crisis counseling and traumatic events treatment planner.* New York: John Wiley.

Kroeger, C., & Beck, J. (Eds.). (1996). *Women, abuse, and the Bible: How scripture can be used to hurt or heal.* Grand Rapids: Baker.

Kroeger, C., & Beck, J. (1998). *Healing the hurting: Giving hope and help to abused women.* Grand Rapids: Baker.

LaGreca, A. et al. (Eds.). (2002). *Helping children cope with disasters and terrorism.* Washington: APA.

Lampin, L. (1999). *God and the victim: Theological reflections on evil, victimization, justice, and forgiveness.* Grand Rapids: Eerdmans.

Larson, J., & Lochman, J. (2002). *Helping schoolchildren cope with anger: A cognitive-behavioral approach.* New York: Guilford.

Latela, M. (2001). *Healing the abusive family: Beyond survival.* Ligouri, MO: Liguori.

Lattanzi-Licht, M., & Doka, K. (Eds.). (2003). *Living with grief: Coping with public tragedy.* Washington, DC: HFA.

LaViolette, A., & Barnett, O. (2000). *It could happen to anyone: Why battered women stay* (2nd ed.). Thousand Oaks, CA: Sage.

Lazoritz, S., & Palusci, V. (Eds.). (2001). *The shaken-baby syndrome: A multidisciplinary approach.* Binghamton, NY: Haworth Press.

Lee, I., & Sylvester, K. (1996). *When Mommy got hurt: A story for young children about domestic violence.* Indianapolis: Kidsrights.

Leslie, K. (2003). *When violence is no stranger: Pastoral counseling with survivors of acquaintance rape.* Minneapolis: Fortress.

Lester, A. (1985). *Pastoral care with children in crisis.* Louisville: Westminster.

Levi, B. (1991). *Dating violence: Young women in danger.* Seattle: Seal Press.

Levi, B. (1998). *In love and in danger: A teen's guide to breaking free of abusive relationships.* Seattle: Seal Press.

Lewis, G. (1993). *Critical incident stress and trauma in the workplace: Recognition . . . response . . . recovery.* New York: Accelerated Development.

Lewis, N., & Fortune, M. (1999). *Remembering conquest: Feminist/womanist perspectives on religion, colonization and sexual violence.* Binghamton, NY: Haworth Press.

Lindholm, A. et al. (2002). *After a murder: A workbook for grieving kids.* Portland, OR: Dougy Center.

Lindsay, M., & Lester, D. (2004). *Suicide by cop: Committing suicide by provoking police to shoot you.* Amityville: Baywood.

Lindy, J., & Lifton, R. (Eds.). (2001). *Beyond invisible walls: The psychological legacy of Soviet trauma.* New York: Brunner-Routledge.

Livingston, D. (2002). *Healing violent men: A model for Christian communities.* Minneapolis: Augsburg-Fortress.

APPENDIX C / 315

Livingstone, D. (2001, 2002). *Redemption of the shattered: A teenager's healing journey through Sandtray Therapy.* San Mateo, CA: Bob Livingstone.

Lobel, K. (Ed.). (1986). *Naming the violence: Speaking out about lesbian battering.* Seattle: Seal.

Lord, J. H., & Frogge, S. (1997). *Trauma death and death notification: Clergy and funeral directors* (rev.). Washington, DC: U.S. Department of Justice, Office for Victims of Crime.

Marcell, J. (2001). *Elder rage – or – Take my father . . . please! How to survive caring for aging parents.* Irvine, CA: Impressive Press.

Marsella, A. et al. (Eds.). (1996). *Ethnocultural aspects of post-traumatic stress disorder: Issues, research and clinical applications.* Washington: APA.

Martin, T., & Doka, K. (2000). *Men don't cry . . . women do: Transcending gender stereotypes of grief.* New York: Brunner/Mazel.

Matsakis, A. (1998). *Trust after trauma: A guide to relationships for survivors and those who love them.* Oakland: New Harbinger.

McCann, J. (2002). *Threats in schools: A practical guide for managing violence.* Binghamton, NY: Haworth Press.

McClintock, K. (2001). *Sexual shame: An urgent call to healing.* Minneapolis: Fortress.

McDill, S. R., & McDill, L. (1991). *Dangerous marriage: Breaking the cycle of domestic violence.* Grand Rapids: Revel.

McNish, J. (2004). *Transforming shame: A pastoral response.* Binghamton, NY: Haworth Press.

Means, J. J. (2002). *Trauma & evil: Healing the wounded soul.* Minneapolis: Fortress.

Meeks, L., Page, R., & Heit, P. (1995). *Violence prevention.* Columbus: Glencoe/McGraw-Hill.

Miedzian, M. (1991/2002). *Boys will be boys: Breaking the link between masculinity and violence.* Harpswell, ME: Anchor.

Miles, A. (2000). *Domestic violence: What every pastor needs to know.* Minneapolis: Augsburg.

Miles, A. (2002). *Violence in families: What every Christian needs to know.* Minneapolis: Augsburg.

Miller, M. (1995). *No visible wounds: Identifying nonphysical abuse of women by their men.* New York: Fawcett Columbine.

Miller-Perrin, C., & Perrin, R. (1999). *Child maltreatment: An introduction.* Thousand Oaks, CA: Sage.

Mills, L. (2003). *Insult to injury.* Princeton: Princeton University Press.

Mitchell, J., & Everl, G. (1996). *Critical incident stress debriefing: An operations manual for the prevention of traumatic stress among emergency services and disaster workers.* Ellicott City, MD: Chevron.

Mollon, P. (2002). *Remembering trauma: A psychotherapist's guide in memory & illusion* (2nd ed.). London/Philadelphia: Whur Publishing (Taylor & Francis).

Morgan, J. (Ed.). (1997). *Readings in thanatology.* Amityville: Baywood.

Mullings, J., Marquart, J., & Hartley, D. (Eds.). (2003). *The victimization of children: Emerging issues.* Binghamton, NY: Haworth Press.

Munday, J. (2004). *Justice for Marlys: A family's twenty year search for a killer.* Minneapolis: University of Minnesota Press.

316 / PERSPECTIVES ON VIOLENCE AND VIOLENT DEATH

Munoz-Kiene, M. (2002). *Big bad news! Terrorism. Hate crime. Gang violence. War* (English & Spanish). Omaha: Centering.

Murray, J. (2000). *But I love him: Protecting your teen daughter from controlling, abusive dating relationships.* New York: HarperCollins.

Myers, D. (1994). *Disaster responses and recovery: A handbook for mental health professionals.* Rockville: MDL Center for Mental Health Studies.

Myers, D., & Wee, D. (2004). *Disaster—Mental health resources: A primer for practitioners.* New York: Brunner-Routledge.

Nadeau, J. (1998). *Families making sense of death.* Thousand Oaks, CA: Sage.

Nader, K., Dubrow, N., & Stumm, H. (1999). *Honouring differences: Cultural issues in the treatment of trauma & loss.* New York: Brunner/Routledge.

Nason-Clark, N. (1994). *The battered wife: How Christians confront family violence.* Louisville: Westminster John Knox Press.

Naylor, P. (1991). *King of the playground.* New York: Aladdin.

Nelson, T. (compiler). (2001). *Walking to tears: Losing a loved one to violence.* San Jose: Writers Club Press.

Neuger, C. (2001). *Counseling women: A narrative, pastoral approach.* Minneapolis: Fortress.

O'Connor, T., & Pallone, N. (Eds.). (2002). *Religion, the community, and the rehabilitation of criminal offenders.* Binghamton, NY: Haworth Press.

Ochberg, F. (1988). *Post-traumatic therapy and victims of violence.* New York: Brunner-Mazel.

Office for Victims of Crime. (2000). *Responding to terrorism victims: Oklahoma City and beyond.* Washington: U.S. Department of Justice.

Palermo, G. (2003). *The faces of violence.* Springfield: Charles C. Thomas.

Parkes, C. et al. (Eds.). (1997). *Death and bereavement across cultures.* New York: Routledge.

Paton, D., Violanti, J., & Smith, L. (2003). *Promoting capabilities to manage post-traumatic stress.* Springfield, IL: Charles C. Thomas.

Pearlman, L., & Saakvitne, K. (1995). *Trauma and the therapist: Counter-transference and vicarious traumatization in psychotherapy with incest.* New York: Norton.

Pellegrini, R., & Sarbin, T. (Eds.). (2002). *Between fathers and sons: Critical incident narratives in the development of men's lives.* Binghamton, NY: Haworth Press.

Perline, I., & Goldschmidt, J. (2004). *The psychology of law and workplace violence.* Springfield, IL: Charles C. Thomas.

Peter, V. (2000). *Parents & kids talking about school violence.* Boys Town: Boys Town Press.

Peter, V. (2002). *Parenting after September 11, 2001.* Boys Town: Boys Town Press.

Pipher, M. (1994). *Reviving Ophelia: Saving the selves of adolescent girls.* New York: Ballantine.

Poling, J., & Neuger, C. (2003). *Men's work in preventing violence against women.* New York: Haworth.

Pollack, W. (2000). *Real boys' voices.* New York : Random House.

Precin, P. (Ed.). (2003). *Surviving 9/11: Impact and experiences of occupational therapy practitioners.* Binghamton, NY: Haworth Press.

Prendergast, W. (2004). *Treating sex offenders: A guide to clinical practice with adults, clerics, children and adolescents* (2nd ed.). Binghamton, NY: Haworth Press.

Quindlen, A. (1988). *Black and blue.* New York: Random House.

Radomsky, N. (1995). *Lost voices: Women, chronic pain, and abuse.* Binghamton, NY: Haworth Press.

Randall, P. (2001). *Bullying in adulthood: Assessing the bullies and their victims.* New York: Brunner-Routledge.

Rando, T. (1993). *Treatment of complicated mourning.* Champaign: Research.

Raphael, B. (1986). *When disaster strikes: How individuals and communities cope with catastrophe.* New York: Basic.

Rashkow, I. (2000). *Taboo or not taboo: Sexuality and family in the Hebrew Bible.* Minneapolis: Fortress.

Redmon, L. (1990). *Surviving when someone you love was murdered.* Clearwater: Psychological Consultation.

Renzetti, C. (Ed.). (1996). *Violence in gay and lesbian domestic partnerships.* Binghamton, NY: Haworth Press.

Resick, P. (2001). *Stress and trauma.* New York Psychology Press (Taylor & Francis).

Reyes, C., Rudman, W., & Hewitt, C. (Eds.). (2002). *Domestic violence and health care: Policies and prevention.* Binghamton, NY: Haworth Press.

Righthand, S., Kerr, B., & Drach, K. (2003). *Child maltreatment risk assessments: An evaluation guide.* Binghamton, NY: Haworth Press.

Ritter, K., & O'Neill, C. (1996). *Righteous religion: Unmasking the illusions of Fundamentalism and authoritarian Catholicism.* Binghamton, NY: Haworth Press.

Rogers, D. (2002). *Pastoral care for post-traumatic stress disorder: Healing the shattered soul.* Binghamton, NY: Haworth Press.

Rosenbloom, D., & Williams, M. (1999). *Life after trauma: A workbook for healing.* New York: Guilford.

Rotschild, B. (2000). *The body remembers: The psychophysiology of trauma and trauma treatment.* New York: W. W. Norton.

Rowatt, G. W. Jr. (2001). *Adolescents in crisis: A guide for parents, teachers, ministers and counselors.* Louisville: Westminster John Knox Press.

Rubel, B. (2000). *But I didn't get to say goodbye: For parents and professionals helping child suicide survivors.* Kendall Park, NJ: Griefwork Center.

Russell, D. (1982). *Rape in marriage.* Bloomington: Indiana University Press.

Rynearson, E. (2001). *Retelling violent death.* Philadelphia: Brunner-Routledge.

Salloum, A. (1998). *Reactions: A workbook to help young people who are experiencing trauma and grief.* Omaha: Centering.

Sampselle, C. (1996). *Violent against women.* New York: Taylor & Francis.

Schornstein, S. (1997). *Domestic violence and health care: What every professional needs to know.* Thousand Oaks, CA: Sage.

Schwarz, R. (2002). *Tools for transforming trauma.* New York/London: Brunner-Routledge.

Selekman, M. (2002). *Living on the razor's edge: Solution-oriented brief family therapy with self-harming adolescents.* New York: W. W. Norton.

Shapiro, L. (1994). *The very angry day that Amy didn't have.* Secaucus: Childswork Childsplay.

Sharp, S., & Cowie, H. (1998). *Counseling and supporting children in distress.* Thousand Oaks, CA: Sage.

318 / PERSPECTIVES ON VIOLENCE AND VIOLENT DEATH

Sherlock, P. (2003). *Taking back our lives: Reflections for survivors of childhood abuse.* Chicago: ACTA.

Shipway, L. (2004). *Domestic violence: A handbook for healthcare professionals.* London/ New York: Routledge.

Silva, R. (Ed.). (2000, 2004). *Post-traumatic stress disorders in children & adolescents* (Handbook). New York: W. W. Norton.

Silverman, P. (2000). *Never too young to know: Death in children's lives.* New York: Oxford University Press.

Sinclair, N. D. (1993). *Horrific trauma: A pastoral response to the post-traumatic stress disorder.* Binghamton, NY: Haworth Press.

Smith, H. I. (2002). *The grief care guide: Resources for counseling and leading small groups.* Kansas City: Beacon Hill Press of Kansas City.

Sobrino, J. (2004). *Where is God? Earthquake, terrorism, barbarity, and hope.* Maryknoll: Orbis.

Sofield, L., Juliano, C., & Hammett, R. (1990). *Design for wholeness: Dealing with anger, learning to forgive, building self-esteem.* Notre Dame: Ave Maria Press.

Solomon, M., & Siegel, D. (Eds.). (2002). *Healing trauma: Attachment, mind, body, and brain.* New York: W. W. Norton.

Spungen, D. (1998). *Homicide: The hidden victims: A guide for professionals.* Thousand Oaks, CA: Sage.

Stacey, W. (1983). *The family secret: Domestic violence in America.* Boston: Beacon.

Stamm, B. (Ed.). (1995). *Secondary traumatic stress: Self-care issues for clinicians, researchers & educators.* Lutherville, MD: Sidran.

Stangler, M. (1995). *Striving to be . . . violence free: A guidebook for creating a safety plan.* St. Louis Park, MN: Perspectives.

Steele, W. (1999, 2003). *A trauma is like no other experience: A booklet for teens.* Grosse Pointe Woods, MI: The National Institute for Trauma and Loss in Children.

Steele, W., & Raider, M. (2001). *Structured sensory intervention for traumatized children, adolescents and parents: Strategies to alleviate trauma.* Lewiston, NY: Edwin Mellon Press.

Stetson, B. (2003). *Living victims, stolen lives: Parents of murdered children speak to America.* Amityville: Baywood.

Stevenson, R. (Ed.). (1994/2002). *What will we do? Preparing a school community to cope with crises.* Amityville: Baywood.

Stevenson-Moessner, J. (Ed.). (2000). *In her own time: Women and developmental issues in pastoral care.* Minneapolis: Fortress.

Stott, S. (2001). *Out of the shadows: Help for men who have been sexually assaulted.* Dorset, UK: Russell House.

Stout, N. (2004). *Where is God in my suffering?* St. Meinrad: Abbey Press.

Straus, M. (1994). *Violence in the lives in adolescents.* New York: W. W. Norton.

Tedeschi, R., & Calhoun, L. (1995). *Trauma and transformation: Growing in the aftermath of suffering.* Thousand Oaks, CA: Sage.

Tehrani, N. (2000). *Workplace trauma: Concepts, assessment & intervention.* New York: Taylor & Francis.

Teipen, K. (2003). *When someone who hurts you dies.* St. Meinrad: Abbey Press.

Turnbull, S. (2000). *Who lives happily ever after? A handbook for families whose child has died violently.* Omaha: Centering.

APPENDIX C / 319

Valent, P. (1994). *Child survivors of the holocaust.* New York: Brunner-Routledge.

VanderKolk, E. et al. (Eds.). (1996). *Traumatic stress: The effects of overwhelming experience on mind, body and society.* New York: Guilford.

Vanderhaar, G. (1998). *Beyond violence: In the spirit of the non-violent Christ.* Mystic: Twenty-Third.

Viano, E. (1996). *Intimate violence.* New York: Taylor & Francis.

Walker, L. (Ed.). (1979, 2000). *The battered woman syndrome.* New York: Springer.

Webb, N. B. (1993). *Helping bereaved children.* New York: Guilford.

Webb, N. B. (Ed.). (2004). *Mass trauma and violence: Helping families and children cope.* New York: Guilford.

Weeks, O. D., & Johnson, C. (2001). *When all the friends have gone: A guide for aftercare providers.* Amityville: Baywood.

Weems, R. (1995). *Battered love: Marriage, sex, and violence in the Hebrew prophets.* Minneapolis: Fortress.

Wekerle, C., & Wall, A. M. (2002). *The violence and addiction equation: Theoretical and clinical issues in substance abuse and relationship violence.* New York: Brunner-Routledge.

West, C. (Ed.). (2002). *Violence in the lives of Black women: Battered, black and blue.* Binghamton, NY: Haworth Press.

Williams, M., & Sommer, J. Jr. (Eds.). (2002). *Simple and complex post-traumatic stress disorder: Strategies for comprehensive treatment in clinical practice.* Binghamton, NY: Haworth Press.

Wilson, J., & Thomas, R. (2004). *Empathy in the treatment of trauma & PTSD.* New York: Brunner-Routledge.

Wink, W. (1992). *Engaging the powers: Discernment and resistance in a world of domination.* Minneapolis: Fortress.

Worden, J. W. (2002). *Grief counseling and grief therapy: A handbook for the mental health practitioner* (3rd ed.). New York: Springer.

Worthington, E. (Ed.). (1998). *Dimensions of forgiveness: Psychological research and theological perspectives.* Philadelphia: Templeton Foundation Press.

Wright, K. (2001). *Religious abuse: A pastor explores the many ways religion can hurt as well as heal.* Kelowna, BC, Canada: Northstone.

Young, B., & Blake, D. (Eds.). (1999). *Group treatments for post-traumatic stress disorder.* New York: Brunner/Mazel.

Zimmerman, M. (1995). *Take and make holy: Honoring the sacred in the healing journey of abuse survivors.* Chicago: Liturgical Training.

Zinner, E., & Williams, M. (1999). *When a community weeps: Case studies in group survivorship.* New York: Brunner/Mazel.

Contributors

Fernando Cabrera is an educator, chaplain, and pastor. He is the program director of the Graduate Counseling Program at Mercy College, New York. He is also a chaplain for the Latin American Chaplain Association and the Kings County SPCC Child Protective Law Enforcement Agency. He is the founder and senior pastor of New Life Outreach International in the Bronx, New York. He serves as a Community Board member in district number seven in the Bronx and is an executive board member for the Hispanic and Jewish Relations Committee for the Borough President of the Bronx.

Jay Caponigro is the Director of the Robinson Community Learning Center, a 4-year-old outreach initiative of the University of Notre Dame in South Bend, Indiana. The Robinson Center provides educational opportunities in underserved communities, as well as violence-prevention programming with schools and area partners. Before joining Notre Dame's staff, Caponigro was a community organizer with the Industrial Areas Foundation, before going on to serve as executive director and lead organizer of Chicago's Southwest Organizing Project from 1995–1999. There he was responsible for creating an organization of 25 churches and schools on the city's racially diverse southwest side where Take Ten was launched community-wide. Working with lay and clerical leaders, Caponigro helped build coalitions to reduce youth violence, improve adult education, reduce racism, and provide job-training opportunities for disadvantaged populations. At the Robinson Center, Mr. Caponigro has been principal investigator for two federal grants from the U.S. Departments of Justice and of Housing and Urban Development. He currently manages a staff of 10, in addition to managing a volunteer base of over 250 individuals. Caponigro is a graduate of Notre Dame (BA majoring in Government and International Studies) and serves on various local boards at the University and in the community related to education, violence, and labor and religion issues. He consults with local and regional organizations on broad-based organizing and leadership development, in addition to administering two community-based learning courses for students at Notre Dame.

Rachel A. Coleman has a BA in Environmental Science and Public Policy from Harvard College. She is currently a doctoral student in clinical psychology

322 / PERSPECTIVES ON VIOLENCE AND VIOLENT DEATH

at the University of Memphis. Her primary interests include the role of the relationship in psychotherapy, constructivist theory, and Buddhism.

Inge B. Corless, RN, PhD, FAAN, is a graduate of the Bellevue Schools of Nursing, Boston University (BSN), University of Rhode Island (MA), and Brown University (PhD). She completed postdoctoral training at the University of California–San Francisco as a Robert Wood Johnson Clinical Fellow. Widely published in death and dying and palliative care and also in HIV/AIDS, Dr. Corless has served as a coinvestigator on a Robert Wood Johnson funded project, TNEEL, for end-of-life education for undergraduate nursing students. Dr. Corless has also been funded by the Division of Nursing to develop a graduate specialty in HIV/AIDS nursing. The courses, including HIV/AIDS Epidemiology, Pathophysiology, and Symptom Management, have been revised and are being taught in a distance-learning format. Dr. Corless spent a sabbatical in South Africa conducting research on adherence to medications in HIV/AIDS and in TB. As a member of the UCSF HIV/AIDS Nursing Research Network, Dr. Corless has conducted research on symptom management and in particular, cognitive impairment and fatigue. She currently serves as a member of the Research Committee for the National Hospice and Palliative Care Organization and on various editorial boards. Her most recent book (with coeditors Barbara Germino and Mary Pittman Lindeman) is *Dying, Death, and Bereavement: A Challenge for Living.*

Joseph M. Currier, MA, LCPC, is a doctoral student in clinical psychology at the University of Memphis. He graduated from Wheaton College with an MA in clinical psychology. Before coming to Memphis, he worked as a psychotherapist for several years on the south side of Chicago. His primary interests include clinical work with children and adolescents, traumatic loss, treatment of childhood grief, and psychodynamic and constructivist theories of psychotherapy.

Reverend Richard B. Gilbert, PhD, DMin, LLD, BCC, CT, Director of Chaplaincy Services, Sherman Health Systems, Elgin, Illinois and executive director of the World Pastoral Care Center. Dick is an Anglican priest, Board Certified Chaplain, Certified Thanatologist, and serves on the Board of Directors of ADEC and the editorial boards for *Healing Ministry Journal* and *The America Journal of Palliative Care and Hospice.* He is a regular contributor to several professional and bereavement journals, a speaker, consultant and pastoral guide, and a resource specialist. He is the author of four books, including *Finding Your Way After Your Parent Dies: Hope for Adults* (Ave Maria Press) and as editor, *Healthcare & Spirituality: Listening, Assessing, Caring.* He has contributed to six other books, including his current project, *Healing the Holy Helpers: Healthy Clergy for the Third Millennium.* He did his clinical residency (CPE) at the University of Michigan Medical Center, earned his Doctor of Ministry in 1999 through the Graduate Theological Foundation and his PhD through the same

CONTRIBUTORS / 323

school in cooperation with Rewley House, Oxford University. He is the Book Review editor for *Illness, Crisis, & Loss*. He has worked closely with his wife, Sharon, now Director of Volunteers at Sherman Hospital, who ran women's programs, domestic violence shelters, as well as advocacy and training for courts, law officers and agencies for over 20 years. Rev. Gilbert has worked as a client advocate in crisis situations and as a counselor and bereavement specialist with many victims and their families.

Jason M. Holland received his BA from the University of Tennessee and is currently a doctoral student in clinical psychology at the University of Memphis. His primary interests include constructivist approaches to grief and loss and common factors in psychotherapy.

Tim Kullman is currently an instructor in the Sociology Department at the University of Wisconsin–La Crosse. He teaches courses in sociology, criminal justice, and global studies. His current research interests include the sociology of religion, religious extremism, and terrorism. Kullman has co-authored the book *Facing Terror: The Government's Response to Contemporary Extremists in America* with Dr. Jim Rodgers from the University Press of America. He wrote the chapter Networks of Hate in Understanding Terrorism: Threats in an Uncertain World, and he wrote the chapter Modernity and Conflict Theorists in Reason, Conflict and Power: Modern Political and Social Thought from 1688 to the Present.

Carr Maher [Editor's Note: Carr Maher is a pen name used by the author of two of the chapters in this book] is a graduate of the University of Michigan (BS Mathematics and BA English). As it was the fashion at the time, he was drafted into the U.S. Army after graduation and actually found he enjoyed it, serving two tours in Southeast Asia. When he returned to civilian life, he was accepted into a Masters program at the University of North Carolina. He was also accepted on the NYPD and did both successfully. He served as a patrolman in Harlem and lower Manhattan before being accepted to the elite Emergency Service Unit and became one of the first trained "talkers" for the new Hostage Negotiation Unit. During a leave from the NYPD, he earned a PhD from the University of Pennsylvania. He participated in courses at Columbia University and worked his way up through the ranks of the Police Department until his retirement. He has been a freelance journalist and a professional speechwriter for the past 15 years. He is presently married to his fourth wife and lives in semiseclusion in New York City, where he is rebuilding an old farmhouse that he had the misfortune to inherit. He splits his time between that and his writing.

Kathleen Malley-Morrison is a Professor of Psychology in the Program in Human Development, Boston University. Since completing a postdoctoral fellowship in family violence at Children's Hospital in Boston, she has focused primarily on issues in family violence. She is coauthor (with Anne P. Copeland) of *Studying*

324 / PERSPECTIVES ON VIOLENCE AND VIOLENT DEATH

Families (Sage, 1991), author (with Denise A. Hines) of *Family violence in a cultural perspective* (Sage, 2004), and co-author (with Denise A. Hines) of *Family Violence in the United States: Defining, Understanding, and Combating Abuse* (Sage, 2004). She also edited *International Perspectives on Family Violence and Abuse* (Erlbaum, 2004).

Barbara Melamed is currently Professor and Program Director of the MS Psychology degree at Mercy College in the division of social and behavioral sciences. She was formerly Dean of the Graduate School of Psychology at Yeshiva University and held appointments at the Albert Einstein College of Medicine in Psychiatry and Social Medicine and Epidemiology. Her research interests have focused on stress under situations that are often traumatic and involve the entire family system. She has produced film media to help prepare children for surgical procedures. She was the founding director of the Behavioral Medicine Clinic at the University of Florida and at Yeshiva University. Her research contributions are in the area of war trauma, including the Bosnian-Croatian War; the assassination of Premier Rabin in Jerusalem and the terrorist bus bombings; and currently the psychological consequences of the World Trade Center attack. She has represented the social-science interests relating to war trauma by participating in National Conferences and scientific-review panels, which focus on trauma recovery and bereavement issues. She holds degrees from the University of Michigan (BS Psychology), athe University of Wisconsin (MS Psychology and PhD Clinical Psychology, Social and Personality Development, and Psychophysiology).

Robert A. Neimeyer, PhD, is Professor and Director of Psychotherapy in the Department of Psychology, University of Memphis, where he also maintains an active clinical practice. Since completing his doctoral training at the University of Nebraska in 1982, he has published 20 books, including *Meaning Reconstruction and the Experience of Loss*, and *Lessons of Loss: A Guide to Coping* and serves as Editor of the journal, *Death Studies*. The author of over 200 articles and book chapters, he is currently working to advance a more adequate theory of grieving as a meaning-making process, both in his published work and through his frequent professional workshops for national and international audiences. Neimeyer served as a member of the American Psychological Association's Task Force on End-of-Life Issues and chair of the International Work Group on Death, Dying, & Bereavement. In recognition of his scholarly contributions, he has been granted the Eminent Faculty Award by the University of Memphis, made a Fellow of the Clinical Psychology Division of the American Psychological Association, and given the Research Recognition Award by the Association for Death Education and Counseling.

Kim Overdyck is the Associate Director of Prevention Programs at the Robinson Community Learning Center, an outreach project of the University of Notre Dame in South Bend, Indiana. She is also the project coordinator of Take Ten—a violence prevention program that provides children with positive alternatives to violence—in local schools, community centers, and at the St. Joseph County Boys and Girls Club sites. Her academic qualifications are as follows: BA majoring in Political Science and Law (1998) and LLB (2000) both from the University of Cape Town, South Africa; MA in Peace Studies, with a concentration in International Human Rights Law (2002), University of Notre Dame, USA. She passed the General Council of the Bar of South Africa National Bar Examination and has been admitted as an Advocate/Litigator with right of appearance to the High Court of South Africa. Before working at the Robinson Center, Ms. Overdyck was a member of the South African Police Service and was assigned as a detective to the Child Protection Unit, where she investigated adult rapes and all crimes committed against children under the age of 14. She is a founding and board member of the Youth Justice Project and is on the program committee of the new Family Justice Center. She is also a co-facilitator and presenter at the annual High School Educators conference at St. Mary's College, Notre Dame. The conference is entitled "The InterCultural Promise: Forming a New Generation of Woman Leaders." She coteaches a community-based learning course on violence and children at Notre Dame. She also volunteers at the Center for Community Justice in Elkhart, Indiana as a mediator for the Victim Offender Reconciliation Program (VORP).

Colin Murray Parkes, OBE MD FRCPsych, is a psychiatrist, researcher, and author of *Bereavement: Studies of Grief in Adult Life,* first published in 1972, now in its third edition, and many other books and articles on bereavement, trauma, disasters, attachment, and loss. He has been a consultant psychiatrist to St Christopher's Hospice since 1966 and Life President of Cruse Bereavement Care. He has served as a consultant following disasters in the United Kingdom, Rwanda (after genocide), New York (after 9/11) and the Indian Ocean (after the 2004 tsunami). He served on International Work Groups on Bereavement, Disasters, Violence and Violent Death and The Cycle of Violence. Awarded OBE by H M the Queen in 1996 for services to bereaved people. He is the father of Jenny Parkes, also a contributor to this work.

Jenny Parkes has worked with children in challenging social settings for almost 20 years, as a researcher, an educational psychologist, and as a teacher. Her PhD research, completed in 2005, focused on children's experiences of living with conflict and violence in South Africa and on working with children's perspectives in developing violence-prevention strategies. Currently she is developing the academic, policy and practice applications for children and violence prevention in South Africa, the United Kingdom and internationally, through a postdoctoral research fellowship at the Thomas Coram Research Unit, University of London, a leading center for research on children and young people in the United Kingdom.

Kimberly A. Rapoza is an instructor of Psychology in the Behavioral Sciences Department at Mercy College. Past awards include a Clara Mayo Award, used to support a doctoral dissertation examining the predictors of relationship violence in dating couples. As a member of an international research team, Dr. Rapoza also is engaged in a series of ongoing research projects on family violence, utilizing cross-cultural and human rights perspectives. She also was a contributing author for *International Perspectives on Family Violence and Abuse* (Erlbaum, 2004), providing an examination of cultural, legal, and attitudinal influences on family violence in the United States. Her work has been presented at the American Psychological Association, the American Psychological Society and the Eastern Psychological Association.

Phyllis R. Silverman, PhD, is currently a Scholar-in-Residence at Brandeis University Women's Studies Research Center and Professor Emerita at the MGH Institute of Health Professions. She developed the idea of Widow-to-Widow that led her to advocate for mutual help among the bereaved. She was Co-Principal Investigator and Project Director of the Harvard/MGH Child Bereavement Study. She is applying the findings from her research in her work as a volunteer in the Children's Room: A Center for Grieving Children and Adolescents in Arlington, MA. Her books include *Never Too Young to Know: Death in Children's Lives*. With Dennis Klass and Steven Nickman, she coedited *Continuing Bonds: New Understandings of Grief.* Her most recent book is a new edition of *Widow-to-Widow: How the Bereaved Help One Another.*

Neil Thompson, PhD, is Professor of Applied Social Studies at Staffordshire University in the United Kingdom and managing director of Avenue Consulting Ltd (www.avenueconsulting.co.uk). He has over 100 publications to his name, including bestselling textbooks. Neil works in the fields of social work and human relations. Following a successful career in social work, Neil plays a major role in shaping social work theory and practice while also making a contribution to our understanding of human relations issues in the workplace: equality and diversity, stress, bullying and harassment, conflict management, loss, grief, and trauma.

Kimberly A. Vogt is a Professor of Sociology and Chair of the department of Sociology and Archaeology at the University of Wisconsin-La Crosse. She earned a BA from Alfred University, Alfred, NY; and a MA and PhD from the University of New Hampshire, Durham, NH. Her research interests include youth homicide, hate crime, and health risk behaviors among gay, lesbian, bisexual and transgender youth. She is an active member of the Homicide Research Working Group, an international group of homicide researchers, and serves on the editorial board of the journal *Homicide Studies*.

Gregory Paul Wegner received his PhD in Curriculum and Instruction at the University of Wisconsin-Madison in 1988. As a Friedrich Ebert Scholar (1983–1984), Wegner gained initial experience writing history while working

CONTRIBUTORS / 327

in the archives of the then divided Germany. Among his research interests are Nazi education and Holocaust education in Germany and the United States. He currently teaches in the Department of Educational Studies at the University of Wisconsin–La Crosse. Wegner's latest work includes the book, *Anti-Semitism and Schooling Under the Third Reich*. He is currently researching and translating the work of an obscure anti-Semitic Nazi propagandist named Johann von Leers via archives in Russia, Germany, Israel, and the United States. Wegner dedicates his chapter to the memory of countless children who met their deaths at the hands of Nazi brutality and citizen apathy.

Index

Abrahams, Shafiq, 286, 287
Acceptance of violence,
    assumptions/principles about, 297
Acceptance/trust as a coping tool, 249
Afghanistan, 83-84, 86, 91
African Americans and homicide, 137,
    138, 140-141, 144-145
    See also "Talk it Out! Wait it Out!
    Take Ten: . . ."
Agreements and breaking cycles of
    violence, 227-228, 234
AIDS quilt panels, 256
Airplane disasters, 120
    See also "Hispanic Families and Mass
    Casualties: . . ."
Albert (prince), 231
Al Qaeda, 86
    See also "Religious Violence and
    Weapons of Mass Destruction"
Alternatives to/coping with violence.
    See "Coping with Violent Death:
    The Role of Spirituality"; "From
    Violence to Peace: Posthomicide
    Memorials"; "Making and
    Breaking the Cycles of Violence";
    "Talk it Out! Wait it Out!: Take
    Ten . . ."
American Airlines. *See* "Hispanic
    Families and Mass
    Casualties: . . ."
American Civil War, 231
Anger
    coping with violent death, 246

[Anger]
    epidemic, 53-54
    toward God, clergy bearing brunt of
    anger, 31-33, 35, 37
    September 11th terrorist attacks in
    U.S., 217
    Take Ten initiative, 280
Animal side of human nature, belief that
    violence comes from the, 13
Anthrax, 88
Anti-Ballistic Missile Treaty, 87
Anxious/ambivalent attachment style,
    153, 159, 171
Anxious/avoidant attachment style, 153
Apartheid, 236
Arendt, Hannah, 80
Art, 249
Asahara, Shoko, 81-82, 87-89
Assumptions/principles concerning
    violence, a statement of
    acceptance of violence, 297
    committee members, IWG, 291
    communal societal responses to violent
    death, 303
    definitions, 292
    education, 299-300, 302
    effects of violence, 296-297
    goals, 292
    individual responses to violent death,
    302-303
    intervention, 300-301
    justice system, 301-302
    overview, 295

330 / PERSPECTIVES ON VIOLENCE AND VIOLENT DEATH

[Assumptions/principles concerning violence, a statement of]
power and leadership, 298-299
preamble, 292-293
public communication, 301
restitution, 302
society, violence and, 298
statements on violence/violent death, 293-294
Ataturk, Kemal, 84
Attachment theory. *See* "Grief and Attachment Within the Context of Family Violence"
Aum Shinrikyo Movement. *See* "Religious Violence and Weapons of Mass Destruction"
Auschwitz, 283
See also "Violence and the Dehumanization of Victims in Auschwitz . . ."
Avoidant attachment, 171
Awareness (open) and breaking cycles of violence, 231-232
Azzam, Abdullah, 83, 86

Balance in one's life, finding a, 250
Banking networks and underground weapons networks, 87
Al-Banna, Hasan, 83-85
Barowski, Tadeusz, 60, 68, 70-71, 75
Being and Nothingness . . . (Sartre), 45
Bereavement and grief, distinguishing between, 5
See also individual subject headings
"Bereavement Following Violent Death: . . ." (Currier, Holland, Coleman & Neimeyer)
community's reactions to the bereaved, 178
complicated grief, 179-181, 194
Core Bereavement Items, 188-192, 194-195
discussion, 193-196
implications, clinical, 196-197
interpersonal implications, 182-185, 193

["Bereavement Following Violent Death: . . ." (Currier, Holland, Coleman & Neimeyer)]
intrapersonal implications, 178-182
Inventory of Complicated Grief, 186-187, 189-192, 194-195
limitations and future directions, 197-198
loss, understanding how we deal with, 177
meaning-making process, 181-182, 188, 192-193
methods, study, 186-189
overview, 177-178
results, study, 189-193
social support systems, 182-184
stigma attached to suicide/murder/accident, 184
study aims, 185
traumatic distress, 179-181
violent death characterized by violence/violation/volition, 177
Berenbaum, Michael, 70
Bethel College, 275
Bible, the, 27-28
bin Laden, Osama, 83, 86, 90
Biological weapons, 88-89
See also "Religious Violence and Weapons of Mass Destruction"
Boas, Jacob, 73
Bonding and relationships, 130, 240-241
Borghesani, Anne E., 262
Bosnian-Croatian War, 204
Boston's Operation Ceasefire (homicide prevention), 147
Botulinum toxin, 88
Brain damage and violent behavior, 224
Brandeis, Friedl D., 73
Brief Symptom Inventory, 208, 212
Bronson, Charles, 8
Brooklyn Society for Ethical Culture, 257-258
Brothers Grimm, 8
Brown, Louis B., 255, 261, 262
Buchanan, Pat, 3

INDEX / 331

Buddha Sakyamuni, 82
Bulletin of Atomic Scientists, 87
Bumper-sticker solutions to violence,
12-13

Cabrera, Fernando, x
Caliphate, Islamic, 83-84
Cantor Fitzgerald, 204
Caponigro, Jay, xi, 272
Caring/sharing, we all need to taught, 251
Carr, Wesley, 35
Cartoon violence, 8
Causes of/means to inflict violence,
inability to distinguish between,
6-7, 12-13
Ceasefire (homicide prevention),
Boston's Operation, 147
Center for Epidemiological Depression
Scale (CEDS), 211-212
Centers for Disease Control (CDC), 137,
285
Central Intelligence Agency (CIA), 90
Challenger Space Shuttle tragedy, 209
"Characteristics of Homicide: . . ." (Vogt)
children, 137-140
cultural influences, 142-143, 146-147
elderly, the, 142, 146
gender differences, 137, 139
grief and bereavement, 145-146
integrated theory, 145
middle age, 141-142, 146
overview, 135
racial differences, 137
reducing homicide rates, approaches
used in, 147-148
social support systems, 148
sociological explanations, 142-145
summary/conclusions, 146-148
teenagers and young adults, 140-141
trends in risk by age group
(1976-2002), 135, 136
Chemical, biological, radiological, and
nuclear weapons (CBRN), 90
See also "Religious Violence and
Weapons of Mass Destruction," 90
Chery, Clementina, 255, 261, 262

Chery, Joseph, 255, 261
Chicken Soup for the Kid's Soul
(Rosenberg), 279
Children
corporal punishment in schools, the
abolition of, 227
homicides of, 137-140
Nazi mass murder, 71-74
play as a method of coping, 250
as teachers, 251
See also "Good Violence/Bad
Violence . . ."; "Grief and Attach-
ment Within the Context of
Family Violence"; "Resisting the
Magnet: A Study of South
African . . ."; "Talk it Out! Wait
it Out! Take Ten: . . ."
Christianity. See "Violence in the Family:
Spirituality/Religion . . ."
Christianity Today, 33
Civil wars, 225, 231
Clan/tribal violence, 225
Clinginess and attachment
theory/domestic violence, 159
Closure concept has little meaning for
family members, 256
Codependence and the clergy, 26-27
Codes (destructive) and breaking cycles
of violence, 232-234
Cohen, Richard, 271
Cohen, Roger, 283
Cold War and good/bad violence, 10
Coleman, Rachel A., x
Colonialism and the Middle East,
83, 85
Columbine High School, 6, 11, 260
Communication
assumptions/principles about violence
and, 301
conflict as a central part of, 49-50
cycles of violence, breaking, 228
Take Ten initiative, 280-281
Community characteristics increasing
probability of youth violence,
285-286
Complicated grief following violent
death, 179-181, 194

332 / PERSPECTIVES ON VIOLENCE AND VIOLENT DEATH

Concentration and death camps, distinction between, 62
See also "Violence and the Dehumanization of Victims in Auschwitz . . ."
"Conflict and Violence in the Workplace: . . ." (Thompson)
conflict as a part of everyday reality, 48-51
existentialism, 45-48
guidelines for handling conflict/violence, 55
ontology, 46-47
phenomenology, 46
reading, guide to further, 56
summary/conclusions, 56, 307
violence, 52-54
Conflict Resolution Education (CRE), 268-269
Constantine (emperor), 234
Contingency and existentialism, 47, 51, 55
Contracts and breaking cycles of violence, 234
"Coping with Violent Death: The Role of Spirituality" (Cox)
anger, 246
bonding and relationships, 240-241
choices that lead to health coping, 246
denial/disbelief, 246
experience loss, things to do with those who, 249-250
good and bad days, there will be, 243
grief and violent death, 241-242
grow through loss, how do we, 247-248
guilt, 246-247
healthy grieving, ways to help other develop styles of, 248-249
lack of coping skills, 242
opportunity, each loss is an, 247
others do not cope in the same way that we do, 243
overview, 239-240

["Coping with Violent Death: The Role of Spirituality" (Cox)]
questions each of us need to ask ourselves, 247
response to loss, 246-247
sadness, 247
seasons of life, loss/growth and the, 245
skills needed, coping, 242-243
spiritual growth as a means of coping, 244-245
summary/conclusions, 252-253, 307-308
unhealthy ways of coping, 246
Core Bereavement Items (CBI), 188-192, 194-195
Corless, Inge, xi
Corporal punishment in schools, the abolition of, 227
Coups, 225
Courage to Teach, The (Palmer), 267
Covictims and homicides, 146
Cox, Gerry, xi
Cozzens, Donald, 35
Crayon Box that Talked, The (DeRolf & Letzig), 282
Criminal enterprises, globalization and, 90, 92
Crisis situations. See "Hispanic Families and Mass Casualties: . . ."; "Silent Night, Violent Night: . . ."; "Violence in Our Own Backyard: September 11 . . ."
Crowd control, nonlethal methods of, 227
Crusades, 80
Cuban Missile Crisis, 232
Cultural norms and domestic violence, 27-28
Culture and homicide, 142-143, 146-147
Curriculum review and coping with violence in schools, 15
See also "Talk it Out! Wait it Out! Take Ten: . . ."
Currier, Joseph M., x
Cycle of crisis response and coping with violence in schools, 15-16

INDEX / 333

Cycles of violence, ending the. *See* "Making and Breaking the Cycles of Violence"
Czech Republic, 267

Death, violent. *See* Violent death
Death Studies, 226
Definitions of violence, 4-7, 292
Dehumanization. *See* "Violence and the Dehumanization of Victims in Auschwitz . . ."
Delinquency and homicide victimization, relationship between, 183
Dempsey, Kathleen M., 262-263
Denial, 246
Denominational structures and domestic abuse, 24-25
Dependence and attachment theory/domestic violence, 159
Depression and September 11th terrorist attacks in U.S., 207, 211, 213-214, 216
Despair and attachment theory, 152
Des Pres, Terrence, 66
Destruction of the European Jews, The (Hilberg), 60
Detachment and attachment theory, 152
Diagnostic and Statistical Manual of Mental Disorders (DSM-IV), 154, 178, 210
Disabled people and Nazi mass murder, 62
Disbelief, 246
Disenfranchised grief, 37, 183
Disorganized/disoriented behavior and attachment theory, 153-154, 157, 158, 160
"Document on Violence and Grief," 4
Domestic violence, 10, 141, 146, 157-161
See also "Grief and Attachment Within the Context of Family Violence"; "Silent Night, Violent Night: . . ."; "Violence in the Family: Spirituality/Religion . . ."
Doomsday Clock, 87, 91
Drama, 249

Dreams, we all need to be taught to try and live our, 252
Drink-drugs-violence repertoire, 99-100
Drowned and the Saved, The (Levi), 67

Ebola virus, 88
Education about violence, 13-16, 299-300, 302
See also "Talk it Out! Wait it Out! Take Ten: . . ."
Egypt, 83
Eldercide, 142, 146
Emotionally withdrawn/inhibited attachment disorder, 154
Emotional support and violent deaths, 182-184
Encouragement as a coping tool, 251-252
Endocrine imbalances and violent behavior, 224
England, 10, 83, 84, 86, 229-231, 234
"Evangelical Clergy and Wife Abuse: Knowledge and Response," 31
Existentialism. *See* "Conflict and Violence in the Workplace: . . ."

False memory syndrome, 228
Familial Patriarchal Belief Scale, 28
Families, 224
See also Domestic violence; "From Violence to Peace: Posthomicide Memorials"; "Grief and Attachment Within the Context of Family Violence"; "Hispanic Families and Mass Casualties: . . ."; "Violence in the Family: Spirituality/Religion . . ."
Farouk (King), 84
Fearful attachment, 160-161, 169-171
Fear (Pickova), 74
Federal Emergency Management Agency (FEMA), 15
Films/motion pictures, 8-9
Firearms, 6-7, 12, 147-148, 162, 271
Flinker, Moshe, 73

334 / PERSPECTIVES ON VIOLENCE AND VIOLENT DEATH

Food in Hispanic cultures, 123-124
Ford, Harrison, 8-9
Forgiveness as a coping tool, 250
France, 83
Frank, Anne, 72-73
Freire, Paulo, 269
Fresno State University, 257
Friendship, 249
"From Violence to Peace: Posthomicide
    Memorials" (Corless &
    Silverman)
  Borghesani, Anne E., 262
  Brown, Louis D., 262
  change happen, making, 259-261
  Dempsey, Kathleen M., 262-263
  Garden of Peace (Boston, MA), 258-259
  McKie, Jesse S., 263
  overview, 255
  remembering, ways of, 255-258
Full Metal Jacket, 127

Gallipoli Peace Park, 257
Gandhi, Mahatma, 9, 233-234
Gangs, 102, 103, 225
Garden of Peace and Remembrance,
    257-258
  See also "From Violence to Peace:
    Posthomicide Memorials"
Gender
  attachment theory/domestic violence,
    170, 171
  homicide, 137, 139
  September 11th terrorist attacks in
    U.S., 207
Gibson, Mel, 8
Gilbert, Richard, ix
Giuliani, Rudy, 120
Globalization and religious violence,
    86-87, 90, 92
"Good Violence/Bad Violence . . ."
    (Stevenson)
  answers to problems of violence,
    people seeking, 3-4
  causes of/means to inflict violence,
    inability to distinguish between,
    6-7

["Good Violence/Bad Violence . . ."
    (Stevenson)]
  definitions of violence, 4-7
  domestic violence, 10
  guns, debate over, 6-7
  International Work Group on Death,
    Dying, and Bereavement, 4
  motion pictures, 8-9
  move on after a violent death,
    suggestions to help grieving
    individuals, 20
  multiple factors, violence due to, 11
  schools/children and impact of violence
    (after an event)
  happened, what exactly, 16
  level of the violence, what was the,
    16
  perpetrator(s) of the violence, what
    do we know about the, 17
  responses to the violence, what were
    the, 18
  survivors need an opportunity to
    process/give meaning to the
    violence, 19
  survivors' reactions, 18-19
  trigger of the violence, what was
    immediate, 17-18
  schools/children and impact of violence
    (anticipated events)
  causes of/means to inflict violence,
    inability to distinguish between,
    12-13
  connection between students/staff,
    create a, 13-14
  curriculum, reexamine the, 15
  cycle of crisis response, 15-16
  death tolls have escalated, 11
  education about violence, 15
  guidelines for coping with violence,
    13-16
  identify members of school
    community, 14
  lockdowns, 12
  overview, 10-11
  safe zones, declaring, 12
  security personnel, 15
  zero tolerance for violence, 15

INDEX / 335

["Good Violence/Bad Violence . . ."
(Stevenson)]
summary/conclusions, 21, 305-306
tolerance for violence as a means of
solving problems, an increasing, 3
violent death, grieving a, 19-20
wars/weapons of mass destruction, 9-10
Gorbachev, Mikhail, 90
Goremba Peace Park, 257
Government representatives and dealing
with mass casualties, 122-123
"Grief and Attachment Within the
Context of Family Violence"
(Rapoza & Malley-Morrison)
attachment/attachment theory, roots of,
152-154
childhood maltreatment, 157-158
continuity between attachment style
developed in childhood and adult
behavior, 154, 171-172
female participants, 170, 171
homicide, child/domestic, 161-165
intimate violence, 159-161
origin/expression/progression of grief,
155-156
overview, 151-152
preoccupied/fearful attachment and
grief reactions, 169-170
regression analyses, the results of,
168-170
resilient, individuals are very, 172
summary/conclusions, 169-172
testing relationship paths predicted
within empirical model, 166-167
witnessing domestic violence, 157-158,
170-171
Grief and bereavement, distinguishing
between, 5
See also individual subject headings
"Grief and Guilt in the Military" (Maher)
guilt, a soldier's, 130-132
sight, the sense of, 127-128
smell, the sense of, 129
sound, the sense of, 128-129
survivor's guilt, 131-132
taste, the sense of, 129
touch, the sense of, 130

Guilt, 130-132, 246-247
Guns, 6-7, 12, 147-148, 162, 271
Gypsies, 62

Hamza, Khidhir, 90
Hannity, Sean, 12
Harmony, the fallacy of, 48-49
Harmony and security, 250
Havel, Václav, 267
*Healing the Holy Helpers: Healthy
Clergy for the Third Millennium*
(Gilbert), 35
Health care issues, 30, 121-122
Hell and existentialism, 47, 50-51,
53
Hey Little Ant (Hoose, Hoose & Tilley),
282
Heyman, Eva, 73
Hilberg, Raul, 60
"Hispanic Families and Mass
Casualties: . . ." (Cabrera)
debriefing the debriefer, 125
follow up, 124-125
food court, invitation to a, 123-124
overview, 119-120
privately, meet, 120-121
rules, set the, 121
stories of family members, listening to,
124
summary/conclusions, 125-126,
306-307
team, meet with a, 121-123
Hispanic identity and September 11th
terrorist attacks in U.S., 207
Hitler, Adolf, 61
Hoge, Dean, 35
Holland, Jason M., x
Holocaust, the, 256-257
See also "Violence and the
Dehumanization of Victims in
Auschwitz . . ."
Homicide
attachment theory, 161-165
cycles of violence, breaking, 229-230
delinquency and homicide
victimization, 183

336 / PERSPECTIVES ON VIOLENCE AND VIOLENT DEATH

[Homicide]
See also "Characteristics of
Homicide: . . ."; "From Violence
to Peace: Posthomicide
Memorials"
Homosexuals, 28-29, 62
Hope, each life must have, 251
Hopi tribe, 251
Hormone changes/imbalances and
aggressive/violent behavior, 224
Human rights and breaking cycles of
violence, 234
Humor, 249
Hussein, Saddam, 10
Husserl, Edmund, 46

Identity and existentialism, 48, 53, 55
India, 87
Indiana University of South Bend, 275
Indiscriminate/disinhibited attachment
disorder, 154
Infants, homicides of, 138, 139
Infants and attachment theory, 152-154
Inflammatory strategies and breaking
cycles of violence, 234-236
Informal Value Transfer Systems (IVTS),
89
Insurance funding and domestic violence
counseling, 30
Integrated models analyzing homicides,
145
Intergenerational transmission of
violence/attachment styles,
158
International Peace Garden, 257
International Work Group on Death,
Dying, and Bereavement (IWG),
4, 226
See also Assumptions/principles
concerning violence, a statement
of
Interpersonal skills and dealing with
workplace violence, 55
In the Shade of the Qur'an (Qutb), 85
Intimate partner violence (IPV). *See*
Domestic violence

Inventory of Complicated Grief (ICG),
186-187, 189-192, 194-195
Iran, 80, 83-84, 86
Iraq, invasion of, 9, 10, 203
Islam, 28
See also "Religious Violence and
Weapons of Mass Destruction"
Islam: The Religion of the Future (Qutb),
85
Issues in School Violence Research, 7
IWG. *See* International Work Group on
Death, Dying, and Bereavement

Jacobs, Michael, 66-67
Japan, 257
Japanese Garden of Peace, 257
Jardins de l'Unesco, 257
Jealousy and attachment theory/domestic
violence, 159-160
Jihad, the concept of, 84, 86
Joan B. Kroc Institute for International
Peace Studies, 288
Journaling, 249
Journal of Death and Dying, 4
Justice system, assumptions/principles
about violence and the, 301-302

Kapsa, James, 268, 270
Kennedy, John F., 232
Khomeini, Ayatollah, 80, 83, 86
Khrushchev, Nikita, 232
Kierkegaard, Søren, 49
King, Martin L., Jr., 9
King's College, 4
Kremer, S. Lillian, 72
Kristol, William, 3
Kullman, Timothy, x, 10
Kuriyama Peace Park, 257

Langer, Lawrence, 67, 72
Language and communication in Nazi
death camps, 67
Language of the family used when
dealing with mass casualties, 123

INDEX / 337

Law enforcement officials and dealing with mass casualties, 122
See also "Silent Night, Violent Night: . . ."
Leadership, assumptions/principles concerning violence and, 298-299
Lee Chicago Public Elementary School, 271
Legislation and breaking cycles of violence, 228, 234, 237
Legitimizing authorities and breaking cycles of violence, 230-232
Lennon, John, 258
Levi, Primo, 60, 66-68, 75
Limbaugh, Rush, 12
Listening as a coping tool, 251
Lockdowns in schools, 12
Long-term distress, violent death associated with, 180
Loomer, Bernard, 267
Love, 250
Luther, Martin, 60-61

Maher, Carr, x
Majsterck, Dian, 287
"Making and Breaking the Cycles of Violence" (Parkes)
family and interpersonal level, 224
individual level, 224
international level, 226
model of cycle of violence that crosses levels of social unit
codes, destructive, 232-234
immediate responses to violence, 229-230
International Work Group on Death, Dying and Bereavement, 226
legitimizing authorities, 230-232
perception of violent behavior, 228-229
polarizing/inflammatory strategies, 234-236
violent behavior, 226-228
national level, 225
overview, 223-224
small group/community level, 224-225
summary/conclusions, 237

Malley-Morrison, Kathleen, x
Malloy, Edward, 272
Managed care and domestic violence counseling, 30
Mandela, Nelson, 236, 265
Man's Search for Meaning (Frankl), 59
Marital tensions leading to alcohol/physical abuse, 224
Marriage guidance counselors, 234
Marriage Role Expectations Inventory, 28
Marshall, George C., 235
Masochism, 52
Mathews, Nancy, 272
Matsumoto, Chizuo, 81-82, 87-89
Abdul-Ala Mawdudi, Sayyid, 83, 85-86
McKie, Jesse S., 263
McKie, Judy K., 263
Meaning-making process for dealing with violent death, 181-182, 188, 192-193
Media, the, 4, 228
Memorials and coping with violence in schools, 14
See also "From Violence to Peace: Posthomicide Memorials"
Mental health workers and dealing with mass casualties, 121-122
Mentally ill and Nazi mass murder, 62
Mercy College, 7-8, 204-205
See also "Violence in Our Own Backyard: September 11 . . ."
Merthyr Gazette, 229
Middle East. *See* "Religious Violence and Weapons of Mass Destruction"
Miles, Al, 26
Milestones, Social Justice in Islam (Qutb), 85
Military personnel. *See* "Grief and Guilt in the Military"
Miller, James E., 245
Minority groups and homicide, 144-145
Miracles, we need to be taught the power of, 252
Monte, Morgan, 273, 279
Mother's Against Drunk Driving, 260-261
Motion pictures, 8-9

338 / PERSPECTIVES ON VIOLENCE AND VIOLENT DEATH

Mr. Peabody's Apples (Madonna & Long), 280-281
Muhammad (Prophet), 83
Muhammad Reza Pahlavi, 86
Mujahedeen, 83-84, 86
Murder. *See* Homicide
Muselmann and Nazi mass murder, 67
Music, 249, 256
Muslim Brotherhood, 82-85
My Lai Peace Park, 257

Nadeau, Janice W., 245
Nason-Clark, Nancy, 31, 36
Nasser, Gamal A., 84, 85
National Aeronautics and Space Administration (NASA), 209
National Intelligence Council, 92
National Museum of the Pacific War, 257
National Rifle Association (NRA), 6
Native Americans, 251
Navajo tribe, 251
Nazi Germany, 203, 235, 283
    See also "Violence and the Dehumanization of Victims in Auschwitz . . ."
Negotiations, police and crisis, 107-117
Neimeyer, Robert A., x
Neonaticides, 139
Nimitz, Chester W., 257
9/11 terrorist attacks in U.S., 89, 119, 120
    See also "Violence in Our Own Backyard: September 11 . . ."
Nostradamus, 81
Notification, homicide-death, 146
Nuclear weapons, 10, 257
    See also "Religious Violence and Weapons of Mass Destruction"
Nuremberg Laws (1935), 61
Nuremberg Trials, 59
Nyberg, David, 267

Objectivity/subjectivity and existentialism, 46, 47, 55
Office of Victims of Crime, The, 146

Oil, Persian Gulf, 83
Oklahoma City bombing, 209
One Flew over the Cuckoo's Nest, 235
One Generation After (Wiesel), 59
"On The Jews and Their Lies" (Luther), 60
Ontology, 46-47
Open awareness and breaking cycles of violence, 231-232
O'Reilly, Katelyn, 277
Osama bin Laden, 83, 86, 90
Ottoman Empire, 83
Overdyck, Kim, xi, 276

Pahlavi, Muhammad Reza, 86
Pakistan, 85, 87
Palestine, 28
Palmer, Parker, 267
Palmerston, Lord, 231
Paranoid schizophrenia, 224
Parkes, Colin M., xi
Parkes, Jenny, x
Parry, Anne, 265, 269, 270
Peace parks/symbols. *See* "From Violence to Peace: Posthomicide Memorials"
Peer leaders and coping with violence in schools, 13-14
"People Who Walked On" (Barowski), 70-71
Perceptions (unbiased) and breaking cycles of violence, 228-229
Persian Gulf, 83, 203
Peterson, Eugene, 35
Phenomenology, 46
Phosgene, 88
Pickova, Eva, 74
Play as a method of coping, 250
Pledge Against Gun Violence Day, 271
Po'a, 81
Poland, 61, 62
    See also "Violence and the Dehumanization of Victims in Auschwitz . . ."
Polarizing strategies and breaking cycles of violence, 234-236

Police officers and unexpected violence, 107-117
Postmodernist thinking, 45
Poststructuralist thought, 45
Posttraumatic Stress Disorder Checklist, 208
Post-traumatic stress disorder (PTSD), 162-163, 178-179, 185
  See also "Violence in Our Own Backyard: September 11 . . ."
Poverty and violence, 144, 285-286
Power/control
  assumptions/principles about violence and, 298-299
  cycles of violence, breaking the, 230-232
  shaping the experience of conflict, 50-51
  South African children associating violence with, 102-103
  Take Ten initiative, 267-268
Power Over Power (Nyberg), 267
Prayer as a coping tool, 250
Predatory violence repertoire, 99-100
Premenstrual tension and violent behavior, 224
Preoccupied attachment, 160-161, 169-170
Prince Albert, 231
Problem solving and Take Ten initiative, 281-282
Protest and attachment theory, 152
Psychological battles taking the place of physical conflict, 225
Psychospiritual approach to critical incidents. *See* "Hispanic Families and Mass Casualties: . . ."
Public communication, assumptions/principles about violence and, 301
Punishment/engagement and breaking cycles of violence, rules of, 227

Al Qaeda, 86
Queen Victoria, 231
Quran, the, 83, 85
Qutb, Sayyid, 83-85

Rabin, Itzhak, 204
Race and homicide, 137, 144-145
Rando, Therese, 33, 37
Rapoza, Kimberly A., x
Raymond of Aguilers, 80
Reconstructionist movements, religious, 28, 30
Red Lake High School, 11
Relational power, 50
"Relational Power" (Loomer), 267
Religion/spirituality
  anti-Semitic traditions, 60-61
  Christianity, Middle East rejects, 83
  mass casualties, dealing with, 122
  Nazi mass murder, 73
  prayer as a coping tool, 250
  reconstructionist movements, 28, 30
  September 11th terrorist attacks in U.S., 219
  Take Ten initiative, 284
  violent acts defended using, 10
  See also "Coping with Violent Death: The Role of Spirituality"; "Hispanic Families and Mass Casualties: . . ."; "Violence in the Family: Spirituality/Religion . . ."
"Religious Violence and Weapons of Mass Destruction" (Kullman)
  Al Qaeda's quest for WMD, 89-91
  apocalyptic goals, 80-81
  Asahara, Shoko, 81-82, 87-89
  Aum Shinrikyo's quest for WMD, 87-89
  banking networks, 87
  globalization policies/practices, 86-87
  history has many examples of slaughter in name of religion, 79-80
  ideological influences on Aum Shinrikyo, 81-82
  ideological influences on Qaeda, 82-86
  scientific spirituality, 82, 88
  summary/conclusions, 91-92
  technical development of the implements of violence, 80

340 / PERSPECTIVES ON VIOLENCE AND VIOLENT DEATH

"Resisting the Magnet: A Study of South African . . ." (Parkes)
attraction of violence, 101-103
control/connection/coherence, 104-105
graphic imagery, 100
overview, 97-98
perspectives are socially constructed, 98-99
power/control, violence associated with, 102-103
repels, violence that, 99-101, 103
summary/conclusions, 105
Responsibility and existentialism, 47-48
Restitution, assumptions/principles about violence and, 302
Revolutions, 225
Ridge, Tom, 91
Rituals, 250, 256
See also "From Violence to Peace: Posthomicide Memorials"
Robelli, John, 229
Robinson Community Learning Center (RCLC), 272-273
Roma people, 62
Roth, John, 70
Rubinowicz, David, 73
Rudashevski, Yitzhak, 73
Russell, John, 231
Russia, 28
Rwanda, 203, 228, 231

Sacred place, create a, 249
Sadism, 52-53
Sadness and coping with a violent death, 247
Sadomasochistic sexual relationships, 224
Safe zones at schools, declaring, 12, 265-266, 284
Santa Fe Indian School, 288
Sarin, 88, 89
Sartre, Jean-Paul, 45, 52
Al Sa'ud, Muhammad, 83
Saudi Arabia, 90
Scapegoating and breaking cycles of violence, 234-235
Schächter, Madame, 64

School-Based Promotion of Social Competence, 268-269
Schools, 228
See also "Good Violence/Bad Violence . . ."; "Resisting the Magnet: A Study of South African . . ."; "Talk it Out! Wait it Out! Take Ten: . . ."
Schwarzenegger, Arnold, 8
Scientific spirituality, 82, 88
Seasons of life, loss/growth and the, 245
Securely attached attachment style, 153
Security personnel and coping with violence in schools, 15
Separation distress as a response to a violent death, 179
September 11th terrorist attacks in U.S., 89, 119, 120, 228, 234
See also "Violence in Our Own Backyard: September 11 . . ."
Shah of Iran, 86
Sharing/caring, we all need to taught, 251
Shiva (Hindu god), 81
Sight, combat and the sense of, 127-128
"Silent Night, Violent Night: . . ." (Maher), 107-117
Silverman, Phyllis R., xi
Sinti people, 62
Smell, combat and the sense of, 129
Social support systems, 29-32, 148, 182-184, 274-275
Society, assumptions/principles about violence and, 298
Sodium cyanide, 88
Sound, combat and the sense of, 128-129
South Africa, 236, 285-287
See also "Resisting the Magnet: A Study of South African . . ."
Southwest Organizing Project (SWOP), 271, 272
Soviet Union, 62, 83-84, 86, 87, 90, 91
Spider and the Fly, The (Howitt & DiTerlizzi), 283
Spirituality, definitions of, 31
See also Relig listings
Spungen, Deborah, 145-146
St. Adalbert Catholic School, 272-273

INDEX / 341

St. Mary's College, 275
St. Mary's Star of the Sea Catholic
    School, 271
Stallone, Sylvester, 8
Stern, Fritz, 283
Stern, Jessica, 90
Stevenson, Robert G., ix
Stigma attached to suicide/murder, 184
Storytelling, 249
Strategic Arms Reduction Treaty
    (START), 87
Strawberry Fields Peace Garden, 258
Students Health and Welfare Centres
    Organisation (SHAWCO), 287
Subculture of Violence, The (Wolfgang &
    Ferracuti), 142-143
Subjectivity/objectivity and existen-
    tialism, 46, 47, 55
Sudan, 90
Sudden infant death syndrome (SIDS),
    184
Suicide, 184-185
Support systems/services, 29-32, 148,
    182-184, 274-275
Survivor's guilt, war and, 131-132
Switzerland, 7, 12
Symbols of safety and coping with
    violence in schools, 14
Syria, 83

Take Ten initiative. *See* "Talk it Out!
    Wait it Out! Take Ten: . . ."
"Talk it Out! Wait it Out! Take Ten: . . ."
    (Overdyck & Caponigro)
    assessing the scale of violence and
        conditions for change, 285-287
    community characteristics increasing
        probability of youth violence,
        285-286
    community support, building, 274-275
    Conflict Resolution Education,
        268-269
    curriculum and activities
        anger management, 280
        communication, effective, 280-281
        conflict and violence, 278

["Talk it Out! Wait it Out! Take Ten: . . ."
    (Overdyck & Caponigro)]
    fair and assertive behavior,
        279-280
    overview, 276-278
    perspectives, trading, 282-283
    problem solving, 281-282
    values and principles, 279
    walk away, knowing when to,
        283-284
definition of violence, inclusive,
    266
enormity of the problem, 265
ground rules, 270
history/background, 269-270
next stage, the, 284-285
post-script, 288
power and the learning environment,
    267-268
principles, ten, 270-272
South Bend, Take Ten arrives in,
    272-274
Students Health and Welfare Centres
    Organisation, 287
summary/conclusions, 287-288
training, 275-276
transferring program to a foreign
    environment, 266-267
Violence-Free Zone, 265-266, 284
Taste, combat and the sense of, 129
Ibn Taymiyya, 83, 85
Teenagers, homicides of, 140-141
Temple, Henry J., 231
Terezin concentration camp, poetry/art
    from children in, 73-74
Therapeutic communities and breaking
    cycles of violence, 235
*This Way to the Gas, Ladies and
    Gentlemen* (Barowski), 70
Thompson, Neil, ix
Threat, definition of, 5
Tibetan Peace Garden, 257
Tobin, Evelyn, 262
Toddlers, homicides of, 138, 139
Touch, combat and the sense of, 130
Trains and Nazi mass murder,
    63-66

342 / PERSPECTIVES ON VIOLENCE AND VIOLENT DEATH

Traumatic distress as a response to a violent death, 179-181
Traumatized and being bereaved, difference between being, 33
Traverso, Enzo, 62, 75
Trent, 231
Tribal/clan violence, 225
TWA, 120

United Nations, 226-227, 231
United States, 10, 86, 87, 231
    See also "Violence in Our Own Backyard: September 11 . . ."
University of Cape Town, 286
University of Notre Dame, 272-273, 277, 288
University of Western Cape, 286

Victoria (queen), 231
Vietnam, 203
Vietnam War Memorial, 257
"Violence and the Dehumanization of Victims in Auschwitz . . ." (Wegner)
    children, voices of the, 71-74
    concentration and death camps, distinction between, 62
    dehumanization as a legal principle, 60-63
    good and evil, no easy categorization of, 70
    linguistic differences, 67
    literature, the role of, 60
    overview, 59
    professional habit motivating persecution, 62-63
    summary/conclusions, 74-75
    survival, the question of, 63-71
    trains, 63-66
    See also Assumptions/principles concerning violence, a statement of
Violence-Free Zones in schools, 12, 265-266, 284

"Violence in Our Own Backyard: September 11 . . ." (Melamed)
    active coping (positive reattribution of the event), 218
    anger, 217
    avoidance, 218-219
    coping strategies, 207-208, 212-213, 217, 218
    depression, clinical, 211, 213-214, 216
    discussion, 215-216
    intrusions/flashbacks, 216-217
    invulnerability of U.S. shattered, 205
    literature, review of the, 206-209
    Mercy College, 204-205
    methods, study, 210-212
    overview, 203-204
    participant characteristics, 210
    passive coping, 217
    posttraumatic stress disorder, 214-215
    questions posed, research, 206
    religiosity, 219
    results, study, 212-215
    two years later (2003), 216-219
"Violence in the Family: Spirituality/ Religion . . ." (Gilbert)
    anger toward God, clergy bearing brunt of, 31-33, 35, 37
    bible used to justify violence, 27-28
    clergy's need for inner growth, 38-39
    cultural norms, 27-28
    denominational structures, 24-25
    disenfranchised grief, 37
    faith, spiritual dilemma and the loss of, 29-39
    homosexuals as victimized group, 28-29
    male headship sets stage for domestic violence, 24
    overview, 23-24
    pastoral care and responses, 31-39
    praxis (to do list for caregivers), 39-42
    scriptures/teachings, examining, 23-24
    summary/conclusions, 42, 306
    support services shifting between clergy and community services, 29-32

INDEX / 343

["Violence in the Family: Spirituality/ Religion . . ." (Gilbert)]
time/safety needed to explore all of what is being experienced, 33
traumatized and being bereaved, difference between being, 33
universality of domestic abuse, denying the, 25-28
victimization as contradictory to mainline religions, 34
Violent death, 3, 19-20, 294
See also "Bereavement Following Violent Death: . . ."; "Characteristics of Homicide: . . ."; "Coping with Violent Death: The Role of Spirituality"; "From Violence to Peace: Posthomicide Memorials"; "Grief and Guilt in the Military"; "Violence and the Dehumanization of Victims in Auschwitz . . "; "Violence in Our Own Backyard: September 11 . . ."
Vogt, Kimberly, x

Walking a away from a fight and Take Ten initiative, 283-284

War, 9-10, 204, 225-226, 256-257
See also "Grief and Guilt in the Military"
Weapons of mass destruction (WMD), 10, 257
See also "Religious Violence and Weapons of Mass Destruction"
Wegner, Gregory P., ix, 10
Wiesel, Elie, 59, 60, 64, 66, 68, 71-73, 75
Willis, Bruce, 8
Winter Grief, Summer Grace: Returning to Life After a Loved One Dies (Miller), 245
Witness, 8-9
Witnessing domestic violence, attachment theory and, 157-158, 170-171
WMD. *See* Weapons of mass destruction
Workplace violence. *See* "Conflict and Violence in the Workplace: . . ."
World Health Organization (WHO), 135
World War II, 9, 235
WT Grant Consortium, 268-269

Yes to Peace Garden, 257

Al-Zawahiri, Ayman, 86, 90
Zero tolerance at schools, 15, 17, 265-266

SELECT TITLES FROM THE

Death, Value and Meaning Series

Series Editor, Dale A. Lund (former Series Editor: John D. Morgan)

WRESTLING WITH THE ANGEL
Literary Writings and Reflections on
Death, Dying and Bereavement
Kent Koppelman

STEP INTO OUR LIVES AT THE
FUNERAL HOME
Jo Michaelson

A COP DOC'S GUIDE TO PUBLIC SAFETY
COMPLEX TRAUMA SYNDROME
Using Five Police Personality Styles
Daniel Rudofossi

LOSS, GRIEF AND TRAUMA
IN THE WORKPLACE
Neil Thompson

DEATH AND BEREAVEMENT AROUND
THE WORLD, VOLUME 5
Reflective Essays
*Edited by John D. Morgan, Pittu Laungani
and Stephen Palmer*

FREEDOM TO CHOOSE
How to Make End-of-Life Decisions
on Your Own Terms
George M. Burnell

PERSPECTIVES ON VIOLENCE
AND VIOLENT DEATH
Edited by Robert G. Stevenson and Gerry R. Cox

WORKING WITH TRAUMATIZED
POLICE OFFICER-PATIENTS
A Clinician's Guide to Complex PTSD
Syndromes in Public Safety Professionals
Daniel Rudofossi